S0-AQI-900

The Everyday Resilience of the City

New Security Challenges Series

General Editor: **Stuart Croft**, Professor of International Security in the Department of Politics and International Studies at the University of Warwick, UK, and Director of the ESRC's New Security Challenges Programme.

The last decade demonstrated that threats to security vary greatly in their causes and manifestations, and that they invite interest and demand responses from the social sciences, civil society and a very broad policy community. In the past, the avoidance of war was the primary objective, but with the end of the Cold War the retention of military defence as the centrepiece of international security agenda became untenable. There has been, therefore, a significant shift in emphasis away from traditional approaches to security to a new agenda that talks of the softer side of security, in terms of human security, economic security and environmental security. The topical *New Security Challenges Series* reflects this pressing political and research agenda.

Titles include:

Jon Coaffee, David Murakami Wood and Peter Rogers
THE EVERYDAY RESILIENCE OF THE CITY
How Cities Respond to Terrorism and Disaster

Christopher Farrington (*editor*)
GLOBAL CHANGE, CIVIL SOCIETY AND THE NORTHERN IRELAND PEACE PROCESS
Implementing the Political Settlement

Kevin Gillan, Jenny Pickerill and Frank Webster
ANTI-WAR ACTIVISM
New Media and Protest in the Information Age

Andrew Hoskins and Ben O'Loughlin
TELEVISION AND TERROR
Conflicting Times and the Crisis of News Discourse

Michael Pugh, Neil Cooper and Mandy Turner (*editors*)
CRITICAL PERSPECTIVES ON THE POLITICAL ECONOMY OF PEACEBUILDING

Brian Rappert
BIOTECHNOLOGY, SECURITY AND THE SEARCH FOR LIMITS
An Inquiry into Research and Methods

Brian Rappert (*editor*)
TECHNOLOGY AND SECURITY
Governing Threats in the New Millennium

New Security Challenges Series
Series Standing Order ISBN 978–0–230–00216–6 (hardback) and
ISBN 978–0–230–00217–3 (paperback)
You can receive future titles in this series as they are published by placing a standing order. Please contact your bookseller or, in case of difficulty, write to us at the address below with your name and address, the title of the series and the ISBN quoted above.

Customer Services Department, Macmillan Distribution Ltd, Houndmills, Basingstoke, Hampshire RG21 6XS, England

---

The Everyday Resilience of the City

How Cities Respond to Terrorism and Disaster

Jon Coaffee
Senior Lecturer in Spatial Planning and Urban Regeneration
University of Manchester, UK

David Murakami Wood
Lecturer, School of Architecture, Planning and Landscape
Newcastle University, UK

and

Peter Rogers
Lecturer in the Sociology of Law
Macquarie University, Australia

© Jon Coaffee, David Murakami Wood and Peter Rogers 2009

All rights reserved. No reproduction, copy or transmission of this publication may be made without written permission.

No portion of this publication may be reproduced, copied or transmitted save with written permission or in accordance with the provisions of the Copyright, Designs and Patents Act 1988, or under the terms of any licence permitting limited copying issued by the Copyright Licensing Agency, Saffron House, 6-10 Kirby Street, London EC1N 8TS.

Any person who does any unauthorized act in relation to this publication may be liable to criminal prosecution and civil claims for damages.

The authors have asserted their rights to be identified as the authors of this work in accordance with the Copyright, Designs and Patents Act 1988.

First published 2009 by
PALGRAVE MACMILLAN

Palgrave Macmillan in the UK is an imprint of Macmillan Publishers Limited, registered in England, company number 785998, of Houndmills, Basingstoke, Hampshire RG21 6XS.

Palgrave Macmillan in the US is a division of St Martin's Press LLC, 175 Fifth Avenue, New York, NY 10010.

Palgrave Macmillan is the global academic imprint of the above companies and has companies and representatives throughout the world.

Palgrave® and Macmillan® are registered trademarks in the United States, the United Kingdom, Europe and other countries.

ISBN-13: 978–0–230–54673–8 hardback
ISBN-10: 0–230–54673–0   hardback

This book is printed on paper suitable for recycling and made from fully managed and sustained forest sources. Logging, pulping and manufacturing processes are expected to conform to the environmental regulations of the country of origin.

A catalogue record for this book is available from the British Library.

Library of Congress Cataloging-in-Publication Data
Coaffee, Jon.
   The everyday resilience of the city : how cities respond to terrorism and disaster / Jon Coaffee, David Murakami Wood and Peter Rogers.
      p.   cm. — (New security challenges series)
   Includes bibliographical references and index.
   ISBN 978–0–230–54673–8 (alk. paper)
   1. City planning.   2. Terrorism—Prevention.   3. Public buildings—Security measures.   4. Crime prevention and architectural design.   5. Emergency management.   6. Natural disasters.   I. Wood, David Murakami.   II. Rogers, Peter.   III. Title.
   HT166.C528 2009
   307.1′216—dc22   2008030133

10   9   8   7   6   5   4   3   2   1
18   17   16   15   14   13   12   11   10   09

Printed and bound in Great Britain by
CPI Antony Rowe, Chippenham and Eastbourne

Contents

List of Boxes, Figures, Plates and Tables

Boxes

Figures

Plates

Tables

Acknowledgments

The idea for this book began in 2004 at a time when the UK Government was enacting changes to the way in which traditional emergency planning was carried out. At this time we were all working in the Global Urban Research Unit of the School of Architecture, Planning and Landscape at Newcastle University, UK, and undertaking research in a variety of areas associated with counter-terrorism, surveillance, urban regeneration and management and participatory practices. The funding for the project originally entitled, *The Everyday Resilience of the City – How Provincial Cities Respond to Threat*, came from the Economic and Social Research Council's *New Security Challenges* programme directed by Stuart Croft from the University of Warwick. The research that has gone into this book, although largely carried out by ourselves, has been helped along the way by a host of academic colleagues, a great number of policy makers and practitioners in the fields of security, emergency planning, policing and other professions connected to resiliency issues, as well as support from family and friends.

We would particularly like to acknowledge the assistance of a number of postgraduate student researchers – Katy Blareau, Anna Leech, James McAllister Jones and Jonathan Parsons – who helped in the collection of early data and literature reviewing for this project. Likewise we owe a debt to a host of academic colleagues across the globe – Steve Graham (Durham), Stuart Croft (Warwick), Harry Richardson (USC), Larry Vale (MIT), John Gold (Oxford Brookes), Lee Bosher (Loughborough), Ces Moore (Birmingham), David Fletcher (Newcastle), Paul O'Hare, Marian Hawkesworth and Ralf Brand (Manchester), the Surveillance Studies Network, the Editorial Board of *Surveillance & Society* and Chris Allen (Manchester Metropolitan) for advice and supportive comments as this research has proceeded and this book has been written.

Jon Coaffee
David Murakami Wood
Peter Rogers

Notes on Contributors

Jon Coaffee is a Senior Lecturer in Spatial Planning and Urban Regeneration at the Centre for Urban Policy Studies, at the University of Manchester, UK. He has published widely on issues related to the social and economic future of cities and especially the impact of terrorism on the functioning and management of urban areas.

David Murakami Wood is a Lecturer at the Global Urban Research Unit, School of Architecture Planning and Landscape, Newcastle University, UK. He works mainly on surveillance and the city, and is a founder and Managing Editor of the journal, *Surveillance & Society*, and a founder and trustee of the Surveillance Studies Network.

Peter Rogers is a Lecturer in the Sociology of Law at Macquarie University in Sydney, Australia. He founded the British Sociological Association Urban Theory and Research Study Group and has sat on the BSA Council. He has published primarily on the themes of urban security, civil contingencies and terrorism, minority participation and citizenship and democracy.

1
Introduction

In recent years resilience has emerged as a key concept in public policy. After September 11 in particular, resilience has become an increasingly central organizing metaphor within the policy-making process and in the expanding institutional framework of national security and disaster preparedness and mitigation. As it has evolved, resilience has begun to infiltrate a host of additional, more loosely connected, social and economic policies. This growth in importance has been underpinned by the political prioritization of the safety and security of communities against an array of perceived hazards and threats, including terrorism, disease pandemic and global warming–related flooding. These priorities have been focused on cities because of the particular vulnerability of densely populated political, economic and cultural centres.

The push for resilience is thus a response to existential or material vulnerability, insecurity and, ultimately, change. Whilst contemporary society is often characterized as one in which we live with risk and in which risk management has become the dominant impulse (Beck, 2002), many contemporary studies of resilience, especially those that deal with Less Developed Countries (LDC) place vulnerability at their heart (for example, Pelling, 2003 and Bankoff *et al.*, 2004). Oliver-Smith (2004), in the latter collection, argues that vulnerability is a fundamentally political–ecological concept, in that it relates to the multi-dimensional relationship between people and their environment. On the other hand, resilience can be defined as a socio-technical or even technocentric concept in many of its versions – it is characterized by an interest in structure and in preserving 'things' indeed in the case of urban resilience, the 'city' itself, drawing on organicist or systems theory concepts of urbanity. Timmerman (1981, p. 5), for example, saw resilience 'as the capacity to adapt to stress from hazards and the ability

1

to recover quickly from their impacts'. Pelling (2003, p. 5) offers a subtle adjustment, defining resilience as 'the capacity to adjust to threats and mitigate or avoid harm'. From an engineering perspective, resilience is defined simply as the measure of the recovery time of a system (Correia *et al.*, 1987), whereas the United Nations (2004) expands this cybernetic conception to the capacity of a system, community or society, to resist or to change in order that it may obtain an acceptable level of functioning and structure. From a national policy perspective the UK Government claims that 'resilience means ensuring that the country is prepared to detect, prevent and respond with speed and certainty to major emergencies, including terrorist attacks' (ODPM, 2004). At the urban level, the idea of 'Critical Infrastructure Protection' (CIP) or the protection of 'lifelines' is now common, the former being enshrined in US national policy (White House, 2003). For example, Godschalk (2003, p. 137) argues that 'resilient cities are constructed to be strong and flexible, rather than brittle and fragile. Their lifeline systems of roads, utilities and other support facilities are designed to continue functioning in the face of rising water, high winds, shaking ground, and terrorist attacks'.

Particularly in the United Kingdom, in the recent past, resilience has been bound up with the idea of civil defence, the 'means and methods of protecting the civil population', as Campbell (1982, p. 15) noted during the height of the second Cold War. However, resilience is also not synonymous with 'defence' as traditionally understood. For example, Campbell (1982, p. 447) noted in the context of the threat of nuclear war that 'we are substantially defenceless' against particular forms of threat despite enormous resources being put into deterrence work. Little (2004, p. 57) also makes a similar point when talking about more recent events in that:

> The tragic events of September 11 made it abundantly clear that there are some scenarios for which direct defence is neither practical nor realistic and that it is difficult, if not impossible, to prevent destructive acts by persons unconcerned with their own safety or survival.

In short, developing resilience to threat has limits; it is impossible to be resilient against every conceivable threat. As Little further notes, 'threats are unpredictable and the full range of threats probably unknowable. We will never be able to anticipate all possible threats and even if we could, there is not enough money to deploy technologies to address them' (ibid.).

Little's assumption of the central role of technology is not unusual. Many of the strategies grouped together under the label of resilience are founded on either the introduction of technologies of defence, control and surveillance, or making design modifications to urban form. However, one of the main arguments that this book makes is that throughout history the protection of the city has been integral to the development of social relations and institutional frameworks at multiple interlocking levels. More recently such developments have become increasingly individualized with the idea of a comprehensive (if not paranoid) security-dominated view that encompasses all scales from national to individual (see Safir and Whitman, 2003). Our argument is that resilience is most effective when it involves a mutual and accountable network of civic institutions, agencies and individual citizens working in partnership towards common goals within a common strategy.

Resilience: past to present

Whilst cities have always been the engines of human civilization and all the positive, vibrant and productive life that this entails (Hall, 1998), it is undoubtedly the case that cities have also been both vulnerable and at the same time acted as defended and controlled centres of power and of power projection. Although resilience has become the new metaphor employed by many to describe and frame a counter-response to threat, many of its characteristics are not new and indeed date back to the development of the first cities. Cities always sought resilience to the hazards they have faced. In this sense, resilience has been core to urbanism. Glaesar and Shapiro (2001, p. 6) argue,

> The first, and probably most important, interaction between warfare and urban development is that historically cities have provided protection against land-based attackers. Cities have the dual advantages of large numbers and walls and thus, holding the size of the attack constant, it is much better to be in a city than alone in the hinterland.

This role is exemplified by the physical boundary of the 'city wall' which maintained its importance from the origins of many cities until the modern period. City walls have not only defined urban spaces, but have been used as a tool by the ruling class to control the population inside them. For example, Raco (2003, p. 1872) argues that 'controlling places has long been a central element of the broader responsibilities of the (welfare) state'.

At the same time, cities have always been sites for both strategic and opportunistic violence, in what Glaesar and Shapiro term 'the target effect', where 'cities have historically been rich targets for looting bandits or terrorists seeking to maximize damage' (2001, p. 3). Throughout history, cities have been partially or entirely destroyed. This has been the result of natural hazards and deliberate acts of policy as much as war. Cities have vanished, moved, been rebuilt and defended in the face of many threats and events. Cities continue to be sites for both strategic and opportunistic violence. Many cities have experienced substantial warfare and destruction, and many remain in situations of conflict and unrest, even subject to extreme forms of violence or 'urbicide' – 'the deliberate wrecking or killing of the city' (Graham, 2003, p. 63).

However, the contemporary city requires openness and complex interlinkages in a variety of regional, national and global flowspaces (Castells, 1996). It can no longer respond with external fortification or abandonment and retreat. It is the continuing centrality of cities in Twenty-First Century life, the concentration of wealth and key societal functions that also makes contemporary cities vulnerable to natural hazards (Henstra *et al.*, 2004) and attractive of human threats such as terrorism (Coaffee, 2003). For example, Bugliarelio (2003, p. 500) comments on the 'threat-rich' nature of cities:

> Within cities, such threats find a target-rich environment – a complex interacting system of people, buildings, infrastructures (utilities, roads, railroads, ports, airports), hospitals, schools, churches, businesses, government, and military bases, with patterns of work, business, home life, leisure, and shopping activities that, all together, define a city's way of life.

Cities thus have many particular features which make them attractive to attack and vulnerable to natural hazards. As David Godschalk (2003, p. 136) noted of cities, 'their architectural structures, population concentrations, places of assembly, and interconnected infrastructure systems, put them at high risk to floods, earthquakes, hurricanes, and terrorist attacks'.

Resilience and the government of cities

The central premise of this book is that security-induced notions of resilience have become a core idea around which threat-response policy is increasingly produced and mobilized at a variety of spatial scales. The recent emergence of resilience as a core concept in policy development has its roots primarily within new security challenges linked to the terrorist threat emerging after September 11 2001, which, it is argued, requires a dramatic rethinking of existing systems of defence and emergency management. The ideas that emerged to deal with this threat sought to embrace proactive contingency management, and utilized resilience as a core concept with could link together counter-terrorism and civil contingency concerns.

Although the idea of resilience is not attached exclusively to counter-terrorism, in much of the political rhetoric the Twenty-First Century is already being breathlessly classed as the 'age of terror' (Lyon, 2003a). The vulnerabilities of cities to terrorism, and how best to address them, have been subject to considerable discussion, debate and reflexive defensive measures in response to what is seen as the next 'inevitable' attack. We should caution, however, that we do not subscribe to the popular (and particularly US) view that September 11 'changed the world', although counter-responses have in some cases been dramatic in order to 'defend the homeland' and offer reassurances to populations that the state has 'the situation under control'.

In considering this, we draw in particular on Michel Foucault's theory of governmentality, in which government is considered as 'the conduct of conduct' (Foucault, 1991). We do not do this to draw wider theoretical implications, which have been well developed elsewhere, particularly by Mitchell Dean (1999) and Nikolas Rose (1996; 2000), but rather to develop a critical discussion of the implementation of urban resilience strategies.

We do this for three reasons. First because, as Dean (1999, p. 13) argues, governmentality simply provides a continuum which connects the exercise of power and authority with the construction of individual and personal identity. It links the conduct of formal government to the conduct of the economy and to the conduct of the citizen. Second, because governmentality highlights the rise of desocialized forms of control based on expertise (Rose, 1993). Finally, as Hunt (2003) emphasizes, because governmentality theory makes clear that Foucault always regarded sovereign power (force), surveillance (discipline) and government (conduct) as three sides of a triangle, not as a progression. Whilst Foucault's work on the development of modern subjectivity traced the way in which disciplinary surveillance developed in modernity, his work never intended the implication that this one form of governmentality entirely replaced sovereign authority. We hope that the emphasis on the deep history of urban vulnerability, risk and resilience combined with detailed empirical studies of contemporary examples will demonstrate this to be the case.

Any study of governmentality must therefore consider these aspects as coexisting even though one or other of them may predominate at any particular time. This happens continuously through periods of surge and retreat in response to specific events and political–economic priorities. In particular, we are concerned here with ideas of what might be referred to as advanced liberal or neoliberal governmentality, wherein responsibility is shifted from the central state both upwards to supranational organizations and downwards to agencies, local government and citizens. This process of responsibilization demands that such actors play an increasingly active role in their own self-government and risk management (Lemke, 2002).

In summary, we see three key and interrelated trajectories which feed into and upon the development of urban resilience, and which thread through the book.

First, the management of multiple risks, through the development of enhanced institutional and actuarial capacity – that is the ability to both pre-emptively identify and respond to threats.

Second, the idea of urban territorial control, whereby the material and virtual form of the city is treated both as a source of risk and as a solution to its mitigation.

Finally, the emergence of a surveillance society (Lyon, 1994; 2003b), wherein risk assessment and management are applied to the population resulting in deliberate or incidental forms of social control.

The structure of the book

This book reflects the findings from a two-year research project funded by the United Kingdom's Economic and Social Research Council under the *New Security Challenges* Programme. This was a programme of work which aimed to promote innovative and up-to-date research into security that moved beyond the traditional preoccupation with military conflict between states, and aimed to define a more comprehensive and comprehensible agenda that would make better sense of contemporary security. Although this book is focused upon the UK experience, it draws where possible on comparison with international examples.

For too many works on contemporary resilience and security, the historical context is limited to a commonplace observation that there is of course a long history and a brief summary of the accepted wisdom.

Whilst this book intends to focus on a very particular study of the development of resilience in modern Britain, we argue that tracing the deeper development of both the discursive and the material aspects of the vulnerability and resilience of the city is vital to understanding the roots of contemporary dilemmas, and also safeguards against making too many claims of their complete novelty.

We thus spend several chapters developing a historical perspective. In Chapters 2 and 3, we cover the background to contemporary concepts of urban resilience through the historical transformations in concepts of the city and what it means to defend a city from outside threats and to control it from the inside. These two chapters take a *longue durée* sweep from the ancient world up to the beginning of the Twentieth Century. Then in Chapter 4 we focus on the Twentieth Century into the Cold War period, where the abandonment of cities became a more distinct possibility and plans for evacuation and retreat (out of cities or underground) became priorities for both civil and military authorities, and when the long experience of rebuilding cities after natural disaster increasingly merged with military perspectives to create new understandings of how cities could recover.

After tracing the deep historical background of urban resilience, we will focus on the introduction, operation and impact of resilience policy as applied to urban areas in the United Kingdom. We are particularly interested in how, in the contemporary city, ideas of resilience become normalized and become an aspect of the everyday urban life. This is a relatively unexplored area of enquiry. The academic and policy literature focuses almost without exception upon key actors seeking to defend major global cities under threat, especially from forms of terrorism. Such defensive and security strategies are explicitly portrayed and appear well publicized. However, what most of the current literature fails to address are a set of key questions linked to the everyday practice of resilience and how this reflects and generates new forms of governmentality.

In Chapters 5 and 6, we show how urban design and planning were employed from the 1960s onwards to try to address both the causes and the practice of crime, disorder and incivility. Through the manipulation of space, pioneers like Oscar Newman argued that places could be created that would discourage unwanted behaviours and encourage 'good citizenship'. In parallel, the rise of electronic surveillance within cities and in the virtual space of databases offered new ways of controlling places and people. We also show how such measures were deployed in attempts to counter the threat of terrorism prior to September 11.

The attacks on the World Trade Center and the Pentagon on September 11 2001 for many constitute a turning point in urban security and defence. Whilst we would caution against generalizing arguments about this event, in Chapters 7–10 we show that a new infrastructure and politics of resilience has emerged in the United Kingdom in response to the perception of a new security landscape. These have occurred across a range of institutions with a role in the governance of urban space. This is not simply a matter of national response but a new multi-tier structure at regional, sub-regional and local levels. We argue that a new governance architecture around resilience has been created with a new set of powers, bodies and multi-agency connections in order to deal more effectively with emerging threats, not just from terrorism but also from climate change and disease. These have merged responsibility for response to civil disturbance, terrorism and natural disaster for the first time in Britain.

Finally, in Chapters 11 and 12, we consider what this means. We focus down on the everyday aspects of the rolling-out of resilience policy in the United Kingdom, relating this in particular to governmentality theory and the idea of responsibilization. We identify three drivers of militarism, modernism and managerialism, with the latter seeking in particular to decentralize risk management responsibilities to a range of stakeholders. We also connect the rise of resilience to neoliberal urban regeneration agendas, arguing that increasingly security is part of a place-branding process used to market the city. In conclusion, we question what could be the future of resilience itself, and if there is an appropriate form and scale of resilience response. We ask whether in becoming subordinate to global rhetorics of risk, fear and competition, 'resilient' might, like 'competitive' or 'sustainable', become just another meaningless label to stick to policy statements, or whether it can become a term around which genuinely new and beneficial agendas may emerge.

2
The Vulnerable City in History

Urban resilience assumes the persistence of the city. However, this notion that cities *should* persist or be resilient was by no means taken for granted in earlier times. The fact that cities could fall, could vanish entirely or be moved to be rebuilt elsewhere was an accepted notion in many parts of the pre-modern world. Partly this derives from a world-view more intimately aware of the mortality and vulnerability of the human body. Many early religions emphasized the fleeting nature of life and the existence of suffering (whatever its cause) and the possibility of any kind of reconciliation with this world only possible through some form of acceptance, referred to in the *Tao-Te-Ching* of ancient China as *wu wei* (lit. no action) (Lao Tzu, 1963). The prevalence of the acceptance of change can be seen not just in Taoism but also in Indian Hinduism and Buddhism and in the pre-Socratic philosophers in ancient Greece, particularly Heraclitus. If change is regarded as the fundamental nature of the world, then attempts to 'fix' anything can only be temporary.

Whilst one finds in later systems of thought more emphasis on stasis, for example, in Plato, the notion of the original form and of the perfect urban 'Republic', and in early Christianity, the rise of the notion of the 'City of God', these expressions of urban stability are proto-utopian – they are literally no place on earth, but in some idealized realm beyond humanity or after death. The religious imagination is frequently linked to the experience of war and disaster (Cohn, 2001). Forms of anti-urbanism often play a strong role, with the earthly city often associated with moral decline, license and disorder in opposition to either a heavenly city or just as frequently a gentler, bucolic rural existence.

Moral concern about the city persists throughout history and in every culture and is often connected to how disaster is perceived by the moral imagination. The story of the destruction of Sodom and Gomorrah in *Genesis* is merely one famous example, where the immorality of cities is held to account for their destruction. Indeed Augustine's (2003 [413–426]) *De Civitate Dei* was written at a time of immense catastrophic change and insecurity, just after the sack of Rome by the Vandals in 410, and the purpose of the work was at least partly to serve as a warning against the earthly political ambition that had just seen the greatest city on earth laid to waste.

Religion could serve as comfort to the suffering, whatever its prescriptions: McNeil (1976) argued that the rise of Buddhism in China from the First Century BCE had much to do with the experience of the devastation of disease epidemics. The rise of the cult of the *flagellatii* in late mediaeval Europe can be traced directly to the belief that the plague was a punishment upon mankind for sin (Camporesi, 1988). One can also find De Boer and Sanders (2005) arguing that the rise of the eschatological Buddhist sect, founded by Nichiren, can be linked to a critique of the *bakufu* (military government) of Minamoto no Yoritomo, which included blaming it for the strong of Thirteenth Century earthquakes that affected the capital of Kamakura.[1]

The purely moral explanation for the disastrous destruction of cities began to decline from the enlightenment in Europe, and particularly the Lisbon earthquake of 1755 and its consideration by contemporary intellectuals. It was, as Dynes (1999) comments, probably the first time that such an event became generally agreed to be the product of a natural phenomenon, as Voltaire argued, rather than the product of divine providence as Rousseau claimed.

With the current growth of attention to global environmental problems and terrorism, we have seen a return to an interest in 'fundamental' causes of disaster and this has meant many a revisionist reinterpretation of destruction and at its extreme, a 'catastrophism' in popular history, exemplified by David Key's only very partially substantiated hypothesis that the global environmental impacts of a massive volcanic eruption in 535/536 CE led to the decline of European civilizations and the mediaeval 'dark ages' (Keys, 2000).

Given the acceptance of 'moral destruction' or active encouragement of apocalypse by so many belief systems for so much of human history, and the massive vulnerability of cities to natural disaster and war for much of this time, it is perhaps as important to explain why cities have been *obdurate* – why so many persisted and continue to persist for so long – before one is able to discuss planned 'resilience'. This chapter traces the history of the destruction of the city and the variety of responses, from abandonment to rebuilding; and considers attempts to protect the city against external threats, both natural hazards and war.

The vulnerability of cities before modernity

War, decline and downfall

The destruction of Rome that prompted Augustine to write was followed by the unravelling of Roman civilization. In some cases, cities flourished only so long as their links to a central authority could be maintained and the decline of the empire resulted in the degradation or decline of cities previously under either occupation or protection. Thus in the Western Empire, cities were often abandoned entirely, as in Britannia, and the country subjected to waves of invasion from Northern Germanic tribes, or declined precipitously and were eventually replaced as centres of power by local lords based in fortified castles in the country, as in Gallia (France) (Anderson, 1996 [1974]).

John Haldon's (1999) analysis of the fate of the Eastern Roman Empire that became Byzantium shows that because of ongoing insecurity and almost continuous warfare and the presence of troops, cities also declined or retreated to the boundaries of their fortified *kastron* (citadel) leaving the extramural settlements largely undefended. For those cities with more extensive fortifications, they shrunk within their walled boundaries leaving large open areas where troops were often temporally billeted as they passed through.

Sometimes the decline of cities reflected the collapse of entire civilizations or societies. Such an outcome was more likely in much earlier periods when human populations were less densely distributed and whole societies could be effectively isolated. For example, the Duvarech'e civilization in what is now Uzbehkistan remains only as traces of beautifully designed cities in the desert. However, the greatest ever extinction of urban civilization was probably the result of the aggressive colonial expansion of Europe, particularly in the Americas. The Spanish invasion of Central and South America, and the British and French colonization of the North, led to the destruction of cities – and civilizations – of all levels of sophistication (see Wright, 1992).

Cities were often deliberately targeted for attack and destruction. Some city-state cultures developed effective siege tactics, particularly the Assyrians, and later the Romans, with increasingly elaborate technologies of siege warfare from rams to catapults (see Campbell, 2006; Kern, 1999). In China, siege warfare had developed alongside the centralizing state as mass battle replaced aristocratic combat in the Ch'eng Chou Period, in the Third Century BCE (Gernet, 1985). Cities after sieges were often treated brutally. In the ancient Near and Middle East, cities were razed to the ground and symbolically ploughed, or sown with plants or minerals, to symbolize their reconversion to agricultural or unusable land. Their inhabitants were frequently tortured, raped and killed. Ridley (1986) gives the examples of the Hittite capital of Hattusa in 2000 BCE, and the destruction of Taidu by the Assyrians 750 years later, and the famous razing of Carthage in 126 CE by a Roman army under Scipio Africanus resulted in similar actual and symbolic destruction and most of its inhabitants being sold into slavery (Raven, 1993). However, stories of razing or destroying cities after battles or sieges were often exaggerated and sometimes referred only to the destruction of walls or towers, so care is needed with many accounts (see Kern, 1999). Sieges also involved the demoralization and killing of inhabitants by any means necessary, including the use of flooding, fire and disease (see below).

Siege warfare was constant in the mediaeval period in Europe; however, the practice of the siege, as with many aspects of the conduct of war, became increasingly formalized. Tilly (1992) describes how in the context of the fighting between Islamic and Christian forces in Southern France and Spain sieges came to acquire rules of conduct which would lead to approximately three different outcomes, either complete freedom (although under new rulers) for those cities that gave in willingly without fighting or enforced expulsion for those that resisted for a few days or weeks; or finally, death or enslavement, followed sometimes by pillage and razing for cities that had to be stormed. Of course, for cities that resisted successfully, the outcome could still be calamitous in terms of disease and starvation.

Perhaps one of the best described of all sieges we have is that of Constantinople (the former Byzantium, now Istanbul) in 1453 (Runciman, 1990 [1965]). The siege of the last great city of the Eastern Roman Empire by the Ottoman forces lasted for almost two months between April and May. The city was finally stormed on 28 May and thereafter followed three days of pillage in which the city was devastated and many of the inhabitants slaughtered or driven away.[2]

Battles did occur inside Jerusalem and other cities during the Crusades, but only very occasionally were whole wars fought largely in cities. In Japan, during the age of military rule that characterized the mediaeval period after 1185, cities were regarded customarily as 'neutral ground' by lords and their *samurai* retainers (Souyri, 2002). However the

Ōnin War which took place from 1467 to 1477 devastated the imperial city of Kyoto, with two main factions based in separate halves of the city and contesting strategic buildings or just fighting in the streets. Much of the city was destroyed by fire and at times almost completely deserted by the normal populace, and the city itself changed hands several times during the conflict (Varley, 1967). As Souyri comments, there were 'no winners or losers' (p. 169), except Kyoto itself (see below). Street warfare of this nature was rare and confined to civil wars and revolution until the Twentieth Century, and did not very often result in such urban destruction until the advent of urban terrorism and state 'urbicide' in the 1990s (Graham, 2002).

From natural events to disasters

The relationship of cities to natural events is a complex one. Whilst a purely social constructionist view of natural events cannot hold (for a political–ecological critique, see Chapter 7), that many events become hazardous or disastrous is undoubtedly as much a consequence of the patterns and intensities of human activity. Indeed most of the disasters suffered by urban centres can be seen as consequential to the very existence of cities. The increasing concentration of people, resources and simply constructed buildings and infrastructure means that any natural hazard, whether it be geological, hydrological or climatic, is likely to affect a greater number of people and result in more fatalities and injuries. Further, the materials and techniques of construction, and the contents, of cities affect the level of death and disruption and result in new hazards, like fire or radioactive materials, which may intensify further the effects of any natural event. Human activities have also created new forms of disaster; in particular, the movement and mutation of bacteria and viruses between animals and humans, the concentration of people in cities and the technologies of transport between them aids the spread of outbreaks and their transformation into epidemics and pandemics (McNeil, 1976).

Natural geological disasters (volcanoes, earthquakes and associated landslides and tsunamis) have proved the downfall of many cities (see de Boer and Sanders, 2002; McGuire *et al.*, 2000), not simply those that are well known like the covering of the Roman city of Pompeii under the ash and lava of Mount Vesuvius and the deaths of around 20,000 people. Other volcanic-related catastrophes to befall major cities in the ancient world include the destruction of the Minoan civilization on Crete, and probably other cities in the region, following the eruption of the Santorini volcano and the subsequent tsunami (Antonopoulos, 1992). Earthquakes have been far more devastating. Various attempts at full chronologies of ancient earthquakes have been made (see, for example, Ganse and Nelson, 1982). In ancient Greece, the massive quake that hit Sparta in 464 BCE 'while not immediately affecting Sparta's prominence, had a catalytic role in its decline' (de Boer and Sanders, 2005, p. 45). The whole region from the Middle East through the Mediterranean was always prone to earthquakes. Alexandria was famously destroyed in 365 by a *tsunami* (in Japanese 'harbour wave') following a massive earthquake epicentred in Crete, which also destroyed the Roman city of Kourion on Cyprus and Argos in Greece, amongst many others (Sorren, 1985). This was only the first of an unusually dense clustering of earthquakes in the region that may or may not have been connected (Stiros, 2001), but which also included the devastation of Antioch and severe damage to Constantinople (Byzantium) (see Downey, 1955; 1958). Another spate of earthquakes affected the Middle East in the Twelfth Century, including that of 1138 which, according to some sources, entirely destroyed the major trading Levantine centre of Aleppo (Ambraseys, 2004).

In the early modern period in Europe, there were two particularly devastating earthquakes affecting urban areas. The first was in Sicily, destroying Catania in 1693 with the loss of 11,900 in the city itself and perhaps 60,000 lives in total. Although the city had been hit by a quake in 1169 during the Twelfth Century spasm, the layout had remained fundamentally the same; however, the 1169 quake totally obliterated the old morphology (Azzaro *et al.*, 1999). The most important quake was undoubtedly that which destroyed Lisbon in 1755 (Chester, 2001). Although it killed fewer in the city of Lisbon than in Catania, it also destroyed much of the old urban fabric and it killed up to 300,000 in the whole country. In addition, Lisbon's relatively greater centrality in the cultural world of the Eighteenth Century enlightenment meant that it had much further reaching social effects, as we have seen; indeed it has been called the 'first modern disaster' (Dynes, 1997).

The most devastating recorded quakes have all been in China, in particular the Ming dynasty Shaanxi Earthquake of 1556 which killed an estimated 830,000 people and destroyed several cities. Due to its positions on the intersection of several tectonic plates, Japan also has a long history of both volcanism and earthquakes. In the mediaeval period, the most serious Japanese urban earthquake disasters were in Kamakura in 1257 and 1293, the latter which was estimated to have killed over 20,000

people or between a quarter and one-third of the population according to the former Emperor Hanazono's contemporary record (see Goble,
1995). In Japan, it was not always the earthquakes themselves that
caused the most urban devastation, rather than it was frequently the
resulting fires, or the tsunami from offshore earthquakes that caused
most damage to coastal cities. Kamakura was hit twice again by such disasters after its rebuilding, in 1369 and 1494 (de Boer and Sanders, 2005).
Japanese cities developed sophisticated systems for monitoring of fire
outbreaks that produced particular social relations (see Chapter 3).

Environmental hazards from weather and water have always been one
of the major factors in urban development and vulnerability. Flooding was both the lifeblood of and the greatest threat to the Egyptian
civilizations of the Nile valley and Delta. There was an intimate relationship with agricultural practices and also city development and flood
risk. Mesopotamian cities were built on marshlands that were partially
drained using a network of canals. Christiensen (1993) showed how
successive civilizations and cities in the Middle East rose and fell in relationship to water, irrigation and water-borne disease; for example, in the
Tenth and Eleventh Century BCE, the people of the cities of the Shiraz
region of modern Iran were recorded as suffering from what appears to
be the effects of endemic malaria and other problems connected partly
at least to the poor management of water resources.

For ancient China, catastrophic flooding was endemic on the crowded
river floodplains of the Yangtse and Huangho, and the complex inter-
action of natural and human process, including urban development,
was all involved, as Elvin (1998) has argued, 'Chinese-style pre-modern
hydro-agrarian city-driven economic development was the main source
of environmental difficulty and disaster in the modern period' (p. 736).
In contrast, in the Netherlands, a country mostly below sea level and
afflicted by numerous disastrous floods and storm surges, the systems for
flood control led to the development of a highly efficient social system,
as with preparedness for fire in Japan (Chapter 3).

Flooding could become a weapon of war. In China, with so many
dykes and canals managing the flow of water, finding the key point to
flood out an army, a city or even an entire province was a not an infre-
quent tactical move from ancient times into the Twentieth Century.
Dongjing (later Kaifeng), capital of the Southern Sung dynasty, was hit
by floods in the Twelfth Century (Johnson, 1995). Heberer and Jakobi
(2000) remind us not only of the siege of Kaifeng in 1642, during which
a dyke was opened and 900,000 people in the city and surrounding area
were killed, but also of the same tactic used by Chiang Kai-shek in 1938,

who in an effort to stop the Japanese advance destroyed 11 cities and killed approximately the same number of people.

The natural variations of climate have perhaps been more important than previously thought. Weiss and Bradley (2001) argue that the collapse of a range of early urban societies in both the old and new worlds have resulted from climate change. For example, a regional period of drought and cooling may have contributed to the collapse of 'the Akkadian empire of Mesopotamia, the pyramid-constructing Old Kingdom civilization of Egypt, the Harappan 3B civilization of the Indus valley, and the Early Bronze III civilizations of Palestine, Greece, and Crete' in around 2300BCE (p. 609). In the Americas, climate-change-related cycles of drought and flooding destroyed the capital city of the Moche in the late Sixth Century BCE.

Sometimes environmental changes have been blamed on the demands of urban civilization. Goodchild (1952) argued that there had been desertification of croplands and decline of grain growing in North Africa towards the end of the Roman period. This area was the 'granary of the empire' (Raven, 1993) and this decline has been posited as crucial in its collapse; however, more detailed recent studies by Barker (2002) found 'no significant evidence for humanly-induced environmental degradation' (p. 503) in the area. But the effects of forest clearance, the intensification of agriculture and urbanization undoubtedly contributed to climate change more generally even in the ancient world (see Reale and Dirmeyer, 2000).

Cities were also crucibles of disease. Whilst cities were still relatively isolated, outbreaks could be relatively contained; however, as trading and transport links intensified not only did cities grow in size and sophistication towards integrated 'world systems' (Abu-Lughod, 1989; Braudel, 1986), they also became vulnerable to outbreaks transforming into epidemics or even pandemics. McNeil (1976) showed how the impact of bubonic and pneumonic plagues spread mainly through the land and sea trade routes that linked East Asia and Europe via South-East Asia, India, Arabia, the Mediterranean, devastating the populations of cities from Callicut through Hormuz and Genoa to London. In Europe, up to one-third of the entire population died between 1346 and 1350 (McNeil, 1976). This was the most severe but neither the first nor the last disease pandemic. Sometimes such pandemics could occur through the exposure of previously distant and disconnected people lacking in immunity to diseases that were relatively common and harmless elsewhere, as happened in the Americas after contact with Europeans (McNeil, 1976).

However, as with other natural hazards, diseases could also be manipulated as a weapon of war. Biological warfare has a long history (see Guillemin, 2005), perhaps beginning with the Hittites (Trevisanato, 2007). The relationship between cities, plague and warfare was also crucial in 1346: the initial entry point of the plague into Europe was probably the city of Caffa, when the disease spread from the Mongol armies besieging it to the inhabitants, perhaps deliberately by the catapulting of the bodies of infected victims over the walls (Derbes, 1966; Wheelis, 2002).

Throughout history then, cities have been vulnerable and have suffered in a huge variety of ways. Natural hazards have been disastrous for cities or turned into disasters through their interaction with human society. Human activities, notably war, have created their own sets of catastrophic results for urban areas, or used and intensified natural hazards. Yet cities survived and multiplied. In the next section, we look at the ways in which urban authorities and populations have responded to both the threat and impact of disasters.

Responding to disaster

Innovation, moving and rebuilding

Disasters did neither inevitably destroy cities or societies, nor indeed produce decline. Cities are obdurate and resilience, although a contemporary development in explicit policy rhetoric and practice has always been implicit in responding to disaster and is perhaps as old as cities themselves. In their discussion of changes to urban form and civic governance structures in response to natural hazards, Vale and Campenella (2005) show how disaster can act as a 'stimulus' to encourage postdisaster rebuilding and innovation and further that urban authorities often emphasize 'that their city has come back stronger than ever' (2005, p. 17).

However, in a major revaluation of the traditionally accepted view of cities beset by catastrophe, Torrence and Grattan (2002) and Grattan (2006) have gone even further and argued that disasters, and volcanoes in particular, are very rarely destructive of human civilization, indeed they may act as a spur to progress. Certainly, even serious catastrophes could pace the way for the emergence of major city-states as has been shown for the massive population movements that led to the rise of the Mesoamerican urban centres of Teotihuacan and Cholula after a series of volcanic eruptions in rural regions (Plunket and Uruñuela, 2006). This was not just congregation for safety, but the ceremonial functions of the urban centres themselves with their pyramidal volcano-like temples were also symbolic acts of resilience.

Disaster could even mean that some cities were moved either politically or even physically. The climatic disasters that afflicted the Moche capital in the late Sixth Century BCE resulted in 'a major northward and inland shift in Mochica geopolitics and population' (Shimada *et al.*, 1991, p. 251) with major urban centres including the capital moving to new locations. There is some evidence to suggest that the ancient Egyptian capital city of Pirramesse was moved to Tanis when a branch of the Nile dried up (Abdallatif *et al.*, 2003).

As we have seen, decline or even abandonment was a common response to natural disaster and war in the ancient world, true even of thriving imperial foundations like the Roman cities of North Africa, once Roman power in the region was seriously disrupted. However, rulers often abandoned old cities and created new ones, entirely unforced. The rulers of Chinese dynasties frequently built new capitals, displacing the old, which whilst often not disappearing would certainly become far less important. This continued up until the colonial period in many parts of East and South-East Asia; for example, in Mataram Java, the capital (*negara*) was moved three times before 1755 (Steinberg, 1987). The rationales included the need to nullify the power base of previous rulers, whose supporters might be tempted to rise up and overthrow the new masters, and sometimes because of such rebellion. However, it seems that, just as with the design of ancient Asian cities, spiritual motivations played just as large a part (see below). The creation of new capitals made a return with the rise of modernist utopianism; however, capital cities like Canberra or Brasilia never threatened to overturn the influence of existing cities in their respective countries. However, in countries which are threatened by disaster, plans for shifting the capital persist in public discourse: for example, in 1992, a resolution was passed in the Japanese parliament to move the capital (or at least government functions) from crowded, polluted and earthquake-threatened Tokyo to some more suitable location (Takamura and Tone, 2003), and after September 11 we saw many responses arguing for concentrated decentralization of government functions (see Chapter 8).

Although in the ancient period sites were often abandoned, just as frequently many cities were simply rebuilt, and by the mediaeval period when cities were more common and far more connected through world systems of trade, politics and culture, rebuilding was normal. In some cases, though settlements persisted or regrew on the same or nearby sites, it would be hard to describe them as the same 'city'. What is now modern New Delhi, for example, was rebuilt at least eight times over thousands of years, each rebuilding in a slightly different location (see Frykenberg, 1986).

Where cities had developed a strong enough social and economic base independent of the ruler, either being downgraded or struck by disaster was not necessarily the end of the city. Witness, for example, the contrasting fortunes of Nara, Kyoto, Kamakura and Edo (Tokyo) in Japan, all of which were built in different periods as capital cities. Nara for a long time remained the spiritual powerbase of ancient Japanese civilization even after Kyoto became the capital. However, Kyoto gradually assumed this role too, and its continued prominence owes much to the economy built around the cultural assets that came from its courtly and religious centrality, despite the intense destruction of the Ōnin War and the loss of its imperial and bureaucratic functions. The city remains for many the 'true' home of the Imperial family and the Imperial palace at Kyoto remained extant (and empty) even after the palace in Tokyo had been destroyed. Nara gradually faded to the status of a provincial town. Kamakura was at least partly chosen as the administrative capital of the *Shogun* in the middle ages, due to its naturally defended position on the coast behind mountains; however, it was exactly this position that also made it vulnerable to tsunami. Kamakura never developed the critical mass needed to evolve into a modern city and despite recovering from the devastating earthquakes and tsunamis of the Thirteenth Century onwards did indeed decline as Edo rose, and now is almost enveloped by the ever-increasing suburbs of megacity Tokyo. Edo itself was hit by the Great Meireki Fire in 1657 and a devastating earthquake and fire in 1707; however, the city was simply rebuilt and expanded.

Defending the city: wars and walls

Whilst it is possible to write a history of the city that plays down the influence of defence – as does Marxist anthropologist Adam Southall (1998) in favour of arguments based on Marx's four modes of production – most accounts of the origin of cities stress how much fortification and warfare are bound up with its origins and development. From Max Weber's classic 1921 account onwards, the contribution of fortification has been recognized. Weber argued that 'the city in the past, in Antiquity and the Middle Ages, was also a special fortress or garrison' (1966 [1921], p. 75). James Tracey agrees that 'the earliest settlements that archaeological research commonly recognizes as cities are also the earliest cities known to have been walled' (2000, p. 1).

However, the prominence and causality of defence in relation to many other factors varies in these accounts. The origin of cities and the reasons for their rise (and fall) are manifold. For example, we can find followers of Paul Virilio, like Nerhuis (1991), portraying the origin of the city wall as a response to the speed of warriors in chariots; however, this seems not to be a historically generalizable argument.

However, surrounding walls, often referred to with the French term, *enceinte*, can certainly not be taken as definitional for the city. Weber acknowledges that walls as a property of cities 'was not universal even in the past' and that further the 'city was not the sole nor the oldest fortress' (1966 [1921], p. 75). Very large-scale fortifications do not have to be associated with the city at all – one only has to think of fortified lines like China's *chang cheng* – Great Wall, lit. 'Long Wall' (Waldron, 1990) – or the coast-to-coast fortifications of the Romans in Britain.[3] There were in fact many more, especially in ancient Mesoamerica, for example the Tlaxcalan frontier wall (Haussig, 1992). In more recent times, the frontier wall has made an unwelcome return, whether it be along the border between the United States and Mexico[4] or the 'security fence' that is turning unresolved invasion and settlement into facts on the ground in Israel/Palestine (Yiftachel, 2006 – see also Chapter 6).

The search for origins is further complicated by Keeley's (1996) claim that scholars' perceptions of the role of war and of walls and when both arose are still often conditioned by what are often unconscious prejudgements based on either Hobbes' (2006 [1651]) position of 'warre' as the natural state of man or Rousseau's (1999 [1755]) conception of the state of nature poisoned by civilization. A recent overview of the history of cities by Reader (2004) stresses that 'warfare did not provoke the rise of cities generally'; (p. 51) indeed many of the first cities for which we have detailed archaeological evidence show few signs of either defensive or aggressive preparations.

This is true of Caral in South America and Çatal Hüyük in Anatolia, although analysts like de la Croix (1972) have argued that in the latter case, the outer ring of houses had largely blank faces on the external side which he regarded as a kind of proto-*enceinte*. However, whether this reflected a need for defence, an internal orientation or symbolism of some other kind, we have no way of knowing for sure. In the case of Caral (Solis *et al.*, 2001; see also Stanish, 2001), there appears to be no evidence of any defensive preparation, nor any aggression. No traces of either fortification or weaponry have been found, and it appears that organized warfare perhaps did not emerge, as a widespread phenomenon, until a much later date in the history of Central and South

American cities (Haas *et al.*, 2004). War seems to have been subsequent to the founding of cities.

This, therefore, might seem to support Lewis Mumford's (1961) classic account of the history of cities. Adopting a psychoanalytic approach, he argued that war was an outcome of cities rather than cities an outcome of war. For Mumford, relying on accounts from *The Epic of Gilgamesh* and other Babylonian myths, the key to this was the transformation of hunters, and particularly male hunters into warriors through their role as protectors of increasingly settled farming communities. Whether or not organized agriculture was a cause or a result of urbanization, this hypothesis would seem to be quite attractive. He then traces the origins of war to the assertion of 'sovereign powers' by egotistical political rulers who were displacing earlier cooperative or religious institutions. The walling of cities then provides 'a permanent structure to the paranoid claims and delusions of kingship, augmenting suspicion, hostility, non-cooperation, and the division of labor and castes' (p. 46). In other words the walled city was, at least potentially, a pathological entity.

Whether or not one accepts the social psychological interpretation, one can certainly see that walls and defences are social order written into material form, a key feature of Sack's (1986) understanding of human territoriality (see also Chapter 5). It is certainly the case that many material forms of territorialization serve both explicit and implicit symbolic purposes (see also Gold and Revill, 1999). Further, the same complex and varying combination of protection (care) and domination (control) still characterizes the understanding and debates around all aspects of defence, urban resilience and surveillance today (see Lyon, 2007).

However, Mumford's polemical account, while provocative, is exactly the kind of argument that Keeley would see as a direct descendent of Rousseau. Although he is keen to stress otherwise, Mumford clearly dreams of a time before war and an urban civilization before walls. We have seen that there is evidence for the latter; however, for the former there is much less. Keeley argues that archaeologists and anthropologists have been guilty of misinterpretation, giving many examples of prehistoric and even pre-urban defensive palisades and ditches, not simply animal enclosures as was believed until recently. He argues,

> Small-scale societies do not 'neglect' fortifications, but the social and economic conditions requisite for undertaking such construction are seldom met by bands and tribes. Even when the necessary social conditions exist, the level of threat maybe too low to justify the cost.
> (Keeley, 1996, p. 58)

Thus, fortifications were not unknown or beyond the supposedly peaceful imaginations of primitive peoples, but were a function of the availability and organization of labour, the resources (either environmental or capital) and the level of existential or actual threat.

Many cities were established as centres for storage and trade, thus the wall represented the protection and enclosure of wealth. This meant that strategies for dealing with even friendly outsiders were productive of walling, but were also not limited to walls. For example, we can see Plato arguing of ancient Athens that visiting traders should be received outside the boundaries of the city, and not in the *agora* (Hall, 1998, pp. 38–40), and this spatial separation became a policy in many city-states, with delineated and often fortified spaces established inside or outside the city for foreigners, the mad, the ill and the troublesome (see Chapter 3).

What this means is that the relationship between war, defence and cities varies. In some places, walls preceded cities and sometimes even substantially walled settlements never really became cities, as in many of the eastern North American indigenous pallisaded settlements (Milner, 2000). In some places cities preceded walls, as in ancient Greece (see below), and in some places, city walls were never felt necessary, as in ancient Mesoamerica, where the cities of the Aztecs were largely open to the surprised armies of the Spanish conquistadors of the Sixteenth Century (Haussig, 1992). Martin van Creveld (1991) argues that the urban *enceinte* developed in countries unable to build massive defensive lines. However, just taking the case of Roman Britain, the opposite would seem to be true – as the external threat to Roman occupation came from one clear direction, the fortified line was perhaps seen as more efficient than walling every single urban settlement.

If fortifications do not seem to have a straight correspondence to the city *qua* city, are they a result of some other factor, for example the relationship of the city to statehood? Here again, the situation is complex. Mogens Herman Hansen, perhaps the world's leading authority on city-states, argues that 'urbanization and state formation go hand in hand, but the relation between the two phenomena differs' (Hansen, 2000a, p. 15) between a state containing many towns or 'macro-state', as in ancient Egypt and the Inca civilization of South America, and the 'city-state', which sometimes builds into a 'city-state culture' of interacting city-states, whether these be equal or hierarchical. Hansen argues that 'war between city states is endemic' (p. 17) and that city-states always have an army of some kind, but that even so, fortification is not a necessary corollary – although they are 'often walled' (p. 19). However, the highly governmentally, socially and architecturally sophisticated, and often violent, city-states of the Aztecs in pre-Columbian central America for the most part did without any kind of fortification (Bray, 1972). Violent coercion, whether war or the threat of war, however is almost certainly intimately connected to the rise of statehood (Tilly, 1992). The concept that the state is the entity which possesses the monopoly of the legitimate means of violence is almost always an *ex post facto* justification: 'legitimated' might be a more exact term.

What we can say is that fortification against outside threat was frequently intertwined with the development of city and of centralized authority. However, this diversity is not evenly spread in geographical or temporal terms. Fortification became important in many entirely unconnected places and times. Our knowledge is of course complicated by the fact that the further back we go the more we are forced to rely solely on physical evidence, with fewer written records. Of the ancient Assyrian city of Assur, Larsen comments, 'Assur was in fact surrounded by walls, but we have no knowledge about military affairs at all' (p. 83). We lack the social contextual evidence necessary to understand the meanings of fortification and the rationales and purposes of both defensive and aggressive preparation. Of course, material evidence is itself often temporally ambiguous, as 'the remains of fortifications are inherently difficult to date' (Cornell, 2000, p. 217).

We know most about the ancient cities of the Middle East, China and of course those of Greece and Rome; however, newer research is extending the scope of our understanding. For example, Graham Connah (2000a,b) shows how several African cities developed often quite complex networks of walls, in particular Benin, and the Hausa centre of Kano, which has also been well described by Robert Griffith (2000). Many other places remain less well studied: research into ancient cities of the former Soviet Union (like the Duvarech'e mentioned earlier) and the borderlands of Afghanistan are sparse, beset by nationalistic politics (Kohl and Fawcett, 1995) and there are few translations (but see Kohl, 1985, for an earlier summary).

In ancient Greece and Rome, the patterns of urban development and their relationship to defence were complex. Owens (1999) shows that early archaic Greek cities were built largely on sites that were naturally defensive, with the exception of some like old Smyrna, which were therefore the first to acquire partial walls in later Ninth Century BC. However, it was not until the Sixth Century BC that urban fortification became more widespread. Cooper (2000) agrees saying that 'most Greek cities did not begin with fortifications' (p. 156). The Etruscans in Italy were fortifying settlements by the next century, but Owens argues that there were key differences in the style of wall and what was defended. In ancient Greece, walls 'weave and deviate, encompassing the outlying hills and other features' (p. 150) with no connection to streetscape or even to the official 'gates' of the city. Although Owens considers this to be possibly to allow urban expansion, the example of Pirene, where the walls include even an 'inaccessible acropolis', indicates that perhaps one reason was the inclusion of local sacred sites and not simply the protection of population or government. In any case this made Greek city walls less effective in practice in times of actual war, which were frequent (Hansen, 2000b) and the construction of more effective military 'cross-walls' was often necessary.

Hansen shows that even in the later classical period, for the city-states, or *poleis*, 'the construction of city walls was a relatively late phenomenon, and that many poleis never had a fortified acropolis or a wall around the urban centre' (Hansen, 2000b, p. 157). In the Hellenistic period many of the most significant *poleis* were coastal and their communications and warfare when it came via the sea. However, by this time, 'almost all poleis were surrounded by a circuit wall' (Hansen, 2000b, p. 162). The famous exception was Sparta, unwalled and yet at the same time the most militarized and the most xenophobic (Gat, 2002; Hansen, 2000b). Perhaps the fearsome and unpleasant reputation of the Spartans obviated the need for fortification, in particular their use of hidden human defences (see Chapter 3).

Walls became more common in all the regions of what is now Italy from around the Fifth Century BC, probably due to repeated invasion by Gallic tribes. However, it was not until the period of the later Roman republic that 'a walled enceinte, complete with towers and formal gateways, was an essential symbol of city-status' (Cornell, 2000, p. 218; following Gabba, 1994). The Roman *municipia* were therefore unlike the Greek *poleis* partly defined by their possession of walls, and in addition the walls were 'fully integrated urban defences with the city plan and the street system' (Owens, 1999, p. 151). This continued with Imperial Rome, and there is during this period not only evidence of extensive building of more sophisticated fortifications, in many different shapes that reflected innovation in both defensive thinking and the particular military threat, but a more general social militarization (Campbell, 2002). These fortifications were not always as impressive as the earlier constructions, often put up in haste in response to threat, and in particular those on the more distant frontiers of the expanding empire often lacked proper stonework (Owens, 1999). However, the fortifications were all part of a programme of pacification, which as Bachrach (2000) shows, frequently made the inhabitants directly responsible for the maintenance of walls.

In ancient China, the imperial city followed a distinct morphology. Whilst there were changes and developments in the way in the specifics of the plan, the broad framework remained unchanged over millennia (Chang, 1970; Steinhardt, 1999). The plan included walls from the beginning; in fact the ancient Chinese character for city, *cheng*, is also the word for wall. Non-imperial cities were often *shi*, or market-towns. The modern word *chengshi* combines the two and preserves the clear hierarchy of types of cities in ancient China, where the merchant class were considered to be parasitic and below even the peasants (see Farmer, 2000). The imperial cities were felt to mirror a celestial model, and this is common throughout East and South-East Asia. For example, Ford (1993) on Indonesian cities and Tanaka and Murakami (2006) on Sendai in Japan, both make reference to the practice of aligning the axis of the city to key sacred mountains (*yama-ate* in Japanese).

In ancient China – and early Japanese capitals which drew on the Chinese influence (see Karan, 1997) – the plan of imperial cities was particularly connected to the cardinal directions and the number four, and consequently 'every Chinese imperial city is encased by four outer walls, which meet at right angles to form a rectangle' (Steinhardt, 1999, p. 6) and this was 'the fundamental feature of the Chinese imperial city' (ibid.). That this pattern was 'divine' rather than mundane is evidenced by its persistence long after the discovery of gunpowder and improvements in tactics and military engineering. The latter did influence fortification, however, in the shape of additional walls beyond the square ramparts of the *cheng*. Freed from the requirements of celestial geometry, these *mamian* or *yangma* were often curved or zigzagged (Steinhardt, 1999), and *shi* often had these forms of fortification too. Chinese cities also often acquired moats in the Yangshao period, largely to protect against horses, though these were also frequently part of complex flood defences (Elvin, 1998).

Ancient Indian walls also appeared to be largely for non-military purposes; however, this had more to do with the conduct of warfare. The walls of Delhi 'were at times defensive, but more often symbolic because warfare, with one exception, was waged on the plains well outside of Delhi's gates' (Asher 2000, p. 249).

Changes to fortification and the increasing obduracy of the city

Over time, cities have become increasingly obdurate and less transient entities. However, the development of city walls did not always work in a linear direction of increasing fortification and stronger physical defences; there have been periods of decline. Many factors are involved in why urban fortifications change and these do not necessarily result in the destruction or decline of the city, and many less immediately catastrophic processes are often involved.

One sometimes positive reason is the lessening of existential or actual threat. In contrast to the earlier years of conquest, the peace – which was admittedly imposed – in areas of the Roman Empire led to the decline of existing walls in many places. Both Owens (1999) and Hansen (2000b) agree that the *pax Romana* led to the decline of city walls through lack of maintenance in Greece in the early centuries CE.

Another major reason is the very success and expansion of the city. The growth of suburbs in Rome is well documented and in earlier periods the walls of the city were continually rebuilt further in increasing circles (Richmond, 1930), as was common in many cities from ancient to the early modern period. However, in many cases the suburbs began to grow faster than walls could be built. In many colonial areas subject to military occupation, residential areas were never enclosed at all, as Johnson (1973) notes of the Roman settlements in Gaul, 'the city wall can hardly have enclosed anything other than the main administrative buildings' (p. 219).

However, one of the main reasons is simply due to new technologies and practices of warfare. As the purpose of this chapter is to trace the roots of the resilient city, we do not intend to cover the detail of changes in fortification techniques. What is worth noting is how little the technologies of fortification changes in most places in the world beyond the initial burst of walling until the advent of modern techniques of warfare (McNeil, 1982; Parker, 1996). Then, confronted by siege guns, walls increasingly became elaborate and sophisticated. The key development was the angle bastion which, when put together, created a star-shaped fortification first outlined by Leon Battista Alberti (1991 [1485]), and later known as the *trace italienne* (see also De La Croix, 1963).

Geoffrey Parker (1996) argued that the *trace italienne* was the most important defensive development in the history of warfare and one of three military innovations (along with the massive increase in army size, which could be said to be a development of the standing army in the late Middle Ages, and the rapid development of firearms) that represented a 'military revolution' that effectively laid the foundations for the rise of the West and its colonial conquest of much of the rest of the world. Partly at least this was because, as Arnold (1995) notes in a detailed study of the Gonzaga lords of Mantua and Monferrat in late Sixteenth and early Seventeenth Centuries, 'the cost of taking a sophisticated fortress eclipsed the considerable expense of constructing one' (p. 220). This then, as McNeil (1982) had previously argued, meant that smaller states could hold out against imperial powers, which only added to the economic pressures for any expanding proto-nation-state to look outside of Europe. This meant land war in Europe shifted away from city back to the pitched battles in fields and even more formalized rules of engagement (Fuller, 1992) which only slowly unravelled, reaching their nadir in Flanders in the First World War. What finally ended this phase were further waves of military technological innovation, first with the development of new kinds of fortification, and the return to the targeting of cities with the advent of the aerial bombardment in the Twentieth Century (see Chapter 4).

This chapter has concentrated on the external threats to the city and the way in which largely sovereign authorities responded to this through territorial responses such as fortification. However, as we have hinted throughout, the threats to the city and in particular the threats to those sovereign authorities were not just from outside but also from within. The city wall served as much to contain populations where they could be more easily ruled. It is to the history of this internal urban order that we now turn.

3
Resilience and Social Control in the City

In the last chapter we considered the vulnerability and obduracy of cities in the face of external natural hazards, war and disaster. In this chapter we look at the internal threats to the city. As we shall see, internal social and spatial control has always been present. However, several factors made the concentration on internal discipline even more important in the modern period. Technologies of fortification and the rise of the nation-state rendered siege warfare and external attacks on cities increasingly expensive and difficult. The new rationalism and the science of the improvement of humanity, combined with industrialization, massive in-migration and the emergence of a large urban working class meant that the urban elites instituted new measures which combined social and spatial control with paternalistic care reflected in the institutions and architectures of the modern age: factories, schools, police, armies, mass housing and so on.

Discussion of order in recent years has been dominated by Michel Foucault's (1977) influential thesis on the uses of surveillance and the evolution of modern subjectivity. Foucault argued that, at least in Western society, the period of the enlightenment from the Seventeenth Century onwards, marked a key moment in the history of ideas about power. Recognizing, as Hobbes and Mumford did, the importance of 'sovereign power' in the pre-modern era, Foucault argued that during this time other, the organization and monitoring of people in spatial and social institutions became more prevalent in assuring social order.

For the pre-modern period Foucault argued that order was ensured by the often arbitrary and spectacular use of violent coercion, whether through war or indeed torture and punishment, exile and captivity. This slowly gave way to more subtle methods aimed at the improvement of the person based on new rational and scientific methods of surveillance or discipline. It is a persuasive story in terms of the particular impact of the enlightenment on Western Europe. However, if one tries to turn it into a generalized account of human social development, it is subject to all kinds of historical and geographical problems, especially if one considers the relationship of the city, threat and order in a long-term and global perspective.

This chapter has three parts. The first covers the relationship of natural hazards and social order, as many systems of social order developed in response to persistent threats. The second moves on to consider the spatial forms of control through internal fortification, ghettos and gaols. Finally, the third part deals with the generation and enforcement of moral order and proper conduct, through moral suasion, spies and informers and the rise of modern policing.

Natural hazards and social order

The role that natural hazards have played in the development of urban social order and control processes is often underestimated by analysts of security and social control. For example, the biggest surveillance network in Tokugawa-period Edo (Tokyo) was not connected to human movement or war, but to the real threat of fire (Murakami Wood *et al.*, 2007). Apart from temples, the fire watchtowers were the only constructions that protruded significantly above the generally low roofline of the city. Japanese buildings were almost all based around wood with heavy tiled roofs, which made collapse in earthquakes and resultant fires common, but also made rebuilding easier (see Sorensen, 2002). Like the upkeep of walls in Roman Gaul this was the responsibility of townspeople themselves rather than government. Complex neighbourhood social structures around fire regulation developed, intersecting with other neighbourhood responsibilities. The complexities meant that whilst the regulation of urban space and social relations was still strictly hierarchical, with a chain of command from the *shogun* down to the *goningumi* (five-family groups) that formed the lowest level of order, it was not necessarily directly coercive instead becoming the basis for an intense and mutual regulation of behaviour (Takashi, 1994).

This can be compared to the Dutch 'polder model' of governance that evolved during the early mediaeval period to cope with the threat of flooding (de Vries, 1974; Kaijser, 2002). Jan de Vries (1974) showed how the development of the great commercial centres like Amsterdam was initially dependent on the cooperative rural water-management systems that had evolved since the Twelfth Century. The cities became the engines of mercantile growth using the system of drainage and canals based on the technologies and artificial landscapes of rural communities.

Japan and the Netherlands evolved systems of social order to cope with natural hazards over long periods of time; however, in many other places, particularly disastrous natural events altered urban societies forever. The systems of disease control in Italy in response to the plague pandemic of 1346–1350 were perhaps the key example in the development of urban governance in Europe (Porter, 1999).

Foucault (1977) argues that there was an ongoing concern with leprosy and the socio-spatial regulation of lepers. Porter's survey of the history of disease control supports this as a key example of how in pre-modern societies 'individual and collective behaviour was regulated for the benefit of elite community health' (p. 27). However, the plague changed things. In some European mediaeval nations, lepers were regarded as legally and spiritually dead. Similar spatial controls existed in India and Japan for the segregation of 'untouchable' castes who were either diseased, in social exile for crimes committed or simply worked in 'unclean' professions (for example, butchery or night-soil collection). Leprosy was relatively uncommon when compared to the plague and thus the measures were both more extreme and more generalized. Extreme measures included the complete closure of cities in voluntary 'quarantine' (lit. a 40-day period) as was carried out by Ragusa (Dubrovnik), Venice and Marseilles, amongst others.

However, most of the measures to prevent the spread of the plague were not designed around medical priorities but 'were aimed at containing the panic, social breakdown and civil disorder which the epidemic threatened to create' (Porter, 1999, p. 37). The nature of the urban government of Italy at this time meant that 'the rulers of these inland city-states had sufficient power to impose strict policing upon their citizens, enforce it through armed militia and by using the religious authorities to provide surveillance and intelligence' (Porter, 1999, p. 36). The Gonzaga rulers of Mantua, for example, banned all citizens from travelling to plague areas, and did not allow travellers back into the city. Other city-states followed the leprosy model and instituted *lazaretto* (plague camps) outside the city, or sometimes posted guards beyond the walls to intercept potentially plague-carrying travellers.

The plague created a generalized upheaval leading to social transformation throughout Europe. In the United Kingdom, rulers were concerned that the shortage or workers would lead to higher wage demands and movement of labour untied to rural manorial or urban guild authority, which led to the regulation of so-called 'sturdy beggars' (that is, the new mobile casual labourer) after the plague. These regulations set off a wave of uprising throughout the Fourteenth and Fifteenth Centuries, starting with the Peasant's Revolt (Dobson, 1983). The rebels burned large areas of London, including the properties of particular Lords.

This explains why the plague model of disease control also spread far beyond the Italian city-states and led ultimately to consolidation of power and the outlines of new national bureaucracies. As Porter (1999) shows, into the early modern period, plague and health regulations and semi-permanent boards of health were increasingly used as excuses to control the growing urban poor.[1] Ultimately, this combined concern for urban health and social unrest would lead to the birth of epidemiology and the urban census in Eighteenth Century UK and France, and to the emergence of town planning in the early Twentieth Century.

Architecture and internal order in the pre-modern city

We have already noted that walls and defences are social orders written into material form, and have seen how the exterior walls were connected to forms of state and of war, but how did urban architecture relate to internal urban order? In her survey of the use of the grid street pattern, Jill Grant (2001) argued that there was no necessary connection between spatial layout and social order; however, it is undoubtedly true that there were frequently rationales relating to internal order behind the planned city.

The first things to consider are entrances and gates, which were equally important as the city walls. Gates are symbolic markers of passage, delineating territory and the passage between inside and out, and in early cities, between law and civilization and the area beyond their reach. For example, as Augustin Berque (1993) shows, many Japanese cities had prominent gates but without significant walls. The gates themselves often tell security stories, as Lieberman (1991) demonstrated with his study of the Arsenale gate in Venice, which was as much a collection of architectural references which created a myth of stability and order as it was an entrance.

However, as breaks in the wall or just a barrier, gates are pinch-points, and filters, a spatial location for social sorting. Gates allow for both constraints on who may enter or leave a city and control over how one may do so. They provide a place for counting, for checking of goods and possessions, for verification or identification, for disease control and for taxation and the enforcement of fines and punishments.

Some were elaborate. The Golden Gate of Constantinople was one of many in the three sets of tiered walls that defended the city in the middle ages, serving a number of functions that demonstrate both the symbolic and practical importance of gateways into the city. Sporting over 192 towers, ancillary moats and passageways, it was the cornerstone of the city's military defence. O'Shea (2006), in his architectural history of Islam and Christendom in the Mediterranean, notes that whilst the Golden Gate played an important role in the victory march of the Christian campaigns from the city, it had long since been stripped of ornamentation and blocked up 'not only because there had been no Byzantine triumphs to celebrate for centuries, but, quite simply, as a defensive measure. The magnificent structure was incorporated into the land walls, and the maze of courtyards and towers that had sprung up about it made it the lynchpin of the fortifications' (O'Shea, 2006: p. 264).

In China, from ancient times up until the Twentieth Century, the outer walls and gates of cities were only the first part of the story of how urban space was divided: Chinese cities were internally walled, gated and monitored (Steinhardt, 1999). Beijing before the communist revolution was the zenith of this kind of divided, controlled city (Dray-Novey, 1993). The city had a series of concentric internal walls separating the city by the importance of its inhabitants. In the centre was Emperor's Forbidden City, surrounded by the Imperial City containing the high administration. Beyond was the Inner City, home to lower level retainers, and then the Outer City. Within these areas, individual *hutongs* (alleys) had *zhalan*, wooden lattice gates, on to the main streets, which were guarded and closed at night. In the Inner City, these were supplemented by more than 700 permanent guard posts, *duibo*.

In Japan, in the Sixteenth and Seventeenth Centuries, the *daimyo* (lords) were building *joka-machi*, castle cities. These varied in style and design, but in many cases the city that grew was either built or grew up around the castle were effectively part of the defence of the castle. The best example of this type was the capital, Tokugawa period *Edo* (Tokyo). With its spiral structure centred on the shogun's castle, and mazy streets with frequent dead-ends and T-junctions, it was not based on the traditional Chinese-style grid, but designed to be impenetrable and inaccessible to outside invaders (Jinnai, 1995). This has contributed to the rather incidental nature of streets in Japan (Shelton, 1999), which in many cases remain narrow alleys leftover from other uses. Unfortunately, this left Edo even more vulnerable to the threat of fire, and when the opportunity for rebuilding the city presented itself, the alleys were widened into roads, on such neighbourhoods replaced entirely.

However, this spatial confusion did not mean that the city lacked order. Edo's urban space, like that of Beijing, was intensely surveilled. The different caste groups were spatially separated in different areas of the city radiating from the core, with often strict regulations about movement from speed to means of mobility – only samurai or lords were allowed to travel by horse for example. The various *machi* or *cho* (neighbourhoods) were further divided by *kido* (gates) across their entrances or at bridges, watched from guard houses (*kido banya*) (Jinnai, 1995; Takashi, 1994). The modern *koban* (police boxes) occupy many of the same sites (Murakami Wood *et al.*, 2007).

In the modern period in Europe when nation-states asserted control over former city-states, many cities were redesigned partly to allow the penetration of state military forces to suppress urban uprising, as well as to allow air to circulate, which was felt to prevent the presence of miasmas believed to carry disease. Wide boulevards radiating from central open spaces were symbols of new power (and the central spaces often contained triumphal arches, symbolic gateways), but they also allowed both the public parading of troops as demonstration of sovereign power, and their rapid deployment in times of revolt. In the Nineteenth Century, Paris was completely redesigned by Baron Haussman, whose plan is a classic example of the new opened city (see Benjamin, 1999).[2] In place of the walls came new tactics of policing (see below), and during the Nineteenth Century the city acquired for some time a spatial order that was not dissimilar to the *koban* system in Tokyo, with small police posts every 200 metres in the central parts of Paris (Kettering, 1994).

Ghettos and gaols

We have seen that from the earliest times, there was concern about how to deal with 'outsiders' in the city, even those who were not aggressive. Many city-states had special areas reserved for traders. Sometimes this was a matter of convenience, for example the *khan* or *wikala* of the Islamic trading cities where foreign merchants tended to be spatially located were in most cases about easy access to both markets and accommodation, as Um (2003) has demonstrated in the case of the trading port of Mocha in modern Yemen. This kind of jumbled urban landscape was seen as much less convenient when outsiders took control, as in the colonial period. The British in many cases took it upon themselves to apply new concepts of town planning in the early Twentieth Centuries, as was the case with the rebuilding of Zanzibar (Bissell, 2000), and Lutyens' New Delhi (Frykenberg, 1986) with the justification of hygiene, in this case, as in the case of the great plague, as much moral and political as medical.

However, in many places, outsiders, even those more permanently resident, had long been far more spatially controlled. Jews were regarded with suspicion throughout mediaeval Europe, and had been entirely expelled from several states, including England in 1297 and Spain in 1492. However, it was in Venice that Jewish communities were both most controlled and then later, most liberated (Ravid, 1976; see also Davis and Ravid, 2001). The *ghetto nuovo* (lit. new quarter) was established in 1516 following several measures including the compulsory wearing of yellow hats.

In the areas of Poland and Byelorussia under Russian occupation from the Eighteenth Century, Jews were also restricted in a multi-level framework of control, not just to particular areas of cities, but to particular cities in a particular area, known as the Pale (see Wirth, 1998). Of course, the ghettos of Eastern Europe took on new and even more sinister significance in the Twentieth Century as the Nazi regime concentrated the Jewish populations still further in these confined urban neighbourhoods, as a prelude to transportation to work and extermination camps.

City walls also became less significant with the rise of the nation-state and the protection of elite interests by division within the city became correspondingly more significant. In Paris the old walls were torn down in 1667, and from this time onwards new forms of internal division and monitoring (including policing; see below) became more important (Williams, 1979). The London of the Victorian period was full of divisions and street barriers, perhaps around 230 in 1867 (Atkins, 1993) for example around the City of London, and the wealthy Bedford estate, which were often policed by private guards who monitored entrants and sometimes charged tolls. In the west end of London, these constituted a 'guilded cage' (p. 266) for the elite inhabitants, and were only removed after significant public and parliamentary campaigning that led to the 1894 London Building Act.

It is hardly surprising that in the United States with its much stronger emphasis on independent private property ownership, entirely private streets should also have been found. In the second half of the Nineteenth Century, these became particularly common in St Louis and New Orleans (Savage, 1987), and in the former became almost like cities within cities, although the motivation behind their building had more to do with upper-middle-class frustration at the inadequacy of urban infrastructure than with concerns for keeping the poor out, as in London (Beito and Smith, 1990). This took place against the backdrop of growing suburbanization and particularly class-divided cities, which had left the largely immigrant working classes in inner-city slums. As Boyer (1978) remarks, 'abandoned by the wealthier classes, the old urban centres increasingly became the domain of newcomers divided by language, religion and tradition, but often united in poverty and a pitiful lack of preparation for urban existence' (p. 124). These conditions inevitably gave rise to both conventional and organized crime, with gang loyalties providing the ordering processes, and to massive labour unrest.

However, there were by now increasing places to put the 'troublesome' poor. Gaols had always existed and were used extensively in the Roman empire (Peters, 1995), but in most cities in the world until the modern period, they were reserved simply for those either awaiting trial or punishment, or those at the mercy of their captors for some debt or ransom. Fairweather (1975) defined this era, which he ended in the late mediaeval period as one of revenge and repression, and both Foucault's (1977) and Spierenberg's (1995) assessments would appear to agree. Melossi and Pavarini (1981) attribute the development squarely to changes in the mode of production in Western Europe from the Sixteenth Century, and indeed as we will see, the control of labour and the labouring classes did play a major part in the new schemes of confinement. However, Jean Dunbabin (2002) has more recently and persuasively argued that the transformation from retribution began in Europe during the juridical revolution that occurred from the Eleventh Century, but even so this was far from complete by the late mediaeval period.

It is certainly true, however, that practices like spectacular punishment, whether bodily, from branding to public execution, or inflicted on property, like house demolition in Athens (Peters, 1995) tended to predominate over the expensive and invisible use of imprisonment as criminal punishment. This was true in non-western societies too. Edo under the Tokugawa shogunate was a society of rigid status enforced by visible bodily punishment (scaring, tattooing or mutilation), exile, outcasting to *hinin* (lit. non-human) status and summary execution, as the main punishments (Howell, 2005). This strict ordering even persisted within the jailhouses where prisoners awaiting sentence were kept (Botsman, 2005).

As we have seen in the discussion of the effect of the plague, and indeed of the Jews, in most parts of the world, the challenge to urban order was perceived as arising from mobile and unfixed people – those who did not fit within the social and spatial hierarchy. The wealthy or productive mobile could be controlled in ghettos; however, the poor and vagrant posed a different problem. In London, mediaeval laws tried to send them back to their manorial place of origin (Dobson, 1983), and in Tokugawa-period Edo, the original response to the increasing migration to Edo of the place-less and work-less in the late Seventeenth and early Eighteenth Century was first to get the city-dwellers to force them out, then later to be registered as *hinin* in a particular place, and therefore subject to the internal controls of *hinin* society. Botsman (2005) describes how the pressures this created, particularly the concerns about the increasing population and spatial concentration of what later were called the *burakumin* (outcastes), led to the creation of special 'stockade for labourers'. This was effectively a camp on the edges of the city, where healthy men of working age who had come to the city to seek economic betterment, were interned and forced to work. This stockade was also used as a preliminary for the much older solution of exile or transportation. Many people were sent to the northern island of Hokkaido, which was then being colonized by the Japanese, to open up the land to agriculture or work in the mines.

Transportation was a 'solution' to the problem of population growth of the urban proletariat used by the colonial powers in Europe too from the Seventeenth Century, particularly by Britain, which sent convicts first to the American colonies, and thereafter to Australia (see Hirst, 1995). However, throughout western Europe, places of confinement for debtors, for the mad, the vagrant and the unemployed were also established from the late Sixteenth Century with the Bridewell insitutions in the United Kingdom and the *Rasphuis* in Amsterdam (1595–) (Fairweather, 1975; Ignatieff, 1978; Melossi and Pavarini, 1981).

Workhouses evolved out of these 'houses of correction' and from then on the use of imprisonment, with work, as punishment, and of course as social control, spread especially through the Hanseatic cities of Northern Europe, as well as through Catholic religious reform in the mid-Seventeenth Century in Florence and Northern Italy, and by the Quakers in Pennsylvania in the United States. However, the workhouse, which combined the punishment of criminals, debtors, with the simply unfortunate from the unemployed to those whose families could not look after them (Spierenberg, 1995), was never an adequate solution.

Foucault's (1977) analysis of the transition in the conception of the person that thereafter occurred involved not only the prison, but also the soldier, police and general militarization, as well as the emerging mechanical-biological science of the body, exemplified in La Mettrie's *L'Homme-machine*. These knowledges produced the idea that the body was trainable and improvable through repetitive disciplinary practices. Foucault's argument is that 'in the course of the seventeenth and eighteenth centuries, the disciplines became general formulas of domination' (1977, p. 137). Time and space would be divided to enclose but also partition, which involved both understanding the person and managing them in institutions (like medicine, factories and schools) and particular spatial formations (like military camps or the prison). Foucault used Bentham's Panopticon as simply the most powerful architectural exemplar, important because it was envisaged as a permanent structure for reinforcing order by self-surveillance. Rather than punish, it was to train the soul, to 'responsibilize' the person (see Chapters 1 and 11, where we discuss how Foucault developed the notion much more explicitly in his work on governmentality).

The Panopticon was never actually built in the form Bentham intended. In fact what came to be called 'panopticons' in prison design were simply circular prisons that retained none of the emphasis on light and visibility and instead were built of heavy stone walls with the usual locked doors (for an architectural description, see Fairweather, 1975). The moral content and humanistic intent of the Panopticon vanished very quickly.

However, it was the persistence and infiltration into wider society of the *idea* of surveillance that Foucault emphasized. In this we can see the notion of prisons as locations which should be under observation and rational disciplinary practices as spreading to surprising places. The vector for the spread of the panoptic idea was again, colonialism. The British in Asia in particular, away from the supervision of parliament and the inquiries of groups of reformers, experimented with urban and prison design for security (and new kinds of policing, as we shall see below). During the period of the Meiji restoration in Japan at the end of the Nineteenth Century, the new administration sent out many different groups of progressive administrators to learn from Western societies, in particular Prussia, France, the United States and Britain. As both Maeda Ai (2004 [1981]) and Daniel Botsman (2005) have shown, in law and penalty the Meiji were influenced in particular by the desire to be seen as worthy of 'civilized' imperialism. Prison design was transformed by the form and practices of colonial prisons of British Hong Kong and Singapore, not least because they were prisons for Asians. The changes affected even the language of confinement; the word for prison shifted to *kangoku* (surveillance gaol) (Maeda, 2004).

We have seen how the internal order of the city was enforced through the use of external and internal walls, barriers, banishment and exile and finally to the use of ghettos, gaols and the prison. However, these material orders were never enough. Particularly from the late mediaeval period into the modern period, the concern with the moral order of cities led to the increasing use of both moral messages from state and national authorities and the use of informers and police to keep urban order.

New moral orders

If the great plague infected social thought (Porter, 1999) and the Lisbon earthquake had continued to resonate long after the tremors had died down (de Boer and Sanders, 2005), one of the ways in which these affects were felt was in the shift in thinking about the proper order of society away from fatalism in the face of disaster and disruption towards the assessment of risk and solution of risk and hazard. However, the decline of 'providence' as an explanation did not mean that morality ceased to be part of social thought.

The enlightenment had produced by the Nineteenth Century new 'social sciences', aimed at applying the rationality of natural science to this collective entity produced in the new industrial cities, or more accurately at controlling the potentially disruptive influence of a new mass of people seeking work in the city. In London, they were referred to variously as the 'dangerous classes', the 'criminal classes' or most disparagingly of all, the 'residuum' (Jones, 1971).

Moral order had long been a major concern of urban authorities. Alan Hunt (1996; 1999) has developed a history of moral regulation of consumption in Europe and argues that 'moral regulation projects have been key vehicles for the articulation of the politics of the middle classes' (2004, p. 563). In early modern Japan, Sheldon Garon (1997) has shown how the soft control of state *kyōka* (lit. moral suasion) policies, designed to bring urban inhabitants – felt to lack traditional rural communal values – together in joint associations for mutual support and surveillance. Likewise, the moral order of cities was a major concern in a newly urbanizing Nineteenth Century United States of America. Paul Boyer's classic account (1978) enumerates the multiple schemes for its address, including the mass movements of urban improvers: from temperance leagues and anti-gambling groups, through clubs and societies to deal with 'idleness' like the Young Men's Christian Association (YMCA), to schemes for model communities (see also Smith, 1995). One might see in these schemes the beginning of what Pelling (2003) argues is the most effective form of urban resilience: the dense webs of community and civic institutions of a genuine 'civil society', which can be far more successful at surviving disruption and disaster than hierarchical control. However, as we have seen with prisons, hierarchical control was the other side of the coin at this time, and prisons were filled through the use of police, whose introduction was often followed by an intense reaction from the public of exactly the socially disruptive nature that urban elites had feared.

Police and informers

There is little space here to get into detailed arguments about the origins of the Police; however, we would generally agree with Brogden's (1987) assessment that until recently many accounts were beset by ethnocentrism; however, they were also fixated on transformations that happened in the modern period in Western Europe. This was certainly an important and transformative time, but to suggest that every organization concerned with urban social control before this period is something totally different from the 'new police' is unfair and too self-justificatory. Spatial and generalized moral social control has almost always been supplemented by forms of policing and surveillance, whether military or civil, uniformed or undercover.

In the unwalled ancient Greek city of Sparta, the outer line of defence of the city was effectively provided by the *krypteia*, an institution which has variously been described as citizenship education, a secret service, a commando school and a wild hunt, but had elements of all of these (see Heater, 2004). Membership was compulsory for two years for all men under 30, as well as being a military training process, the very existence and increasingly reputed cruelty of the *krypteia* served to chill any thoughts of regime change.

However, the spatial form of internal urban structure could also be highly influential on the kinds of policing systems that were developed. Ling (1990) describes how in Roman cities there was no system of naming or numbering of streets and this would have made all kinds of bureaucratic controls very difficult. This meant that state control was less dependent on the development of highly formalized bureaucracies than on human informants. In ancient Rome, these included the Augustinian *frumentarii* (lit. corn collectors). They have been called 'the Roman secret service' (Sinnigen, 1961), but became a kind of political police about whom there were frequent complaints for their effect on liberty and freedom of thought and expression. They were abolished under Diocletian but their replacements, the *agentes in rebus* (lit. general agents), were perhaps even worse (Sheldon, 2005). Of course, the presence of vast numbers of uniformed soldiers (and veterans) could and did function as internal agents of discipline; however, disaffected current and former soldiers were just as likely to be a threat to order (see Africa, 1971; Campbell, 2002). Indeed the initial purpose of the *frumentarii* was to keep order within the army, but in such a militarized society, it was perhaps inevitable that this would spread into broader urban social control.

Early modern Japan was far more spatially and socially controlled, as we have seen, but even so, Edo had a system of *meakashi* (lit. sharp-eyes) (Botsman, 2005), informants who were typically freed criminals and who operated in networks under their own bosses. Notorious for their own abuses of their position, these dubious characters were replaced by the *tesaki* (lit. fingertips) in the Eighteenth Century, of which there were 381 with over 1000 subordinates at the time of the Meiji Restoration.

The Ottoman Empire, which lasted into the Twentieth Century, suffered from the problems of a militarized society as much as ancient Rome (see Raymond, 1991) and its policing systems were remarkably similar to those of the much earlier Roman imperium. Swanson (1972) describes how several organizations had policing functions, including the *Janissary* guards, originally slaves and warriors from conquered territories, whose role was to keep military order in the Empire and who, like the Samurai in Japan, gradually became more bureaucratized and less martial as time went on. In Istanbul (Constantinople), several overlapping sets of secret police operated, nominally all under the control of the Grand Vizier, including the *Böjek Bashis*, who dealt with thieves, and the *Salma Chebdil Chokadaris*, who enforced punishment on infringers of Islamic *Sharia* law. In all major cities of the empire, the Janissaries also operated both a daytime 'beat' police service and control over trading practices – as Brogden observed, commercial policing is often downplayed – and a night watch which enforced the law that no one was allowed outside in the city without a lantern.

In most cities of the world then, either or both of military police or religio-political police (sometimes called *haute police* due to their role in protecting the regime) were the norm. However, it is undeniable that throughout Europe from the Seventeenth Century, more formal systems of policing began to be established. These were not particularly a product of industrialization as was long contended. We have seen how policing, formal and informal, has existed as a result of the felt need to manage the risks of social disorder (or even revolution) in increasingly populous and culturally diverse urban centres. The new police in Europe were a product initially of the merging of enlightenment rationalism and absolutist authority, and were also connected to the demands of the new technologies of warfare (Raeff, 1972). This laid the grounds for the interventionist and welfarist states that would emerge in the Nineteenth and Twentieth Centuries.

Raeff contended that the new 'policing' originated in the French and Prussian interest in internal order and a regulated society, in the latter case, through numerous *kanzeleiordnungen* (lit. chancellery orders) and later *polizeiordnungen* (lit. policing orders) (Raeff, 1972). In Berlin, the new officials were able to be drawn from existing (mediaeval) guild structures, which combined with a spatial ordering of administrative quarters and districts meant a relatively cheap solution. In Russia, however, the absence of these institutions meant a very centralized and expensive police service (Raeff, 1972). The connection of policing to the centre almost inevitably led to an over-powerful role for political police throughout the late Russian empire and into the Twentieth Century (see Brower, 1986).

The conditions of industrialization were already in place in the Eighteenth Century, and yet in his famous study of the pre-revolutionary Paris police, Alan Williams (1979) showed that the essential function of this organization was as a social espionage systems based on networks of informers, which also acted as a bureau of censorship. In other words, this was a political police remarkably like those of the great imperial capitals of Beijing, Edo or St Petersburg, and much less 'modern' in many ways than those of Istanbul. One might have expected this to change after the Revolution but in fact it did not, and in the period of the *terreur* Robespierre made great use of the facilities and resources of the police (ibid.). The investigation of 'low crime', in other words the concerns of ordinary people, did not become a more important area until the establishment of the *Sûreté* in 1812 and then the *Sergents de Ville* in 1854, under Napolean III (Williams, 2006).

The French system, eventually settling to a basic division between an armed gendarmerie and a civilian police, became a model for policing across Southern Europe and the Mediterranean world. Sometimes, this was imposed through occupation. In the Papal cities of pre-Risorgemento Italy, the Papal court police, the *sbirri*, who had performed a set of oppressive functions that combined those of the various Ottoman police, were transformed into a uniformed police under Napolean III's regime and eventually evolved into a French-style dual police system (Hughes, 1994). Sometimes, the threat of French power prompted change in pre-emptive imitation. For example, in the Ottoman Empire, the power of the Janissaries in relation to the Sultan eventually led to their abolition in 1826 and the evolution of a civil police force formalized in 1870, with a form of armed military 'gendarmerie' still keeping order outside Istanbul (Swanson, 1972). Ironically as the Empire declined in the early Twentieth Century, and the rulers feared a communist uprising, policing reverted back to a more political model.

Britain was somewhat different. Palmer (1988) argued that the London elite were horrified by the intrusive functions of the Parisian police, and it took a long time for anything like an organized police to be established in British cities. There were two major factors which speeded the process: urban population growth and the experience of colonialism. As in the United States, the first was the rapid urbanization and pressures placed upon the burgeoning urban society in the Eighteenth Century by the expansion of the industrial urban poor (Taylor, 1997). This was combined, as in ancient Rome, with the influx of injured or unemployed soldiers returning from wars, in this case with Napoleonic France. Despite the widespread urban disorder of the period, rural life was relatively unchanged and landowners often hired soldiers as organized militias on private estates. However, in the city the *nouveau riche* elites were nervous of the threat of disorder (and at worst, revolution in the French style) to their positions, persons and properties from the new masses of morally problematic poor (see Jones, 1971). Certain magistrates of London in the Eighteenth Century had been acting in a similar fashion to the rural landowners in hiring enforcers and detectives to bring people before the courts, including the famous Bow Street Runners; however, it was not until 1829 that Robert Peel established a Metropolitan police force, independent of both crown and parliament, with a specific remit for crime prevention under the English Common Law.

The new police were not necessarily popular with either the working classes or with the elites whose interests they were supposed to serve. In the United States, police were employed to break up the strikes and demonstrations which characterized the late Nineteenth Century. The key point in this era of discontent occurred in 1886 at Haymarket Square in Chicago, the city that was at the time, 'the disorderly embodiment of instability, growth and change' (Smith, 1995, p. 7 – see also Harring, 1983). When police tried to break up a large demonstration, they were attacked by a home-made anarchist bomb, which killed one and injured many more, but the police response was to kill four protestors and again, injure others.

Initially the British police were also disliked. It was not just the monitoring and sometimes suppressing of mass protest or meetings of reformers' groups, however, but in the everyday practices of targeting the urban poor that created dissatisfaction. As Taylor comments, 'the practice of "moving on" men in the street was highly unpopular and impinged on large numbers' (p. 99).

Colonial policing and the rise of political police

However, the other reason for the transformation of policing was at first entirely unconnected to London or Paris. It was based in the cities of India, Africa and South-East Asia and Ireland. In the interaction with Western modernism in the colonial period, the social ordering practices of both colonizing and colonized cities were also transformed. We have already seen how other aspirational colonial states, such as Japan, were changed. However, there were strong connections between colonial law enforcement and the emergence of political police in Western Europe; in other words, the colonized countries acted as experimental proving grounds for new techniques of urban spatial and social order, before the application of the 'lessons' of control in the colonies could be 'brought home' to the cities of the colonial nations. Palmer's (1988) comparative work on the Irish and English police is instructive here as is Tony Bunyan's (1977) and Bernard Porter's (1987) research on the evolution of political police. Bunyan and Porter both argued that the experience of policing India and Ireland led to the establishment of the 'Special Branch' of the Metropolitan Police in 1881, in particular the anxiety after the 1857 Indian 'Mutiny' which led to the establishment of the India Office 'Political and Secret Department', and the Fenian uprising of 1867. So although the supposedly racial reasons for the problems of control were emphasized in public (Anderson and Killingray, 1991), behind the scenes the class dimensions were recognized and more generic 'lessons learned'. The latter also emphasize how the policing of colonial order concentrated for the most part upon the protection of white property, which evolved independently from the practices in British cities but ended up looking remarkably similar: for example, foot patrols, fingerprinting, forensics and detective work.

However, there were large differences too. The moral questions of drunkenness and gambling were of particular concern where 'other races' were involved, and the emergence of very particular forms of regulation like the so-called 'Indian List' in Ontario (Genosko and Thompson, 2005; see also Sturgis, 1991) was particular to the colonies. Likewise the way in which the British adapted the caste system of the Punjab to their own notions of the dangerous classes by classifying thousands of Punjabis as hereditary criminals (Major, 1999).

Surveillance and identification

It was clear to many early modern writers especially to those from the nation-states with absolutist regimes, that the state and the law had the right to the identity of its citizens. The influential Prussian thinker, Johann Gottlieb Fichte, wrote in 1796 that 'no one must remain unknown to the police' (quoted in Groebner, 2007, p. 229). Groebner shows the complexity of establishing identity in the pre-modern period, and how this was at different times and in different places dependent on marks on the skin like scars and deliberate bodily markings, or alternatively on signifiers carried with the person, like seals and letters of safe conduct.

However in the modern period, along with new ways of confining and new organizations for the detection and control of those worthy of confinement, ways of establishing identity and character became an even larger concern for the elites. Once again the link with industrialism is weak, as this informatization of urban social control did not occur in the Eighteenth Century, as Higgs (2004) remarks on Britain, 'long after the creation of an industrial society, policing in England was based very little on information' (p. 97).

Instead, this surveillance surge took place in the later part of Nineteenth Century, the period of moral panic at the sheer rise in numbers of the unoccupied urban poor. This was a time of huge growth in interest in social classification across all fields from the intellectual to the spatial which included developments as diverse as the Dewey decimal system for books in 1876 and Taylor's scientific approach to the most efficient positioning of workers in factories (Bowker and Star, 1999). The new rational approaches also meant the application of science and new technologies to the problem of order in the massively growing cities of Europe and America.

There were many differences in approach. Alan Sekula (1986) argues that Alphonse Bertillon of the Paris police, whose *bertillonage* combined photographs and written information, was seeking to identify individuals whereas, with his method of composite photography, the British eugenicist Francis Galton, was attempting to find the 'criminal type'. This would establish some general rules for identifying *all* criminals as a group in the manner of the castes of India or Japan. This would provide 'a gauge of the intentions or capabilities of the other' (ibid., p. 13), and allow the development of 'distinctions between incorrigible and pliant criminals and the disciplined conversion of the reformable into "useful" proletarians' (ibid., p. 14).

However, Galton was not just interested in broad typographies, he was also an enthusiast of fingerprinting for identification, and published a text on the subject in 1892. Bertillonage declined because it was too complicated and thorough for the information retrieval systems of the time, and it was fingerprinting in the end that proved to have the best combination of convenience and reliability (Finn, 2005). Here again, there was a link to colonial practice: the first use of fingerprinting was in the Indian police as the British authorities claimed that Indians all looked the same (Higgs, 2004).

Many of the attempts at classificatory identification were ludicrously pseudo-scientific and racist, and some were discredited within decades, for example the practice of phrenology (the measurement of the topology of the head) (Parssinen, 1974; Van Wyhe, 2004). Galton aimed at producing evidence for his political contention that the unfit should be bred out of the population before Britons degenerated into Africans. However, as Sekula (1986) observes, his composite photographs just 'dissolved the boundary between the criminal and the working-class poor, the residuum that so haunted the imagination of the late Victorian bourgeoisie' (p. 50). His proudest achievement was the classification of 'the Jewish type' (Green, 1984; Sekula, 1986). It was an obsession which would return to haunt the Twentieth Century.

Towards the Twentieth Century

Internal spatial separation, policing and the rise in 'scientific' methods of identification were part of a contemporary Euro-American trend towards defining the new threat to cities as from (possibly hereditary) classes of people, for example 'criminals' (see Wetzell, 2000). Concern with the inherent and possibly revolutionary threat of 'dangerous classes', and the efforts of elites to separate themselves from them, came up against the more socially inclusive and welfarist thinking which was to gain increasing prominence in the mid-Twentieth Century (see Chapter 3). However, it is no exaggeration to say that the combination of these developments of rebuilding and privatization of space with surveillance of suspicious groups may have set the tone for thinking about urban resilience, threat, crime and disorder in the late Twentieth Century (see Chapters 5 and 6). In the middle of all of this, however, there was again war, but war of a kind that threatened to remove any possibility of defending the city.

4
The Threat of Total Devastation

In the previous two chapters we have examined the nature of both threats to cities and urban order and responses to those threats into the modern period. However, the nature of threat, external defences and the internal control of cities all changed remarkably during the Twentieth Century. Towards the end of the Nineteenth and beginning of the Twentieth Century, the urban revolutions that had been feared by urban elites were actually successful in some places, as in Russia (thereafter the Soviet Union). The control of colonies also became more tenuous as independence movements grew stronger and European economies were overstretched by the costs of maintaining order and successive world wars. Internal control and surveillance reached their greatest intensities in the nations and empires that had overthrown their previous regimes: in the Soviet Union, Nazi Germany and Fascist Italy. However, it was only after the Second World War (WW2) that the nadir of the totalitarian surveillance state would be reached in the German Democratic Republic.

Although warfare became increasingly industrialized and increased hugely in its intensity, cities had become open and increasingly connected centres for industrial power rather than defended spaces. Industrialization also made cities huge, and natural events became correspondingly more disastrous. Cities once again became targets for destruction in war. In the First World War (WW1), cities were not under permanent threat; however, the rise of airpower had not gone unnoticed. Thereafter, the vertical became increasingly important and cities became targets for attack from above, first by aircraft, and then by long-distance missiles. Even though WW2 and after saw instances of siege warfare, for example with Stalingrad and Berlin, the threat of annihilation of cities without any possibility of defence – made real in WW2 by the fire-bombing of Dresden, London, Tokyo and others and particularly by the atomic bombing of Hiroshima and Nagasaki – made the abandonment of cities, once again, a more distinct possibility. Plans for evacuation, retreat (out of cities or underground) became priorities for both civil and military authorities in the post-WW2 period.

This chapter is divided into three parts. The first considers the impact of natural disasters on increasingly connected cities. The second analyses the combined changes in industry and warfare that led to an age of industrial war. Finally, the response of urban and national authorities is considered from civil defence through the possibility of abandonment to the growth of an increasingly paranoid urban surveillance.

Natural disasters of the early Twentieth Century and their consequences

Disasters in the Twentieth Century were less localized. It was not that any direct destruction was necessarily greater, although this tended to be the case where cities were expanding rapidly with poor infrastructure and building standards. However, by the early 1900s, the networks of economic relationships linking cities in the mediaeval and early modern period had started to become more integrated into a single world system of capitalism (Wallerstein, 1989), which before WW1 was dealing in volumes and values of trade that were greater than at any time before or indeed for many years afterwards (Hirst and Thompson, 1999). This can be illustrated in the San Francisco earthquake of 1906. The Lisbon earthquake might have reverberated culturally, but the after-effects of the San Francisco quake plunged the United States into an economic recession (Odell and Wiedenmeir, 2004). It also sparked a transformation of government preparedness and recovery.

The earthquake itself, which struck on 18 April 1906, was one of the biggest ever though not as disastrous in terms of loss of life as earlier quakes, with no more than 3000 people in total dying in the whole area and maybe as few as 700 out of a population of more than 400,000 (USGS, nd.). However, as the majority of buildings were still wooden, it was the ensuing fire that destroyed most of the centre of the city, and caused most of the damage which was estimated (much later) to have cost around $400,000,000 (NOAA, quote in USGS nd.). However, it was the insurance claims that caused the economic disaster, and they demonstrated that cities were now bound up in trade and finance linkages that made urban disasters resonate much more widely than ever before (Odell and Wiedenmeir, 2004).

The San Francisco quake was also significant because of the response in many areas. Although nation-state bureaucracies had been growing for some years, the earthquake contributed to the development of more specialized national agencies and systems of accountability for learning lessons from such disasters and implementing them. It also increased the role of academic scientific expertise. For example, the Report of the State Earthquake commission set up by scientists immediately after the quake was initially funded by a private charity, the Carnegie Institution of Washington (Lawson, 1969 [1908]); however, it came to be regarded as a model for government inquiries into disaster and resulted in the setting up of the Seismological Society of America (Rubey, 1969). The earthquake's economic consequences also led to the creation of modern economic management systems to help minimize the vulnerabilities that were created through the interdependence of financial flows, eventually leading to the creation of the Federal Reserve System (Odell and Wiedenmeir, 2004).

The lessons were not learnt everywhere immediately. Although there had been Japanese seismologists involved in the Carnegie report, the major threats to cities continued to come from the combination of ill-supported urban growth and natural events. The *Kantō Daishinsai* (Great Kanto Earthquake) and subsequent fire struck Tokyo and the surrounding area in 1923, killing around 140,000 (Davison, 1925, quoting contemporary Japanese sources, gives just under 100,000). Tokyo, even more than San Francisco, was a city of wood. We have seen how Tokyo, during the Edo period, had developed complex social systems for disaster prevention and the watching of fire in particular. However, these were of little use in such a devastating disaster and the state had not developed effective prevention or relief systems.

The politics of rebuilding Tokyo after the *Kantō Daishinsai* illustrate just how quickly the lessons of the quake dissipated. The central theme of the plans adopted was to drive great avenues through the old city in Hausmanesque fashion, and it is clear that the impetus was as much about creating the perception of a modern city ready for economic growth as creating firebreaks in the urban form (Jinnai, 1987; Schencking, 2006; Sorensen, 2002). The rebuilding was best by political arguments and compensations policies to landowners that allowed cheap and still wooden-framed temporary buildings to be put up in return for the land lost to the new roads. The post-earthquake rebuilding therefore intensified the problems of over-dense, poorly built housing outside of the new main streets.

The quake once again showed the role of the new class of scientific experts (perhaps one of the long-term consequences of Lisbon). Academic journals now existed where experts could share their observations on disaster, and which would in turn influence policy. One such expert, Charles Davison, writing in the British *Geographical Journal* in 1925, argued that 'it is doubtful that another on the same scale will ever occur again, for there is no city now existing with so many wooden houses as Tokyo possessed in 1923' (p. 41). However, as shall see, he was not correct. The continuity of the Japanese city as a wooden construction would lead to a special place for it in the history of thinking not just about natural disaster, but about deliberate destruction in war, which is where we shall now turn.

Industrial war and the city

David Hounshell (1984) famously showed how the origins of the Fordist mass production line lay in the creation of standardized parts for the French military in the late Eighteenth Century. It was the Americans at the armouries of Springfield and Harpers Ferry, who adopted this with most vigour, and arms manufacturer, Samuel Colt, who took this further than anyone else with the development of almost entirely machine-produced rifles and hand-guns (see also Ruttan, 2006). These developments meant major changes in the tactics of war like camouflage uniforms and dispersion on the battlefield (Van Creveld, 1991) and the advent of the railway-driven *blitzkrieg* (see Black, 1998).

Yet despite this, strategy in land warfare was still recognizably Napoleonic even in WW2 (Van Creveld, 1991). What changed were five factors: the scale of war; the growth of armoured seapower (beyond the scope of this book); the role of defensive fortification; the impact of air-power, which would see a renewed threat of destruction to cities; and finally, the deliberate targeting of civilians for annihilation.

The scale of war: the Twentieth Century haemoclysm[1]

War by the beginning of the Twentieth Century was huge in scale, economic importance and social impact. Initiated by the move to mass mobilization that began with the French Revolutionary forces in the late 1790s, the numbers of men in uniform exceeded four million in Europe in 1900. However, the real arms race had not even started. Its role in fermenting the First World War is still unclear – the theory that there is an inherent propensity to war in investment in armaments (Anderton, 1990) is still open to debate. However, it is undoubtedly true that nations had devoted huge resources to war by this time, with the united Germany having engaged in a massive naval build-up since the late 1890s which led to naval competition with Britain in particular (see Hamilton and Herwig, 2003; Henig, 2001; Strachan, 2000). More than ever before too, the economic capacity of nations to wage war was increased: Black (1998) emphasizes the role of American industrial capacity in determining the outcome of the war, at least on the Western front.

The destruction of the war was equally massive and industrial in its scale. It would appear to have killed about 15 million people, up to nine million of them troops (Black, 1998; White, 2005a). Added to this was the massive global influenza pandemic which killed perhaps 50 or even 100 million of the battered and weakened population in the years immediately afterwards the war (Johnson and Mueller, 2002). Finally, the economic after-effects of WW1 and the conditions of the peace imposed upon Germany in particular sent inflation sky-high, contributed to the Great Depression and ultimately to war once again (Hobsbaum, 1994). However, the 'war to end all wars' was only half as destructive as WW2, which resulted in the deaths of around 50 million and the majority of them civilians (White, 2005a; see also Mazower, 1998).

The threat of airpower

One of the main changes between 1900 and WW2 was the return of the threat of total destruction to the city from war. Despite the massive death toll, WW1 was a war fought mainly in the fields and on the sea. However, the signs of the change to come had been visible long before. The Montgolfier brothers had flown a hot balloon in 1783 in Paris, and the French military had already created a corps of *aerostations* by the late 1790s (Fuller, 1992; Hyde, 1976). These were largely used for reconnaissance; however, in 1849, there was the first recorded bombing of city from the air when Venice was attacked by Austrian balloonists (Buckley, 1999; Ziegler, 1994).

Most Western powers had balloon corps of some kind by the late Nineteenth Century but they were not taken very seriously as weapons platforms, not least because they could not be guided independent of the wind direction. The invention of the dirigible airship by Santos-Dumont and more significantly the Zeppelin in Germany meant a genuinely new threat to armies and to cities. Many of the prophecies of war in Clarke's (1966) excellent survey of the fiction of this time envisaged cities destroyed by flying machines and there were panics in

Britain and the United States about 'phantom airships' (Gollin, 1981). The development of the heavier-than-air aeroplane meant that natural defences were now on their way to being useless: when Louis Bleriot crossed the channel in 1906, Lord Northcliffe, owner of the *Daily Mail* newspaper, remarked that Britain was no longer an island (Edgerton, 1991; Hyde, 1976).

The First World War saw attacks on cities by both airships and aeroplanes and, although these were not intense by later standards, 'by war's end, bombs had hit every capital of the European powers except Rome' (Sherry, 1987, p. 13). As Sherry remarks, in WW1, aerial bombardment was felt to be more significant as a reflection of a decline in moral values rather than a serious strategy. For that reason many dismissed it, including famously, Winston Churchill, as simply a form of 'terrorization of the civil population' (quoted in Sherry, 1987, p. 5), which would ultimately be unsuccessful. In total, only 1413 people were killed in Britain, mainly in London, and most of these were during the last 18 months of the war when the German forces turned to their new *Gotha* aeroplanes instead of the *Zeppelin* (O'Brien, 1955).

The 1920s was, as Sherry claims, 'the golden age of speculation about the aeroplane' (1987, p. 23), and saw visionary plans across the world for air warfare. Azar Gat (1998) argues that these were essentially modernist visions of fast, clean and efficient killing that would end wars quickly. In the United States, General Billy Mitchell argued the case for the combination of gas and air warfare as the means to destroy the population of cities without destroying the structure.[2] He had no time for the moral arguments about terrorization of civilians, writing as early as 1921 that:

> the only way a war can be brought to a successful conclusion in the case of determined resistance is to carry the war into the enemy's country; and in modern times, this may mean attacking his whole population, means of production, and subsistence.
>
> (quoted in Spaatz, 1947)

That General Spaatz was still quoting Mitchell approvingly after the horrors of indiscriminate bombing of WW2 shows how far away the world was from Edwardian concerns about moral decline. And Mitchell foresaw those horrors too: for him the lessons of the 1923 Tokyo earthquake and fire were not to do with recovery and resilience, but rather that 'these towns are built largely of wood and paper to resist the devastations of earthquakes and form the greatest aerial targets the world has ever seen' (quoted in Sherry, 1987, p. 58). The city was now the object of attack for its own sake.

By the 1930s, many nation-states had developed the types of aircraft necessary for strategic bombing. Contradicting Churchill's earlier assessment, Stanley Baldwin warned in the British House of Commons in 1932 that 'the bomber will always get through', and further that this changed the nature of warfare, 'the only defence is in offence, which means that you have to kill more women and more children more quickly than the enemy if you want to save yourselves' (*Hansard*, 10 November 1932).

Even the hint of their use could lead to drastic action. Sherry (1987) makes it clear that it was the United States's open movement of bombers to the Pacific that led to Japan's surprise attack on Pearl Harbour. Of course, Japan already knew what bombers could do, having used them in its invasion of China, and by now the whole world was aware. Initially, it was easy to condemn as it was only the Fascists and Nazis who used bombers against cities and civilians. First, there was Mussolini in his pointless imperial adventure in Abyssinia, and then most notoriously the Nazi Vulture Squadron destroyed the Basque city of Guernica in support of Franco's Falangists in the Spanish Civil War in 1937.

However, depressingly, Baldwin was to be proved correct and terrorization of the civil population was to be the most significant feature of war in the Twentieth Century from the 1930s. Bombing of cities was a strategy adopted by all, even if they disapproved of its use by 'the other side'. The panic caused amongst the US urban elite by a few small homemade bombs thrown by anarchists at the end of the Nineteenth Century was to be nothing to what the elite of all nations meted out on the unfortunate urban populations of cities in WW2.

Mitchell's boast about Japanese cities fulfilled itself: they were repeatedly attacked with conventional and incendiary bombs, culminating in the intense fire-bombings of Tokyo in 1945 that left between 100,000 and 125,000 people dead. The single raid of 9 March is estimated to have had a death toll of 84,000 perhaps the largest single death toll from any single conventional aerial attack (White, 2005b). This time the city would be rebuilt in steel and concrete, ironically under American occupation (see Dower, 2000). Western cities suffered almost as much from aerial bombardment. In Britain, London suffered casualties of around 20,000 in the Blitz, and Coventry a little less than half that number, yet the city survived and this was celebrated in an act of almost instantaneously created official mythology (UKMI, 1941). In Germany, Dresden and Hamburg together lost about 80,000 in RAF fire-bombings in 1943 and 1945, and Berlin around the same as London under American raids. US cities in contrast, were untouched.

In a long-term perspective, the most obvious and devastating threat to the city came from the atomic bomb. A possibility ever since the atom was split in the 1920s, the bomb was the product of a massive mobilization of scientists by the US state (Jungk, 1958; Rhodes, 1986), racing against a similar mobilization in Germany (Powers, 2000). Led by Robert Oppenheimer, the US 'Manhattan Project' succeeded too late to use the weapon in Europe, and instead two bombs were dropped on the cities of Hiroshima and Nagasaki in Japan,[3] instantly killing around 80,000 and 45,000, respectively, and condemning at least as many more again to painful slow deaths from the effects of radiation. The blast that was 'brighter than a thousand suns' (Jungk, 1958) cast a long shadow over cities for the rest of the century, and new means of delivery made even the bomber seem amateur.

Exterminations, old and new

However, despite the impact of airpower and the atomic bomb on the city, none of the immediate death tolls were anywhere near the levels of first of all, the Holocaust, or the old-fashioned siege warfare that characterized the Eastern front in the Soviet Union.

The deliberate genocide of Jews, Slavs and Romany people as well as the mass killing of homosexuals, communists and political enemies led to the deaths of over ten million (almost five million of those being Jewish). Naimark (2007) makes the case that the exterminations cannot really be separated from the way that the war was conducted by the Nazis. Military historians have tended to attempt to keep them separate, seemingly out of some misguided belief that there is still, after all the history of the Twentieth Century, some elusive form of honourable war as opposed to something worse: genocide, terrorism, ethnic cleansing. However, the Nazis were seeking a 'purified' empire, and this necessarily involved total war and total annihilation of its perceived enemies within and without: this was *vernichtungskreig* (lit. race war) (Mazower, 1998). If war and cities have been intertwined, the Holocaust also involved the extreme possibilities of developments that were key to urbanity and civilization. They took the logic of internal division of the ghetto and the expulsions of the Middle Ages, and combined them with the military concentration camp that had been invented by the British in the Boer War (itself of a lineage including the lazaretto and the prison), and the industrial methods of the factory (Sofsky, 1997). On the fringes of the old Pale of Settlement, the *endlösung* (lit. final solution) brought together the latest innovations in gas warfare with the newest technologies of surveillance and information management in the use of IBM Hollerith machines to organize the condemned (Black, 2002) in vast prison-factories devoted to the production line slaughter of its worker-prisoners. If there was ever any real humanitarian use for aerial bombing, it was surely to destroy the death camps or at least the railways and supply lines that led to them; however, the allies knew and did nothing (see Neufeld and Berenbaum, 2000).

Not everything in WW2 was high-technology extermination. The epic sieges of the Eastern Front between Germany and the Soviet Union were mediaeval methods at modern scales. Leningrad and Stalingrad alone cost around 850,000 and 750,000 lives respectively, and these were only a proportion of the deaths resulting from Hitler's massive Operation Barbarossa (see Weinberg, 1994). The street-by-street urban fighting that took place in Berlin and other German cities as the war came to an end was also the bloodiest of its type ever seen. It was quite clear by the end of WW2 that the city offered no protection against a determined attacker and its civilization and diversity no protection against oppression. If its original purpose had indeed been pathological as Munford claimed (see Chapter 2), the city was now pathetic: utterly wide-open, divided, defenceless and more vulnerable than it had ever been.

The city in a MAD world

The renewed vulnerability of the city persisted and even intensified after WW2. It was made most plain by the advent of nuclear weapons, but it was the combination of nuclear weapons with newly developed rocket technologies that made this a persistent threat. The Nazi V1 and V2 rockets made more of a psychological than a military impact in WW2 (see King and Kutta, 2003); however, it was the capture of Nazi plans and the leading rocket scientists like Wernher Von Braun by the Americans that led to this apocalyptic technological combination (Neufeld, 1995).

The development of the Intercontinental Ballistic Missile (ICBM), launched from land or submarine or aircraft, meant that no city anywhere on earth could consider itself safe. Would this mean the end of cities? Freedman (1989) showed how in the early 1960s, there was a proposed policy of 'city-avoidance' by the United States, when ICBM sites rather than cities were considered to be the primary target. However, this did not last, and for the USSR, 'the notion of "Marquis of Queensbury rules for the conduct of nuclear war" was treated with derision' (p. 241).

Some thought a nuclear war winnable and there were at least five occasions when US presidents made direct threats of nuclear attack between 1946 and 1970 (see Kaku and Axelrod, 1987). Even during the second Cold War, the veteran analyst, Herman Kahn (1984) reiterated this possibility. Britain briefly considered the idea of becoming a non-nuclear power, but rapidly replaced this with the development of its own nuclear delivery system, the 'Blue Streak' missile, eventually cancelled in 1960 (Hill, 2001). Thereafter, the insistence on maintaining a British nuclear 'deterrent' meant that Britain became increasingly dependent on the United States, and increasingly vulnerable to nuclear attack as what Campbell (1984) called America's 'unsinkable aircraft carrier'.

The political systems that developed to cope recognized an updated version of Baldwin's dictum, 'the missile will always gets through', and the escalation in numbers and power of nuclear and conventional missiles meant the emergence of a stand-off between the two major post-war blocs that lasted until the fall of the Soviet Union, largely bankrupted by the effort, in 1989. 'Mutually Assured Destruction' or MAD meant that no rational government would ever use nuclear missiles because it would result in their total annihilation, however 'successful' their own strike was (Freedman, 1989). Left-wing writer, E.P. Thompson, called it 'exterminism' which he described as 'the final stage of human civilization' (New Left Review, 1982). The world would effectively become a closed system (Edwards, 1996), a kind of city at global level, girded by missiles targeted only at itself.

The resilience of the city to industrial war

Responses to the industrialization of warfare came at many levels. First, there were attempts to control warfare and to give it recognized rules, a development of the informal (and frequently broken) agreements and norms that had existed since the early mediaeval period in Europe.[4] Secondly, there were still attempts to fortify and defend cities and indeed a return to the idea of fortifying whole countries. However, as the threat of airpower and then ICBMs became clear, this was supplemented with civilian preparedness or 'civil defence' to ensure the survival of populations even if the city as an entity could no longer be protected. Then, there were plans for the worst and for the abandonment of cities with no intention of preserving the mass of people. Finally, in the second half of the Twentieth Century, new technologies of early warning later supplemented by satellite monitoring, missile-interception and even space warfare suggested that the threat of annihilation could be averted or defended against even if the MAD strategy failed.

Fortification in the early Twentieth Century

The increasing power of weaponry, and especially mortar and howitzer shells which fell from above, and the extensive, dispersed nature of warfare by the early Twentieth Century meant that the days of the *trace italienne*, and indeed the basic idea of the closed circular fortification, the *enceinte* itself, were finally over. The basic new form which evolved during the Nineteenth Century was the ring or girdle system, where dispersed detached forts were scattered in a circular pattern around what was to be defended (Mallory and Ottar, 1973). They began to contain moveable cupolas for large guns, and the body of the fortification itself was increasingly buried. The new structural building materials of the industrial age like iron, steel and concrete made them more expensive, and they took much longer to construct, with the result that by the time of WW1, many were incomplete and ineffective.

Although there were many very good examples of purely urban defences built along the new principles like those around Liege, Namur and Antwerp in Belgium and Paris in France, fortification was no longer concentrated around major cities, and there was a return to the ancient 'line' system of groups of fortifications on frontiers, or around strategic military positions and supply routes such as bridges and railway lines. Before WW1, the French had constructed a system of frontier fortifications around and between Verdun, Toul, Epinal and Belfort; however, as Mallory and Ottar (1973) remarked, the lessons of warfare in the trenches had a more lasting impact outside of France and despite Verdun's holding out, 'the field fortifications which were developed during 1914–18 in fact proved to be stronger than the permanent fortifications' (p. 33).

Despite this and the growth of tank warfare and airpower, the post-WW1 period saw the largest and most expensive example of the return to the line system, the fortifications constructed under Minister of War, André Maginot. This was a massive system of permanently manned *ouvrages* (underground forts), tunnels, buried artillery positions and banked walls supported by independent electricity supply and power generation. Propaganda talked of it being 'coast to coast'; however, it was far from complete and was bypassed very early in the war in 1940, leaving Paris wide open to occupation. It was, as Mallory and Ottar (1973) concluded, 'an expensive mistake in every possible sense', and indeed despite the fears of the allies over the similar but improved 'West Wall' constructed by the Nazis late in the war, this system too proved nothing more than a delaying tactic (see also Black, 2002). It was a hugely costly one in terms of lives and money, but like the ancient walls they echoed, the message that the lines represented was almost more important, although this message too was less impressive by the time of the ICBM.

This is not to say that walling was thereafter irrelevant. However, it re-emerged in surprising ways. The first was rhetorical. Churchill's remarks in 1946 that an 'iron curtain' was descending across Europe (Hobsbaum, 1994) was not for the most part reflective of any material wall. However, in Berlin, the rhetoric became reality. Berlin was totally within the half of Germany occupied by the Soviet Union yet it had, like Vienna, been divided into four zones after the end of the war. The Soviet Zone became East Berlin, and the French, British and American zones, West Berlin, effectively a 188-square mile urban territorial enclave (see Robinson, 1953, for a contemporary geographical analysis). From 1948 to 1949, Stalin attempted unsuccessfully to blockade West Berlin; however, the two halves were still much interconnected until 1961 when a set of walls, guard posts, barricades and minefields were constructed between and around West Berlin which persisted until 1989 (see Ladd, 1997; and Chapter 5).

Early warning systems

For the most part, it was as much as any state could do to develop early warning systems of aerial assault. Huge concrete sound mirrors had served in the 1920s and early 1930s to concentrate the sounds of approaching places or ships; however, these were rapidly replaced by RADAR in place in both Germany and the United Kingdom by 1939 (Kendal, 2003). Radar was however limited when it came to tracking the launch and flight of ballistic missiles. Brian Stocker (2004) has argued that Ballistic Missile Defence in Britain owes much to the experience of London as the major target of V2 attacks; however just as with its missile programme, its early warning and defence programmes were quickly dominated by the United States. As in the case of the Blue Streak missile programme, this was largely because of the cost of maintaining an independent warning programme. Declassified documents in the National Archives show that the Ballistic Missile Early Warning System (BMEWS) built at the compromise location of Fylingdales, in North Yorkshire, would not have offered much protection to British people. The supposed 30-minute warning offered to the United States, was never more than a 4-minute warning to the United Kingdom, which would not have provided enough time for anyone other than those with immediate access to proper shelters (central government) to escape a nuclear strike (Wood, 2001).

In the 1960s, technologies changed rapidly. Satellites began to supplement ground-based detection systems. The United States had launched its first surveillance satellite in 1959, two years after the first Soviet 'Sputnik' orbit, and by 1966, hundreds of public and secret launches had taken place (Burrows, 1987). The history of satellites designed to provide early warning against missile or other aerial or orbital assault is a tangled web beset by secrecy. As with the ground-based BMEWS, Britain relied on the American systems, including the MIDAS operated from 1960 until 1963 (Richelson, 1999); the Defence Support Program (DSP) (1970–1997); and most recently, the Space-Based Infra-Red System (SBIRS), part of the National Missile Defense (NMD) programme, which also included upgrading BMEWS with huge pyramidal Phased-Array Radars. In the United Kingdom the SBIRS component, like that of the DSP programme before it, is based at Menwith Hill, the massive US National Security Agency site in North Yorkshire (Bamford, 1983; Wood, 2001). The irony remains that no 'defence' systems against Ballistic Missiles yet offer anything of that nature. Despite the rhetoric of the Star Wars programme in the 1980s, US Space Command in the 1990s and the few tests of ballistic missile-killing missiles, early warning is still the predominant purpose. And early warning has always had a complex politics, bound up with issues of social order and civil defence, which is where we now turn.

The evolution of civil defence in the United Kingdom

As we have seen, neither international agreements nor fortifications nor early warning were able to prevent the destruction of cities or defend them from targeting in practice, and nation-states and within them urban authorities had to develop plans for the safeguarding of populations in worst-case scenarios. Given the focus of the rest of the book, we will concentrate here largely on the British experience.

Britain maintained a strong tradition of volunteerism which had persisted from the Victorian times (Roberts, 2004), a form of normatively moral self-reliance which saw misfortune as the fault of the unfortunate. The result for urban defence was (and remains) a reliance on guidelines, codes of practice, local implementation and voluntary associations. The idea persisted that preventing public panic and preserving the state was more important than providing genuine protection for people, as is noted by critical investigators such as Tom Harrisson (1976) and Duncan Campbell (1982), as well as more conventional academic analysis such as that of Lawrence Vale (1987). Thus the volunteer responsibility has always been backed by the threat of force embodied in the use of states of exception or emergency powers.

Most agree that the response to bombing raids on London in the First World War was belated and bewildered. The officially sanctioned report on civil defence in Britain published by HMSO in 1955, admits that 'the Government only gave in gradually and reluctantly to demands for public warnings in London', and that when it did concede to public pressure, the measures were 'somewhat primitive' (O'Brien, 1955, p. 10). The description given makes this seem somewhat of an understatement:

> Warnings were distributed partly by maroons (or sound bombs) fired into the air, and partly by policemen on foot, on bicycles, or in cars carryings *Take Cover* placards and blowing whistles of sounding horns. (ibid.)

Although later some public buildings were designated as shelters in the capital, it was left to local authorities elsewhere, and many people in any case preferred the sanctuary of the underground, or to leave the city for the suburbs or the country, if they could.

After WW1, a new Air Raid Precautions Sub-Committee was eventually established in 1924. It concentrated very much on likely attacks on London, and came up with a rather arbitrary estimate of how many people were likely to die per tonne of bombs, 50, a figure which continued to be the basis of policy into WW2. It is also notable that their first report persisted in arguing that air raids did not warrant public warning as a general rule (O'Brien, 1955). The committee spent more time debating the possibility of moving the seat of government, though at this time, complete evacuation was not felt necessary or desirable.

A small ARP department was eventually created and the first ARP Circular was finally issued on the 9 July 1935. It was exemplary of the volunteeristic approach, as O'Brien notes:

> The decision to graft the structure on to normal local government meant that the immediate problem was to persuade local authorities [in this case country councils] to draw up A.R.P. schemes, and ordinary citizens to give voluntary service (p. 56).

In particular there was 'a straightforward refusal' (O'Brien, 1955, p. 58) to provide any kind of public bomb shelters, a decision which was justified on grounds of the (entirely unproven) effectiveness of home-made shelters.

The Department concentrated mainly on producing advice and inspecting the efforts of the County Councils, producing leaflets like *The Protection Of Your Home Against Air Raids* (1938 – see O'Brien, 1955, pp. 150–1). Duncan Campbell reports the eminent socialist scientist, J.B.S. Haldane's barbed but entirely accurate assessment that it 'does not distinguish sharply between an air raid and a picnic' (Haldane, 1938, in Campbell, 1982, p. 98). For most people in WW2, the Anderson Shelter named after Sir John Anderson, ARP committee chair from 1938, offered their best hope of survival. This was effectively an earth-covered corrugated-iron shed in the back garden, however, when well constructed, although often damp and uncomfortable, it did provide some protection against conventional blasts. Later in WW2, the Morrison Shelter, an internal shelter based around a metal table-like frame, named after government minister, Herbert Morrison, was produced in the millions (Campbell, 1982; O'Brien, 1955).

Campbell also notes the continuity between *The Protection of Your Home Against Air Raids* and the subsequent *Advising the Householder on Protection Against Nuclear Attack* (1963) and the infamous *Protect and Survive* (1976, 1980). The emphasis in all these documents is that people will be most likely to survive any kind of attack if they hide under what amounts to a normal house door propped up against in internal wall and have enough food and entertainment. They were above all expected to 'Stay at Home' and rely on the local authority who 'will best be able to help you in war' (UKCOI, 1980, p. 7). This attitude persists into the more recent advice on responding to emergencies as we shall see in Chapters 10 and 12.

The question of more protective public shelters was always controversial. Although a Structural Precautions Committee had been set up in 1936 (Meisel, 1994), a special conference in 1939 under Lord Hailey to consider the issue of public deep shelters did not endorse the scheme, arguing in particular that their provision 'might create a "shelter mentality" which would interfere with essential war-production' (O'Brien, 1955, p. 192). As Harrisson (1976) remarks, 'the class structures of pre-war, pre-welfare, Britain played a major part in determining the precautions taken for the population as a whole' (p. 39), and there were many contemporary critics, especially on the left, particularly The Left Book Club, which included Haldane, and also radical architects who came up with plans for workable mass deep shelters (Meisel, 1994).

The consequences of the lower classes rejecting in any way the war aims of the elite were always of major concern. O'Brien (1955) reports several occasions during the war when this was discussed at top-level meetings, with the ARP Department frequently despairing at the 'irrational' decisions of ordinary people in air raids. The experience of air raids was, however, creating new kinds of sociality amongst people of which the government was at this time not greatly aware (Meisel, 1994).

However, deep shelters *were* already being built, but for political leaders and civil servants (Campbell, 1982; see also Trench and Hillman, 1984). Started in 1933 at various government locations, by 1940 the network of tunnels and bunkers under Whitehall was, as Hillman and Trench describe it, a 'troglodyte city' (p. 195) under central London. The London County Council and some outlying authorities, notably Finsbury, did construct public shelters (Trench and Hillman, 1984), and eventually the central government was persuaded enough to build eight deep shelters under tube stations, though not all were finished (Campbell, 1982).

We have seen how internal urban order has frequently been linked to aggressive goals and the threat of natural disaster and hazard. Both O'Brien (1955) and Duncan Campbell (1982) link civil defence to the maintenance of public order more broadly, emphasizing the importance of the *Emergency Powers Act* (1920) which effectively made permanent emergency WW1 regulations embodied in the *Defence of the Realm Act* (1914). However, the former is more supportive of state aims. The initial spur to the passing of the EPA had been the combination of the massive growth of industrial trade unions during the war, which had doubled in size from four to eight million members, combined with the Russian revolution and the fear that such an event could occur in any country (Desmarais, 1971; see also Bonner, 1985; Hobsbaum, 1994). The Act effectively legitimized the actions of two government committees, The Strike Committee and the Supply and Transport Committee (STC) which had been set up to crush industrial unrest at the war's end. The latter became the Emergencies Committee, which later was renamed the Civil Contingencies Committee after the 1972 Miner's Strike (Campbell, 1982; Whelan, 1979).

The intent of the act was clear in its application. It was invoked a total of five times up until 1970 (Whelan, 1979), always on occasions involving labour disputes: the 1920 strikes, the General Strike of 1926, the dockers' strike of 1948, the railway strike of 1955 and the seamen's strike of 1966 (Thorpe, 2001). It of course also remained in force throughout WW2, but its use became markedly more common in the turbulent years of the 1970s at the end of the 'Golden Age' of capitalism (Hobsbaum, 1994), when it was used six times in ten years (Whelan, 1979).

The 1920 EPA divided Britain into 11 regions, under the control of a regional Commissioner, giving special powers including their use of the military to preserve order and ensure supply of goods and services. O'Brien shows how the Air Raid Precautions Committee took on the example of the EPA to structure its operations. Regional ARP Commissioners took office in August, 1939 although the exact boundaries of their 11 regions were not settled until 1941. They were given very large powers, but only in the event of the local government structure breaking down (O'Brien, 1955), which never happened during WW2.

In fact the most powerful bodies in the ARP system remained the Local Authorities and the most significant individuals in the emergency bureaucracy set up in the war were the local ARP Controllers who were responsible for 'nearly all precautions affecting people' (Harrisson, 1976, p. 83), most of whom were town clerks, with a quarter being police Chief Constables (ibid.). They operated out of control centres under which were report centres and at the base, the Warden Posts. These were staffed by Air Raid Wardens, the most visible element of WW2 ARP precautions. Some 400,000 of these wardens were paid, the rest of the almost 1.4 million were not, which also included the Fire Wardens, ambulance crews and other volunteers.

In the immediate post-war period, nothing revolutionary occurred with regard to civil defence: the 1948 *Civil Defence Act* reiterated the WW2 system. A Civil Defence Corps (CDC) would be created, envisaged as having over 300,000 volunteers, which it did by 1954, and the same regional structures would eventually be used as the basis for Regional Seats of Governance (RSGs), which would take over *all* government functions in the event of a nuclear attack (Campell, 1982), although this was denied at the time (Vale, 1987).

The 1948 structure and the efforts at pursuing it were roundly condemned by a 1953 House of Commons Select Committee report on Civil Defence. However, what was equally vital in changing things was a secret report on the actual likely effects of the dropping of the new hydrogen bombs on Britain (Hughes, 2003). The 1955 Strath Report showed that Britain's civil and military defence would be utterly inadequate for the new age of warfare. Thereafter there was an internal argument within government over the necessity of maintaining civilian involvement in defence in any way. It was an argument which was won by those on the side of reducing civil defence provisions. As Vale (1987) argues, nuclear deterrence was emphasized as the main form of defence and civil defence gradually lost its importance and its budgets until in 1968, the CDC was abolished and civil defence put on a 'care and maintenance' basis. There are some analyses which claim that the decline of civil defence was a product of the 1970s lobbying of peace groups, to which local authorities gave in (Hilliard, 1986); however, this is clearly mistaken, given that central support for civil defence was effectively abandoned. Local Authorities were left to fund it and it is therefore unsurprising that many who recognized the futility of any nuclear civil defence strategy devoted their budgets instead to other emergency management priorities. This was also encouraged, as Vale (1987) points out, from the very first of the many Home Office Emergency Services circulars that was issued in 1972.

However, far more controversial were the 1973 *Home Defence Planning Assumptions*, which had as their first aim the securing of the United Kingdom 'against any internal threat' (Vale, 1987, p. 139) This was as Whelan (1979) so clearly showed the era in which the economic and political control of the state reached its lowest ebb in Britain, with the 1920 Emergency Powers Act being used more in a single decade than it had ever been before. However, the EPA had also been supplemented twice during the 1960s, once by the 1964 Emergency Powers Act, and even before this by the secret 1962 Emergency Power (Defence) Act rushed through in the aftermath of the Cuban Missile Crisis (Jones, 2005).

The shelter debate was also revisited during the Cold War with the same conclusions as in WW2. Quite comprehensive guidance on how to build your own nuclear shelter was eventually issued for those who wished to build one (UKHO, 1982), but public shelters were not generally provided. Combined with the absence of adequate countrywide warning, this was effectively a death sentence for the vast majority of the urban population in the event of a nuclear war. As Vale concluded in 1987, 'British policymakers have done little to meet the challenges of nuclear age civil defence' (p. 151). Officials were more protected as Campbell (1982) showed, with each RSG supposedly having a secure underground bunker. London's bunkers were even more extended and some of the WW2 Deep Shelters commandeered for official use. Many functions were also given emergency back-up outside of the city (see below). However, as Vale (1987) argues, the actual protection offered to officials by the RSG bunkers was limited and none would have withstood a blast. There might have been a lack of concern for ordinary people but there has always been an amateurishness and cost-cutting mentality about preparedness in Britain that extends even to the protection of state officials. Or perhaps they too were just not important enough.

Evacuation and abandonment

That the schemes for deterrence, early warning and civil defence might not be enough was widely recognized. Visionaries such as H.G. Wells, in his novel, *The Shape of Things to Come* (1933), envisaged the rational cities of the future to be constructed entirely underground, but only after the lesson of devastating air war had led to the destruction and abandonment of the cities above ground.

In WW2, mass evacuation had only ever been seen as temporary and prioritized children and the elderly. With the advent of the ICBM, plans did develop during the latter part of the Twentieth Century for abandonment of cities to destruction and the evacuation of key military personal to prepared underground facilities in the countryside. The British government built 'secret underground cities' to use McCamley's (1988) only slightly exaggerated title, including the massive Spring Quarry complex near Corsham in Wiltshire. This had been extended originally from natural caverns during WW2 for weapons manufacture and storage, and was adapted after the war for use as the wartime central government HQ and later for the intelligence services (Campbell, 1982).

Alternative communications were developed in secret, for example, in Britain from 1954, the *Backbone* system (Campbell, 1982; see also Wood, 2001). Government communications would be transferred from the Citadel (Whitehall) to the Forest Hill Royal Naval communications site, in close proximity to Menwith Hill in North Yorkshire, which acted as the centre for US Signals Intelligence (SIGINT) operations in Europe from the very start of the Backbone programme.

It is disappointing, but perhaps not surprising, that US military geographer, Thomas Eastler (2005) in his review of the military use of the underground makes little mention of the massive Cold War bunker architectures, preferring to concentrate on the Viet Cong, and the use of caves by contemporary terrorists. In the United States, things went even further than in the United Kingdom. Many major military and law enforcement organizations have underground facilities, and more than this there were serious plans for the mass abandonment of cities in the Cold War period (Farish, 2003; Vanderbilt, 2002). Matt Farish (2003) shows in particular how this period of 'anxious urbanism' that had followed the supremacy of the skyscraper building period of the 1930s led to widespread imaginations of the end of cities, and in the construction of the Interstate Highway system, a plan that was at least partly designed to facilitate the mass evacuation of cities in the event of war. However, the size, decentralization and incoherence of US governance mitigated against workable measures for civil defence and emergency management in the Twentieth Century.

However, not all nations which had more homogenous populations and experience of strong government did better. The Swiss produced what remains the best example of a properly funded and workable combination of civil defence and emergency planning. It is as Vale (1987) summarized 'a rare example of political and technical success in civil defence planning' (p. 121). Further it was carried out openly, against a backdrop of non-nuclear neutrality and total public support:

> The enhanced commitment to civil defence was proposed to the Swiss in a referendum; it is codified into a series of enforceable laws; it is tailored to the needs of both army and industry and it is built into the structure of nearly every house. Swiss civil defence has, with remarkable unobtrusiveness, become part of both the landscape and the national consciousness. (ibid.)

In contrast, Japan, despite all its experience with earthquakes and destruction of its cities, and its similar reputation for social homogeneity and order to Switzerland, did not develop a workable disaster preparedness law until 1971. Even then, when tested in the major *Hanshin Daishinsai* that struck the city of Kobe and the surrounding area in 1995, it was found to be woefully inadequate with the central government systems unable to cope with the disaster (Hashimoto, 2000; Shaw and Goda, 2004). It is also open to question how much the more active methods for disaster prevention through building standards will stand up: there have been recent instances of fraud in the earthquake building certification system (Ogawa *et al.*, 2007), which leads us to suspect wider abuse of the system.

The paranoid reflex

Responding to and preparing for disaster and war was unavoidable in the Twentieth Century. Yet much greater effort was expended on conducting war and causing disaster. This had led to a largely unacknowledged importance for the military and militarized perspectives in all aspects of governance. Campbell's (1982) general thesis that British civil defence has always had a more military and militarizing character would perhaps have been non-mainstream in the 1980s. However, as David Edgerton (2006) has recently and powerfully demonstrated, even in the 1920s, at a time that both contemporary military critics and later historians characterized as lean years, Britain retained the largest military forces of any nation in the world, both relatively and absolutely, and military priorities maintained their importance until the late Twentieth Century. In the mid-century, it was gradually recognized how much of the economy depended on war and its preparation (see de Medeiros, 2003).

The paranoia around the safeguarding of the military-industrial complex was huge, from the control of trade union activity in the United Kingdom, and the rise of McCarthyism and internal espionage in the United States (Davis, 1992; Garber and Walkowitz, 1995) to the extremes of the dictatorships of the Soviet Union and its thousands of miles of Gulags for political prisoners (Appelbaum, 2003) and the Stasi secret police of the German Democratic Republic (see Mazower, 1997). In many ways, the object of security had shifted away from the people (if they indeed ever had been the focus), away from the city, and onto security itself. Security was being secured and made resilient. Everything in the city and every person was therefore a potential threat. This meant a constant shifting between registers of governmentality and the various strategies associated with them: between the moral order of the government of conduct and its focus on welfare and responsibility, the discipline of surveillance which its apparatus of visibility, and the authoritarianism of sovereign power with its violence and territorial control. In the next chapter we focus on the controlling of this risky city, its particular focus on the everyday management of crime and disorder and how such ideas were appropriated for countering terrorist threats.

5
Controlling the Risky City

The threat of Cold War urban abandonment and apocalyptic 'worst-case scenarios' linked to nuclear annihilation provided an overarching rhetoric for post-war emergency planning in many advanced nations. The cities and nations-state of the modern period came under threat from successive crises (of empire, of finance, of social order) and ways had to be found to enable cities to survive in the face of disaster. However, such an ideologically driven rhetoric could not provide for the everyday management of cities. In this context, it was not just the threat of natural disaster but increasingly civil disorder, crime and eventually urban terrorism that was of concern, and led to a series of urban responses whose influence is retained to the current day.

From the 1960s onwards, urban design and planning were employed to try to address both the causes of crime, disorder and incivility and its practice. Through the manipulation of space, planning pioneers like Oscar Newman argued that places could be created that would discourage unwanted behaviours and encourage 'good citizenship'. At the same time, the rise of electronic surveillance within cities and in the virtual space of databases moved the control offered by institutions out into the streets and personal lives. The controlling effects may often be the unintentional by-products of attempts to improve 'flow' and reduce 'risk', but a reconfiguration and reterritorialization of urban order occurred.

Within this context this chapter is divided into four main parts. The first part will highlight the disillusionment that followed the break down of the modern project in part due to the high rates of social segregation and crime and civil disorder that became indelibly associated with large social housing projects, and encouraged the introduction of environmental design measures to combat crime through strategies of territorial control. In particular, this part of the chapter will assess the impact of this on the early genesis of the movement towards creating *defensible space* and territorial control. The second part of the chapter, using examples from Northern Ireland and Israel, will demonstrate how such territorial control approaches were utilized out of the civic context and became 'militarized' to create defensive enclaves in the urban landscape as a response to terrorist attack. The third part highlights how territorial control was increasingly backed up and reinforced by the emergence of closed circuit television cameras (CCTV). The fourth part of the chapter, utilizing the example of Los Angeles, highlights how fortress and surveillance measures became overstated as a result of the rise in a 'culture of fear' in many Western cities; leading to the beginnings of a further fragmentation of the city into a series of supposedly safe and unsafe zones with security increasingly used as a 'strongpoint' of sale.

Territorial security

The geo-political urban strategies of nation-states were largely invisible to ordinary people, and those most involved in the everyday governance of cities, which had their own problems of control. In the late 1960s and early 1970s, defensive architecture and urban design were increasingly used in American cities as a direct response to the urban riots which swept many cities in the late 1960s, as well as the perceived problems associated with the physical design of the modernist high-rise blocks. Such structures were seen as breeding grounds for criminal activity (Jacobs, 1961), often seen as a result of the development of so-called 'indefensible' space (Newman, 1972).

In the last 40 years such defensive measures based on the manipulation of urban design have been developed due to rising crime rates, the escalation of social conflicts related to material inequality, intensifying racial and ethnic tensions, the heightened fear of crime and, of particular relevance to this book, increased attacks by terrorist groups against urban areas. We will highlight in this chapter and the subsequent ones how this has led to an increasingly sophisticated array of fortification, surveillance and security management techniques being deployed by urban authorities, the police and the military to protect perceived urban vulnerabilities.

These urban trends evoke the notion of human territoriality, which is related to the spatial control of a given area by certain social groups. What we mean by territory here is important. Too often territory has been used in a naturalistic way, assuming what is effectively a biological determinist conception of territory, deriving from Hobbes' 'war of all against all' as the natural state. Instead the theory of territoriality that we employ here is derived from geographer Robert Sack's classic work (1986), *Human Territoriality*. For Sack, territory is both the definition of a space and the attempt to influence thinking and behaviour with regard to that space. Here territoriality and the search for social power are intimately connected (p. 5).

Since the 1960s human territoriality has been studied in a number of contexts, but in particular in relation to crime prevention and the impact of defence as a key feature shaping the urban landscape (Flusty, 1994; Gold and Revill, 2000). The territorial analogy has most frequently been used in urban research to describe segregation in terms of 'conflict interpretation', with social groupings reacting to what they perceive as a hostile environment by evoking territoriality through physical barriers such as walls, or creating 'turfs' to preserve the character of a defended area and to instil a sense of cultural solidarity (Clay, 1973; Collinson, 1963).

In the 1960s and early 1970s, vivid examples emerged which highlighted how in certain situations the micro-geography of individual cities could be significantly influenced by territorial imperatives. Perhaps the best-known example of such territorial division was the construction of the Berlin wall in August 1961 to stop the exodus of workers from the Soviet sector in the East of the city to the Western side of the urban area (The American sector). It has been estimated that over 30,000 people a month were emigrating across the city. The 'wall' began as a barbed wire fence but quickly became a solid structure, eight feet tall. Until its 'opening' in 1989 many people were arrested or killed attempting to cross the wall which served as a vivid territorial barrier in a fractured urban landscape and of broader Cold-War geo-political tension (see Ladd, 2005).

Outside of the Cold War stand-off, Belfast in Northern Ireland also became a fractured landscape, this time based on religious sectarian division. Boal's study of the Shankhill/Falls interface in West Belfast in the late 1960s perhaps provides one of the best-known examples of human territorial behaviour, where Protestant and Catholic communities were kept apart by a series of physical barriers (defensive walls, or peace lines) which acted as territorial markers in the urban landscape (Boal, 1969; 1971). Consequently the residential geography of the city became largely fragmented into a series of inclusive 'religious enclaves'.

However, arguably the most notable research undertaken in the last 40 years on human territoriality was related to attempts to reduce criminal behaviour by 'designing out' crime on public housing estates (Jacobs, 1961; Jeffery, 1971; Newman, 1972), which began on large residential estates in the United States and has, over time, been employed across the globe.

The application of territorially for defence

The late 1960s, as John Gold (2007, p. 282) highlights, saw 'storm clouds' forming over modernist planning projects and mass social housing estates it spawned. Such estates themselves had been designed as a solution to the social disorder seen in the ungovernable slums of Nineteenth-Century cities. However, as a design solution removed from the political and economic solutions that poverty and social exclusions actually warranted, such estates became the very opposite of the utopian living spaces they were designed to be, and like their predecessors, evolved into places of high crime and stigmatization. This was a particular acute problem in urban America where the idea of ordered modernist space was 'destabilized by the shifting landscapes associated with post/late modernity' (Haywood, 2004, p. 137).

In the late 1960s and early 1970s, defensive architecture and urban design were increasingly used in such environments as a result of research that indicated a relationship between certain types of environmental design and reduced levels of violence (Gold, 1970). There were also concerns that enhanced urban fortifications were socially and economically destructive (in terms of economic decline of the city centre and social polarization) and that the provision of security was becoming increasingly privatized as individuals, having lost faith with the public authorities to provide a safe environment, increasingly sought to defend themselves and their property. Consumer preferences were thus increasingly beginning to influence the proliferation of anti-crime features at this time:

> The urban environment is being fortified today, not primarily by public decisions, but mainly through a multiplicity of private choices and decisions individuals make in our decentred society. The private market is responding to growing demand for an increasing range of crime control devices and other means of safety. In some cases, safety has become a commodity that is explicitly sold or rented with real estate.
> (ibid., p. 153)

As a result of such concerns, American urban planners and designers looked for relatively unobtrusive strategies to reduce the opportunity for urban crime particularly within residential environments. Initially, an approach called *Crime Prevention through Environmental Design* (CPTED) suggested that the design and arrangement of buildings could create environments, which would discourage normal patterns of social inter-action and encourage criminal behaviours (Jeffery, 1971). The central idea of CPTED was that the built environment could be designed or changed to facilitate social cohesion among residents so that criminal opportunities could be reduced leading to a decrease in crime and fear of crime. As Jeffery (1971, p. 178) stated, 'in order to change crimi-nal behaviour we must change the environment (not rehabilitate the criminal)'.

In the late 1960s and early 1970s architect Oscar Newman also under-took a study of the infamous Pruitt–Igoe public housing estate in St Louis (the city that had pioneered urban separation in the Nineteenth Century) and New York. It was the publication of Newman's (1972) *Defensible Space* that stimulated the most intense debates on the rela-tionship between crime and the built environment and in particular the death of the modernist dream. As Gold (2007, p. 282) noted:

'Defensible space', a spatial concept spun off the 1960s fascination with territoriality and other atavistic concepts, asserted that human beings have deep-seated needs to maintain certain types of bounded spaces in their domestic environments in order to preserve commu-nal harmony. The design of new estates, particularly those involving high-rise blocks of flats, apparently denied these needs and led to all manner of social pathologies.

Newman argued, like others before him, that anonymity in the city ran parallel to rises in crime rate, and drew attention to the increasing sense of anonymity and danger that city life entailed, noting in particular that residents in high rise blocks did not appear to know each other, making neighbourhood organization of crime prevention difficult (see also Wirth, 1928; Jacobs, 1961). Jane Jacobs, for example, in the seminal *The Death and Life of Great American Cities* (1961) had made an influen-tial case that urban design could contribute to diminishing community safety.[1]

In his studies Newman did not rule out the use of security fences or electronic surveillance technologies, but relying on these measures was seen as a last resort if more subtle design solutions were unsuccess-ful (Coaffee, 2003). Newman developed the concept of *defensible space*, which he saw as a 'range of mechanisms – real and symbolic barri-ers... [and] improved opportunities for surveillance – that combine to bring the environment under the control of its residents' (Newman,

1972, p. 3). More practically, Newman (1973, p. 2) argued that defensible space was a means by which the residential environment could be redesigned 'so they can again become liveable and controlled not by the police, but by a community of people who share a common terrain'. Poyner (1983, p. 8) further claimed that defensible space was considered attractive at this time, because the 'emphasis was on the use of the environment to promote residential control and therefore somehow return to a more human and less threatening environment'. In short, defensible space offered an alternative to the array of physical and overt security measures that were increasingly being introduced to American housing at this time.

Newman's ideas were inexorably linked to the late 1960s and early 1970s and reflected a growing interest in the relation between environment and behaviour, and ideas of territoriality. Seen largely through the lens of 'design determinism', defensible space was seen as the physical expression of a social fabric that could defend itself and could arguably be achieved by the manipulation of architectural and design elements. Thus deterring crime was fundamentally about giving would-be intruders a strong sense that if they enter a certain space they are likely to be observed and that they would have difficulty escaping. Newman concluded that outside spaces become more defensible if they are clearly demarcated and surveilled, and that a number interrelated design features contributed to the construction of a secure residential environment (see Box 5.1).

Box 5.1   Elements of defensible space

1. Creating a sense of ownership and community of shared space amongst local residents by the zoning or demarcating of public space – referred to as *territoriality*. Such a 'sense of ownership' might be achieved, for example, through symbolic measures such as signage or physical barriers such as fences;
2. The utilization of environmental design to improve *natural surveillance* for residents;
3. The *image* of the building structures could be altered to avoid the stigma of public housing;
4. The environmental surroundings of residential areas could be altered so that they merged with areas of the city considered safer and enhanced their *milieux*.

Newman's work although criticized for its poor statistical analysis containing 'unverifiable assumptions about causal relationships between physical design and crime' (Gold, 1982, p. 57; see also Cozens *et al.*, 2005), and its omission of the interplay between social and physical variables, subsequently became popular, mainly in the United States, as a concept underlying the design of new residential communities.

Over time the influence of his ideas have spread worldwide, particularly in the United Kingdom where they were applied on similar large high-rise housing estates in the late 1970s and 1980s (Coleman, 1984, 1985; Dawson, 1984; Goodey and Gold, 1987). Although these are often referred to in Jeffery's term – CPTED – these ideas are more closely related to Newman's (Cozens, 2002). More recently second and third generation of CPTED schemes have evolved which increasingly include measures such as access control, tactics such as 'target hardening' and advanced technologies such as CCTV to enhance the formal surveillance of space (Crowe, 2000; Moffat, 1983). In the United Kingdom, for example, in the late 1980s the Association of Chief Police Officers and the Home Office pioneered a new approach to reduce crime called Secured by Design (SBD) which sought to embed CPTED and defensible space ideas into to new build housing developments (Cozens, 2002).[2]

As we shall see in the next sections of this chapter, ideas associated with CPTED and defensible space, have been increasingly utilized in the militarization of parts of the urban landscape in cities under attack from terrorism.

Militarizing defensible space

As we have shown in previous chapters, the history of the city has been bound up with military order, defence and aggressive warfare, and it has not been unusual for the security services – the Army and the Police – to contribute to the urban planning process when radical security issues needed to be embedded within city design. By contrast, ideas developed in the 1970s placed much more emphasis upon the planner and designer to subtly design-in crime-reducing features to residential environments and create defensible space. Those favouring this more subtle approach did not necessarily rule out 'target hardening' or highly fortified methods of securing territoriality, but this was seen as a last resort. However, in the 1970s there were particular situations where more overt and military-style security was required. Such approaches took ideas of CPTED and defensible space out of the residential context and applied them alongside the deployment of barriers to defend commercial centres or in some case entire cities or nations against terrorism. The following parts of this section highlight two such examples, from Northern Ireland and from Israel.

Belfast and the ring of steel

In the British context, defensible space ideas were to have wider adaptations than the residential context. For example, Fred Boal (1975) argued, in relation to the need for anti-terrorist security in Northern Ireland, that the ultimate level of security provision in a city is defensible space with its emphasis on territoriality, existing alongside physical barriers.

Belfast in the 1970s could be seen as a laboratory for radical experiments on the fortification and territorialization of urban space where polarization between different communities became largely institutionalized and intimately connected to the political organization of space (Bryan, 2003; Shirlow and Murtagh, 2006). A number of distinct defended territories were created along sectarian lines to give the occupants of a defined area, or individual buildings, enhanced security. Initially, the segregation was marked by the creation of no-man's lands – places that nobody would live – which separated conflicting territories, and then by razor wire, armoured vehicles, peace walls and a series of police and army checkpoints (ibid., p. 256). Defensible space was the order of the day as 'the apparent permanence of the conflict and the lack of any solutions acceptable to all parties have meant that the ideological divisions have increasingly become a concrete part of the physical environment, creating an ever more militarized landscape' (Jarman, 1993, p. 107).[3] Here, the agencies of security were forced into ever-more securitized military bases and Police stations and were forced to rely on ever more distant surveillance techniques such as listening posts placed on the top of blocks of flats and airborne surveillance through the use of helicopters mounted with cameras (Bryan, 2003).

In Northern Ireland it was in the city centre of Belfast that the most visible militarized security was concentrated. On 18 July 1972 the counter-terrorist security apparatus around Belfast city centre was initiated with new traffic restrictions imposed without warning as barbed wire fences were thrown across the main streets creating a number of defensive segments, with access controlled by the British Army through a series of barriers and vehicle searches (Coaffee, 2003). The city centre in effect became a 'besieged citadel' (Jarman, 1993, p. 115).[4] The drastic security measures were taken due to the unsuccessful attempts by the authorities to tackle the car-bombing of the city centre and can be seen as a radical example of the search for territoriality and defensible space.

The bombing campaign against the city centre peaked in intensity on 21 July 1972, three days after the construction of the cordon, when the Provisional IRA detonated 22 bombs in and around Belfast city centre within the space of 75 minutes. Significantly all the explosions occurred outside the new restricted 'traffic zones' (*Belfast Telegraph* 22 July, p. 1). Despite the devastation, this also highlighted the success of the security cordon against a relatively uniform terrorist tactic: the car bomb. This indicated that the Army and Police's defensive strategy had been successful as far as defending the central business district was concerned. However, fears that the Provisional IRA would continue to plant bombs just outside the security cordon led to more Royal Ulster Constabulary (RUC) Police officers being deployed in such areas. This highlighted a possible disadvantage of such a defensive landscape – namely that by overtly securing one area, the would-be intruder, criminal or terrorist will seek out less well-defended targets – essentially displacing the risk of attack. By 1974 the barbed wire fences encircling the central area had been replaced by a series of tall steel gates (referred to as the ring of steel) and civilian search units were established.[5] We will show in subsequent chapters how the rhetoric of 'rings of steel' has continued to be associated with counter-terrorism techniques and strategies, particularly in London.

As the relative threat of terrorism against Belfast city centre decreased during the 1980s and 1990s, urban planners sought to re-image this 'pariah city' in an attempt to attract businesses back (Neill, 1992; Neill *et al.*, 1995). Reduced levels of security, decreases in the number of terrorist attacks, redevelopment and pedestrianization have subsequently helped to re-invigorate central Belfast.

However, the subsequent re-imaging of Belfast in the 1990s was only partially successful as it was often seen as superficial and not a catalyst to tackling the real and deep-rooted sectarian problems of the city.[6] Neill (1992, p. 9) concluded that Belfast city centre at this time was a place where:

> A post-modernist consumerist kaleidoscope of images floats uncomfortably on top of the squat brutalism of terrorist-proof buildings and the symbolism of the past. It is a condition of visual schizophrenia.

Belfast provides an example of a city with a 'hardened' urban landscape where the spatial configurations within a defined area, especially borders and boundaries, have become more pronounced in an attempt to create territoriality. Although increasing the feeling of safety for those living on the 'interface' areas, this also imposed serious restrictions of access and movement and hence reduced the quality of life in the effected areas (Bollens, 1999). For example, ways in which buildings were delimited from their surroundings through defensive architecture, or ways in which groups have demarcated boundaries to separate their 'turf' from neighbouring ones. As such, the security forces such as the Police and army became 'major agents' in restructuring the urban landscape (Jarman, 1993).

That said, Belfast city centre came 'back from the dead' in the decade following the construction of the ring of steel (Brown, 1985a, p. 10) with a large increase in private sector investment and business vitality correlated to the almost complete eradication of terrorist bombs. Landscape 'softening' or demilitarization also occurred in Belfast through the 1990s as attempts were made to remove territorial barriers and boundaries in order to increase access between previously conflicting territories given the reduced threat from terrorism, and Belfast's increased attempts to re-image itself within the global economy (Brown, 1987). As we shall highlight in the next chapter, the reduction in bombs in Belfast was in part due to changing Provisional IRA tactics that increasingly sought to target London.

The 'hardening' and subsequent 'softening' of the urban landscape of central Belfast since the 1970s has been linked to an assumption that territoriality can be expressed through the built environment. This was initially achieved by the construction of walls, gates and low-tech security cameras, which served to exclude unwanted persons or activities from a defined area. These began to be slowly removed and it was not until mid-1995 that smaller security barriers replaced the remaining gates in the main shopping streets. Indeed any decrease in security was offset by a centralized CCTV scheme, which became operational in December 1995 (Coaffee, 2000). Even during the ongoing 'peace processes' of the 1990s and 2000s Belfast largely remained as segregated and polarized as ever particularly at the interface areas between conflicting territories (Bryan, 2003; Shirlow and Murtagh, 2006).

Israel and the everyday securityscape

Like Belfast in the 1970s and 1980s, Israel during the 1980s and 1990s became synonymous with military-style security, which significantly impacted upon urban land-use, mediated by a series of political forces.

Soffer and Minghi (1986), for example, argued that the link between the military and planning in Israel must be viewed not only in a historical context but also in terms of different scales of intervention (national, regional and local), requiring different elements of security to be implemented (see Table 5.1). As they noted (p. 29),

A security landscape is moulded by the occupancy and utilization of land dominated by security considerations and by the general security expressions of society that have accumulated during history. In other words, a security landscape is a result of the necessity to defend a state (or territory) under certain political processes, ideas and levels of technology over a passage of time within a very specific natural and cultural regional context.[7]

Table 5.1 Security landscape elements in Israel in the 1980s (adapted from Soffer and Minghi, 1986)

Landscape scale	Element	Security elements
Macro-level (national)	*Military*	Border fortifications, airports, ports etc.
	Security and defence	Transport and defence networks, civilian defence, planned population dispersal and emergency planning
	Results of war	Ceremonies and monuments, civilian education and media
Meso-scale (regional)	*Military*	Army camps and training grounds, border security linked to regional conditions, man-made forests
	Security and defence	Regional transport networks and planning and infrastructure
	Results of war	Old fortifications and abandoned villages
Micro-level (local)	*Military*	Army camps and industries (in cities)
	Security and defence	Shelters in rural areas, paved roads within settlements and fields, guard towers, fences around settlements, bomb disposal holes, special architectural planning and material used
	Results of war	Monuments, street sign and parks named after the fallen, poster detailing security in schools and public institutions, guard duty at public buildings, ruins and old fortifications

Such a concern with security has pervaded the country and its cities creating what Azaryahu (2000) referred to as a *securityscape*, 'which pervade Israeli experience of space in terms of impending threats, defence strategies and precautionary measures' (p. 103). Here the concept of security morphed from an overarching concern for national security and its borders to a concept that also sought to connect to issues of personal security and everyday experience as a result of a series of terror attacks in the early 1990s inside Israel, and missile strikes linked to the first Gulf War:

> Whereas 'security' was traditionally aligned with the military and warfare, when terrorism later emerged as a prominent threat to public safety, 'security' was extended to cover spheres of public safety commonly associated with police jurisdiction and activity (ibid., p. 105)

This, it was argued, increased the role of the Police and Army within the planning process which gave the impression of 'protected spaces' symbolized by 'demarcation and fences' which separate the Israelis and Palestinians (ibid., pp. 105–7). It is further argued that 'the urge to design protected spaces' dominated Israeli 'security thinking' (p. 107) although such a need for designed-in territoriality is seen at a number of distinct spatial scales from the militarized borderlands (often a result of incursions into neighbouring territory such as the late 1970s in Lebanon or the building of a 'border fence' around the Gaza strip) to the common construction of 'sealed' security rooms in individual houses to protect occupants from missile strikes, or more latterly from the effects of chemical or biological weapons (a major concern during the first Gulf war in 1991).

Equally the way in which such protected spaces were managed or patrolled has altered especially given the popularity of suicide bombing as terror tactic directed against the urban fabric of Israeli cities. As Azaryahu (2000) noted, a situation, reminiscent of Belfast in the 1970s, emerged which has altered the experience of public space and normalized security checks and an armed presence on the street:

> The transformation of public spaces into protected spaces was also initiated in the early 1970s after a series of bombs in movie theatres, supermarkets and shopping malls. Security personnel employed by the owners were positioned at the entrance to check the personnel bags of people. Accustomed to this security ritual, Israelis open their bags automatically. (p. 111)

Although in this chapter we are concerned with how ideas of territoriality were adopted in the 1970s and 1980s by the military or Police for countering the threat of terrorism, it would be remiss not to mention how the Israeli rhetoric of protected spaces has been perpetuated over time.[8] Whereas in Belfast in the 1980s there was a softening of the defensive military urban landscape, in many parts of Israeli the heightened need for internal and border security has led to an evermore brutal and visible territorial defence, most notably, in response to a heightened risk of suicide bomb attacks coming from the Palestinian territories. Most symbolically, in 2002, the construction of a wall begun through the entire West Bank to seal Israeli cities and Jewish settlements from the Palestinian territory, at a cost of $1.5 billion. 'The Wall' was constructed of '8-metre-high concrete slabs, electric fences, barbed wire, radar, cameras, deep trenches, observation posts and patrol roads' (Weizman, 2007, p. 161). This wall allows access only through armed checkpoints containing x-ray scanners and is patrolled by thousands of security guards. Such high levels of security continues in the everyday spaces of Israeli urban areas with constant bag checks at shopping malls and restaurants, favourite targets of suicide bombers.

The wall – seen by the Israeli's as essential for state security – however has multiple meanings. As Weizman (2007, p. 162) notes, 'the Wall' represents a 'multiplicity of technical, legal and political conflict over issues of territory, demography, water, archaeology, real estate, as well as political concepts such as sovereignty, security and identity'. Moreover, the construction of the wall is viewed by opposition groups as an attempt by the Israeli state to increase their territorial control of the wider region and in particular gain greater influence over its water resources (see Al Tamimi, 2003). Others also see it as an oppressive measure that territorially annexes the impoverished Palestinian communities from their wealthier neighbours. As Juma (2003), an environmental activist in the Palestinian territories, noted:

> You can call it a 'Separation Wall', 'Isolation Wall', 'Colonial Wall', or as we call it the Apartheid wall: but certainly not a 'Security Wall'. Yet none of these names reflect the shocking reality of what the Wall really is. What may not have been clear to some at the beginning of the Wall's construction, when pretences and buzzwords of 'security' and 'fighting terror' were dominant is the Israeli and global discourse, had recently come to the surface... All in all we are witnessing a 21st century version of Apartheid, which will lay siege to Palestinians within fragmented disconnected cantons...

The urban panopticon: the rise of video surveillance

During the 1980, requirements for reinforced territorial security and broader concerns linked to the rise in urban terrorism also saw the increased adoption of electronic surveillance equipment into the civic realm. In particular, video surveillance (or Closed Circuit Television, CCTV) increasingly played a significant role in these various strategies of spatial control. Attempts had been made to utilize film and broadcast television cameras for crime control from very early in the history of television: examples can be found in Nazi Germany (Hempel, 2006), and in post-war Britain, where for the coronation of Queen Elizabeth II in 1952, the police requested the British Broadcasting Corporation to provide them with access to footage for purposes of crowd control but were refused (Williams, 2003).

Yet CCTV's origins are neither exclusively in urban policing nor military surveillance. A significantly underplayed strand in the history of surveillance is that of consumption and leisure, and it is here where CCTV first flourished. It was in the 1960s casinos in the United States, largely to prevent fraud and sharp practice, and thereafter, particularly with the development of videotape, in the massive suburban shopping malls and semi-public spaces that provided the new housing developments with leisure and shopping amenities, that CCTV developed (Norris *et al.*, 2004). Theme parks are also crucial here: the parks owned by the Disney Corporation became important sites for the experimental utilization of private security (in the form of undercover security) and also CCTV (Shearing and Stenning, 1985). This is important because it is the semi-public, closed and controlled world of malls and theme parks that is increasingly seen as providing a model for neoliberal urban renewal initiatives (Sorkin, 1992; see also Chapter 12).

However, for urban spatial control, the United Kingdom was the pioneer of CCTV and remains the 'model' for law enforcement agencies worldwide. CCTV was first introduced in public space in Bournemouth, a resort town on the south coast of Britain in 1985.[9] The year before had seen the Provisional IRA mount a devastating bomb attack on the ruling Conservative Party conference in Brighton, almost killing the Prime Minister, Margaret Thatcher; Bournemouth was to be the venue for the next conference.

That CCTV soon penetrated British towns and cities so thoroughly was not entirely due to the fear of terrorism. The neoliberal relaxation of planning laws and expansion of out-of-town shopping had seen traditional space of consumption in town centres decline. Other fears were also used to justify the installation of CCTV systems: particularly football hooliganism (again a leisure-related rationale), and high-profile crimes against children, in particular the kidnapping and murder of James Bulger in Merseyside, North West England, in 1993. Crucial to this process was the relationship between the central state and the Local Authorities who largely operate the systems, in terms of state funding initially through CCTV Challenge (part of local regeneration schemes called City Challenge) from 1994 to 1999, and then the CCTV Initiative.

Security for sale

In the 1970s and 1980s we saw a progressive creep of the introduction of defensive design and CCTV into urban areas in response to the occurrence and fear of crime and terrorism. In the early 1990s enhanced *defensible space* approaches once again served to influence the design and management of the urban landscape and its internal borders where increasingly 'form follows fear' (Ellin, 1997). For many commentators this was seen as a broader social shift towards a 'culture of fear'. Here it is argued that fear, and in particular fear of crime, is socially constructed.[10] Such a 'culture of fear' is expressed most notably through the built environment creating an ever more common situation where 'virtually every institution – bars, universities, doctors' surgeries, sport, public transportation – takes security very seriously. Burglar alarms, outdoor lights, panic buttons, CCTV cameras and an array of private security personal are testimony to a flourishing market in fear' (Furedi, 2006, p. 3). This, it can be argued, is an unbalanced response, which bares little relation to actual occurrence of crime. This apparently disproportionate approach has led to an ever more security-conscious citizenry and 'militarized' built environment and has important implications for the everyday experience of the city, and in the approach taken by urban authorities to countering the risk of terrorism. This later concern can often be seen starkly in terms of attempts to protect economic interests amidst an all-pervading ambient fear (see also Glassner, 1999).

In the early 1990s, the response of urban authorities to insecurity was in some cases dramatic, especially in North America and in particular Los Angeles (LA), where it was argued that the implementation of crime displacement measures and the surveillance of particular spaces were taken to an extreme. In LA the social and physical fragmentation of the city is often shown to be very pronounced, and which, according to certain commentators at this time, could possibly be setting a precedent for the future of post-industrial cities (see Dear and Flusty, 1998; Haywood, 2004).

During the early 1990s LA assumed a theoretical primacy within urban studies with an overemphasis on its militarization, portraying the city as an urban laboratory for anti-crime measures (much like Belfast during the 1970s). Fortress urbanism was highlighted as the order of the day, as an obsession with security became manifested in the urban landscape with 'the physical form of the city ... divided into fortified cells of affluence and places of terror where police battle the criminalized poor' (Dear and Flusty, 1998, p. 57). However, as Christopherson (1994, p. 420) pointed out, 'there is no doubt that the new fortresslike environments respond to some version of consumer preferences'. For example, it was reported that in 1991 that 16% of Los Angelians were living in 'some form of secured access environment' (Blakely and Snyder, 1995, p. 1) seen as an ultimate lifestyle choice and a dominant feature of contemporary urban life. The emergence of the 'fortress city' also appeared to be about transforming the city in the mirror of middle-class paranoia combined with economic vibrancy. As Haywood (2004) notes in relation to the renaissance of downtown LA, and its apparent blanket security and privatized of public space: 'this was the corporate Los Angeles manning the ramparts in a bid to protect its economic interests by excluding those individuals and groups no longer necessary for (or dangerous to) the perpetuation of profit in the city's new globalized economy' (p. 115).

Mike Davis is perhaps the most cited author on 'Fortress LA'. Davis depicted how, during the 1980s and 1990s, the authorities and private citizen groups in LA responded to the increased fear of crime by 'militarizing' the urban landscape and the multitude of public spaces therein. His dystopian portrayal of LA in *City of Quartz* (1990) and again in *Ecologies of Fear* (1998) provided an alarming indictment of how increasing crime trends were effecting the development and functioning of the contemporary city through the radicalizing of territorial defensive measures, with the increased role played by the Los Angeles Police Department (LAPD) in the development process. As Davis starkly highlights 'in cities like Los Angeles on the hard edge of postmodernity, one observes an unprecedented tendency to merger urban design, architecture and the police apparatus into a single comprehensive security effort' (1990, p. 203). Here the militarization of commercial buildings and their borders became 'strongpoints of sale' (Dear and Flusty, 1998; Flusty, 1994). As the boundaries between the two traditional methods of crime prevention – law enforcement and fortification – have become blurred, defensible space and technological surveillance, once used at a micro-scale level, was being used at a meso and macro level to protect an ever-increasing number of city properties and residences, which was facilitated by the growth in the private security industry. As Davis notes of the increased everyday militarization of the city:

> Welcome to post-liberal Los Angeles, where the defence of luxury lifestyles is transformed into a proliferation of new repressions in space and movement, undergirded by the ubiquitous 'armed response'. This obsession with physical security system, and, collaterally, with architectural policing of social boundaries, has become a zeitgeist for urban restructuring, a master narrative in the emerging built environment of the 1990s. (1990, p. 223)

In *Beyond Blade Runner*, Davis (1992) extrapolated current social, economic and political trends to create a vision for the future city in the year 2019, which in this account had become technologically and physically segregated into zones of protection and surveillance such as high security financial districts and segregated 'gated' communities. In this vision, economic disparities created an urban landscape of cages and wasteland covered by a 'scanscape' of omnipresent surveillance. He argued that defensive strategies already used in LA only needed to be augmented to 'perfect' this vision. Davis (1998) further highlighted the growing tendency for major cities at this time, especially LA, of developing stark conditions of 'spatial apartheid' and the unchecked adoption of methods of social control, and questioned the possible future awaiting such urban conditions:

> But what kind of dystopian cityscape if not Blade Runner's might the unchecked evolution of inequality, crime, and social despair ultimately produce? Instead of following the grain of traditional clichés and seeing the future merely as grotesque...would it not be more fruitful to project existing trends along their current downward-sloping trajectories? (Davis, pp. 359–61)

This dystopian scenario Davis saw as an almost inevitable result of the way in which high levels of visible security, particularly for the middle and upper classes, have become a commodity for sale – a lifestyle choice, fuelled by the constant stream of media pronouncements that fear is all around and the resultant protectionist reflexes, and where defence against the dangerous 'Other' is sought. In *City of Quartz* security was seen as a 'prestige symbol', which provided personal insulation protecting the rich from 'unsavoury groups' (Davis, 1990, p. 224). This commodification and commercialization of security is also a strong theme in *Ecologies of Fear* where as Haywood (2004, p. 129) notes, security and surveillance became as desirable as floor space and acreage:

> Is there any need to explain why *fear* eats the soul of Los Angeles? Only the middle-class dread of progressive taxation exceeds the rent obsession with personal safety and social insulation... which no hope of further public investment in the remediation of underlying social conditions, we are forced instead to make increasingly public and private investments in physical security. The rhetoric of urban reform persists, but the substance is extinct. 'Rebuilding L.A.' simply means padding the bunker. (1998, pp. 363–4)

Many subsequent authors elaborated Davis's work. For example, Flusty (1994) provided a categorization of the different types of fortress urbanism, which he argued, had thrown a blanket of fortified and surveillance security over the entire city. He referred to the spaces of security as 'interdictory space', which are designed to exclude by their function and 'cognitive sensibilities'. A typology of such spaces is shown below in Table 5.2.

Flusty highlighted how such defended spaces, alone or in combination, had pervaded all aspects of urban life, leading to an ever increasing number of highly secure gated communities, bunker architectures and highly policed ghettos in the disadvantaged areas of the city. He also noted how the commercial privatization of space has been taken to an extreme as a strong fear of the public realm leads to highly inclusive business facilities, either in isolation or in self-contained agglomerations.

Table 5.2   Typology of interdictory space (adapted from Flusty, 1994)

Stealthy space	Passively aggressive with space concealed by intervening objects
Slippery space	Space that can only be reached by means of interrupted approaches
Crusty space	Confrontational space surrounded by walls and checkpoints
Prickly space	Areas or objects designed to exclude the unwanted such as unsittable benches in areas with no shade
Jittery space	Space saturated with surveillance devices

In the 1990s the spectre of Belfast-style 'rings of steel' being constructed to protect key strategic areas from violent crime and terrorism was also revived by Davis (1992) who, when prophesying about the prospect for Twenty-First-Century urbanism, noted that within the crime-infested future city the car bomb could well become the ultimate weapon of crime and terror, and predicted that urban authorities might well enact fortress style 'rings of steel' as a counter-response. We will return to the linkages between crime prevention and counter-terrorism in the next chapter.

Although 'Fortress LA' in the 1990s became a powerful vision for the city it is important to realize that there are many ways in which future urbanism in LA may be viewed. For example, critics of Davis have argued that he is portraying only a partial and very dystopian image of the city as one shackled with terror, fear and anxiety and under the constant gaze of surveillance cameras. Others have argued that the overly Marxist concerns of class conflict that attempt to paint a broader conceptual framework of the fortress city have led Davis, and others, to ignore the more everyday experiences and diverse spatial practices linked to and how security intersects with the construction of contemporary urban landscapes (Haywood, 2004).

Towards intensified control

This chapter has highlighted that from the late 1960s to the early 1990s an increased emphasis was given to issues of community safety and controlling risk in urban management and in residential developments, which occurred initially against a broader backdrop of Cold War rhetoric of disaster preparedness. Since this time an array of security solutions have been skilfully and often subtlety integrated into the planning, design and construction of the built environment. The use of the concept of territoriality became popular during this period to explain why urban areas were fragmenting in accordance with concerns over fear of crime and conflict. Although initially ideas of creating defining territory and of creating defensible space were developed for residential environments, such concepts were soon applied in certain locations as a solution to countering the emergent terrorist threat. Likewise, as technology has advanced increased use has been made of electronic surveillance, most notably in the form of CCTV cameras which during the 1980s became more widespread in the United Kingdom and elsewhere. In the early 1990s expressions of how built environment professionals were utilizing ideas of territory, surveillance and fortification for crime-reducing purposes led to a sceptre of the 'fortress city' encapsulated best by depictions of modern day LA.

As the 1990s progressed we saw a further intensification of surveillance and other defensive measures, and at the same time 'planning for the worst' was revived and increasingly linked to the economic future of cities amidst the specific economic targeting by terrorist groups. The next chapter will develop this idea further, arguing that in the 1990s we saw the beginnings of a new approach to emergency and counter-terrorism planning emerge which increasingly sort to focus upon the management of risk alongside design and surveillance solutions.

6
The Intensification of Control: Towards Urban Resilience

In Chapter 5 we highlighted how since the late 1960s an increased emphasis was given to issues of crime prevention, community safety and controlling risk, often in a territorial way, through the design of the built environment. We then argued that these principles during the 1970s and 1980s became more extreme and militarized, and were utilized in very specific ways in certain locations suffering persistent terrorist attack. We further addressed the way in which technological developments, especially linked to the advancement of CCTV, became embedded within a powerful rhetoric of the 'fortress city' where security became a strongpoint of sale.

In this chapter, we argue that these trends were further intensified, refined and expanded in scope in the 1990s, both in relation to crime prevention as well as in response to changing modes of terrorist attacks particularly against economic infrastructure. We will highlight how, during the 1990s, the perpetual fear of crime and the growing threat of terrorism proved a catalyst for the intensification of urban control in a number of ways. First, through protective security and a growth in the construction of 'architectures of fear' (Pawley, 1998), and the creation of 'exclusion zones' or *cordons sanitaires* (Coaffee, 2004) to protect 'at risk' sites and societies; second, in connection to the advance of hi-tech surveillance systems – a surveillance surge (Wood *et al.*, 2003) – with the expansion of existing systems and the adoption of ever more refined technologies; and third, a broader focus upon managerial measures to regulate the public realm, and upon contingency planning, to enable organizations to continue with 'business as usual' as soon as possible after an emergency or attack.

Most notably, in the UK the integration of these design and managerial measures adopted in the financial zones of London in response constant fears of terrorist attack represented the antecedents of 'resilient' approaches that were to more fully evolve in the 2000s in many other cities as a result in the upsurge in urban terrorism following the events of September 11 and the increased frequency of natural disaster events around the globe. This chapter will also highlight how approaches to dealing with terrorist risk begun to move beyond the crude barrier mentality shown other conflict zones like Northern Ireland and Israel (Chapter 5) and embrace aspects of contingency planning in conjunction with less obtrusive approaches to protective security.

Territory and changing reactions to risk

During the 1990s, Ulrich Beck in his risk society thesis argued that in vulnerable areas a 'protectionist reflex' means that 'withdrawal into the safe haven of territoriality becomes an intense temptation' (1999, p. 153). This, as we highlighted in Chapter 5, reflected an urban response to threat of crime, fear of crime, natural disaster and terrorism, which was focused upon exclusive territorial imperatives (Coaffee, 1996).

During the mid-late 1990s there was a further surge in using ideas of territoriality as a crude conflict resolution measure which according to many accounts led to a new 'enclaving' of the city focused upon the defence of spaces where people live and work (Dillon, 1994; Norfolk, 1994). This led to well-established critiques of the city as 'carceral', fragmented, and unjust (Davis, 1990; Marcuse and Kempton, 2002). For example, Merrifield and Swyngedouw (1997) indicated how at this time in advanced Western cities new technologies and consumer preference has led to a dramatic increase in an intensification of social control, where:

> The powerful . . . are now able to insulate themselves in hermetically sealed enclaves, where gated communities and sophisticated modes of surveillance are the order of the day. Concurrently the rich and powerful can decant and steer the poor into clearly demarcated zones in the city, where implicit and explicit forms of social control keep them in place. (p. 11)

For example, by the middle of the 1990s it was reported that in many parts of the United States one-third of new communities were incorporating such fortifying principles into their design and management (Blakely and Snyder, 1995; Dillon, 1994) with similar trends occurring in many other countries (Caldeira, 1996; Doeksen, 1997; Jürgens and

Gnad, 2002a); representing a desire by social groups to achieve 'spatial purification' (Sibley, 1995, p. 77).

More broadly, in the field of urban studies during the mid-1990s, although territoriality was still commonly employed as a descriptive metaphor in relation to the resolution of conflict, more nuanced work was beginning to unpack the impact, and lived reality, of security features employed in the built environment. For example, work in the late 1990s on *Landscapes of Defence* (Coaffee, 1996, 2003; Gold and Revill, 1999, 2000) begun to highlight how the everyday landscape is shaped by defensive considerations, through surveillance practices, overt fortifications, idea boundaries and identity, and through new forms of security governance and management operating in the public and private areas of cities.

Other work on the role of defence in structuring cities also begun to illuminate the way in which the physical built form reflects ongoing social concerns with public safety – trends that appear to be mutually reinforcing. Nan Ellin (1997), for example, edited a series of essays entitled *Architecture of Fear* which examined how:

> This fixation [with security] manifests itself in such efforts... despite the evidence that they do not lessen crime... [and] that such disjointed efforts exacerbate rather than eradicate the sources of fear and insecurity (backcover).

Furthermore, Peter Marcuse (1993, p. 101) argued how city walls can be seen as both 'walls of fear' and 'walls of support', whilst Ellin (1997) noted that whilst 'form follows fear' in the city this relationship can be reversed to one in which fear is seen to follow form.

Others also increasingly used military metaphors to describe the way in which urban managers at this time were developing defensive strategies and utilizing ever-advancing military technology in civic defensive features in response to the evaluation of cities as strategic sites for a spectrum of large-scale destructive interventions and an ever-expanding interest in the vulnerability of cities against natural disasters.

Intensifying urban control

We have argued so far in this book that there are a number of key interlocking themes and approaches – fortification and territoriality, surveillance and control, and management and regulation – which run through the history of urban areas responding to threat, be that from external attack, war, criminal activity, fear of crime, natural disaster or terrorist events. The following sections will highlight the adoption of these approaches with reference to 1990s' urban control strategies *per se* before applying them directly to attempt to 'beat the bombers' in London in the mid-1990s (Coaffee, 2000). This later section will also highlight how approaches to improving preparedness (what we might now term resilience) were beginning to come to the fore in counter-terrorism and security management strategies.

Intensifying fortification

As highlighted in Chapter 5 the 'fortification approach' to contemporary urban security often took the form of turning office blocks, shopping centres and residential communities into territorial enclaves through methods of restricted access, the erection of defensive barriers and reinforced bollards around high-risk sites, and the creation of exclusive enclaves.

The desire for fortified territories in the city meant that during the later parts of the 1990s, particularly in urban America, an 'architecture of paranoia' (Brown, 1995) enveloped many areas of the city with defensible space principles increasingly re-introduced in an attempt to make residential communities more 'desirable' (Ellin, 1996; Newman, 1995).

Enhanced fortification at this time, as in other eras of history, helped enhanced segregation in the controlled city through an array of ever-more sophisticated physical and technological measures and new configurations of stakeholders. Often the explicit aim (or at least outcome) was to exclude the sections of society deemed a threat to a particular way of life or those that would hinder the orderly flow of commercial activity, what Flusty (1994) highlighted as the erosion of 'spatial justice' in the city. In this new enclaved city, access control and boundary reinforcement were paramount and access and egress were highly regulated (see Oc and Tiesdell, 1997).

The surveillance approach

The fortification approach was often complemented by enhanced surveillance practices in particular, CCTV. Giles Deleuze's groundbreaking essay *Postscript on the Societies of Control* (1992) argued that since the end of the Second World War a new society, the society of control, has replaced the pre-war disciplinary society where 'enclosures' maintained order through the controls of wages and discipline. In the society of control, technological controls transform social ordering with individualization replaced by 'passwords' and electronic cards. These, it is argued, are read by computer, allowing or denying access to information and protecting entry into disparate social worlds and urban neighbourhoods (Coaffee, 2005). In short, virtual control, and therefore virtual imprisonment through technically maintained access, has moved out of the bureaucratic institutions and into the public sphere. A host of studies in the 1990s served to illuminate similar concerns focusing on how CCTV reorders urban life such as David Lyon's (1994) *The Electronic Eye*, Simon Davies' (1996a) *Big Brother* and Clive Norris and Gary Armstrong's (1999) *The Maximum Surveillance Society*. We should also note that the rise of CCTV itself as an everyday urban phenomenon is intimately linked to a re-appropriation of military technologies. As Coleman (2004, p. 200) highlights, 'the end of the Cold War and the buttressing of military-come-surveillance industries with public money have enabled the camera surveillance industry to turn its expertise towards the high street'.

In the United Kingdom during the 1990s, the surveillance approach was intensified in large part due to a series of terrorist bombs, and rises in city centre crime rates which encouraged many more local authorities and private businesses to install security cameras. This in effect became another 'surveillance surge' (Wood *et al.*, 2003) which followed a gradual 'creep' (Marx, 1988) in the growth of CCTV. More broadly, the demand for CCTV was in response to its supposed benefits for increasing the 'quality of life' in cities: deterring crime; the freeing-up of police manpower, which can then be redeployed; and possible insurance discounts which could be obtained (Horne, 1996). However, the rise in CCTV appeared to be linked more to fear of crime and perceptions of insecurity as much as with actual occurrence, with citizens and businesspeople arguing that they feel safer in areas 'protected' by CCTV.

During the mid-1990s, CCTV became the police's favoured crime preventative measure having 'more of an impact on the evolution of law enforcement policy than just about any technological initiative in the last two decades' (Davies, 1996b, p. 328; see Fyfe and Bannister, 1996). During the mid-1990s around 200,000 cameras were put in place in UK urban areas, many of which are erected in high-rent commercial areas (Davies, 1996b, p. 328) representing a 550% increase of CCTV in commercial centres between 1994 and 1999 (Williams and Johnstone, 2000). Overall, between 1992 and 2002 it is estimated that over £3 billion was spent on CCTV installation and maintenance in the United Kingdom (McCahill and Norris, 2002).

Despite this 'surveillance surge' a lot of evidence at this time pointed to the visual deterrent of CCTV rather than its protective potential (Millward, 1996). Warning signs that were commonly displayed indicated that the area was under CCTV surveillance further reinforced the deterrent value of CCTV. That said, the installation of CCTV schemes did facilitate increased linkages between local business, local authority planners, town and city centre managers and the Police in relation to issues of crime prevention (Durham, 1995). For these reasons CCTV schemes remained popular with the majority of the public and it was commonly highlighted in the 1990s that 80–90% of town centre users support the introduction of CCTV (McCahill and Norris, 2002). Others highlighted how CCTV was 'waved aloft by police and politicians as if it were a technological Holy Grail, and its promises chanted like a mantra as a primary solution for urban dysfunction' (Davies, 1996a, p. 328). Indeed, CCTV increasingly became a key part of a wider narrative or urban renaissance and was almost ubiquitously embedded with the regeneration schemes. As Coleman (2004, p. 200):

> The entrepreneurial city is fostering a new urban aesthetic emerging around the creation of privatized spaces for consumption within which proponents of CCTV elaborate a form of 'regeneration-speak' that provides 'confidence' to consumers, tourists and investors... In the UK, regeneration strategies regularly promote the development and funding of street safety initiatives in which street camera surveillance figures prominently. (ibid.)

The mid-1990s also saw the first concentrated and widespread critical reaction to social and democratic concerns about CCTV, with many studies highlighting the negative impacts of CCTV relating to how it reorders and controls urban life (Lyon, 1994) creating 'a collection of surveillant nodes designed to impose a particular model of conduct and disciplinary adherence on its inhabitants' (Soja, 1995, p. 25). In this sense the rise of CCTV was often critiqued though ideas of the Panoptican (Chapter 3) – seen as a metaphor for control of urban space (Bosovic, 1995; Marx, 1985) – which, it was argued, was now being extended beyond the confines of individual buildings and institutions and into the public realm. The plethora of surveillance technologies within the city were seen to evoke fears of an Orwellian society based on 'Big Brother', or rather a variety of 'Little Brothers' (Lyon, 1994, p. 53). As Davies (1996a, p. 17) noted at this time, 'CCTV... creates a means of enforcing public order on an unprecedented scale'. For many

CCTV also became a key part of everyday urban life – 'the fifth utility' – an integral part of the infrastructure of out cities alongside, water, gas, electricity and ICT networks (Graham, 1999). Regulation in the United Kingdom was minimal until 1998, and thus whilst CCTV was expanding it was also able to be normalized as an expected feature of public space (Graham *et al.*, 1996). Thereafter CCTV was subject to some nominal legal requirements through the Crime and Disorder Act Human Rights Act and Data Protection Act (all 1998), the first of which was in any case largely designed to promote and co-ordinate further expansion of CCTV. In addition the United Kingdom historically lacked any constitutional right of privacy in public spaces. The presence of this right (and other forms of constitutional protection) has made the growth of CCTV in many other countries much slower (Gras, 2004).

Urban management

Whereas in the 1970s and 1980s the focus on crime prevention was explicitly focused upon designing out crime (and terrorism) with only an implicit managerial dimension, during the 1990s this less-prioritized management element was increasingly developed. Here the central argument was that protective security alone is not enough and can only make urban areas safer if complemented by managerial measures (Oc and Tiesdell, 1997). Here, we can conceive of management strategies in a number of ways: Police-led; through public-private partnerships including the key role of businesses; agency driven, incorporating the role of city and town centre management; and in terms of the deployment of private security.

As highlighted in Chapter 5, traditionally the response to crime and terrorism from the 1970s onwards had focused upon the role of the Police and/or security services, arguing that crime can be reduced by implementation of greater legal controls with greater numbers of Police who have more power to shape the built environment (Grogger and Weatherford, 1995; Rubenstein, 1973). In particular, research in the 1990s begun to highlight how the Police strategically use notion of territoriality to control areas of the city (see Herbert 1996; 1998). The importance of territoriality stated Herbert (1997b, p. 399) intensifies as power is resisted: 'contested spaces preoccupy the police most'. He highlighted how Police strategies involved creating boundaries and restricting access as they seek to regulate space showing how the 'power of the Police is inserted within the fabric of the city' (Herbert, 1997a, pp. 6–7).

Increasingly, as the 1990s progressed, we saw the integration of business communities and policing in developing strategies for creating safe and secure urban areas. For example, in the United Kingdom, Section 17 of the 1998 Crime and Disorder Act (Home Office, 1998) placed a statutory duty on local authorities and Police services to prepare and publish a crime audit to reflect broader concerns such as community safety and sustainable development. Importantly Section 17 also stresses that this must be down with consultation with local communities.

Furthermore, upon Police advice, individual business were increasingly active in developing appropriate risk management strategies and in developing and contingency and emergency plans, especially in financial districts. Likewise, the banding together of a number of businesses in order to enact area-based security strategies (for example, pub-watch schemes) were beginning to become increasingly common at this time.

Sometimes such strategies were formalized under particular local legislation such as Business Improvement Districts (Hoyt, 2005) which often had an explicit remit to develop safer public and private spaces. In other instances, beginning in the 1990s, we saw the rise of town or city centre management (TCM/CCM) which has had a significant impact upon the regulation and control of public space, and in particular could be seen as a tool of social regulation (Rogers and Coaffee, 2005). This highlighted a tendency for actively categorizing desirable and undesirable groups, with the consumer seen as the 'preferred user...in preference to those perceived as anti-social and "unaesthetic"' (Reeve, 1996, p. 69).

Alongside both the increased involvement of businesses and private urban managers, there was also a crucial and expanded role for private security firms in influencing the maintenance of public and private spaces. During the 1990s and beyond, the private security and risk management industries grew at a fast rate (Ericson and Haggerty, 1997; Loader, 1997). For example, Jones and Newburn (1998) indicated that the number of people working in private security in the mid-1990s now approximated to that of the 43 police forces in England and Wales.[1] At this time it was frequently argued that the popularity of security features, expressed by the increased privatization of space according to the preferences of the rich and powerful, helped to fuel the growth of the private security industry (Sorkin, 1995; Lees, 1998).

This evolving dynamic of social control through management and regulation was expressed by a number of commentators as being 'revanchist' in origin, although this symbiosis between urban revitalization and the retrofitting of defence and control feature was not seen as a new phenomenon. For example, Neil Smith (1996) argued that this coupling of urban rejuvenation and what he called 'urban revanchism' had historical as well as contemporary precedents, in which ruling authorities have used a combination of moral authority and military strategies to retain public order in the city. In making his argument Smith drew on the analogy of the right-wing French political movement of the Nineteenth Century. This political movement of the petit-bourgeoisie – reactionary, nationalist and anti-working class – was associated with a vengeful and repressive response to the failed revolutionary challenge of the Paris Commune. Smith suggested that a similarly aggressive attack on the urban poor could be seen emerging in contemporary gentrification and through zero-tolerance policing approaches being pioneered in New York. Subsequent to Smith's work, the revanchism concept has been illuminated by a number of scholars who have also highlighted the unjust nature of many urban defence and security strategies (Holden and Iveson, 2003), particularly for less powerful and less economically viable citizens, or 'unsightly user demographics' (Rogers and Coaffee, 2005, p. 324; see also Atkinson, 2003; Belinda and Helms, 2003). In particular, the impact of new 'revanchist' urbanism on minority groups such as buskers, street entertainers, leafleters, beggars, skateboarders and the homeless has been commented on widely (Cooper, 1998; Fyfe, 1998; Rogers, 2006). One such study by MacLeod (2002) highlighted the conflict between urban entrepreneurialism and alternative uses of public spaces in Glasgow and argued that 'relationships between entrepreneurial governance, downtown renaissance and the active systems of surveillance... are intertwined with the advance of the revanchist city' (p. 603). This, he argued, led to a situation where and increase in the regulatory management of urban areas and the creation of 'new civic spaces [which] appear to be concealing more active geographies of displacement and marginality' (MacLeod, 2002, p. 613).

In this chapter, so far we have discussed how, in the 1990s there has been an intensification of control which has had an impact on the design (fortification and surveillance) and management of urban spaces. The discussion thus far has primarily focused on issues of community safety rather than on security for counter-terrorism. It is to this latter concern that this chapter now turns. We will highlight how London in the 1990s became perhaps the key global example of how a city might defend itself from terrorism: through a combination of urban design, integrated management, the implementation of advanced military-style technologies and strategic territorial thinking. The proceeding section will also highlight how, at this time, other global cities, most notably New York and Tokyo, were also beginning to confront the impact of new forms of terrorism particularly focused upon their economic and financial districts.

Changing terrorist targeting and tactics

In the early 1990s important financial centres became prime targets of terrorist attack because of their vast array of new 'designer' office buildings, their increasingly cosmopolitan business communities and the significant media attention and publicity that could be obtained by the terrorists (Coaffee, 2003). Examples of such commercial target-ing outside of the United Kingdom included attacks in the financial districts of New York in 1993 and Tokyo, Madrid, Paris, Riyadh and Colombo in 1995. In all cases, with the exception of Tokyo, the terror-ist tactics employed utilized vehicle-borne improvised explosive devices (VBIED's) directed against parts of the critical business infrastructure. In Tokyo in 1995, 12 people were killed and many injured as a result of the release of the nerve agent Sarin into the Central Tokyo subway system (see Juergensmeyer, 1997).

Refocusing on urban design to defend the US homeland

In many cases, the response in these global cities to terrorist attack was reactionary, falling back on crude approaches to territorial security, and once again adopting ideas of defensible space (see Chapter 5) as their key *modus operandi*.

The American responses to terror attacks on the World Trade Center in 1993 and the destruction of the Alfred P. Murrah Federal Building in Oklahoma City in 1995 are cases in point. In both these cases the American public became increasingly aware of 'home-grown' terrorism and the role that urban built environment professionals might play in 'terror-proofing' cities.

On 26 February 1993 a vehicle-borne bomb was detonated in a pub-lic parking area below the iconic World Trade Center in central New York City. Six people were killed and over 1000 injured. The impact of this bomb on the psyche of the American public, unused to terrorist attacks, was immeasurable and brought about a swift defensive response (Parachini, 1993) with individual buildings as well as discrete commer-cial districts increasingly attempting to 'design out terrorism' (Coaffee, 2004). As Brown (1995) reported, in the *New York Times* 'barricades and bollards have become the newest accessory on this country's psychic frontier... You might call it the architecture of paranoia. They call it defensible space'. From an emergency management perspective the reaction of the New York Authorities was also considered to be inadequate and *ad hoc* (see later sections of this chapter for a comparison with London).

On 19 April 1995 the Alfred P. Murrah Federal Building in central Oklahoma City was bombed, killing 168 lives and injuring over 800. At the time it was the worst terrorist act on US soil. As a result the US Government passed legislation for increased protective security to be erected around federal buildings as well as debating how individual buildings and urban areas more generally could be 'bomb-proofed'. In particular, there was concern over how the Murrah building had collapsed 'like a pack of cards'; this structural deficiency claimed most of the lives lost. Expert structural engineers were called in to assess how, and why, the building had given way and how similar structures might be hardened to increase resistance against future terrorist threats. For example, Hinman and Hammond (1997) argued that blast resistance could be embedded within buildings and at certain 'at risk' sites such as embassies and that this *should not* be optional for designers. Defending buildings from the effects of blast was not, however, new. As Baer *et al.* (2005, p. 114) highlight, 'blast resistant design specialists and the tools they use to understand explosions are Cold War legacies', although at the time of the Oklahoma attack most of these specialists had little experience of civilian building protection and were usually employed developing hardened missile silos or command bunkers. At the end of the Cold War, and with the continuing threat of terrorism, engineers and architects were increasingly forced to confront designing, not military structures, but civic buildings often, 'with budgetary and aesthetic considerations that were never meant to accommodate blast hardening' (ibid., p. 118). This raised a series of questions that today engineers, architects and urban planners are still attempting to grapple with (see Chapter 11). For example, how do you retrofit blast resistance into existing buildings? How do you restrict access effectively to public buildings? How do you build 'stand-off' areas (setting the building back from the street and putting in place barrier protection, often bollards) in compact urban areas where there is minimal space to do so? How do you convince developers and building owners that they should alter their plans (often at great cost) to include blast resistance? And how do you construct counter-terrorist measures that do not give the impression that you are creating fortified enclaves or bunkers?

Tokyo and a lack of preparedness

In the mid-1990s Japan suffered two major terrorist gas (Sarin) attacks perpetrated by the religious cult Aum Shinrikyo, which exposed the authorities' inability to deal with this type of terrorist attack and posed questions, and huge challenges, for emergency planners, and in particular the First Responders who lacked any experience as to how to deal with this scale of emergency (NATO, 2005).

On 27 June 1994 the mountain town of Matsumoto was subject to a Sarin attack where vaporized gas was released into the evening air. Seven people were killed and over 500 injured by this action, which in hindsight was seen as a practice run for the later attack on the Tokyo subway system on 20 March 1995. The following set of points is amended from an account of the chronology of this later attack taken from a NATO report (2005) which draws on this incident to highlight how the management of the response to terrorist attack requires pre-planning and testing as well as the use of appropriate specialist equipment, all sadly lacking in the Tokyo case (see Box 6.1).

Box 6.1   Shortcomings in the Tokyo response to chemical terrorist attack

- The subway stations attempted to evacuate passengers *en masse*. Fire, police and the emergency medical departments tried to assist the victims; but as they were mostly unprotected, some became victims themselves.

- Although police received emergency calls shortly after the attack, it took another hour before a chemical agent was suspected. Three hours after the attack police and military authorities identified sarin, and it was further hour before the information was shared with other emergency agencies.

- Search and rescue operations were hampered by the fact that there was neither a response plan in place, nor did adequate training to prepare the response personnel for a WMD attack exist.

- No contingency plan existed outside the military. Many of the First Responders on the scene did not have the training to recognize and function in a contaminated environment. This led to the erroneous reaction by the volunteers to rush to the scene trying to help and thereby causing secondary contamination. The

Incident Management made no effort to co-ordinate the provision of resources to each contaminated area, comprised altogether of 15 different subway stations.

- Another significant secondary effect was the impact on hospital care in central Tokyo. Contaminated victims arrived in taxis, busses and on motorbikes, and in turn contaminated emergency rooms at hospitals, causing several to close down ambulance services. Secondary deaths resulted from routine heart attack and stroke victims being denied access to the closest emergency department because it was closed due to sarin contamination or overwhelmed by sarin patients. The prolonged transport time to reach outlying hospitals resulted in several deaths, a model of the secondary and unintended consequences of attacks.

- The pronounced lack of established interagency relationships contributed to the fact that there was no central co-ordination between police, fire department and the public health department.

- The Japanese Self Defense Force was requested to send two experts. But it was unwilling to co-operate with the police.

- Significant *communication problems* became apparent early on and continued for a considerable time. For example, due to information overload, the ambulance control centre could not dispatch emergency medical technicians; drivers of ambulances could not acquire information about the availability of hospital beds; and some First Responders had to use public telephones to communicate with their organizations.

Protecting and preparing UK plc

During the 1990s the threat of economic terrorism received a good deal of attention from international leaders. For example, the British Prime Minister at the time, John Major, cited car-bombings around the globe and the Tokyo subway gas attack as examples of how terrorism affects security and freedom, and stated, perhaps prophetically, that 'it is a problem from which no one can hide and on which we must all co-operate. This is the security challenge of the 21st century' (cited in Jones, 2006).

The threat of terrorist attack in the 1990s served to affect global business centres both materially and symbolically. Urban terrorism created security threats to which municipal and national governments were forced to respond in order to alleviate the fears of their citizens and business community (Coaffee, 2003). As a result security measures similar to those used to 'design out crime' were increasingly introduced, including physical barriers to restrict access, advanced surveillance techniques in the form of security cameras, insurance regulations and blast protection, as well as innumerable indirect measures that operate through activating individual and community responses (ibid.).

In a UK context, the main terrorist threat during the early-mid 1990s came from the Provisional Irish Republican Army (PIRA), with their prime target being the City of London (also known as the 'Square Mile' or 'the City') due to its iconic value as the traditional heart of British imperialism and its economic importance at the centre of the British and global financial system (Rogers, 1996). Large-scale bombs were detonated in the City in the early 1990s as well as a number of smaller devices being discovered before detonation. In addition, in the early-mid 1990s, two further bombings targeted the London Docklands – London's secondary financial centre and seen as a symbolic extension of the City of London.

Risk reduction in 'fortress London'

In the City of London large PIRA bombs exploded in April 1992 and April 1993. Estimates at the time put the bomb damage for each major blast at between £500 and £800 million.[2] In addition, the London Docklands was also targeted by PIRA in November 1992 (unsuccessfully) and successfully in February 1996. Subsequent bomb threats in both financial centres, and the subsequent reaction of London authorities and the Police, served to highlight the use made of both territorial and technological approaches to counter-terrorist security, as well as the role played by well-established continuity and security planning in restricting the impact of these attacks.

The strategic counter-response employed within the City of London in particular, drew heavily on lessons learned from attempts to 'beat the bombers' in Belfast in the 1970s and 1980s with the adoption of territorial approaches to combating terrorism by restricting and monitoring access to vehicular traffic through a series of surveilled checkpoints (Chapter 5).

After the first major London bomb in 1992 such a 'fortified' solution to counter-terrorism was dismissed as an overreaction by the Police and business community. After the second major City bomb in 1993 the adoption of additional security was no longer an option. As such in July 1993 what was referred to in the media as a Belfast-style 'ring of steel' was activated in the City, securing all entrances to the central financial zone (Burns, 1993; Smith, 1993). The entrances into the City were reduced from over 30 to 7 where road-checks manned by armed police were set up.[3]

Attempts were made to balance the adopted security with the economic importance of the City. As it evolved, the City's ring of steel represented a far more symbolic and technologically advanced approach to security, which tried to avoid the 'barrier mentality' of Belfast in favour of less overt security measures which would be more acceptable to the international business community. However, the security cordon provided a highly visible demonstration that the City was taking the terrorist threat seriously and was helpful in reassuring financial industries that they were doing all they could to stop terrorism and avoid business relocation (Donegan, 1992; Jones 1993). Indeed, within London, the ring of steel was promoted to the wider London population in terms of traffic management and environmental improvements which attempted to remove any references to the ongoing terrorist threat (Corporation of London, 1993a,b). The extension to the security cordon, announced in 1997, was also promoted as the 'traffic and environment zone' with no reference made to its counter-terrorism function (Coaffee, 2003). Over time the geographical scale of the security cordon increased over time to a 2001 position where 75% of the Square Mile was covered within the secure zone.[4]

In the City of London the retrofitting of ever-advanced CCTV cameras in both private and public spheres backed up territorial approaches to security. Publicly, the police, through a partnership scheme called Camera Watch, encouraged private companies to install CCTV in liaison with neighbouring businesses. At the entrances of the ring of steel, as well as strategic points around the Square Mile, the most technologically advanced CCTV cameras available at this time were installed (see Plate 6.1). This camera equipment was developed from military technology deployed during the first Gulf war in 1991 and represented an example of where military techniques are deployed in a civilian setting (often linked to the Revolution in Military Affairs literature). In this instance, in February 1997 24-hour Automatic Number Plate Recognition cameras (ANPR) connected to national police databases were installed at the entrances of the security cordon. These digital cameras were capable of processing the information and giving feedback to the operator within four sections (Norris and Armstrong, 1999).

Plate 6.1   ANPR Cameras at the borders of the City of London

In the space of less than a decade, where terrorism had been considered a serious threat, the City of London by the new millennium transformed into the most surveilled space in the United Kingdom, and perhaps the world, with over 1500 surveillance cameras in operation (Coaffee, 2003).

The London Docklands, containing the iconic Canary Wharf complex, was also the focus for counter-terrorist planning through the

1990s. Following the thwarted 1992 attack, managers at Canary Wharf initiated their own 'mini-ring of steel' essentially shutting down access to a private estate within the Docklands complex (Coaffee, 2004). Such an approach combined attempts to strategically 'design-out terrorism' with changing territorial approaches adopted by the Police and private security industry. Security barriers were thrown across the road into and out of the complex, no-parking zones were implemented and a plethora of private CCTV cameras were installed alongside an identity card scheme.

After the 1996 bomb in the southern part of the London Docklands, the business community successfully lobbied the Metropolitan (London) Police to set up an anti-terrorist security cordon to cover the whole of the Docklands – the so-called Iron Collar, modelled on the City of London's approach – amidst similar fears that high-profile businesses might be tempted to relocate away from the area (Coaffee, 2003; Finch, 1996; Hyett, 1996). Subsequently this security cordon was initiated for the whole Dockland peninsula comprising four entry points which at times of high-risk assessment would have armed guards stationed at them. High-resolution ANPR cameras were also installed. The most noticeable difference between the scheme initiated in the Docklands and that in the City was the overt advertising of the Docklands security cordon – 'Security Cordon. Stop if Directed' – on large signs at entry points into the cordon (Plate 6.2) instead of downplaying the zones anti-terrorism purpose, as had been the case in the City of London (Coaffee, 2003).

Prior to September 11 counter-terrorism measures in the United Kingdom were largely deployed to stop vehicle bombs, with defence focused almost exclusively on London's financial zones. Ironically these zones became synonymous with increasing the 'quality of life' where heightened levels of security were a key 'selling point' in attempting to market the affected economic districts to potential investors and tenants (London Chamber of Commerce, 1994; 1996), being seen by the business community as 'rings of confidence' which gave those inside the security zone a feeling of safety and preventing the feared exodus of high-profile tenants to more remote edge-of-city sites (Coaffee, 2004). We will return to this idea of security as a selling point in later chapters, contending that it is a key feature of 'everyday urban resilience'.

The genesis of 'resilient planning' in London

The changing terrorist risk agendas of the 1990s brought about a series of changes in relationships between the way in which the insurance

Plate 6.2   Security cordon advertisement when entering the Isle of Dogs, in the London Docklands

industry viewed the risk of terrorism and the way in which it was perceived by those responsible for the physical security enacted around the financial zones in London. The processes involved can be seen to be subtly supportive of one another as both were concerned with maintaining the reputation of London as a safe and secure business centre. The behaviour of the insurance industry in London at this time can also be seen to have been important in influencing processes that resulted in the increased fortification of the urban landscape, as well as educating business about the risks faced (Coaffee, 2003). Of particular note here is the enhancement of contingency planning which was widely utilized as an anti-terrorism measure in order to improve the ability of businesses in the financial zones to 'bounce back' from a terrorist incident. This was important from an insurance perspective as terrorism insurance covered business interruption as well as material damage (Gloyn, 1993).

There were two main elements to such contingency planning. First, there was crisis recovery planning (CRP) which highlighted how London could bring about a 'business as usual' situation as soon as possible after a large-scale attack (Frost, 1994). This was most noticeably employed in the Square Mile where CRP was initiated at two levels; first in relation to individual companies, and second, in respect to a strategic City-wide plan. After the 1992 St Mary Axe bomb many companies prepared CRPs that made contingency for temporary relocation to peripheral 'disaster recovery space' at short notice. At the time of the Bishopsgate bomb, CRPs instigated by the Corporation of London at a City-wide level were also in evidence. The Corporation's disaster plan had been refined through practice drills and aimed to get people back to work as quickly as possible.

CRPs employed after Bishopsgate were, as noted in the Corporation's *City Research Project* (1995, p. 27), themselves a result of corporate change at a global level to mitigate a variety of risks (not just terrorism) and develop some form of Integrated Emergency Management (IEM). In particular, this research project report noted that 'the large institutions which have taken the most extensive measures have not done so solely because of a specific threat [terrorism] but rather as part of a global scheme, not least to counter infrastructural failure such as power cuts and flooding (another danger in London)'. The Corporation continued by indicating that in their opinion their efforts were superior and more proactive to those in other global financial centres:

> The level of contingency planning both by the Corporation and by individual firms is in contrast to centres such as New York, where the response to the World Trade Center blast [in 1993] was impressive but *ad hoc*. (ibid.)

Furthermore, this report highlighted that at this time, the City viewed the threat of terrorism as something to be proactive against as opposed to just reactive, and that 'the degree of fatalism with regard to officials interviewed in the United States was in contrast to the proactive approach of the City after its first bomb' (ibid.).

The second form of contingency planning employed during the 1990s was the increased importance placed upon developing security plans, which included the risk management response (such as CCTV, access control and stand-off areas and blast protection) that formed the basis of protective security. Security planning, like CRP, at this time can be expressed on two levels: first the private response of individual companies in terms of risk management measures, and second, the co-ordinated response of the police and the local government in constructing strategic security cordons and associated security infrastructure.

As well as developing area-based security strategies, the police, in liaison with the private security sector, set about creating an extra layer of security around individual buildings through the addition of landscape features and the implementation of security strategies. Coaffee (2003, p. 107) noted at the time that:

> Typical security plans adopted at this time aimed to deter an attack and deny the terrorist access to the premises – creating what could be referred to as a 'mini ring of steel' – which served to fortify and 'harden' the urban landscape by altering the spatial configuration of the outside area adjacent to a building, in particular the borders of a building and the immediate surrounds.

There were other precautions that were also taken by many businesses to reduce the effects of a bomb blast such as application of anti-shatter window film, safety glass (a legal requirement under building regulations at certain critical locations), the installation of blast curtains and the construction of internal shelter areas. It was felt that adding such structural considerations in when designing a new building (rather than retrofitting) would cost an additional 0–5% of building cost (Crawford, 1995, p. 18).

The security precautions taken were implemented alongside advice from the Police, security services and in conjunction with Home Office Guidance for *Bombs: Protecting People and Property*, first published in 1994.[5] This guide highlighted how preparation was increasingly playing a part in counter-terrorism thinking within organizations as well as strongly encouraging building occupants to 'participate in the counter-terrorist security planning in your community: communities defeat terrorism' (p. 4).

The Mancunian response

It is now well over a decade since a large terrorist bomb decimated a significant part of central Manchester, North West England, in June 1996. Subsequently the city centre was physically remodelled at a cost well in excess of £1 billion (Williams, 2000).

The post-bomb regeneration and reconstruction experience in Manchester highlights the importance of both attempting to design-in security features to the urban landscape and develop systems of emergency management that could assist recovery from an attack. Manchester authorities, however, approached this task in a very different way from other cities affected by large terrorist attacks. As previously noted, other UK experiences from Belfast (1970s, Chapter 5) and the City of London and London Docklands (1990s, this chapter) led to an emergency planning response which favoured a 'fortress approach' to security with the setting up of 'rings of steel' comprising tall gates, mass camera surveillance and guarded checkpoints (Coaffee, 2004).

The civic leaders in Manchester, given fears that business would relocate away from the city centre, muted setting up a similar security apparatus in the aftermath of the 1996 bomb. Ultimately this did not occur; however, what was generated was a commitment to embed security features into the new regeneration masterplans. For example, this occurred through restricted vehicle access to the central shopping zones, the installation of a centralized CCTV system, the design and integration of 'cordoned-off' areas for high profile (and hence high target risk) buildings and bomb-proof litter bins installed as part of the street furniture (Coaffee and Rogers, 2008).

Such design interventions were also backed up by an expanded emergency planning role for the city council. The subsequent embedding of the need for enhanced preparedness within governance approaches obviously had an additional counter-terrorist purpose, but also boosted the attractiveness of the city centre as a safe and secure commercial district, a middle-class residential environment and a prestigious events and conference venue (Chapter 10).

From an urban management perspective, after the 1996 bomb an independent and privately funded City Centre Management company was also established to represent the views of local business and residents. Subsequently management strategies were developed in liaison with the police and city council to tackle a wide range of security and safety issues, ranging from the rolling-out of street crime warden schemes and the implementation of by-laws to regulate perceived anti-social behaviour, to the retrofitting of security to the newly emerging public realm. Perhaps the most notable aspect of this city centre revival, one that links design, surveillance and management together, has been a surge in the installation of CCTV cameras. This began as a relatively small initiative in 1998 with only 19 cameras dotted around the central city but has expanded in line with regeneration activity. Today over

80 co-ordinated cameras (including ANPR cameras) and hundreds of private cameras have been installed to monitor the city centre, creating the most advanced CCTV system in the United Kingdom outside of central London. In Manchester the aim was simple: to create a permeable surveillance ring around the rejuvenated city centre to improve safety, reduce the fear and occurrence of crime, encourage the influx of shoppers, residents, tourists and businesses and provide protection for critical commercial infrastructure (Coaffee and Rogers, 2008).

Towards a resilient planning of cities

This chapter has sought to highlight how, in the mid-late 1990s, urban areas continued to focus upon issues of crime prevention, often through an intensification of previous territorial techniques of defensible space and CPTED. We have highlighted that as this approach has advanced, the design of space (fortification and surveillance) and management have become increasingly hybridized. We have also argued that such techniques were also increasingly adopted in very specific locations (economic nodes) deemed to be at risk from terrorism.

Such defensive approaches in these instances were not restricted to territorial concerns but were also adopted at the individual building scale, placing great emphasis upon 'target hardening', a subject that was widely critiqued. For example, Martin Pawley (1998, p. 148) argued at this time that, as a result of an upsurge in urban terrorism, especially against 'the highly serviced and vulnerable built environment of the modern world', the new-wave of signature buildings could be replaced by an 'architecture of terror' as a result of security needs. Citing examples from Israel, Sri Lanka, North America, Spain and the United Kingdom, he prophesied that such structures could well take on an 'anonymous' design to make them less of an iconic target. He emphasized that, once this security-oriented planning became established, it would be difficult to withdraw unless the terrorist threat significantly decreased (Coaffee, 2006).

Likewise we have highlighted the broader strategic impact of crime management and counter-terrorism policy which at this time was highly focused in particular risk 'hot spots'. This gave the overall urban landscape a fractured and fragmented feel with the protected zones increasingly disconnected to the overall city; a form which Graham and Marvin (2001) referred to as 'splintered urbanism'.

Above all we have argued that the responses in New York, Oklahoma City, Tokyo, London and Manchester to terrorist risk during the 1990s elicited a growing awareness of the need to be proactive and prepared for a catastrophic incident. In subsequent chapters, we will highlight how this 'anticipatory' requirement was further 'ratcheted up' after the events of September 11 for both terrorist and non-terrorist threats. In other words, we are arguing that September 11 did not, as many have claimed, 'change the world' and develop new trends in terms of urban defences, but merely reinforced existing and historically rooted trends. As we discuss in the next chapters, the latest incarnation of the defensive city is increasingly focused on the ideas, language and rhetoric of 'resilience' which has increasingly been adopted in many countries to characterize emergency-planning procedures and as a 'catch-all' phrase for how urban areas, and their managers, can deal with contemporary terrorist attacks or other disasters.

7
States of Protection and Emergency: The Rise of Resilience

In recent years the concept of 'resilience' has become central to the discussion of shifting social and political histories and the framework of agents and agencies operating under the guise of national security and disaster mitigation. The use of 'resilience' as a conceptual metaphor in the language of such policy, and as an active rationale for the *modus operandi* of governance underpinning domestic emergency, is becoming increasingly pervasive (Buckle *et al.*, 2000).

As we will argue, in this and subsequent chapters, in the post-September 11 world, not only were new or modified solutions to contemporary forms of terrorist risk (and other forms of risk such as from natural hazards) sought, but new ways of managing this process initiated. As we noted in Chapter 6, this is not inferring that September 11 altered existing threat-response in the dramatic ways that many have claimed. Rather we argue here that in the tradition of reflexive practice, a rethinking and re-evaluation of risks, hazards and threats, and how to counter them, has emerged. As Molotch and McClain (2003, p. 679) argue, 'the attacks of September 11th indicate a new kind of threat to urban security and imply the need for new urban knowledge's or at least fresh ways to apply older understandings'. Likewise Ulrich Beck (2003) argued that in the light of September 11 we need a new vocabulary to articulate how we manage and govern in an ever-expanding 'risk society' in that: 'we live, think and act in concepts that are historically obsolete but which nonetheless continue to govern our thinking and acting' (p. 256).

We argue in this chapter that emergency responses and counter-terrorism processes are increasingly adopting a new vocabulary – around the term resilience – which attempts to convey a response which is *proactive* as well as *reactive*, and which has in-built adaptability or 'bouncebackability' (Coaffee, 2006) to deal with the fluid nature of the range of security challenges faced by many nations and their urban areas.

We will also argue that as the idea of resilience has become embedded within this security and civil contingencies policy context it has been attached to a range of risk-related policy pronouncements across a range of policies often only loosely related security and social order. In this sense resilience is a versatile metaphor, a 'floating signifier' and a 'translation term' – defined by Gold and Revill (1999, p. 235) as a term which 'allows connections to be made between different stands of research with common terminology and consistent threads of analysis, without needing to make assumptions that the phenomena under investigation are the product of similar processes that apply regardless of cultural context'.

Of particular concern in this chapter are the issues of how, and why, the concept of resilience has emerged as a key policy metaphor underpinning the reaction of the state to the ongoing terrorist threat and other emergencies? We also question if this 'new language' of emergency planning is reflected in changing strategic guidance in nation-states considered to be at high risk from disruptive challenges, and whether or not this changes the emphasis of what constitutes an emergency or threat? We additionally ask how such changes in strategy are coming to inform the emerging structures, policies and practices which can be seen to target the 'improvement' of social and civil resilience to a range of crises?

To develop these arguments we adopt a model developed by Pickett *et al.* (2004) for unpacking what they termed 'cities of resilience'. This model highlights how a key 'emergent metaphor' to describe a raft of policy initiatives (in this case resilience as applied to national security and emergency planning policy) has evolved, through step-change from an initial 'generative metaphor' in a range of relatively unconnected fields of enquiry (see Figure 7.1). The transformative process will highlight how the 'meaning' of the term resilience has been appropriated by policy-makers in order to refine the 'model' of UK policy and strategy in relation to risks, hazards and threats.

Within this context this chapter is split into two main parts. The first part unpacks the conceptual etymology of the term resilience. By developing a detailed assessment of the original meaning(s) of resilience

Generative metaphor ⟶ Meaning ⟶ Model ⟶ Emergent metaphor

Figure 7.1   Process of conceptual transition as a policy step-change

in academic enquiry, the concept of resilience can then be grounded in the contexts of disaster management, contemporary security policy and social and economic considerations of the consequences of high-risk and high-profile emergencies. Unpacking the metaphorical rhetoric that underpins and validates the current approaches to resilience gives a solid grounding for reassessment of the strategic and political agenda through which resilience policy is increasingly applied in the current context.

Secondly, and specifically from a UK perspective, we look at some of the disruptive events that stimulated a review of emergency planning and national security policy in the early 2000s and thus informed the 'emergent' rhetoric of resilience. This enables a constructive review of how ideas of resilience have become embedded within emerging governance approaches for emergency preparedness, and in particular, for facilitating increased interoperability between agencies at a range of scales (the specifics of which in the UK context are detailed in subsequent chapters).

Unpacking meaning, model and metaphor through 'resilience'

A conceptual context as to why resilience has emerged as a key policy driver in emergency planning can be offered through examples of how resilience has been used in prior research across different disciplines. Whilst by no means comprehensive, the purpose of the following appraisal is to illustrate the range of definitions deployed in different research contexts (particularly ecology and psychology) and by demonstrating the range of issues resilience can be applied to.

Ecological resilience

One of the most significant academic uses of the term 'resilience' in an analytical research context can be attributed to C.S. Holling (1973), who introduced the term to the analysis of ecological systems. Specifically, ecological resilience was defined as:

> ...the amount of disturbance that an ecosystem could withstand without changing self-organized processes and structures (defined as alternative stable states).
>
> (cited in Gunderson, 2000, p. 425)

Ecological resilience in this form has a conceptual emphasis on 'resistance' framed as 'the magnitude of disturbance that can be absorbed before a system changes its structure' (Adger, 2000, p. 349). Likewise, 'engineering' resilience in ecology is seen as the duration taken for a 'return to the steady state following a perturbation' (Gunderson *et al.*, 2002, p. 530), giving a temporal context to the *process* of resilience.

The conceptual emphasis of resilience is here fairly consistent, broadly drawn as the systemic resistance to external influences and the ability of that system to return to a new steady or stable state of relative normality. However, there are a variety of ways in which these concepts have been applied across the biological and environmental sciences, for example relating to: marine reef ecosystems and the 'vulnerability' of reefs to bleaching by water temperature change (Obura, 2004); the challenges facing, and contributions made by, specific species to broader ecosystemic resilience (Davic and Welsh Jr. 2004); as a dynamic element in 'carrying capacity' between ecosystems (del Monte-Luna *et al.*, 2004); and extending towards social research by charting community conflict as a result of exposure to 'environmental hazards' (Shriver and Kennedy, 2005). The uses of resilience in ecology are thus complex and varied, reflecting subtly different aspects of its meaning in different cases.

In both research and policy the way in which the concept of resilience is applied has noticeable affects on the type of output generated. A good example of this is in the conceptual drift in the focus from environmental 'hazards' towards human oriented 'disasters':

> The hazards orientation encourages attention to the beneficial as well as the adverse affects of natural variations...Research which focuses almost exclusively on the disaster end of the spectrum tends to increase emphases on the search for both social culpability or blame; description of physical risks involved; and the emergency and short-term humanitarian response.
>
> (White *et al.*, 2001, pp. 84–5)

It can be argued that this is one of many small, but significant, changes to research practices into disaster management, and as a key thread of resilience this is vital to following the changing emphasis of strategy and policy. In short, as the meaning of what constitutes a disaster is redefined so too are the boundaries of what constitutes the appropriate policy response.

The meaning of resilience as an ecological concept has developed in both critical theory and applied research over time. Where previously the emphasis was focussed on ecological science and environmental ethics, there are now conceptual links to be made between the meaning of resilience in ecological research and the contemporary social and institutional responses to emergencies, particularly through the understanding of hazardous natural disaster events.

A useful theoretical framework for understanding the changing usage of ecological resilience can be derived from the previously introduced work of Pickett *et al.* (2004) in attempting to bridge the disciplines of ecological theory, socio-economic research and planning practice. By focusing on the 'vernacular metaphorical origin' of resilience in ecology (ibid., p. 373) and using the 'generative metaphor' of ecological resilience, Pickett *et al.* have developed a methodological tool for unpacking connections between disparate systems, using resilience as the integrative tool for understanding metropolitan urban social ecosystems.

As a contributor to a 'generative metaphor' this framework of ecological resilience helps to demonstrate a number of key issues of relevance to this discussion; first, that the term resilience has had, and continues to have, a broad range of applications in ecological theory and research; secondly, that the application of the concept has a significant effect on the paradigms of research and practice, with multiple variations stemming from notions of 'hazard', 'vulnerability', 'risk', 'resistance' and so on; and thirdly that in the ecological definition resilience is defined by change or 'perturbation' within a specific site or 'ecosystem', increasingly with an implicit negative connotation, whether that be through the duration of resistance before a response is manifest *or* the time taken to return to a stable or 'steady' state of comparative normality in the post-event period.

Psychological resilience

Building on ecological approaches to resilience there is also a related body of work investigating aspects of resilience in psychological research and practice. This field has, over time, addressed a wide range of resiliency issues, such as the resilience of parents to stress (Heiman, 2002), definitions of 'quality of life' (Lawford and Eiser, 2001) and responses to loss and trauma (Bonanno, 2004). For example, Margaret Whaller (2001) places the origins of the term resilience within the study and practice of psychiatry, linked to the assessment of those 'at risk' and specifically 'at risk youth'[1] or 'children'. She noted that:

> Resilience was initially conceptualized as the resultant personality traits or coping styles that seemed to make some children continue to develop along a positive developmental trajectory even when confronted with considerable adversity.
>
> (Whaller, 2001, p. 291)

Connecting with discourses of 'risk' and 'protection', resilience can be used here in similar terms 'to describe individuals who adapt to extraordinary circumstances, achieving positive and unexpected outcomes in the face of adversity' (Fraser *et al.*, 1999, p. 136). So, in a psychological sense, resilience is not simply about resistance and response to a perturbation, it also encapsulates the potential for a *positive* outcome arising, in part, from the exposure of an individual or group to adverse circumstances or events. Despite using a very different frame of reference this is echoed in the orientation of natural hazards research. As shown in a study by Shriver and Kennedy (2005), environmental contamination of a residential area led to psychological reactions throughout the community – through, in this case, the 'ambiguity of harm' – and thus impacted upon the social organization of the community, generating polarized viewpoints of how best to manage the resultant tensions. This study connected the three areas of ecological resilience: as contamination of an ecosystem (the community); with psychological resilience (the reaction to unknown danger); with social resilience (the organization of the community in response to threat).

By focusing on the individual or collective communal response to exposure, links can be made to the ability of people to react positively to negative events, thus making resilience a *quality* towards which to aspire. This principle can be seen to run through many aspects of the 'emergent metaphor' of resilience underpinning modern policy. For example, hailing the resilience of New Yorkers following September 11 (Bonanno, 2004; Bonanno *et al.*, 2006) or Londoners subsequent to the July bombings in 2005 (Wessely, 2005).[2]

These subtle variations in how we might think about resilience show that both ecological and psychological areas contribute to the development and understanding of the broader concept. Whilst ecology focuses predominantly on broader ecosystemic issues, the focus of psychological resilience is on the human individual or community, providing a useful link to social application.

Connecting resiliency concepts to disaster management

In developing these conceptual cross-disciplinary connections there are two key interpretations to the idea of resilience we can further develop here which have been applied to highlight aspects of resilience in practice. By relating previous ecological and psychological under-standings towards understanding 'social' or 'community' resilience, and 'economic' resilience, links can be made towards rethinking the most appropriate ways to organize disaster management.

With regard to social resilience, Carpenter *et al.* (2001) linked ecologi-cal research with resilience in 'socio-ecological systems' thus connecting ecology to social processes by assessing the 'adaptive cycle' and 'adaptive capacity' of a range of systems. Adger (2000), in researching the links between social and ecological resilience, also argued that one way in which this can be encouraged is by 'focusing on the links between social stability (of populations within social systems) and resource depen-dency' (p. 351) – which yields a better awareness of how specific institu-tions as 'modes of socialized behaviour' and 'more formal structures of governance and law' (ibid.) can be grounded in the local ecology.

In the context of urban environmental risk, Mark Pelling (2003) in *The Vulnerability of Cities* argued that the 'adaptive potential' of indi-viduals and communities is related to two types of 'human response': first, coping strategies where social networks may be mobilized to reduce the negative impact of an event; and second, institutional modification which 'aims to alter the institutional framework of a city using polit-ical influence to create political space for at-risk actors to argue their case' (p. 62). This latter response is of course problematic in situations where there is institutional inertia and a lack of willingness to change, or where change is moving apace, particularly linked to privatization and the hollowing out of the state (see, for example, Adger, 2000). In summary, argues Pelling:

> The retreat of the state and expansion of the private sector and civil society in cities worldwide has created an opportunity for new institutional forms and networks to be created that can enhance a city's ability to deal with vulnerability and environmental hazard (pp. 63–4).

Another key connection to be made across fields of enquiry, and a key contribution of the social sciences to the debate, can be found in the related concept of 'community resilience' where a number of researchers have attempted to model the human response to natural disaster (Creamer, 1994; Van den Eyde and Veno, 1999). For example, Paton *et al.* (2001, p. 158) have argued that 'the orientation of work in this area [disaster management] has progressively moved from a deficit or pathological paradigm, to one emphasizing community resilience', with Tobin (1999) further arguing that community resilience is one of the 'holy grails' to obtain for successful disaster recovery.

Others have argued that, by adding the caveat of cultural and social processes to the discussion of resilience, the balance of resiliency policy can be reoriented away from analysis of deterministic legislative and technological processes, and increasingly grounded in the more meaningful experience of the world by citizens, often absent from debates in the disaster mitigation literature (Durodie and Wessely, 2002). As Durodie (2005) further notes:

> Policy makers and emergency planners must learn from the literature examining human behaviour in disasters. The relevant research shows that professionals should incorporate community responses to particular crises within their actions, rather than seeking to supplant these because they consider them ill-informed or less productive ... Actions to enhance the benefits of spontaneous association, as well as to develop a sense of purpose and trust across society are, at such times, just as important as effective technical responses. (p. 4)

In understanding the emerging urban experience of 'perturbation' in the context of a new mode of resilience governance, it becomes clear, due in part to the emphasis of disaster on the assignation of blame, but also to the prevalence of risk, that the management of response to events and ensuring social stability places extreme pressure on the formal structures of governance. The unpredictable power of natural forces to impact upon or affect social relations and systems of governance has recently been highlighted, and a call for new understandings of 'environmental hazard' as 'natural disaster', and the need for new ways of coping, is widely acknowledged. Whilst natural disasters and environmental hazards are far from being exclusively urban experiences, the recent surge in events affecting large-scale conurbations, in both the developing and developed world, has seen a significant shift towards unpacking the adaptive capacity of governance institutions and communities, and how this might be utilized as part of developing a new 'urban resilience' (Bull-Kamanga *et al.*, 2003; Pelling and High, 2005).[3] In this sense social or community resilience is seen very much as the participation of citizens in the process of making the state more resilient and to help manage threats and 'conditions of uncertainty'. Here the argument is that shared and co-ordinated action can reduce collective vulnerability.

The second major link that we wish to make to resilience is through the notion of economy. In travel and tourism the concept and measurement of 'economic' resilience is central to the sustainability of locations, areas and regions. In its broadest sense economic resilience has tended to relate to small nation-states and their ability to generate a comparatively high Gross National Product (GNP) in the face of fluctuating global economic conditions. A good summary of this application can be drawn from the study and indexing of economic 'vulnerability' amongst small island nation-states, for example the Singaporean phenomenon (Brigulio, 2004; Brigulio *et al.*, 2005). The index of economic resilience presented by Brigulio *et al.* comprises of (a) macro-economic stability, (b) micro-economic market efficiency, (c) good governance, and (d) social development to measure the economic success of a nation-state (through GDP) in the context of its inherent vulnerabilities – noting also that man-made policies can be seen as a main contributor to success in overcoming vulnerability in high-risk locations (ibid., p. 18). We noted in Chapter 2 there is also historical evidence, back to the most ancient times, that natural hazards can spark social innovation and new urban developments.

More conceptually, Adam Rose (2007) has made strong links between ideas of economic resilience and the multi-disciplinary and contextual dimensions of natural and man-made disasters, in his redefinition of economic resilience as 'the ability of an entity or system to maintain function (for example, continue producing) when shocked' (p. 384). This approach moves firmly into the context of emergency prevention, response, management and mitigation, and draws on both ecological and engineering resilience as metaphorical basis for organizing the resilience process. Economic resilience in this sense becomes the ability of nation-states and governance agencies to embed a disaster mitigation process into the everyday practice of governing, ensuring the ability of nation-state to continue operating within the global economy at a regular capacity. Links can also be made to the infrastructural connotations of environmental imbalance through disaster management, for example the failure of utilities, transport or energy in the event of an urban perturbation and the shift towards business continuity and supply-chain management (Rose, 2007, p. 385). As we have seen in Chapter 4, the absence of such processes and the unanticipated economic links from shock of the San Francisco earthquake and fire of

1906, led to a nationwide recession. A more recent example of these connections can be seen in the reactions of the US energy industry in the aftermath of Hurricane Katrina (Hess, 2005). This type of approach grounds the understanding of disaster events as disruptions to the flow of capital where resilience becomes measurable through the assessment *post ex facto* of economic disruption in the affected location (Rose 2003, 2004; Greenberg *et al.*, 2007).

Such analysis can also be used to highlight how a city's ability to restore 'businesses as usual' after a disaster can be seen in terms of economic competitiveness. We saw in the last chapter how London was able to market this ability as a positive trait after terrorist attacks in the 1990s. Likewise, commentators after the September 11 attacks have shown how New York was seen as economically resilient. Howard Chernick (2005, p. ix) in *Resilient City* showed how 'fear that New York's competitive economic position in the world economy would deteriorate as firms fled the city proved to be unfounded' despite a massive reduction in rentable office space and job losses of over 125,000 in the three years proceeding the attacks. We argued in Chapter 1 that in our view the events of September 11 did not 'change the world' but merely reinforced pre-existing trends in a variety of ways. Chernick's analysis backs up this assumption, in that 'the terrorist attack did accelerate cyclical and long-terms trends that were under way' and whilst showing initially large-scale economic harm, showed little 'permanent damage to New York City as a business location' (p. 9).[4]

The preceding sections have identified a variety of areas of research where the use of the term resilience has been employed – ecology, psychology and in terms of social, community and economic resilience in disaster management, all of which have applicability when assessing how and why resilience has been generated in the key language of Governments, particularly in the United Kingdom, to underpin the rhetoric of new and emergent forms of planning for terrorist threats or other disruptive challenges. It is to the deployment of 'resilience' into this emerging policy nexus that we now turn.

Step-change in the meaning, model and metaphor of resilience

Managing tensions related to emerging threats and risk events is the role of disaster management and emergency planners at a range of scales in differing national contexts. It is into this emerging field of policy that the new concept of resilience is now most frequently deployed in order to bring together the activities of key actors, agencies and institutions.

It is therefore important to appreciate how the roles and responsibilities of those associated with emergency planning and disaster management have been reconceptualized in recent years, both in terms of the language underpinning policy, as suggested above, as well as in the strategic policy and everyday practices informed by the language of emerging 'resilience' policy.

In understanding and applying these changes it is useful to demonstrate how the above redefinition of strategic 'resilience' policy can be driven through the theoretical framework introduced at the beginning of this chapter. Figure 7.2 below, charts the way in which resilience policy has emerged from generative metaphors and been redefined and reapplied in a new socio-political context – where many aspects of UK policy were focusing on response to the ongoing terrorist threat as well as existing concerns about the lack of preparedness within the emergency planning system to cope with natural disaster or large-scale

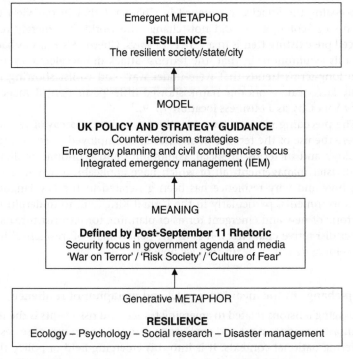

Figure 7.2 Resilience applied to the context of changes in contemporary emergency planning policy

disruptive events. In this model we also highlight, that over time, ideas of resilience for emergency planning and disaster management has been broadened out to intersect with other previously separate areas of public policy, particularly around social order and control, which might be seen as only loosely connected to concerns about terrorism or natural disaster.

Figure 7.2 shows that following on from the generative metaphor of resilience the next level, that of 'meaning', is focused through the specific paradigm of inquiry as well as the evolving research context: in this case, in the post-September 11 era it can be argued that resilience as a generative metaphor has been focused through such general ideas as the 'war on terror', 'new security challenges' and the 'culture of fear', resulting in the perceived need for a change in the operation of the specific practices of emergency planners and disaster managers.

These practices then form the 'model', as a 'layer of connotation' through which the 'core meaning' is 'translated' to 'a real or proposed situation' (Pickett *et al.*, 2004, p. 370). In this case, the new meaning of resilience is translated into governmetalizing strategies – policy documents and legislation – around counter-terrorism and civil contingencies. This has occurred within a broader context of a move towards developing an emergent 'structure of resilience' in the United Kingdom around Integrated Emergency Management (IEM) which 'comprises six related activities: anticipation, assessment, prevention, preparation, response and recovery' (UK Resilience, 2005a). These can be seen as characteristics of the generative metaphor arising from the refined meaning of resilience which underpins the emergence of new, structured governance models, where:

> Resilience means ensuring that the country is prepared to detect, prevent and respond with speed and certainty to major emergencies, including terrorist attack.
>
> (ODPM, 2004)

This emergent metaphor of resilience operates at a range of scales from the macro (a resilient society or a resilient nation-state) through the meso level (as resilient regions or resilient cities) to the micro-level (resilient communities and resilient individuals). More importantly the metaphorical 'step-change' in understanding resilience, and its emergence as a body of strategic governance and policy, suggests the increasing influential *process* of resilience can be defined broadly as the ability of a system of any kind to either absorb or respond to negative external influences or to more generalized experiences of perturbation.

Rethinking emergency planning policy – towards resilience policy

In this chapter the primary concern has been with the conceptual evolution of the defining characteristics of new policies of 'resilience' as the emergent metaphor which underpins the new UK policy framework for emergency preparedness.

Until recently in the United Kingdom, the emergency planning system had for many years been considered 'fit for purpose' with a predominantly reactive focus on response to events as they occurred, driven locally with 'central government quite willing to let local agencies deal with emergencies' (O'Brien and Reid, 2005, p. 353). In more recent years, it has been suggested that the increased complexity of disasters and their impact have necessitated a rethink in the priorities of civil defence and civil protection (Alexander, 2002), supporting the changing paradigms of emergency planning suggested here through our analysis of 'resilience'.

Defence, protection and contingencies

The Civil Defence in Peacetime Act 1986 and the Local Government and Housing Act 1989 recognized the need for a change in the management of emergencies from the strategic emphasis at the time on 'civil defence' (Rockett, 1994, p. 48). As we have seen in Chapter 4, the Cold War system had seen emergency planning as a wartime concern underpinned by a rhetoric emphasizing the 'management of civil populations in the face of actual or potential aggression' (Alexander, 2002, p. 209). The key concern and subject of this system was the potential consequences of open warfare and hostile relations with the Soviet Union, but after the fall of the USSR and a series of high-profile domestic civil disasters, pressure was raised for Government to address the applicability of this method of planning to new social and civil emergencies (Smith, 2003, p. 410). The above mentioned Acts allowed civil defence resources, which had previously been the province of the military, to be mobilized in peacetime, and engendered a shift towards giving Fire and Civil Defence Authorities the ability to co-ordinate district and borough emergency planning in periods where military threat was not the primary or highest risk. Recognition that updating this legislation was required helped to introduce a new rhetoric emphasizing 'civil protection' 'through the gradual realization that it is not effective, or efficient, to manage civil emergencies such as floods and transportation crashes by military means' (Alexander, 2002, p. 210).

The rhetoric of 'civil protection' was itself brought under scrutiny in the United Kingdom in the late 1980s and early 1990s by the high profile of a number of tragic rail crashes, ferry accidents and football stadium disasters. Concerns were once again raised regarding the ability of the existing emergency planning system to respond to disasters (Smith, 2003, p. 410). Despite subsequent Government reviews in 1989 and 1991, little impact registered upon the structure and finance of the emergency planning system. Furthermore, the funding for peacetime preparedness was not a central issue on the UK political agenda at this time and updating and reforming of emergency planning remained 'tomorrows work' in a complex state of infrastructural limbo compounded by legislative inadequacies, funding cuts and organizational problems. For example, Walker and Broderick (2006, p. 275) highlight that funding in this area had been periodically reduced from 1991 as 'part of a peace divided at the end of the Cold War'.

Meaningful changes in the system were only triggered in 2000 and 2001 after another series of high-profile regional and international emergency crises. Calls for a review of the performance and management of emergency planning swiftly followed leading to a new review of what is now commonly referred to as 'civil contingencies'. In the United Kingdom this policy review built on what has been referred to anecdotally by practitioners as the '3 Fs': the *fuel* protests (blockades of oil refineries, go-slow convoys on motorways), the outbreak of the *Foot and Mouth* Disease and a number of serious *flooding* incidents. The combination of these 'disaster' events led to questions being posed regarding 'who was in charge' of emergency responses, and the need for a meaningful peacetime response to 'civil contingencies', as opposed to the previously over-simple rhetoric's of defence and protection. Furthermore, these events were not all local in nature, thus the regional and national inability to co-ordinate response was brought into sharp focus as a failure of Central Government.

It was argued that state privatization, local and regional governance reorganization and a general 'hollowing out of the state' had left a disorganized 'chain of command', which lacked authoritative leadership and appropriate resources (Smith, 2003). The long-overdue review of emergency planning procedures began in early 2001 and was completed by the end of that year, during which time responsibility for civil contingency planning was shifted from the locally fragmented Home Office Emergency Planning Department to the emergent Cabinet Office's national body – the Civil Contingencies Secretariat (CCS) in July 2001 (see Chapter 8). With *carte-blanche* to reform the emergency planning system, this new body appeared better equipped to co-ordinate a response across different branches of Government and to streamline the channels of communication and control during civil emergencies (Smith, 2003, pp. 412–14). However, as this review progressed, a series of disaster events – incorporating a Foot and Mouth Disease epidemic and, most notably, the September 11 terror attacks – dramatically changed the landscape of UK emergency planning giving new and significant impetus to the agenda of improvement and reorganization.

This 'upping the ante' in disaster management was felt around the globe. In the United States there had been ongoing and heated debate about the ability of the American state, and its population, to response to subsequent acts of large-scale terrorism. This has moved away from a focus on building construction that emerged in the mid-1990s as a key concern (Chapter 6) to focus upon more holistic strategies for protecting high-risk areas, although it is still questionable whether the required level of 'resilience' has been obtained. For example, Stephen Flynn in *Edge of Disaster* (2007) paints a picture of an American nation still unprepared for dealing with a major catastrophe. He argues that terrorism cannot always be predicted and that more effort and resources must be put into preparedness training, infrastructure protection and the building of community and economic resilience. In short, argues Flynn, resilience should become the 'national motto' as Americans seek to embed protective security and disaster management measures into national organizations and the collective psyche:

> When it comes to dealing with the risk of a disaster, as a nation we should be thinking about it as we do seat belts. Identifying and embracing pragmatic measures that reduce the consequences of unexpected events is not a defeatist position. It is the smart thing to do. A resilient society is one that won't fall apart in the face of adversity. Protecting property and successfully evacuating populations that are potentially in harm's way lessen a … disaster's destructive impact. Making infrastructures resilient makes them less attractive for terrorists. And preparing for the worst makes the worst less likely to happen. (ibid., p. 154)

The United States undoubtedly took the global lead in the legislative reform around counter-terrorist response, throwing the agenda of civil liberties and state security centre stage with the swift passing of the Uniting and Strengthening America by Providing Appropriate Tools Required to Intercept and Obstruct Terrorism (Patriot) Act 2001. As a centre piece of the American response to terrorist attack, the Patriot Act was also supported with the establishment of the Department of Homeland Security (DHS) in 2002 – with its remit for domestic protection and disaster mitigation. The DHS, however, also acts as a focus for critical appraisal by the civil rights movement in the United States. The accusation from civil liberties lobbies maintains that the federal government has, through the establishment of extra-ordinary bodies for management of these issues and the creation of emergency powers for dealing with terror suspects, contravened the principles of open government; eroded the right to privacy; unjustly targeted immigrants, refugees and minorities for differential policing; and jeopardized the fair and equitable treatment of security detainees (see Chang, 2002; Doherty *et al.*, 2005; Wolfendale, 2007).

There has clearly been a series of step-changes in a range of contexts relating to the emergence of resilience policy. In particular the influence of security on debates around the mitigation of hazards, risks and threats has become more visible. In the United Kingdom (as can be seen in the following chapters) the discussion of response, proactive intervention, preparation and prevention came to the fore through the lens of security requirements. The emphasis was on the need to be prepared in the increasingly risky world of the unknown and versatile aggressor, but also build bridges and collaborative relationships, through this initial impetus of security towards other areas of IEM. One key difference between the American and UK model is that 'UK Resilience' is a wide net cast to encompass a range of civil, natural and anthropogenic risks, hazards and threats from the beginning (see Chapters 9 and 10), whereas in the United States widespread criticism was levied at the Office of Homeland Security for its focus on foreign threats at the risk of indigenous natural hazards (CHSGA, 2006; US House of Representatives, 2006). Another example of differential focus occurs in Australia where the focal point of security is on immigration, border control and foreign relations and is strongly contested (McDonald, 2005). As it appears that the international idiosyncrasies define the structure, means and method of policy directions, consistency is apparent less in the specific policy of the nation-state or government body than it is in the rhetoric underpinning emerging policies (Milliken, 1999).

In the United Kingdom (and elsewhere) new frameworks for understanding risks have now emerged, reinvigorating the aspects of defence and security as opposed to protection which had been underpinning the rhetoric of policy guidance. In other words, as Alexander (2002) notes, we have moved from civil defence to protection and back again. The emergency management process was subsequently broadened to focus upon the emergent threat and counter-terrorist challenges as well as the hazards posed by natural disasters, hence refining the traditional meaning of emergency planning. In late 2001, the regional and national review was thus now elevated to the international stage as counter-terrorist dimensions made reform of preparedness and response a key political priority and significantly sped up both the review process and increased the allocation of resources towards this endeavour.

Subsequent reform of the process of emergency planning in the United Kingdom has been widespread. What were now seen as 'outdated' emergency planning procedures largely based upon crisis management were replaced by new strategic vocabularies, drawing on globalized risk and uncertainty (Beck, 2002; Mythen and Walklate, 2006). New 'ways of working' with a particular vernacular emphasis upon preparedness, prevention and response to attack emphasized the need for 'anticipatory measures taken to increase response and recovery capabilities' (McEntire and Myers, 2004, p. 141). It was in this context that the elasticity of the term resilience came to the fore through the powerful meaning driven by new slogans such as 'the war on terror' the 'culture of fear', but also through emphasis on the potential for a positive return to a new normality, giving a highly emotive rhetoric on which to attach a host of wider issues.

In the United Kingdom the new governance and policy structure that has developed from this emergent conceptual metaphor of 'resilience' has sought to bring together 'the components of the disaster cycle – response, recovery, mitigation and preparedness' (O'Brien and Reid, 2005, p. 354) under the guise of new model of emergency planning, the aim of which is to become fit for purpose to deal with *all* emergencies: natural disasters, human-induced events and terrorist attack. However, this model of resilience appears to be largely driven by new security concerns proceeding September 11, drawing less on the environmental hazards and socially constructed disasters. Although, there is a wide range of events that can be constituted as a disaster in an uncertain world, policy continues to emphasize the urban terror attack as the driver behind a much larger and potentially more sinister redefinition of what constitutes threat in a resilient society.

Many commentators have expressed concern over the prioritization of terrorist-related threats. As O'Brien and Reid (2005, p. 359) note in relation to the United Kingdom: 'resilience in the face of international terrorism is an obvious current priority...but wider considerations should not be consumed by this current single course of threat'. Equally, as Alexander (2002, p. 211) highlights, terrorism has a significantly and wide-reaching influence on emergency planning practice:

> It is a curious paradox that terrorism now dominates world thinking despite the fact that natural and technological disasters of the more usual kind have not become less serious and remains vastly dominant in terms of size and frequency of their collective impact.

Furthermore, from an American perspective, Flynn (2007, p. xviii) argues that the overlooking of higher-probability and higher-consequence risk from natural disaster at the expense of terrorism has wide-ranging implications for society at large:

> ...there is something fundamentally wrong with expending virtually all of our intellectual energies, political capital and resources on combating terrorists when a daunting array of perils is more likely to injure or kill us... From a potential victim's standpoints it does not matter how your life is being threatened; what matters is that reasonable measures have been taken both to protect you from that threat and to assist you when you are in trouble. The folly of a myopic focus on terrorism became abundantly clear when Hurricane Katrina struck New Orleans.

We shall see in subsequent chapters, how, from a UK perspective, this discussion of what threats should be prioritized was played out in practice whilst local and regional governments sought to establish new ways of organizing and dealing with generic disaster preparedness and response.

Characterizing the emerging metaphor of resilience

'Preparedness', 'prevention' and 'response' are key characteristics of the emergent metaphor of resilience in the new security and contingency-driven meaning and model of UK emergency planning. The 'bounce-backability' (Coaffee, 2006) through the formalization of IEM improves, in theory at least, the resistance of the system to negative external perturbation. This occurs through improving the communication and co-ordination of multi-agency response, but also through improving public communication, technologies of response and the legislative power of the controlling Government institutions and public services tasked with minimizing disorder. The newly emergent metaphor of resilience thus moves beyond the negative connotations associated with emergency planning as civil defence – a metaphor that can be seen as highly reactive and tied to 'finger pointing' and the assignation of *de facto* blame or responsibility post-crisis. This sits in opposition to current understandings of resilience as preparing, preventing and thus protecting, through improved disaster mitigation processes emanating from the individual, businesses, the city and the nation.

This 'new' approach views emergency planning and disaster management as an integrative and holistic exercise which is seen as a collective responsibility. As Trim (2005) notes, 'new approaches and initiatives need to be discovered with respect to solving disasters (and preventing disasters), that revolve around co-operation of government officials, military and police force representatives, staff from non-governmental organizations and international companies, and various emergency operatives' (p. 244). It is this capacity which current UK resilience legislation and policy guidance is attempting to embed within policy communities at a variety of scales, by addressing concerns over the role of local government and partner agencies in civil protection (Coles, 1998). This is most notably driven through strategic guidance in the form of the Civil Contingencies Act of 2004, which received Royal assent in November 2005. The Act formalized new requirements as statutory obligations and emphasizes the pivotal role of local government in emergency planning, preparedness and response (Daws, 2005). The detail of this Act and the links to wider security policy will be addressed in the next chapter.

The final shift away from defence and protection, and towards a new rhetoric of resilience policy can be addressed through a number of 'threads' or dimensions around which the concept of resilience can be articulated, which differ from traditional notions of emergency planning and disaster recovery (Coaffee, 2006). These are introduced here and will be revisited in greater detail in Chapters 8–11.

First, there has been a move towards greater preparedness rather than reactive disaster management, stimulated by new security challenges and natural catastrophes. The recent criticism of the US federal Government in the aftermath of Hurricane Katrina for the lack of preparatory planning and disaster response, attests to the requirement of this move (see, for example, Gotham, 2007). Traditionally, most of the emergency planners' arsenal was linked to reacting to a disaster once it has happened and to developing appropriate plans to create 'a business as usual' situation as soon as possible. In contrast, more contemporary approaches view resilience as both reactive *and* proactive. Others support this idea in relation to the embedding of notions of a fluid form of resilience into the urban development process. As David Godschalk (2003) argued:

> Resilient cities are constructed to be strong and flexible rather than brittle and fragile...their lifeline systems of roads, utilities and other support facilities are designed to continue functioning in the face of rising water, high winds, shaking ground and terrorist attacks. (p. 137)

Second, there has been a broadening of the emergency planning agenda, to cover not just disaster recovery from natural and environmental hazards or accidents and war, but to focus specifically on new security challenges. Most countries have only recently begun to appreciate the global nature of the threats posed by both natural hazards and technological accidents, and importantly in the post-September 11 era, incidents of catastrophic terrorism which have worldwide impacts.

The contemporary terrorist threat has also fundamentally altered the established agendas of emergency planning. On one hand, a far greater variety of threats now present itself. Concerns about how terrorists might use deadly chemical and nuclear materials, biological agents or the internet in attack have promoted a review of 'are we prepared?' Similarly, the damage inflicted by September 11 has prompted questions about the adequacy of current contingency planning arrangements, insurance policies and business continuity cover.

Third, the key role of institutional resilience has been promoted in different tiers of government; this emphasizes holistic and multi-agency solutions to risk management to be undertaken by Governments, service sectors and other emergency managers to create strong and transparent institutional arrangements to protect complex infrastructural systems. This, however, is not just about co-ordinated thinking and multi-agency working *per se* but rather about such 'joined-up thinking' occurring at the appropriate spatial scale. Whereas traditionally, localities, more often than not, have been responsible for both pinpointing potential target risks and pulling together the appropriate response, new larger-scale risk events have necessitated a rethink about the appropriateness of this institutional infrastructure (Chapter 8).

Emergency or 'resilience' planning is now becoming a highly influential area of strategic policy in other areas of Government as the importance of developing robust processes and procedures for managing risk. In short, the intent is to embed resilience within the culture of Government to provide organizational and 'business' continuity and broader economic resilience (Chang *et al.*, 2002; Coaffee and Murakami Wood, 2006). Here economic resilience of this type relates specifically to the sustainability of key functions, the facilitation of existing process within an organization and the ability of an organization or system to perform despite potential negative external influences (Chen and Siems, 2004). In this sense, importance is increasingly placed upon risk assessment through 'horizon scanning' and the detection and response to emergent threats and disaster events, in a way that assures stakeholders or investors that all is 'under control' and that the company has the ability to 'bounce back' from such disruptions. For example, Sheffi (2005) in *The Resilient Enterprise*, explores how the response to disruptions that occur in private sector business functioning is focusing not only on security that might be deployed but on 'corporate resilience' and how it is possible that investments made to embed such resilience might in turn be beneficial in terms of 'competitive advantage'.

A key example of 'continuity' in this sense can be seen in the more recent preparation of institutions for human or avian influenza pandemics. Here there has been much emphasis on the cross-training of staff to ensure the availability of relevant expertise, and creating procedures for delivering services under stress of highly depleted workforces, in other words upon organizational resilience. This is seen as an urgent priority with experts agreeing that there is a high probability of a pandemic in the near future. The last major 'flu' pandemic to hit the United Kingdom in 1918 cost 228,000 lives in the United Kingdom and an estimated 20–40 million worldwide. Current Government estimate claims a pandemic could claim between 50,000 and 75,000 lives (Cabinet Office, 2008, pp. 13–14).

This pandemic threat, like the fear of terrorism, has led to a widening of the influence of resilience and the importance of this term as a means for securing wider change in the culture and processes of governance in the United Kingdom. In an international context, the role of disease is increasing in importance within the framework of emergency preparedness that is now emerging given the potential of an international viral pandemic to pose massively larger threats that global terrorism. A number of high-profile health threats in differing contexts have shown that the resilience and embedded systems for the interruption of pandemic 'chains of transmission' are now vital in a global context, and that 'inadequate surveillance and response capacity in a single country can endanger national populations and the public health security of the entire world' (Heyman and Rodier, 2004).[5]

Securing the rhetoric of resilience

In recent years, and within a multi-disciplinary field of enquiry, 'resilience' has come forth as a key 'buzzword' in policy and practice and has led to a range of primarily urban-oriented research assessing the response to terrorist risk in the city (Coaffee, 2003; 2004), the 'vulnerability' of cities to natural disasters (Pelling, 2003) and the 'recovery' of cities and states from emergencies and disaster events (Vale and Campanella, 2005). Such research has also been given further policy credence by the increase of dramatic government rhetoric, suggesting that 'the danger is disorder. And in today's world, it can now spread like contagion' (Blair, 2003).

A key point to make in understanding the broader implications of resilience as a generative metaphor is that the scope of influence of the concept now transcends emergency planning and civil contingencies. Whilst at once developing the systems and structures of national, regional and local governance around the themes of disaster/emergency response, recovery, mitigation and preparedness, the new resilient governance infrastructure can also be seen to extend through other related policy initiatives into a range of everyday spaces and experiences into a much wider array of policies (see Figure 7.2).

The perpetual sense of danger and uncertainty unpinning this rhetoric gives emotive validity to the assertion of state leaders that they are 'doing the right thing' for citizens and 'making them safer'. Despite which, the media rhetoric continues to espouse dangers and criticism of certain Government agendas, particularly recurring around themes of detention periods for suspected terrorists, immigration and migration, cultural conflict in local communities, and the means and method of communicating with the wider public about threats they face. Emerging research, highlighted and developed in proceeding chapters in this book, touches on these themes including; the national policy agenda of secure and resilient governance in the United Kingdom (Chapter 8); implications of this reformation for broader democratic governance at regional and local levels (Chapters 9 and 10); and the impacts of resilience policy on everyday urban practice and experience in a number of ways (Chapter 11). The aim of 'resilience' policy therefore appears to link the impetus of wider strategic guidance, policies and emerging governance structures, and locally driven initiatives, with the appearance and reality of shifting democratic structures directed towards ensuring that 'disorder' in all its forms has as little impact on the everyday experiences of citizens and the everyday functioning of the urban societies and economies (see Chapters 10 and 11).

The concept and rhetoric of resilience is a multi-dimensional and cross-disciplinary concern with broad applications extending vastly beyond a reworked framework of emergency planning within which it has been generated as an emergent metaphor. In the context of security and emergency planning the emergent metaphor of resilience that has emerged from prior ecological and psychological research encapsulates the ability to both bounce back – that is the elasticity of a system in the form of its positive 'adaptive capacity' (Carpenter *et al.*, 2001, pp. 766–7) – and resist change, retaining its standard functions of organization (Adger, 2000, p. 349). Where resilience significantly differs from previous ideas of civil protection and civil defence in the context of strategic policy is in the affirmation of a positive and proactive outcome – the return to a 'new normality' – subsequent to an event or perturbation, drawing from psychological and metaphorical applications and applying this rhetoric to 'more formal structures of governance and law' (ibid., p. 351).

A new policy context has emerged from this process of change in the strategic deployment of the rhetoric of resilience in policies affecting civil contingency, counter-terrorism and emergency planning, and requires a rethinking of the debates surrounding these discourses. This fluid policy context helps us in understanding the boundaries of resilient society both in the context of emergency planning for practitioners and in unpacking questions for the wider civil liberties of everyday citizens in the resilient nation-states, cities and resilient societies of the future. The next chapter develops this discussion in more depth, analysing the UK national policy context for civil contingencies and counter-terrorism focusing on the use of resilience as the dominant interpretation and conceptual metaphor for the management of threats of different types and forms.

8
The UK National Response

For many years commentators have discussed the costs and benefits of urban authorities adopting counter-terrorism measures in the face of real or perceived terrorist threats; and we have shown, historically, how principles of fortress architecture and defensible space were used by the security forces to territorially control designated areas at threat from terrorism.

Similar sentiments to this 'fortress urbanism' rhetoric have been commonplace after September 11 where the destructive damage caused and insurance losses accumulated were unprecedented for a terrorist attack. September 11 also brought to the fore wider concerns about different types of potentially 'catastrophic' terrorism (Carter *et al.*, 1998; Laqueur, 1996) where threat (not just from terrorism) can only be managed, not completely eradicated. This was the context in which new emergency planning regimes were developed (Chapter 7).

We do, however, need to be careful when ascribing the events of September 11 as the *start* of a new and dramatic militarized urban counter-terror response. Rather, like others we argued that the 'war on terrorism' has been used as a 'prism being used to conflate and further legitimize dynamics that *already* were militarizing urban space' (Warren, 2002, p. 614). Post September 11, new terrorist realities have led in some cases to new and dramatic urban counter-responses based on fortification as well as increasingly sophisticated military threat-response technology. For example, Graham (2002, p. 589) has highlighted how the events of September 11 have served to influence the technological and physical infrastructure of targeted cities where 'urban flows can be scrutinized through military perspectives so that the inevitable fragilities and vulnerabilities they produce can be significantly reduced'. He continued by arguing that 'military and geopolitical security now penetrate utterly into practices surrounding governance, design and planning of cities and region' (p. 589).

We should also be wary of reactionary comments made after September 11 which predicted the demise of the skyscraper (Kunstler and Salingaros, 2001), the changing functionality of urban centres, the 'shrinkage of urban space' as communities seek the sanctuary of purpose built enclosures (Savitch, 2008) and the potential for terrorism to lead to a new counter-urbanization trend amongst business and wealthier citizens in search of 'space and security' (Vidler, 2001).

Although a lot has been written about how the design of urban areas might offer solutions to reduce the threat from terrorism – either through enhanced fortifications or the adoption of ever-more sophisticated surveillance techniques – it is in the realms of forward-looking emergency planning that perhaps the greatest changes, and challenges, lie. In this sense, an emergency was defined by the UK Government as 'a situation or series of events that threatens or causes serious damage to human welfare, the environment or security' (UK Resilience Guidance, 2005, p. 1). Here three different levels of 'emergency' were identified which initiate a different strategic chain of command for dealing with events on the ground. These are detailed in Table 8.1.

Table 8.1   Levels of UK emergency

Level of emergency	Management implication
Catastrophic emergency (Level 3)	A high and potentially widespread impact and requires immediate central government *direction* and support such as a September 11 scale terrorist attack in the United Kingdom, or a Chernobyl scale industrial accident. The response would be led from COBR(A) and harnessing all possible resources. The Cabinet Office would chair preparatory meetings of officials although other departments might assume control addressing specific aspects of the response.
Serious emergency (Level 2)	Has, or threatens, a wide and prolonged impact requiring sustained central government *co-ordination* and support from many departments and agencies, including the regional tier in England and, where appropriate, the devolved administrations. Such challenges would include a major terrorist attack or serious outbreak of animal disease. In England and for reserved issues elsewhere in Great Britain, the central government response would be led from COBR under

	the direction of the Home Secretary or a nominated lead Minister. The Cabinet Office or the government department responsible for overall management of the Government response (the Lead Government Department or LGD) would normally chair meetings of officials.
Significant emergency (Level 1)	A narrower focus requiring central government *support* primarily from a lead government department or devolved administration in addition to the work of the emergency services, local authorities and other organizations as part of their normal day-to-day activities. An emergency of this scale in England or affecting reserved issues elsewhere in Great Britain would not normally involve the full activation of COBR(A). In England, the regional tier is likely to have some input, if only to report on the impact of the emergency across their area or to monitor the situation and provide an interface with the local Strategic Co-ordination Group. Examples of emergencies on this scale could include prison riots, severe weather, or a terrorist incident with limited consequences.

Source: Amended from UK Resilience Guidance (2005, p. 2).

This table highlights the different roles – directive, co-ordinative or supportive – that the national Government is expected to fulfill. Government engagement in response to emergencies is directly related to the potential geographical spread of an emergency. For example, localized incidents can be dealt with at local and regional levels. Regional emergency response can largely be facilitated by the regional tier acting as a conduit between central and local responders (Chapter 9). An emergency which is deemed significant but still only level 1 (such as widespread weather abnormalities) would be led by the national level but would not activate COBR(A) (Cabinet Office Briefing Room A in Downing Street which deals with the United Kingdom's emergency response in a national crisis). COBR(A) is only activated at levels 2 and 3 where coverage of the emergency is pan-regional or national. Finally, national response will be co-ordinated by the so-called Lead Government Department (LGD) model, where 'one department or devolved administration takes overall responsibility for co-ordinating, handling and presentation. Individual departments and devolved administration remain responsible for their policy areas' (ibid., p. 6). This LGD model, as Walker and Broderick (2006, p. 235) note, 'reflects a resilience strategy which is [aiming] to spread involvement and responsibility amongst potentially all departments, a strategy which was followed even during the total war of 1939–1945 (see Chapter 4; see also O'Brien, 1955).

To respond to a wide array of potential emergencies the United Kingdom has in recent years created a whole new governance architecture around resilience, with September 11 contributing greatly to the urgency of being prepared for emergencies; a lesson further emphasized by the difficulty of response to unexpected natural disasters from around the globe, such as *Hurricane Katrina* (2005) and the Indian Ocean Tsunami (2004).[1] In the United Kingdom, resilience planning has been developed through civil contingencies and counter-terrorism legislation and guidance, and a new set of powers, bodies and multi-agency connections has been created to manage these issues. It is in the connected realms of national civil contingency and counter-terror management that this chapter will focus.

As we argued in Chapter 7, from a UK perspective, the idea of creating resilience against terrorist attack and natural hazards has brought forth the recognition of the need to rethink the outdated emergency planning system and place increased emphasis upon holistic and multi-agency solutions to risk management. Such collaboration, it was argued, should to be undertaken by Government at all levels, service sectors and other emergency managers.

Importantly, we must remember the historical and political management context in which the proposed change was articulated: that of the UK state being seen historically as one of the most centralized in Europe (Goldsmith, 2002), where local governments in particular have been instruments for implementing the will of central Government. Although the incumbent Labour Governments have argued that local decision-making is more accountable to local people and less constrained by the state, there is still the distinct impression in many fields of policy that central control remains a strong centralist tendency (Wilson, 2003). In this situation national Government often appear to offer local government more autonomy and a genuine 'partnership' role but only in a highly conditioned way based on funding and the following of prescriptive national guidance.

Within the context of developing increased resilience in the United Kingdom, there are a number of 'guiding principles' of governance and partnership working that, UK Resilience Guidance (2005, p. 4) noted, were required so that 'emergencies can 'be managed flexibly to reflect circumstances at the time' (see Box 8.1).

Box 8.1   The guiding governance principles of UK Resilience

Preparedness – All those individuals and organizations that might have to respond to emergencies should be properly prepared, including having clarity of roles and responsibilities.

Continuity – Response to emergencies should be grounded in the existing functions of organizations and familiar ways of working, albeit delivered at a greater tempo, on a larger scale and in more testing circumstances.

Subsidiarity – Decisions should be taken at the lowest appropriate level, with co-ordination at the highest necessary level. Local responders should be the building block of response on any scale.

Direction – Clarity of purpose should be delivered through a strategic aim and supporting objectives that are agreed and understood by all involved to prioritize and focus the response.

Integration – Effective co-ordination should be exercised between and within organizations and tiers of response as well as timely access to appropriate guidance and appropriate support for the local or regional level.

Communication – Good two-way communication is critical to an effective response. Reliable information must be passed correctly and without delay between those who need to know, including the public.

Co-operation – Positive engagement based on mutual trust and understanding will facilitate information sharing and deliver effective solutions to issues arising.

Anticipation – Risk identification and analysis is needed of potential direct and indirect developments to anticipate and thus manage the consequences.

Developing a multi-scalar resilience is not just about co-ordinated thinking and multi-agency working *per se* but rather about such 'joined-up thinking' occurring at the appropriate scale. In the United Kingdom this was an exercise led from the centre of Government with a focus upon achieving a consistent level of 'resilience' across the United Kingdom, particularly from terrorist attack, but also a system that was able to respond effectively to other forms of emergency or threat. There was thus a renewed focus upon Integrated Emergency Management (IEM) whereby the arrangements for all emergency management are assimilated to ensure that the organizations and agencies responding to a disaster can do so in a co-ordinated way both internally – in terms of intra-organizational co-operation – as well as with co-responding organizations. IEM had been a broad approach, 'an aid-memoire more than a blueprint' (Walker and Broderick, 2006, p. 252) since 1992 when the Government first published a detailed booklet called *Dealing with Disasters*. This was revised, updated and republished in 2003 by the Cabinet Office (ibid.).

To develop a consistent degree of resilience throughout the United Kingdom, national resilience management has evolved largely as a strategic rather than directive tier, in a Foucauldian sense 'of governing at a distance', with a requirement to co-ordinate central government action at different tiers in emergency response. However, such an appearance of decentralized control is balanced so that executive authority can be manifest during the national or larger scale crisis.

Whereas in some countries (most notably the United States with the establishment of the Department of Homeland Security) a 'single response framework' has been developed to deal with the ongoing threat from terrorism (Gregory, 2007, p. 333), in the United Kingdom the strategic foci at the national level since 2001 has been twofold. First, there has been a focus upon updating and reforming the system and structure of emergency planning legalization that was largely a remnant from the Cold War (Chapters 4 and 7); and second, the development of a national counter-terrorism strategy (and associated legalization). These two major streams of work have produced key pieces of national policy: the Civil Contingencies Act (2004) and the Countering International Terrorism Strategy (2006). These are conceptualized in Figure 8.1. This diagram highlights the two main strands involved in developing 'UK resilience', which will be unpacked in the following discussion. The key point to note here is that although there appears to be similarities between the two streams (particularly in relation to a focus on preparedness), in reality, as they have developed they have often worked in isolated silos, and been led by different branches of National Government. That said, common to both has been the need to embed resilience to threats and hazards into the culture of governance, as the driving force behind reform.

Within the context described above the remainder of this chapter is divided into three key parts. First we will highlight the impact of

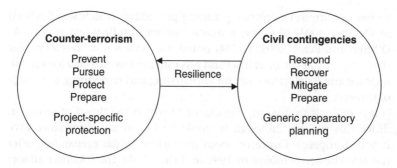

Figure 8.1 The UK national resilience policy context

the development, and introduction, of the Civil Contingencies Secretariat (CCS) and the 2004 Civil Contingencies Act (CCA) which began to popularize the resilience terminology and use it regularly in relation to the ability to 'bounce back' from disruptive challenges. The second part of the chapter will focus primarily on the 'security' aspect of resilience, namely the development of a national counter-terrorism strategy (known in government circles as CONTEST) which developed from 2003, and was published finally in July 2006. The third part of the chapter draws together the practical implications of the rolling-out of the CCA and CONTEST and highlights the challenges that faced UK Resilience as this evolved.

Developing resilience to emergencies

As we saw in Chapters 4 and 5, the system of emergency management had remained relatively unchanged for a nearly half a decade with recent incidents of serious flooding incidents, the occurrence and spread of foot and mouth disease and fuel protests on the UK motorway network (the '3 Fs') exposing this system as outdated and in need of serious overhaul. It was in early 2001, importantly before the terrorist attacks in New York and Washington, that national Government initiated a review of the emergency planning process, led in the first instance by the Home Office and then transferred to a newly formed specialist branch of Government which was located in the Cabinet Office, and which was responsible for co-ordinating policy and strategy across Government departments. This new unit, the Civil Contingencies Secretariat (CSS), was initially tasked with a consultation exercise focusing on the review of current emergency planning procedures which was finalized in October 2001. This was a multi-scale and multi-threat review. As O'Brien and Read (2005, p. 354) noted, the review was 'much broader than response at the local level and was intended to establish a national, regional and local framework for anticipating and responding to a range of threats'.

It is difficult to quantify the extent to which the threat of terrorism drove this process, although it would be fair to say it certainly gave it added impetus. Concerns about the lack of initial preparation after the Manchester bombing in 1996 and the World Trade Center attacks in 2001 clearly focused the Government's mind on developing an IEM system that could cope with significant terror attacks. As the Home Secretary declared in November 2001, in the light of September 11, our 'objective is to do everything that can be done to enhance our resilience' (cited in Walker and Broderick, 2006, p. 46).

In leading the reform of emergency planning, the CSS adopted the vocabulary of resilience to describe this new and evolving process as it purveyed a holistic, positive and proactive approach. Resilience according to the Cabinet Office (2003) was defined as:

The ability to handle disruptive challenges that can lead to or result in crisis...Resilience is built around several key activities. Firstly, risks of disruptive challenge must where possible be identified, either by considering internal weakness or scanning the horizon for external threats. Anticipation allows choices to be made. In some circumstances, it is possible to prevent disruptive challenges occulting by taking action at an early stage. In other cases, planning has to take place to prepare to deal with a disruptive challenge. If the disruption does occur it becomes necessary to respond, and once the situation is brought under control the focus becomes recovery. This cycle – anticipation, prevention, preparation, response and recovery – is at the heart of resilience. (Paragraph 1.1)[2]

As a cross-cutting arm of Government, the CCS has a number of functions and performs a variety of roles (see Box 8.2). Overall though, the primary focus is upon a variety of potentially disruptive challenges 'which could include the impacts of natural hazards such as flooding and foot and mouth disease, major accidents as well as the consequences of terrorist activity' (Cabinet Office, 2007).

Box 8.2 The CCS main areas of activity (Cabinet Office 2007)

- Co-ordinating assessment of risks which could pose a disruptive challenge to the United Kingdom through Horizon Scanning and a periodic UK Risk Assessment;

- Co-ordinating development of generic capabilities to deal with the consequences of disruptive challenges through a cross-Government Capabilities Programme;

- Implementing legislation to support civil resilience in the United Kingdom;

- Providing a centre of excellence for training on Emergency Planning at our Emergency Planning College;

- During a crisis, co-ordinating consequence management to support the Government's response.

These multiple roles cover a wide range of commitments and have been divided into streams and embedded into the Capabilities Programme: an ongoing cross-governmental initiative that is a central part of building resilience across all parts of the United Kingdom. The programme consists of 18 'workstreams' (each led by a Government Department), divided into three thematic groups. First, there are three structural workstreams focusing on national, regional and local capabilities. Second, five which deal with the maintenance of essential services such as food and water, health, utilities, transport and financial services. Finally there are ten 'functional' workstreams, 'dealing respectively with the assessment of risks and consequences; chemical, biological, radiological and nuclear (CBRN) resilience; site clearance; infectious diseases (human); infectious diseases (animal and plant); mass casualties; evacuation and shelter; warning and informing the public; mass fatalities; humanitarian assistance and flooding' (UK Resilience, 2007).

UK Resilience (2007) also make a disclosure about terminology, that 'Capability' is a military term which includes personnel, equipment and training and such matters as plans, doctrine and the concept of operations' (ibid.). This is an illuminating point and reinforces and argument made in previous chapters that increasingly there has been a conflation of civil and military protection, and in particular, that military techniques are being used to scan the 'homeland' for potential threats, vulnerabilities and disruptive challenges. Walker and Broderick (2006, pp. 25–6) make a similar point in that 'the diffuse and complex array of challenges which are shaping the 'resilience' agenda' also tend to blur the traditional boundaries between 'war' and 'peacetime' in policy terms'.

In the light of September 11, the Capabilities Programme, which was initially scoped out in 2002, appeared to be focused upon concerns that the United Kingdom was not ready for a major terrorist attack on the scale of the World Trade Center event. The CCS was, however, very careful to note that their remit was broader than simply counter-terrorist responses and that 'the scope of the programme accordingly extends to the full range of responses to the full range of contingencies likely to face the United Kingdom in the first part of the 21st century' (Cabinet Office, 2007).

An ongoing assessment of the CCS's 18 workstreams has allowed national Government to allocate and reallocate resources for resiliency activities dependent on risk assessment and achieved levels of competence across various branches, and tiers, of Government. Such competence is also tested through a series of live and table-top 'exercises' which are structured around the ongoing review of capabilities.

At the time of writing there have been two Capabilities surveys conducted nationwide to assess resilience capacity at all tiers, and to allow prioritization of workstream funding allocation. The first was a limited regional mapping exercise in 2003/2004 prior to the Civil Contingencies Act, 2004. The second involved a survey of a host of resilience planning stakeholders and was published in the summer of 2006. This survey has highlighted significant improvement across the country, in terms of resiliency. In particular, it has highlighted a number of key issues focused around increased levels of preparedness for terrorism and other threats, and improved multi-agency working (see Box 8.3).

Box 8.3   Overall UK assessment of preparedness (from UK Resilience, 2006b)

- The United Kingdom has a good level of preparedness overall. Where comparisons can be made with the more limited 2003 mapping exercise the local response results demonstrate clear signs of improvement in specific areas, such as in planning to respond to a human influenza pandemic.

- Preparedness for less clear-cut eventualities is well developed: 'generic' capabilities (for example, against the event of a chemical, biological or radiological incident) have benefited from investment and heightened interest.

- Multi-agency co-operation seems to have benefited from emphasis on partnership in the Civil Contingencies Act.

- Although planning for emergencies at the local level is well established and has improved significantly, there is scope for making the review and exercise of plans more systematic.

- Within the essential service workstreams there is a good level of business continuity and crisis management. Planning for specific scenarios is also good but less developed than generic planning.

- There is little regional variation in preparedness; however, there are differences at the local level within regions. This suggests that there are more significant differences in the challenges faced at a local level within any given region, than between regions.

- Central government's core response capabilities are well-developed. Departmental business continuity plans are in place and are being exercised.

The Civil Contingencies Act (CCA) of 2004

The Civil Contingencies Act (Contingency Planning) Regulations were adopted in 2005 by Parliament after going through a number of iterations. The final version, complete with statutory guidance, was released as a document called *Emergency Preparedness* by the Cabinet Office in 2005, which was an enlarged version of the earlier *Dealing with Disaster* guide, but still very much structured around ideas of IEM.[3] The CCA came into force in November 2005.

The CAA for the first time aimed to establish a consistent level of civil protection (resilience) across the United Kingdom. The Act was largely structural in orientation and set out a simple framework which highlighted what resiliency tasks should be performed and by whom, and how co-operation towards this goal should be achieved. This Act was, however, primarily focused on insuring conformance at the local level (sub-regional scale).

The CCA as it has been rolled out aimed to established 'a modern framework for civil protection capable of meeting the challenges of the 21st century' (Security Service, 2006). The Act and its supporting regulations and guidance have, according to Government:

- created a common framework of duties for all organizations that are at the core of emergency planning and response work;
- given local responders a clear set of roles, responsibilities and standards to guide their work;
- mandated structures and processes for partnership working at the local and regional level, and advocated much greater multi-agency integration and collaboration;
- required emergency planning arrangements to be underpinned by systematic assessments of risk and exercised regularly;
- mandated business continuity planning to ensure that local responders can sustain the effectiveness of their functions even in the face of an emergency, and continue to deliver core functions with a minimum of disruption; and
- conferred a duty to raise awareness of emergency management issues in the communities they serve (ibid.).

The Act itself has two main parts. Part 1 focuses upon the development and reinforcement of 'local' arrangements for civil protection, and the establishment of a roles and responsibilities framework for local responders. Part 2, by contrast, is focused far more upon how the state develops a modern framework, including special legislative powers, to react to 'serious emergencies' (Cabinet Office, 2006). We are mainly concerned here with a discussion of Part 1.

In establishing a new statutory framework for civil protection, local responders are seen as the key resilience 'building block'. These are either seen as Category 1 or Category 2 responders. Category 1 responders 'are at the core of emergency response' and 'are subject to a full set of civil protection duties' (ibid.), and include emergency 'blue light' services (Police, Ambulance and Fire) and local authorities. By contrast, Category 2 responders are seen as 'co-operating bodies' who are more likely to be involved in the incident response than central to the preparatory resilience planning work. Examples of Category 2 responders include transport and utility companies and Strategic Health Authorities, although this list has been extended to incorporate some of the broader affected actors (in the infrastructural impact of disaster) who can then be called on if required, for example utilities companies (power, water supply) and increasingly in the private sector (with the focus on business continuity and supply chain management).

Through the CCA, the UK Government has attempted to provide a central strategic direction to developing resilience. In practice though, power was initially delegated, in a co-ordinated way, overseen by the Regional Coordination Unit, to the regional level which is seen as a communication conduit to the local level. In next chapter we will also detail the establishment and impact of 'new' regional tier of resilience governance and focus on how they act as a channel between centre and locality and can influence the evolution of local resilience strategies developed according to CCA guidance.[4]

In the discussion of the multiple tiers of resilience governance to come we focus upon the English experience. It is, however, also important to note that the CCA has also made provision for new emergency planning and civil protection frameworks to be established in the devolved administrations of Scotland, Wales and Northern Ireland, as part of a broader approach to UK resilience.[5] Here in many ways the developed administrations were expected 'to mirror many tasks of the UK-level crisis-mechanisms, as well as fulfilling the same tasks as the English Regional structures' (UK Resilience Guidance, 2005, p. 1).

Although the CCA is largely a structuring device for other Government tiers, it has had influence in certain areas of practice. In particular, it is at the national level that initial 'warning and informing' the public workstreams were operationalized (UK Resilience, 2006a). It is here that the emerging resilience agenda began to receive public acknowledgment, as well as some criticism. The national Government's commitment to educating the public about the 'new' threats faced by international terrorism, and other risks, was highlighted in 2004 a booklet *Preparing for Emergencies: What You Need to Know*. This booklet was delivered to every household in the country to inform the public about the 'self-protection' measures they might take in the event of a chemical, biological, radiological or nuclear (CBRN) attack (Home Office, 2004). Some have, however, argued that such a booklet, despite its focus on the individual and community response, deflected attention away from the contentious issue of the ongoing programme of state reform and regulation of emergency planning and counter-terrorism (Mythen and Walklae, 2006; see also Coaffee and Rogers, 2008). Others have also questioned whether 'the Government [was] more concerned with being seen to be doing the right thing [rather than] genuinely trying to engage the public in this crucial area' (Richards, 2007, p. 289).[6]

The national counter-terrorism strategy

The CCA 2004 was a comprehensive set of guidance that was focused upon enhancing civil protection, predominantly at the local level, based on the development of a set of integrated and relatively generic emergency management procedures. In this Act, the need for enhanced civil protection, although influenced by 'new' threats from terrorism, was broader, seeing the preparation and response to disruptive challenges in more holistic terms. By contrast, the other main strand of developing UK resilience was highly focused upon new forms terrorist threats linked to mass causality no-notice attacks potentially using CBRN materials.

This is not to say that 'traditional' attacks using, for example, vehicle-borne devices were no longer deemed a significant threat, rather, that the nature and scope of the 'attack trajectory' had changed. Likewise, we should not infer that the United Kingdom has never had concerns about mass casualty strikes and attacks by 'violent extremists'. Attacks against the World Trade Center in New York in 1993 and the against the Paris and Tokyo metro systems in 1995 (Chapter 6) precipitated concerns that such techniques might be exported to the United Kingdom, and particularly to London (Coaffee, 2003). More recent attacks around the world, for example in Bali in 2002 and Madrid in 2004, combined with the attacks on the London underground over the summer of 2005, have meant that emergency services and emergency planners (and other stakeholders) have now been tasked with preparing for, coping with and re-bounding from both conventional and unconventional types of terror threat.

Since early 2003, the United Kingdom has had a long-term strategy for developing resilience for counter-terrorism (CONTEST). Its aim is to reduce the risk of terrorism, 'so that people can go about their daily lives freely and with confidence' (HM Government, 2006a, p. 9). This strategy was formalized and laid out in the *Countering International Terrorism: The United Kingdom's Strategy*, published in July 2006 the aim of which was to 'develop and implement plans and programmes to strengthen counter-terrorism capabilities at all levels of Government, the emergency services, businesses and the wider community' (p. 3).

Towards this resiliency objective, as with emergency planning reform, significant extra resources have been utilized; approximately double the pre-September 11 level (ibid.). Equally the partnership rhetoric in counter-terrorism has been strengthened with envisaged co-operation between all Government Departments, links across all governance tiers, and with the emergency services. As with the dissemination of civil contingency legislation, the need to generate public awareness of both the threat and counter-response is of high political priority.

The CONTEST counter-terrorism resilience strategy is divided into four distinct strands: PREVENT, PURSUE, PROTECT and PREPARE, each led by a branch of Government and which are collectively concerned with reducing the threat and vulnerability – and hence risk – from international terrorism (see Figure 8.2). As it proceeds, the following discussion will also highlight the vast number of different dimension involved in the current 'war on terror', and how counter-terrorism policy cuts across, and becomes embedded within, a variety of other public polices.

The Prevent strand

The Prevent strand of CONTEST is concerned with tackling what the Government refers to as 'the radicalization of individuals'. The focus here is both within the United Kingdom and overseas, with the objective of breaking the chain, or 'the conveyor belt', of radicalization, which sustains the international terrorist threat. This has become a controversial area of policy, especially with the emotive language often used to describe it (such as radicals, extremists), and accusations of discrimination against particular racial or ethnic groups (Kaplan, 2006; Poynting and Mason, 2007).

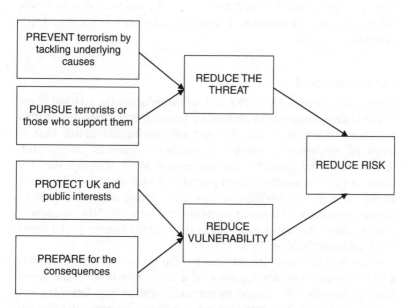

Figure 8.2 The national counter-terrorism strategy (CONTEST)

There are three key aspects to the Prevent strand of CONTEST. First, the need to 'tackle disadvantage' and support community cohesion in particular communities, where breading grounds for radicalization might occur based on structural inequalities and discrimination. This is in many ways a broader policy objective than just counter-terrorism, particularly focused around urban regeneration and the building of cohesive and sustainable communities (Home Office, 2001; ODPM, 2003).[7]

The second aspect of the Prevent strand concerns legislation and pronouncements on 'unacceptable behaviours' which might lead to deportation from the United Kingdom. This aspect of 'Prevent' aims to 'deter those who facilitate terrorism and those who encourage others to become terrorists by changing the environment in which the extremists and those radicalizing others can operate' (Home Office, 2007a).

The third part of the Prevent strand is a longer-term strategy to 'engage in the battle of ideas by challenging the ideologies that extremists believe can justify the use of violence, primarily by helping Muslims who wish to dispute these ideas to do so' (ibid.).[8] Overall, the Prevent strand is very much seen as a enduring strategy, and one which has received added emphasis after the events in London in July 2005 where 'home-grown' suicide bombers set off a series of explosive devices on the London transport network. This long-term strategic goal was given further weight when in early 2008, as part of a national security review, the *Prevent Violent Extremism: A Strategy for Delivery* was published (HM Government, 2008).

The Pursue strand

The Pursue strand of CONTEST focuses on reducing the terrorist threat to the United Kingdom by disrupting terrorist operations. It has three key elements which are largely legal and intelligence based. First, in terms of intelligence gathering, a number of agencies: the Security Service (MI5), the Secret Intelligence Service (SIS or MI6) and the Government Communications Headquarters (GCHQ) – collectively known as the security and intelligence agencies – combine to offer as full a picture as possible of terrorist activities and networks.[9] These agencies work together through a Joint Terrorism Analysis Centre (JTAC) which was established in June 2003.

Secondly, the Pursue strand aims to 'disrupt' and 'frustrate' terrorist attacks through the development of a more robust legal and quasi-legal framework. This strand in particular utilizes the Terrorism Acts of 2000 and 2006. The 2000 Act made it illegal for particular 'known' terrorist groups to operate in the United Kingdom and makes it a criminal offence to incite terrorism or provide training for terrorist purposes. More recent legislation – the 2006 Terrorism Act – enhanced the powers of the 2000 Act and also made it a criminal offence to distribute material that 'glorifies' terrorism. Controversially, the 2006 Act also extended the maximum period a suspected terrorist may be detailed without charge from 14 to 28 days and there have been a host of more recent attempts made by the UK Government to extend this to up to 90 days. The 2006 Act has been condemned by human rights and civil liberty groups as creating 'unacceptably broad speech offences', and representing 'a serious incursion on free speech rights, criminalizing careless talk and banning non-violent political organizations' (Liberty, 2006).

This 'disrupt and frustrate' aspect of the Pursue strand also makes use of the Anti-Terrorism, Crime and Security Act, 2001 by which the assets of suspected terrorists can be frozen. Further, utilizing the recently enacted legislation to allow the deportation of foreign nationals, the Immigration, Asylum and Nationality Act, 2006 introduced a number of counter-terrorism-related measures including 'a good character test' to help predominantly with border security. Finally, the Prevention of Terrorism Act, 2005 allows for the issuing of a 'non-derogating' control order against individuals which might involve restrictions on travel, their use and access to communications equipment, the imposition of curfews, 'house arrest', or in the case of a foreign national, possible deportation.[10] Despite the plethora of counter-terrorism laws produced since the events of September 11, their remains tremendous ambiguity regarding their power and effectiveness (Walker, 2006) and a great deal of concern over implications for civil liberties (Haubrich, 2006).

The final part of the Pursue strand concerns international co-operation. Here the UK Government provides training (from the Ministry of Defense) and funding to other Governments in order to help them build up their own capacity to deal with the ongoing terrorist threat in their own territory. By working with partners and allies overseas it is argued that the United Kingdom can strengthen its intelligence effort and achieve disruption of terrorism outside the United Kingdom.[11]

The Protect strand

The Protect Strand of CONTEST has perhaps been the most high profile and visible stream of the national counter-terrorist response, and concerns reducing the vulnerability of the United Kingdom to terror attack through the increased securitization of UK borders, critical national infrastructure and public 'crowded' places.

Strengthening border security has been a key concern after September 11. A cross-government Department Border Management Programme (BMP) was established by the Government in March 2004 to ensure closer and more effective joint working to strengthen border security and improve 'identity management' whilst minimizing the impact on legitimate 'traffic'. This has involved the adoption of advanced biometric technologies (finger-prints and iris scans) primarily in passports, and fixed radiation detection equipment for screening for the trafficking of illicit radiological materials. Moreover, an e-border programme was launched in 2004 that uses 'systems and technology to ensure that we know much sooner who is entering and leaving' (HM Government, 2006a, p. 23).[12]

The civil liberties and privacy issues related to e-borders have, however, been hotly debated. For example, Privacy International (2005) argued that this 'radical re-organization of border and travel surveillance policy' is highly problematic:

> The new programme will involve the collection of biometrics on visitors to the UK, the generation of vast information stores on all Britons and visitors... This programme does not merely apply to combating terrorism however; it is for use for general policing matters.

The second key aspect of the Protect strand is the defence of key critical national infrastructure, primarily through the dissemination of security advice (to help reduce vulnerability), but also programmes of research and development into effective protective security measures. This aspect of 'Protect' is led by the Centre for the Protection of National Infrastructure (CPNI).[13] Critical national infrastructure (CNI) protection involves a number of separate but interlinked priorities. First, it involves protecting key CNI by working with the private sector, particularly those involved in the provision of utilities – energy and water – and key services such as transport and finance. This has involved the adoption, by the private sector, of new technologies of surveillance. For example, on parts the London Underground in 2004, in response to the Madrid train bombings, high-tech 'smart' CCTV surveillance software (Intelligent Pedestrian Surveillance system, IPS) was rolled out that would, it is claimed, automatically alert operators to suspicious behaviour, unattended packages and potential suicide bombing attempts on the Tube system. The system automatically tracks and integrates 3D images with CCTV video, maps and other real-time information. The implementation of this system followed extensive trials, which initially had little to do with terrorism and predated 2001. The original intention was to develop a crowd flow monitoring system that morphed into something more as its potential to spot those waiting on station platforms to commit suicide was realized (Graham and Wood, 2003). As noted at the time in *New Scientist:*

> It could be the dawn of a new era in surveillance. For the first time, smart software will help CCTV operators spot any abnormal behaviour. The software, which analyses CCTV footage, could help spot suicide attempts, overcrowding, suspect packages and trespassers. The hope is that by automating the prediction or detection of such events security staff... can reach the scene in time to prevent a potential tragedy.
>
> (Hogan, 2003)

Privacy groups have again expressed concerns about this development and about the increasing coverage of monitoring technology such as CCTV, linked to the war on terrorism (Ball and Webster, 2003; Clarke, 2004).

Likewise, more advanced fortification techniques and materials have been advanced by structural engineers to protect key 'at risk' sites. This draws not only on current research and development, but also the experience of other countries developing terror-resistant materials and building structures in the wake of attack (see Chapter 6). In the United Kingdom this includes not only the utility sector, but also iconic sites such as the Houses of Parliament which have put in place a raft of reinforced steel barriers – a ring of steel (see Plate 8.1) – and high-risk sites, such as the United States Embassy in central London where protective bollards have been installed that can withstand the force of a seven-tonne truck travelling at 50 miles per hour. These advanced protective measures have recently replaced the crude placement of concrete 'jersey barriers' – or 'rings of concrete' – put in place in the immediate aftermath of September 11 (Coaffee, 2004).

The advancement of science and technology in the fight against terrorism has also led to the publication of a connected Government strategy intended for use by Government, business, academics as well as 'end users', such as the emergency services: *The United Kingdom Security and Counter-Terrorism Science and Innovation Strategy*, in 2007 (HM Government 2007b). This strategy highlights the volume, as well as multi-disciplinary nature of counter-terrorist research and development in the United Kingdom at the current time. The parts of Government feeding into this strategy are shown in Table 8.2 which highlights the

Plate 8.1 Reinforced steel barriers surround the Houses of Parliament in the Central London 'Government Security Zone'

Table 8.2 Government groups that fed into the 2007 Counter-Terrorism Science and Innovation Strategy

Government department/group	Role/representation
Security Service, Secret Intelligence Service and the Centre for the Protection of National Infrastructure	Responsible for protecting the United Kingdom against threats to national security
Police	Represents police counter-terrorism science and innovation interests through The Association of Chief Police Officers (ACPO)
Office of Science and Innovation	Represents the Government's Chief Scientific Advisor who is responsible for ensuring that Government policy is underpinned by the best possible science and scientific advice
Ministry of Defence	Provides assistance to civil powers in particular on Chemical, Biological, Radiological and Nuclear (CBRN) material and explosives
Joint Terrorism Analysis Centre	National centre for analysis of terrorist threats

Home Office	Leads on overall security and counter-terrorism strategy and co-ordinates delivery of security and counter-terrorism science and innovation
HM Treasury	Ensures counter-terrorism funding is spent effectively and efficiently
Health and Safety Executive	Responsible for the safety of nuclear licensed sites and security issues, and advises on risks from CBR material
Foreign and Commonwealth Office	Supports development of international counter-terrorism science and innovation co-operation
Department for Transport	Ensures transport security
Department of Health	Prepares for dealing with health effects
Department for Environment, Food and Rural Affairs and the Food Standards Agency	Counters threats to environment, agriculture and food
Department for Communities and Local Government	Develops approaches to prevention of terrorism and strengthens the resilience of the regional tier and of the Fire and Rescue service responses to terrorist incidents
Cabinet Office	Supports the Prime Minister on counter-terrorism-related matters

Source: Adapted from HM Government 2007b, p. 3.

numerous Government interests which fed into the Research, Analysis and Development Working Group which devised the strategy.

This strategy addresses, for example, how technologies are being developed and deployed to aid the pursuit and disruption of terrorist organizations; for behavioural profiling; for the protection of key sites; and to aid response and recovery from terrorist attack. The 2007 strategy is also central to identifying current and future (horizon scanning) research priorities, linked to the civil contingencies work on 'Capabilities' (and associated risk profiling at regional and local levels).

We have already noted the civil liberties implications of the growing use of such technologies in everyday urban settings and crowded places which have been the subject of considerable debate. At the same time, the efficacy of technology-focused counter-terrorism policy responses has been called into question and there are warnings about the danger of seeing science and technology as a panacea to more deep-seated social and cultural challenges (Durodie, 2006).

The final element of the Protect strand refers to advice and assistance. Here the Security Services in particular have been disseminating a host

Table 8.3   Top ten security guidelines for business

1. *Carry out a risk assessment* to decide on the threats you might be facing and their likelihood. Identify your vulnerabilities
2. If acquiring or extending premises, *consider security* at the planning stage. It will be cheaper and more effective than adding measures later
3. *Make security awareness part of your organisation's culture* and ensure security is represented at a senior level
4. *Ensure good basic housekeeping* throughout your premises. Keep public areas tidy and well-lit, remove unnecessary furniture and keep garden areas clear
5. *Keep access points to a minimum* and issue staff and visitors with passes. Where possible, do not allow unauthorised vehicles close to your building
6. *Install appropriate physical measures* such as locks, alarms, CCTV surveillance and lighting
7. *Examine your mail-handling procedures,* consider establishing a mailroom away from your main premises
8. When recruiting staff or hiring contractors, *check identities and follow up references*
9. Consider how best to protect your information and *take proper IT security precautions*. Examine your methods for disposing of confidential waste
10. *Plan and test your business continuity plans*, ensuring that you can continue to function without access to your main premises and IT systems.

Source: Adapted from the Security Services, 2006.

of booklets, most notably *Protecting Against Terrorism* (Security Services, 2006) which included a top ten list of tips for business (Table 8.3).

In terms of directive advice, there has also been a rolling-out to all Policing areas of special branch police with an expertise in protective security, so-called Counter-Terrorist Security Advisors (CTSA's) who are trained and tasked by the National Counter Terrorism Security Office (NaCTSO), a specialist police organization co-located with the Security Service in the CPNI. The primary role of CTSA's is to provide counter-terrorism security advice to businesses in relation to both conventional and non-conventional terrorist techniques in order to reduce vulnerability to terrorist threats.

The Prepare strand

The fourth and final strand of the CONTEST strategy is Prepare, perhaps the strand most closely connected with the previous discussions on civil contingences reform. Simply put, the Prepare strand is about 'ensuring that the UK is as ready as it can be for the consequences of a terrorist attack' (HM Government, 2006a, p. 25). This strand is assuming the *inevitability* of an attack and, as such, adopts the rhetoric of resilience:

Achieving this involves developing the *resilience* of the UK to with-stand such attacks. This means improving the ability of the UK to respond effectively to the direct harm caused by a terrorist attack, and in particular to those individuals affected by it; to recover quickly those essential services which are disrupted by an attack; and to absorb and minimize wider indirect disruption.... (ibid., emphasis added)

The Prepare strand also places great focus upon multi-agency, multi-tier and multi-stakeholder working:

A very large number of stakeholders deliver *resilience*, across the public, private and voluntary sectors. It is important that all organizations pull in the same direction if contingency planning is not to be disjointed and inefficient, and if the response to an emergency is to be as effective as possible. The provision of leadership and direction to the *resilience community*, and processes which join-up work at the *local, regional and national levels* of government, and between the public, private and voluntary sectors, is thus of fundamental importance to the Prepare strand. (ibid., emphasis added)

In this sense, the objectives of this strand: to identify risks from terrorism, assess the impact of potential risks; build the capacity and capabilities to respond; and evaluate and test response through simulation, are cross-cutting with the work of the Civil Contingencies Secretariat and embedded within the Civil Contingencies Act, 2004. As such, this strand of CONTEST also points towards IEM and the production of generic plans that might be rolled out to deal with all disaster and emergencies:

Given the vast range of potential terrorist attack scenarios, with a wide range of potential consequences, it is neither practicable nor prudent to plan for every scenario. Instead, planning seeks to build generic capabilities and plans, able to be drawn on flexibly in the response to a wide range of terrorist (and other) events. (ibid.)

At a national level there is also a cross-governmental central crisis management response scenario, linked to an ongoing, publically available terror threat assessment for the United Kingdom. In terms of crisis management a meeting of the Civil Contingencies Committee (CCC) is called – also known as Cabinet Office Briefing Room A, or

COBR(A), after the room where it originally met – and deals with the United Kingdom's emergency response in a national crisis (levels 2/3). COBR(A) does not just convene for terrorism issues (for example, following the September 11 attacks in the United States, the July 7 attack on London and the failed bomb plots on 21 July 2005). It has also met to co-ordinate the response to the fuel protests in 2000, and more recently to discuss the avian flu threat in Scotland (April, 2006).[14]

When COBR(A) meets its first role is to consider whether to invoke the powers contained in part two of the Civil Contingencies Act, which allows considerable powers to be transferred to the executive in times of a serious emergency. This is, however, only likely in the event of a major CBRN incident.[15]

From August 2006 the UK Government has also made public their threat assessment of the risk posed by international terrorism (Intelligence Service, 2006).[16] Their threat levels aim to give a broad indication of the likelihood of a terror attack, based on current intelligence and recent events. The scale used is shown below in Figure 8.3; the current level of which is displayed on the Home Office or MI5 websites. The argument here for public display is broadly in line with the 'warning and informing' stream of civil contingencies work in that 'sharing national threat levels with the general public keeps everyone informed and explains the context for the various security measures we may encounter as we go about our daily lives' (ibid., p. 2). The UK threat level assessment is very similar to the well-known American 'five colour' code equivalent created by the Department of Homeland Security after September 11 in order to keep the terrorist threat publically and permanently visible (Figure 8.3).

The UK terror threat levels	US homeland security advisory system
Critical – an attack is expected imminently	**Severe** – severe risk of terrorist attack (red)
Severe – an attack is highly likely	**High** – high risk of terrorist attack (orange)
Substantial – an attack is a strong possibility	**Elevated** – significant risk of terrorist attacks (yellow)
Moderate – an attack is possible, but not likely	**Guarded** – general risk of terrorist attack (blue)
Low – an attack is unlikely	**Low** – low risk of terrorist attack (green)

Figure 8.3 UK and US terror threat levels

Towards UK resilience

As intimated throughout this chapter, although there appears to be some integration between civil contingencies and counter-terrorist strategy and policy, they operate in very different ways. Equally, within both polices there have been areas prioritized and areas where less priority has been given. For example, during the roll-out of the CCA 2004 there has been a high focus placed upon conformance to statutory obligations, especially at the local level due, to pressures of meeting performance management and for completing full risk assessment for the Capabilities review. Less attention as a result has been placed on stream of public 'warming and informing' and upon ideas of developing resilient communities. In a similar way, the CONTEST strategy as it has evolved has shifted in emphasis. Initially there was a strong focus placed on reactive measures, either through legal means or the implementation of highly visible security systems (to highlight that the Government was responding to public anxieties regarding the threat of terrorism). As the CONTEST strategy has evolved far more attention is now being placed on prevention rather than cure – in other words upon the Prevent strand and in stopping individuals within local communities becoming 'radicalized'. In very recent times and especially after the attacks against London (successfully foiled) and Glasgow airport in the summer of 2007, there has also been a significant emphasis placed within CONTEST upon protecting crowded places and soft targets – such as shopping centres, bars, pubs and clubs and sports stadia (Coaffee, 2008).

In the cases mentioned above the newest priorities place much more emphasis upon the 'public' nature of threat and how we all (Governments at all levels, the private sector, the community and voluntary sector and the general public) have a role to play in reducing the vulnerability to risk, and in mitigating the impact of a disaster event (terrorist related or otherwise) if one occurs. This argument about the nature and impact of 'everyday resilience' will form the basis of much more detailed discussion in Chapter 11.

As it has been rolled out, the UK resilience agenda has been fast moving and fluid. This pace of change has presented a series of challenges in terms of both the directive and communicative roles of national Government. In the last part of this chapter we will highlight some these challenges (which will be explored in far more depth in subsequent chapters). These include a series of governmentality challenges of: governmental co-operation; devolution and sustained funding; partnership working; re-skilling; proportionality; liberty and discrimination; and public disclosure.

Challenges of governmental co-operation

Although the United Kingdom has built up an increased capacity to deal with threat (particularly terrorist related) there are still evident problems of intra-governmental co-operation and collaboration, despite such joined-up working being seen as a precondition for an effective resilience policy. The Lead Government Department model that has been adopted with regard to different strands of work is bureaucratically efficient, but can present challenges of mutual working (Wintour, 2005). More recently a think tank report from DEMOS (2007, p. 13) has argued, there is still a greater need for 'a holistic approach to national security, and that the UK national security framework was in its current state 'incoherent' and 'outdated', and has failed to adopt to the new Twenty-First-Century challenges. This perceived lack of joined-up working was referred to as a 'Cyclops syndrome' (BBC News, 2007b). Here it was further argued that the Government approach was still entrenched in a Cold War way of thinking and focused too much terrorism to the exclusion of other dangers, and lacked co-operation between Government Departments.

Likewise, others have highlighted tensions between local and central working with a command and control management model adopted for the Capabilities review being at odds with the locality approaches favoured for other aspects of the CCA. In this sense, care needs to be taken that centralist tendencies do not destabilize the ability to establish effective local working practices.

Challenges of sustained funding

The civil contingences legislation in particular provides a viable framework for devolving responsibility to local responders, with the regional tier acting as a communicative conduit. But, will the relatively high degree of funding (approximately double pre-September 11 levels for both counter-terrorism and civil contingencies) be retained for resiliency work? Whereas resilience is a key political issue at the current time, future spending plans are periodically reviewed and subject to challenge and change. It is likely the success of resilience policy, particularly at the local level, will be determined by levels of sustained funding and resources released from Whitehall (Gregory, 2007, p. 340).

Challenges of partnership working

The current push towards enhancing resilience involves multi-organizational partnerships with partners drawn from across the public sector, from different tiers of government, the police and emergency services, the community and voluntary sector and private sector organizations. As Lowndes and Skelcher (1998, p. 315) highlight, such multi-agency formation arise within an increasingly fragmented institutional landscape and are seen as the most appropriate way of managing complex problems, although such endeavours have traditionally encountered a host of barriers relating to constraints of time/effort, policy complexity and a lack of suitable training for partnership members. The argument here is that successful partnership working often takes time to develop and become sustainable, and is often beset by mistrust between partners from different cultural backgrounds who use different 'languages', have different degrees of skills and experience and are under different pressures of time and resources. Against this backdrop, establishing neat and tidy multi-stakeholder and multi-scalar partnership working that will easily deliver Government resiliency objectives is likely to be more problematic than perhaps expected, at least in the short term.

Challenges of re-skilling

The challenges faced by the United Kingdom from terrorism and other disruptive challenges are arguably higher than it has been for many decades. In particular, we are told by the Government that the spatial extent of the terror threat has broadened; London is no longer the only 'high risk' area. In this sense there is a great need for training to be implemented, particularly in the provincial cities and regions, to allow re-skilling of responders to occur. This we know from experiences of assessing organizational cultural change, as with the development of effective partnership working, is not necessarily an easy process. How will responders who have been used to operating in a particular way now cope with working in an increasingly high-profile line of work? How successful will they be in acquiring new skills? And just as importantly, how will they 'unlearn' old and outdated repertoires of working? Likewise, how can flexibility of action be embedded within organizations that are used to a relatively stable working environment (the last major change in civil emergency legislation was in 1948)? The need now is for emergency planners and other resilience responders to be able to acquire the skills to work successfully within an ever-changing and complex field.

Challenges of proportionality

As we have highlighted in Chapter 7, the success of Government trying to implement a resilience policy is influenced by its risk assessment. Although civil contingences legislation, in particular, was driven forward at speed by concerns for a lack of capacity in counter-terror response, we need to keep in mind that proportionally far greater threats in terms of likelihood loss of life, cost and disruption, preset themselves with other risks, most notably pandemics. In this sense, we should not let terrorism drive civil contingences and provide its overarching focus and devour a large proportion of the funding. Although the stated aim of both the CCA and CONTEST is to develop preparedness through a system of IEM which is capable of responding to all disruptive challenges, care must be taken to ensure that concerns for terrorist response, especially in parts of the United Kingdom where the likelihood of attack is minimal, do not overshadow genuine attempts to develop more nuanced and localized resilience based on local specificity and localized risk profiling.

Challenges of liberty and discrimination

There are evidently huge civil liberty issues associated with the rolling-out of resilience policy, especially with regard to counter-terrorism. In particular, there are ongoing debates over the use and function of new military threat technologies which are increasingly infused into the urban sphere, blurring the boundaries between civil protection and militarization. Recent scholarship has highlighted that counter-terror measures can contribute to an atmosphere of fear and a culture of surveillance that have consequences for social control and freedom of movement, potentially leading, in an urban context, to a reduction in the democratic involvement in urban planning and often facilitating the increasing militarization of urban design (Graham, 2004; Swanstrom, 2002; Murakami Wood *et al.*, 2006). In the United Kingdom, and elsewhere, there is also a particular risk that counter-terrorism measures, and particularly legal measures, may alienate members of the community with 'hyphenated-citizenship' that feel singled out as threats (Stasiulis & Ross, 2006). There is clearly a need to address the problem of terrorism while remaining attuned to such social and cultural concerns, and balance liberty with the new security challenges (Coaffee *et al.*, 2008).

Challenges of public disclosure

A further challenge facing national policy-makers is regarding the 'warning and informing' stream of both civil contingency and counter-terrorism work. There is a fine line between providing the general public with important personal risk information and 'scaring' them into thinking that they are unprepared for the 'inevitable' attack. The publication of the *Preparing for Emergencies* booklet in 2004 demonstrated that this is a difficult balance to get right. This booklet, part of an £8m government awareness campaign urged the use 'common sense' and the following of practical guidance in the event of a terrorist attack or other disaster situation. In many respects, it was not much different from the guidance issued before WW2 or the *Protect and Survive* booklets of the second Cold War (see Chapter 4), and was treated with as much disdain and ridicule from commentators and many of the public. For example, in response to HM Government's official *Preparing for Emergencies* website,[17] a high-profile spoof site was set up by the 'HM Department for Vague Paranoia', whose main advice was to 'run away'.[18] This was in a long line of satirical responses to the perceived inadequacy of emergency planning in the United Kingdom dating back to Haldane's comments on ARP (air raid precaution) strategy (see Chapter 4) and was perhaps as significant a commentary on how Government risk communication strategy has raised serious questions about the way in which the individual citizen is being increasingly mobilized in pursuit of their own risk management and how such information can ratchet up levels of fear (see Kearon *et al.*, 2007; see also Chapter 11).

Resilience, although a new rhetoric on which to hang a host of emergent emergency planning activity protection issues, is not a new area of activity *per se*. Although the threat of terrorism has been popularly seen to drive this process, deficiencies in the pre-September 11 systems of civil protection were first exposed by more everyday events such as the inadequate and disorganized responses to localized flooding. Recent years have seen vast programmes of reform, directed by Central Government focused upon both civil contingences and counter-terrorism policy, which although containing many overlaps, still undoubtedly require greater integration. Whereas, concerns for counter-terrorism have driven the resilience agenda forward apace, it has not overwhelmed it (although at certain times this is the impression) given other disasters and threats the United Kingdom has recently faced, most notably outbreaks of 'foot and mouth' and 'blue tongue' disease, avian flu, pandemic human influenza and widespread flooding in 2007 alone. As these resiliency practices have evolved, it has been the civil contingences legislation that has had the widest geographical impact, as it is a statutory requirement in all local authority areas which are directed in their task of generating IEM and generic emergency plans via the conduit of a newly established regional tier. Of course, the fluid nature of threat also means that the response frameworks utilized by Government at all tiers will be dynamic in nature and modified as new threats present themselves or weakness in the resilience system is exposed by testing or actual events.

This chapter has set a broad context for the emergence of practical resilience at the strategic level of national policy. The subsequent chapters now turn to consider the multi-scale nature of UK resilience, first thorough an analysis of the regional scale (Chapter 9), then local and sub-regional tier (Chapter 10), before turning our attention to the everyday public experience of resilience policy in urban areas (Chapter 11).

9
The UK Regional Response

The widespread reframing of risk, threat, disaster, hazard and the institutional responsibilities associated with new civil contingency legislation required a comprehensive redrafting of the roles and relationships of a number of Government tiers and agencies. It also required a redressing of the workloads, tasks and duties of key actors involved in emergency planning and resiliency issues.

Having set a broad context and developed a recent history for the rise of resilience and counter-terrorism policy-linked responses to new security challenges (Chapters 7 and 8), we now focus on some of the more specific organizational changes brought forth at the regional scale associated with the introduction of civil contingency legalization, most notably the Civil Contingencies Act (CCA, 2004). Here it is clear that a key element of the Government's drive to create a consistent level of civil protection across the United Kingdom was the introduction of a regional tier in order to integrate the existing local response capabilities and help ensure economies of scale in an event of an emergency being proclaimed, in other words a strong emphasis on preparedness. We should, however, note that this is not the first time a regional scale has been used for emergency planning. We highlighted in Chapter 4 how from the 1920 Emergency Powers Act until after the Second World War a regional presence was in operation, and gave special powers including the use of the military to preserve order and ensure supply of goods and services.

This chapter seeks to unpack the regional resilience tier and is divided into four main parts. First, we focus upon the ongoing push towards regionalism in English Government structures *per se*, arguing that the development of the regional resilience tier is part of a broader process of 'new regionalism' and changing approaches to governmentality. Second, we focus specifically upon the structure of the regional resilience tier and the role of the Government Offices for the Regions in establishing a regional resilience presence. Third, we focus upon the role and remit of regional resilience. The fourth and concluding part of this chapter presents a comparative analysis of the differences between how resilience governance was organized in London in contrast to the other more peripheral regions.

New regionalism and resilience

Throughout recent decades the United Kingdom has gained a reputation as one of the most centralized states in Europe (Jones and MacLeod, 2004). Following the election of the New Labour Government in 1997, a programme of constitutional reform was put in place to modernize the state, based on the principle of subsidiarity: that is that decisions should be taken at the lowest level of competent authority. We might read such an approach in terms of neoliberal governmentality and the expression of power relations between different tiers of government to allow effective and efficient governance to occur. Such an approach at the regional level can be seen to have two competing rationales: first, a political rationale to devolve responsibility in order to allow regionally specific (and hence more effective) policy to evolve and, second a managerial rationale which allows the central Government to administer and control (steer) this process through retaining ultimate power within this process (to govern without governing) by centrally constructed and monitored, but sub-nationally delivered strategies.[1]

For the purposes of this chapter, a key feature of constitutional modernization was the push towards a 'new regionalism' (Amin, 1999; Deas and Ward, 2000) seen by Valler *et al.* (2002, p. 187) as being 'both the scale at which economic activity is increasingly being organized, and the appropriate site at which to define and deliver policy responses'.

Under the post-1997 New Labour Government, 'new regionalism' was most notably enacted in two key ways; first, in 1999, through the formation of Regional Development Agencies in the eight regions outside London in order to create ' "functional regions" that [were] better able to stimulate and manage sustainable economic growth' (Valler *et al.*, 2002, p. 187) and second, and of most importance to the forthcoming discussion, was the bolstered role given to the 'outposts' of Central Government: the Government Offices for the Regions (GORs). GORs were originally set up in 1994 to deliver Government programmes and initiatives at the regional (and local) level, and to help to establish partnerships with relevant organizations (Whitehead, 2003).

The arrival of GORs led to a number of debates about whether or not this amounted to the centralization of power, with Whitehall being able to strategically control regional affairs, or whether it was a more effective way of focusing on specific regional concerns. What became clear as GORs were developing and subsequently evolved was that they established a capacity 'for playing both roles' (Mawson and Spencer, 1997, p. 71), and that 'the regions should provide the administrative building blocks for a more devolved and democratically accountable regional tier of government' (ibid.).

After a change of Government in 1997 the role and remit of GORs begun to change as they were expected to service more Central Government Departments whose expectations of the GOR was that they now develop 'a clear focus on strategic priorities' (HM Treasury, 2006, p. 1). This was to be achieved by a programme of transformational change and streamlining which was set in train in order that they might become more influential bodies and develop a smaller but more focused network of GORs (HM Treasury, 2006). The new key objectives for this GO Network were seen as 'supporting local and regional delivery and promoting flexibility within the devolved decision-making framework' (ibid., p. 2), alongside Regional Development Agencies and local governments.

In short, GORs form a nexus of the civil service and service delivery between national agencies, central government and local authorities:

> Government Office [are] the New Civil Service – 'new' because we provide strategic leadership and operate through partnerships with central, regional and local organizations. We have increased our impact by: rebalancing our teams; increasing the seniority and expertise of staff; and organizing around policy and place. GOs offer simpler, more responsive government based on lean, focussed organizations supported by efficient, effective and shared back office functions. (Government Office Network, 2007)

Overall, the rationale behind 'new regionalism' was the intention to increase the institutional capacity of the regions to act on behalf of the state whilst at the same time making policy increasingly reflective of different sub-national conditions. That said, and perhaps predictably, there appeared to be a focus in the early years of 'new regionalism' with developing the governance framework rather than an emphasis on successful outputs (see, for example, Valler *et al.*, 2002). This, as we shall see in the forthcoming sections, is an accurate characterization of how the resilience stream of regional working that initially developed, and subsequently evolved, in the mid-2000s.

Integrating resilience into the regional agenda

Key to emergency planning modernization was the establishment of the regional presence in resilient planning. As a result of a concentrated programme of regional reform, risk assessment and co-ordination of resources in the event of an emergency became increasingly embedded in the fabric of civil service; not just for the first time as a set of statutory obligations but as a process of multi-agency working. This regional resilience tier was initially enacted in 'interim' form in 2003 and was tasked primarily with co-ordination of local specificities, particularly linked to gaining the co-operation of Category 1 responders; operating as a conduit for information on best practice; and for performance and compliance on the full range of civil contingencies. The key to such regional level reform lay in recognizing the pitfalls of creating an unwanted, unnecessary and additional layer of bureaucracy that would be not be taken seriously by local responders.

A key change in the establishment of the regional tier was the changing nature of the information flow. Previously the focus of communication had been on direct and reactive response-driven processes, whereby COBR(A) acting as 'central command' would be in charge in the event of a large-scale emergency and negotiate with local scene commanders on site. The regional tier now added a conduit for the management of capabilities and preparation. Where this was made most apparent was through the 'firming up' of communicative channels between local and national actors through a regional tier in the form of regional resilience fora and thematic planning subgroups that form the structure of resilient governance in the regions.

The practical aspects of this process forms a key aspect of the discussion to follow, particularly the relationships that emerged from these resilience steering committees on specific issues which acted as expertise 'swap-shops' for highly specialized practitioners. We shall also unpack the tensions between different groups that emerged as a result of this process, many of whom, at the local level, feared the installation of civil servants between central government and local experts as another example of regionalization of government, via 'the back door', and of another obfuscating tier of bureaucracy to be lamented and avoided.

Operational tensions were also apparent during the process of establishing a regional resilience tier. These have become most apparent where institutional ways of working vary between different scales of operation, and as a result of fears that local level operation might be downsized because of the introduction of an additional and higher level tier. The melting pot forged at the regional scale by such links between central and local government is therefore not without its own contestations and resistance, especially where the ongoing rescaling of the state can be linked to the new ways of working encouraged by such systemic reform. This for some at the outset of this reform programme was leading to concerns of over-bureaucratization of the existing systems and pragmatic pessimism of the efficacy of change (see O'Brien & Reid, 2005).

Regionalizing emergency services

One of the key roles in developing resilience policy at the regional level was co-ordinating and managing relationships with Category 1 responders. Category 1 Responders focus on those aspects of resilience that fall within their existing remits and work with other responders to ensure 'joined-up working'. The regionalism agenda, based on a Government Office model, which had led to the introduction of the regional resilience tier, was in parallel, applied as a rationale for further reform of the emergency 'blue light' services.

The proposed regionalization of 'blue light' agencies was one of the most debated issues surrounding the implementation of a regional tier of resilience governance. In particular, between 2005 and 2007 a range of both legal and strategic battles were played out related to the proposed changes to the form and nature of 'improvement' in protective services, which it was proposed, should correspond with civil service reform in relation to civil contingencies. Here proposals were made by Central Government to advance a long-standing agenda for a rationalization of emergency service delivery using a more 'efficient' regional service delivery model. This approach appeared to use the guise of statutory civil protection arrangements as a means to legitimize this process of change; a strategy which was responded to in a number of different ways by each 'blue light' service, and most strenuously by the Police and Fire services.

With regard to the proposal for Police regionalization, a report, *Closing the gap: A review of the 'fitness for purpose' of the current policing structure in England and Wales* (O'Connor, 2005) was commissioned by the Home Office in April 2005. This report demonstrated the intent to 'close' the perceived 'gap' in the ability of national protective services to cope with major incidents, hazards and threats.[2] The overall aim was to create a new resilient force structure for the hazards and threats of the Twenty-First Century.

In assessing the national level of organization fitness it became clear that Central Government felt that very few of the 43 forces in England and Wales met the fully required standard of operational readiness across a number of key 'protective services' areas including counterterrorism and domestic extremism, civil contingencies, and critical incidents.[3]

This report argued that, in order to achieve the best comprehensive level of policing across all areas, 'size' of the police force was critical, and suggested forces should have a minimum officer capability of between 4000 and 6000 officers to optimize service delivery within a business-oriented framework – an essentially rationalized, and in many cases, regional structure. Any proposed police force mergers were, however, postponed until further notice in July 2006 due to a threat of legal challenge and a lack of cross-party political support.

The proposed regionalization of Fire Services was no less controversial. This sat within a broader reassessment of the nature and role of the Fire Service which had been ongoing since the late 1970s but was advanced alongside an ongoing review of resilient services and emergency service delivery undertaken in 2003. The focus from the beginning was more operational than strategic, and focussed on improving services and technological capacity for proactive prevention, as well as dramatically improving the reactive response of the Fire Service to emergencies. A regional model was thus put forward to ensure that 'the right resources in the right place at the right time' would be embedded in the updated statutory framework (ODPM, 2003, p. 7). Two key rationales for this proposed regionalized reform were the increased risk of terrorist attack and experiences of biological hazards with regional and national impact, which heightening awareness of the potential scale of emergency operations. Under this proposal, regional Fire and Rescue management boards would become co-terminous to the GOR regional resilience tier and tasked with a number of functions, including ensuring resilience to emergencies especially potential chemical, biological, radiological or nuclear attacks; establishing regional control rooms; and developing regional training strategies and delivery (ibid., p. 33).

The plan here was to rationalize Fire services from 59 Fire authorities to 21 in total, 12 of these in England and Wales; an initial plan that was strongly opposed by Local Fire Authorities. This resulted in the generation of a counter-plan by Her Majesty's Fire Service Inspectorate (HMFSI) under the title *Regional Control: National Resilience* (2003). Central government adopted many of the elements of this counter-plan, placing more emphasis on the role of Fire Service within counter-terrorism and natural disaster management, as well as Integrated Emergency Management (IEM) and Integrated Risk Management Planning (IRMP). The most significant regional impacts of the resulting compromise were threefold, all of which had a focus on regional and large-scale disruptions. Firstly, the remit of Regional Management Boards (RMB) was tightened in order to offer strategic co-ordination in key areas, liaising with regional resilience operations and effectively mirroring the governance structure of the GOR regional resilience tier. Secondly, the establishment of Regional Control Centres and the 'FiReControl' programme, a project which aims to create nine regional control centres and has presented a central point for the operational aspects of regional resiliency, which in terms of infrastructure have the potential to become embedded in emergency response as the nexus of co-ordination activities. They also have potential to act as the 'Resilience Centre' for other agencies, embedding an operational and infrastructural resilience to the everyday service delivery as well as under extraordinary circumstances. Thirdly, the 'New Dimensions' programme which is part of the Department for Community and Local Government's (DCLGs)[4] contribution to the Government's Civil Contingencies Capabilities Programme. Its aim is to enhance UK preparedness and resilience by improving the capability of the Fire and Rescue Service to respond to major and catastrophic incidents.

However, concerns have been consistently raised by the Fire and Rescue services (and to a lesser extent the police service) about the reality of increased resilience as a result of these changes. There were especial concerns about how proposed changes would impact of 'frontline services'. This reform was also seen by some as an imposition of a masked regionalization agenda from central government (HMFSI, 2004; CLGC, 2006, p. 17). Although this rationalization of the Fire service has raised concerns over a 'forced' regionalization agenda, in practice lessons learned from the response to a number of 'regional' incidents highlight how effective this tier might be for coping with emergency events which has enhanced confidence in the regional tier arrangements within the Fire service. For example, the response to incidents such as the Buncefield fuel depot explosions (December 2005) and the intense regional flooding of recent years (particularly June 2007) has highlighted that the Fire service has played a significant role in the response to region-wide emergency events.

The structure of the regional resilience tier

Regional level co-operation for emergency preparedness and civil protection provides 'a mechanism for improving co-ordination and communication into and out from the centre of government' (Cabinet Office, 2005, p. 168). In order to improve the flow of information to and from local experts and practitioners, the regional level took on new significance, reflected in the strategy of central government towards improving the institutional resiliency of communication between different levels of Government. This proposition suggests that: 'regional government structures [should] provide the platform for a regional role in emergency response where one would add value by improving co-ordination between local and central response' (UK Resilience, 2005a). The structure of governance institutions tasked with co-ordination, as such, must be strong, but flexible, in order to assist and embed collaboration between diverse experts in a variety of institutional contexts, all of which signified a new role for the regional governance agencies.

The role of Government Offices for the Regions (GORs)

In the UK scenario, the need to improve coherence in the established lines of control and communication between the local, regional and national tiers of Government in the event of disaster or emergency has occurred through adding a regional tier to emergency planning, which has been tasked, initially, with the implementation of the CCA to ensure that statutory obligations for preparedness and response were in place by the Capabilities Programme Review in 2006.[5] This has occurred under the auspices and observation of the DCLGs Regional Coordination Unit (RCU) – the strategic control centre for all the Government Offices.

The aim here was for the GORs to act as a link between relevant central government and local government, offering interpretation of specific policy agendas and implementation of a formal and standardized regional policy communication and co-ordination structure. The primary role of the regional tier is thus as a communicative channel between the core and periphery of Government across a broad range of civil contingencies issues. Another central role was in improving cross-agency co-operation which was initiated in many cases by installing Memorandums of Understanding across regional levels for response, and sharing and implementing best practice across the established emergency planning groups at local levels. In developing this regional emergency planning role, the GOR focused primarily was on response to non-terror-related incidents where the civil and emergency services take a more central role than security-related agencies in most of the major aspects of 'soft' resilience such as preparation, planning and recovery. In contrast, security agencies and emergency services liaise more with respect of 'hard' issues such as prevention and response on the ground.

Regional Resilience Teams

To fulfil their role under the CCA, GORs have each established a Regional Resilience Team (RRT) which has been operational in each of the GORs since April 2003. RRTs are intended to act as the first port of call for local authorities and partner agencies in the event of a non-terrorist-related incident.

RRT also form the communicative nexus for the exchange of information and best practice in an increasingly large portfolio of activity connected to aspects of civil contingency. For example, they are expected to liaise, as appropriate, with businesses through the Regional Development Agency, and to wider programmes of GOR work such as planning and transportation, housing, community cohesion and neighbourhood renewal.

RRTs vary in size, scope and effectiveness across the regions, and formed the key channel for the dissemination of statutory benchmarking requirements to local practitioners in the run up to Capabilities Review in 2006. National guidance pertaining to civil contingencies is disseminated from the RRT through previously established networks to key local agencies and practitioners across the full spectrum of civil contingencies.

As is common with the establishment of new governance infrastructure at this level, as RRTs developed they focused predominantly on establishing their institutional architecture, and as such suffered a few growing pains as they sort to establish their 'presence' in the region. Initially, in many cases, local networks cut through this regional communicative tier, accessing information from the centre of Government through previously established and often informal channels, leading some to question the purpose of the regional tier. Likewise the establishment of an RRT was seen by some as a threat to local authority emergency planning units (EPUs) who saw them as more Central than Local Government facing, and who were concerned for the sustainability of the funding for this activity (the establishment of the RRT was a high-profile ventures but political priorities change quickly), as well as unease that much of the intended resources were not being ring-fenced at local level for emergency planning activity (see Chapter 10). In particular, there were also concerns expressed by some local responders that the RRT was about 'central government interference' in 'their' localized emergency planning procedures, a concern that had been expressed in early drafts of the civil contingency legalization:

> At the local level, the RRTs could well be regarded as a means of furthering centralized control over locally elected bodies, while supposedly only having a 'coordination' function after an emergency has been proclaimed. (Joint Committee on Draft Civil Contingencies Bill, 2003)

The often forgotten local EPUs which had for many years been relegated to back-office functions of local authorities initially welcomed the sudden explosion of investment and growth in resources at the regional tier.[6] However, the rapidly expanding portfolio of activity and rising profile of emergency planning at the regional scale caused an initial distrust of the regional agenda amongst some local emergency planning teams. The addition of what appeared, to many, as 'another layer of bureaucracy' seemed initially to significantly undermine the established local relationships. It was also felt by some that the regional tier might devalue the high level of specific local knowledge that had been accumulated, as well as superimpose a centralized structure on the flexible networks of operation and 'best practice' that had been established locally. It is worth remembering that for the most part, the civil servants tasked with setting up, and staffing, the RRTs had little or no emergency planning experience and were hence seen by established local experts as initially 'not fit for purpose and on a steep learning curve'.[7]

However, over time, the role of the RRT as the conduit within the establishment of a solid and formal system of communication between national and local government has undoubtedly allowed for a more robust and consistent conformity across local emergency planning services, giving the distinct impression of a series of communities sharing best practice across agencies. Whilst these networks had previously been largely local and informal, more formal channels of communication were increasingly developed. The result was the creation of a more effective 'communities of practice' amongst resilience responders in terms of generating and sharing multi-agency expertise and learning opportunities.

Whereas, the regional resilience agenda may not have won over all the local practitioners during the initial period of 'high pressure' to meet deadlines for conformance to the CCA, it did encourage the best practice embedded in the existing practices of local practitioners to come forth and be recognized within a renamed, repackaged and formalized communicative structure. Regulatory conformance was, for many, easier to achieve through regional collaborative working championed by RRTs, who co-ordinated the regular meetings of regional operatives to share progress, and reinforced this message of change (see Regional Resilience Forums, below). This *modus operandi* of embedding resilience into the everyday practices of local and regional operators was slowly becoming not simply a statutory obligation of those working within this field, but a 'way of working' in its own right, as recognition of the expertise already in place in localities. It provided a concrete example of where the function of governmentality across the board of regional government had been successfully embedded.

How does the regional scale work?

In practice the implementation of resilience infrastructure was a massive exercise in reforming the structure and operation of the bureaucracy of regional governance and embedding new workstreams. The drive towards developing a consistent degree of regional resilience throughout England, predominantly involved the setting up of two key mechanisms. First, the Regional Resilience Forums (RRFs), which are non-statutory multi-stakeholder bodies that meet on a regular basis, and have responsibility for developing regional capability. Second, the Regional Civil Contingencies Committees (RCCCs) – a mechanism by which a response to a large-scale emergency at the regional scale is operationalized, but only in extreme situations. Whilst the RRF is frequently convened by the RRT the RCCC is only *supported* by the RRT at the GOR level, and co-ordinated by practitioners from across the active agencies in response to a specific event.

RRF are the principal mechanism for multi-agency co-operation on civil contingencies issues at the regional level. Its membership usually comprises around 20, drawn from an array of Category 1 and 2 responders, including senior representation from local public bodies such as constituent Local Authorities, local 'blue light' agencies and Health Authorities, as well as national public bodies and NGOs such as the Environment Agency, the Maritime and Coastguard Agency (where appropriate) and the regional director of Government News Network. Depending on regional circumstances, additional members may be included. The RRT at GOR act as the secretariat for this group. Figure 9.1 provides an example of typical RRF membership.

Chaired by:

Regional Director, Government Office

Core members:

Chief Executive, local authority
Chief Constable, local police force
Chief Fire Officer, local Fire and Rescue Service
Regional Director of Public Health
Regional Director, Environment Agency
Regional Operations Manager, MCA
Appointed representative of the Regional Brigade Commander
Voluntary sector representative
Government News Network
Representative of Regional Assembly

Additional members:

Utilities
Transport operators

Secretariat:

Regional Resilience Team, Government Office

Figure 9.1   A typical example of Regional Resilience Forum membership
Source: Adapted from Cabinet Office (2005, p. 172).

The function of the RRF

The main purpose of the RRF is to 'ensure effective delivery of those elements of regional civil protection that need to be developed in a multi-agency environment' (Cabinet Office, 2005, p. 168). RRF have no role to play in operational responses to emergencies but it is expected that each RRF undertake a series of tasks (see Box 9.1).

Box 9.1   Key tasks for the RRT

- Compilation of agreed regional risk map;
- Consideration of policy initiatives in the area of civil protection that emanate from local and central government and all other relevant sources;
- Facilitation of information sharing and co-operation between its members, including, for example, reports on recent incidents and exercises;

- Sharing, wherever appropriate, of lessons learned from emergencies and exercises in other parts of the United Kingdom and overseas;

- Support for the preparation, by all or some of its members, of multi-agency plans and other documents, including Regional Capability Co-ordination Plans; and

- Co-ordination of multi-agency exercises and other training events.

Source: Cabinet Office, 2005, p. 168.

Simply put, the role of the RRF is to improve co-ordination across the region and between the centre and the region, and improve local response capability. RRFs also seek to improve inter-regional co-ordination support planning for a response capability. These roles are mainly strategic in orientation given the senior membership of the RRF. The everyday activities of the RRF are normally devolved to a series of middle management subgroups which undertake the work and report back to the main RRF.

RRF are also closely connected with Local Resilience Forums (LRFs) through overlapping memberships; formal communications as to how the workstreams and subgroups each tier develops can be co-ordinated (for more information on LRFs, see Chapter 10). Workgroups, for example, focus on specific plans or specific areas of concern such as the resilience of utilities and transport.[8] Likewise the RRF acts with national government in largely a co-operative way. In short 'the RRF works alongside other elements of the multi-agency planning framework at the local and central government levels' (Cabinet Office, 2005, p. 169). Figure 9.2 highlights an example of the structure of the institutional architecture of resilience in the North West Region which highlights links between the RRF and other structures, and the workstreams it has initiated.

Operationally, the resilience infrastructure is focussed through two main streams of subgroups to the RRF:

- Specific capability streams (permanent subgroups), for example, Risk assessment, CBRN, Warning and Informing and others.
- Specific Plan focussed (temporary subgroups), for example, regional resilience plan (RRP), mass fatalities plan, family assistance centres, pandemic flu plan.

The permanent subgroups are specialist meetings of Category 1 and 2 responders on established issues such as long-distance planning,

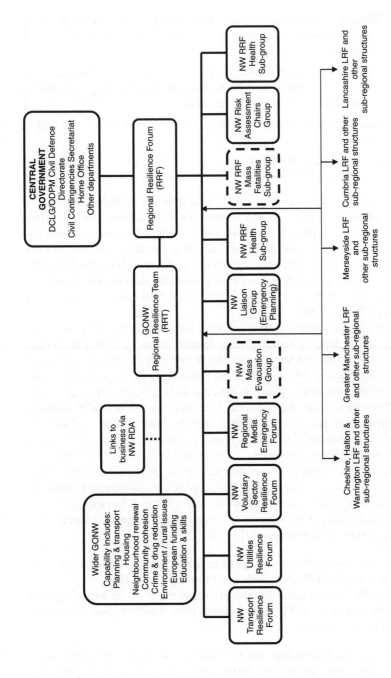

Figure 9.2 The regional resilience tier in North West England (as of 2007)

whereas the temporary groups are convened only for as long as the preparation of the plan is required. Once these work packages and plans are completed, the temporary groups are effectively disbanded, to meet only infrequently and only in regard to updating and identifying aspects of the plans that may need amending.

Of particular importance to the development of RRF has been a series of key tasks that have sought to determine the institutional capacity of the resilience response. These often help guide the subgroups operating underneath the RRF, through which specific elements of the capabilities programme are sub-divided and operationally enacted. For the purposes of our discussion we will focus upon the development of Regional Risk Registers (or assessments); the creation of Regional Response Plans; and the development, and staging, of regional 'exercises'.

Regional Risk Registers

The role of Regional Risk Registers (RRRs) is to build on the local (community) risk registers compiled by practitioners within the LRF structure (see Chapter 10), collating this information into a regional register and allowing for a comprehensive assessment of current and future regional priorities. Interestingly, the RRR that is 'publically' available only lists natural hazards and excludes security-related risks, including top tier COMAH sites such as oil storage and refinery or water distribution and purification plants. To include these sites or related terror threats in risk registers was considered unnecessary and dangerous as it may cause undue alarm in the public with potential knock on dangers to financial markets, such as housing prices and insurability issues in areas affiliated with high risks, or provide a form of target list for potential terrorists.

The resultant RRRs (completed in most regions in 2005 as a lead priority of statutory conformance, but subject to continuous review) highlighted where risk is thought to occur in a particular region, as well as allowing the RRF to prioritize work. This will of course mean that different regions will have different workstream priorities reflective of their overall risk profile. For example, in the North East of England typical risks including flooding and foot and mouth disease (rural and natural hazards) whereas in London the risk priorities are focussed more on terror and security-related issues. This is reflected in the differing progress made on different workstreams within the Capabilities Programme across various regions.

Regional resilience plans

The RRF is also primarily responsible for developing Regional Response Plans. The Cabinet Office (2005, p. 175) has identified three types of regional 'resilience' plan that are generally activated as a result of a serious incident or under high levels of threat: a generic response plan for activating Regional Civil Contingencies Committees (RCCCs) and regional apparatus; a business continuity plan for the Government Office; and Regional Capability Co-ordination Plans, which involve establishing procedures for communicating with the local level, other regions and central government. These plans are developed and 'owned' by the RRF and maintained by the RRT (ibid.).

The rationale behind generic regional response planning is that each region will have a plan to ensure that, should it be necessary, regional crisis management machinery can be activated as smoothly as possible. This will require that capabilities are developed through skills, training and exercising and that procedures are established and communicated to relevant responders.

The second element of regional 'resilience' planning is the Government Office Business Continuity Plan (GOBCP) which has a simple remit to 'make sure that the Government Office can continue to operate its essential functions in an emergency, particularly those which might be necessary for the response to that emergency' (ibid., p. 175).

The third main element of such regional planning is the requirement for the RRF to deliver of Regional Capability Co-ordination Plans (RCCPs), which seek to ensure a consistency of approach in resilience planning by the LRFs and responsible agencies that will be required in the event of an emergency incident effecting more than one LRF simultaneously. In short, the purpose of this type of planning is 'to support local planning, by ensuring that local plans can be scaled up in response to wider impact events ... to deal with emergencies which overwhelm individual local areas' (ibid., pp. 175–6).

Resiliency exercises

Testing emerging resilience plans has been central to the regional resilience agenda, and regional tests for major flooding, CBRN attacks, pandemic influenza and an array of high-profile threats, hazards and risks have been undertaken in recent years. Such exercising is vital to the establishment of resilience and ensuring that systems remain honed and prepared for the emergence of a disaster event. The aim is to ensure all organizations are fully prepared for all types of emergencies and fully conversant with the detail and chain of command within emergency plans (Coaffee and Wood, 2006, p. 511).

Exercises have tended to be of three types carried out across LRF, RRF and RCCC levels of operation: discussion forums to allow plans to be finalized; table-top simulations; and 'live' rehearsals. Table 9.1 gives examples of exercises carried out in the regions outside London, specifically focused on testing procedures for terror-related events.

Most of these exercises are focussed specifically at the regional level but also have a bearing on inter-regional exercises. For example, *Northern Synergy* in January 2006 was the largest counter-terrorist exercise ever held in the United Kingdom and used a scenario exercise based on the Beslan siege in Russia in 2004 (which resulted in the security forces

Table 9.1 Examples of regional level resilience exercises carried out in 2004–2005

Region	Name and date of test	Focus of test
North East	Exercise Merlin Aware October 2005	To establish the function and practice of multi-agency strategic command and staff procedures in the response to, management of and recovery from a Chemical, Biological, Radioactive, Nuclear (CBRN) incident
Yorkshire and the Humber	Breaking Crisis/Bright Future Sept/Oct 2005	This was a multi-phased event for testing emergency response to CBRN events including participation from military and civilian agencies, including Technical Response Force of the British Army, the Police Forces of the Yorkshire region and other partner emergency services. The three phases tested in turn different aspects of the military and emergency services, and local services partnership with the RRF in a series of fictitious potential scenarios
North West	Exercise Diamond Dagger Aug/Sept 2004	A test that involved a range of agencies, not inclusive of all agencies that would be involved in response. This involved co-ordination between local police and military organizations in a test of front-line techniques and technology in the face of a chemical event in a high-risk site

Table 9.1   (Continued)

Region	Name and dateof test	Focus of test
West Mid- lands	Exercise Horizon July 2004	Regional response tests for the RRF command and control structures and deployment of specialist resources in response to CBRN events or incidents. This was followed up with a series of table-top events to ground and share the lessons learned across agencies and provide more meaningful feedback to the national tier
East Mid- lands	Exercise Arctic Sea June 2005	Department of Health pilot testing at regional level for the testing of global influenza pandemic contingency arrangements. This test focused on the response of health agencies and the business continuity of health organization and the general public in the face of a potential pandemic outbreak

Source: UK Resilience, 2005b.

storming the school and the resultant deaths of 344 of the hostages). This exercise provided valuable experience for a wide range of agencies, and enabled them to test their arrangements, and their ability to respond to a very serious terrorist incident. Lessons learned from this and other exercises have been fed into resilience plans for responding to a wide range of terrorist threats to ensure that all agencies involved are prepared to respond to a major terrorist incident.

Outside of the peripheral regions, advanced planning and testing has also occurred in the capital, London. The London region has developed of a series of strategic emergency plans – for example for mass fatality planning, the setting up of Humanitarian Assistance centres and the development of evacuation plans for London (called Operation Sassoon). These plans are regularly validated in table-top or live simulated tests, which also give an opportunity to test standard procedures and assess staff competencies.

Examples of such London-wide tests have included *Exercise Capital Response* in 2002 and *Exercise Capital Focus* in 2003. *Capital Response* was a table-top test which exercised the 'command, control communication and consequence management issues following a catastrophic incident' to ascertain if current structures and provision could cope with an event on the scale of September 11 (London Prepared, 2006). Exercise *Capital Focus* in 2003 tested the revised structures in an exercise designed to trial communication arrangements and information flows between the lead responders and Government.[9]

The most high-profile test conducted in London, to date, was *Exercise Osiris II* in 2003. The aim of which was to test specific elements of the operational response to a chemical attack on the London Underground (simulating similar circumstance to the Tokyo Sarin gas attack of 1995; see Chapter 6). This exercise focused on Bank Junction in the heart of the City of London, and followed a desk-top exercise *Osiris I*. For this day-long test the City of London – London's financial heart – was locked down and London's emergency services were tested for their state of preparedness, their ability to work in a co-ordinated fashion and gave 'blue light' services the opportunity to test the effectiveness of new specialist equipment, including chemical suits.

Further exercises conducted in London in recent years have also included tests with international counterparts in American and Canada,[10] as well as 'rising tide' scenarios (such as pandemic influenza), major power outages in high-risk times (such as mid-winter) as well as systematic testing of communication arrangements between agencies and operatives on the ground following the report of the response to the 7 July 2005 bombings, particularly the exposure of shortcomings in technological compatibility issues on the ground (such as frequency of radios, ability of telecoms to operate underground, and air filtration and circulation systems).[11]

Wider tensions in the reality of RRF Operation

RFFs, as they developed, were perceived as the 'regional presence' of central Government in the region, but as a body without devolved power or responsibility. When RRFs were being established there were inevitable fears about the balance between Central Government control and a more pragmatic and grounded local working style. As they developed it became clear that they were very much a communicative, rather than directive governance structure. Recognizing that the localized expertise of ground level operators was infinitely more valuable than a centrally directive service, the resultant structure of RRFs focussed on a series of attempts to develop mechanism for sharing of best practice, the identification of risks for each region, and the broader conformance through working groups and plan-specific panels underneath the key focal groups.

In the case of the RRF there was initially some confusion over the precise role of the new body. Many local practitioners feared that this added layer of civil service bureaucracy would stultify local working relationships that were often founded on personal relationships across organizations as opposed to formalized 'memoranda of understanding' or obligations. However, under the guidance of a series of well-appointed Directors at the regional tier, the resilient policy structure was rolled out both as a strategic reform as well as the co-ordination of existing competencies. This sought to court locally available expertise rather than superimpose a top-down chain of command from a body of civil servants with little expert knowledge or prior experience of emergency operations.

That said, the co-operation of agencies across a broad range of issues was, at first, sluggish due to the pressures of a timetable for conformance to new obligations that might make the state liable for sanctions or legal actions for failure to protect citizens, but quickly gathered momentum. This 'speeding up' of the process is in part linked to the realization at several levels of operation, that the role of the regional resilience tier was not playing a directive role but performing a function of complementary co-ordination. This was in order to provide the services through which experts could communicate with each other and Central Government, in a more regular and formalized environment. In this situation the emerging RRF offered a new opportunity to develop 'best practice' with increased support from the centre; in effect a more attractive work environment for all concerned.

This was also an arena of practice fraught with potential tensions and institutional differences between organizations with complementary competencies, but differing agendas and practices. Despite the personalities of key individuals that in many cases helped to smooth the process of change, there were some universal concerns over particular aspects of the new structure. The biggest cause of concern and confusion in the early development of the regional tier, and a bone of contention in establishing trust between agencies in the practical operation of resilience as a viable system, was the role and remit of the RCCC to which we now turn.

The Regional Civil Contingencies Committee

The Regional Civil Contingencies Committee (RCCC or 'R triple C') represents the second instance of a significant structural change to the regional operation in IEM. Whereas the RRF had primarily a collaborative remit in policy development, the RCCC focussed on the process of response to a large-scale event such as a significant terrorist attack. An RCCC will only be activated if there is an urgent need for it, either by request of Central Government or by one of the agencies within the region. RCCC are to be formed 'to co-ordinate the regional response to an event which had completely overwhelmed local responders or which had an impact over a wide area' (DCLG Fire and Resilience, 2006). For terrorist incidents the RCCC is activated by the Home Office (Lead Government Department) and/or COBR(A).

As an element of the emerging resilience 'toolbox' of central government, the RCCCs were intended as:

> ...a means of co-ordinating the response to and recovery from an emergency at a regional level in England. While most emergencies are dealt with by local responders, at a local level, recent experience has highlighted that there may be very exceptional circumstances when the response to an emergency would benefit from co-ordination at a regional level. This may be when local response arrangements are overwhelmed, or when the majority of localities within a region are affected. (UK Resilience, 2005a)

Here is where the separation of the strategic co-ordination and the activity of the regional tier in the event of an emergency became unclear in the eyes of many resilience responders. As this new system was emerging it became clear that there was a significant difference between the preparation and strategic *planning* for an emergency and agencies tasked with the *responding* to an event or emergency. The RCCC aimed to plug this gap, in practice, by embedding the capability to provide a regional tier to the co-ordination of response at national, regional and local levels, specifically with regard to wide-area and high-impact emergencies; a need highlighted by the events of September 11 and subsequent July 7 bombings in London, but also as mentioned previously by the flooding and foot and mouth events, which were themselves both regional (in the former case) and national (in the latter case) in the scale of response required.

Whilst, as a result of practice histories, there are some regional variations in the construction of these bodies, the systemic overview is generic in terms of capabilities and workstreams. The RCC is in all cases a multi-agency body that draws on expertise from within the RRF, particularly on senior staff from emergency services, Government Office and private sector partners who are seconded as required to the group

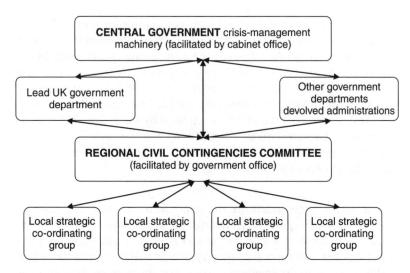

Figure 9.3   Regional co-ordination arrangements in England when an RCCC has been convened (simplified)
Source: Cabinet Office (2005) (adapted).

depending on the context of the emergency event. A simplified model of this can be seen in Figure 9.3.

Significantly, when activated the RCCC acts as a funnel of information, from national bodies such as COBR(A) to local responders through the strategic co-ordination groups.

The RCCC was probably the most problematic of the structural changes at the regional tier, as many local practitioners had previously been used to communicating directly with national level in the event of emergency, with a direct line into COBR(A). The RCCC, for some, even though it was highly unlikely to be activated, created a new barrier between local and national government and was seen as dangerous, particularly as this multiplied the possibility of miscommunication and slowed down the speed of communication between the site of a disaster and the situational response at 'ground zero'. Furthermore, by seconding expertise, the RCCC was seen as a possible drain on vital personnel from related partners and 'hard' Category 1 responders. This was felt most keenly amongst the emergency services whose main responsibility in response is seen as 'hard' site management.

Box 9.2   **Duties required of a RCCCC (UK Resilience, 2005a)**

- Maintaining a strategic picture of the evolving situation within the region;
- Assessing any issues that cannot be resolved at local level;
- Facilitating mutual aid arrangements within the region and, where necessary, between regions;
- Ensuring effective communication between local, regional and national response;
- Identifying regional resource priorities;
- Providing, where appropriate, a regional spokesperson.

Refining the duties of this group, through extensive testing of regional events, table-top exercises and cross-regional training, was a focus of the embedding of the resilient planning and response into regional government. As such the role played by the RCCC does in fact vary depending on the response requirements of the emergency event (see Box 9.2).

The RCCC is in no way a directive body in the 'hard' management of response, and would, if activated, aim to provide a fluent exchange of information, and assist in the co-ordination of smooth transitions from initial response to the recovery phase, where civil services will be more prominent than emergency services, through multi-agency co-operation required at every phase of both response and recovery (should prevention and preparation have failed to circumvent the disaster, hazard or threat).

The key point to note here is that the activation of an RCCC is highly unlikely but an eventuality that must be prepared for. At the time of writing the RCCC mechanism has only been activated once since the development of the regional resilience tier in 2003 in response to serious flooding in Gloucestershire, South-West England, in July 2007.[12]

A pragmatic response to resilient governance in the regions

This chapter has highlighted the structure and function of the regional tier of resilience governance and detailed its obligations under the CCA of 2004. We now turn to the extent to which such structures and processes have developed according to a prescribed and centrally driven model, or a locally/regionally contingent approach.

Undoubtedly, what was required at the regional level was a degree of operational pragmatism. For the public sector *per se* such experientially based pragmatism as an organizing principle is not a new concept, although through the Twentieth Century it has tended to take a back seat to more rational, systemic, technocratic and scientific models of management which, for many, offered a more 'common sense' view of public administration (Coaffee and Headlam, 2008). However, as Snider (2000) highlights, 'implicit pragmatism' has embedded itself within many public sector programmes and organizational policy over time especially in times of 'crisis' and 'overwhelming challenges'. Indeed many have argued that pragmatism has been a key feature of the broad reform and modernization of government agenda perused by the New Labour Government since 1997 – of which regionalism was an explicit part (see, for example, Powell, 2000). Here the focus of policy and practice was on 'what matters is what works' (Southern, 2001) which 'represented a shift from a focus on the institutions of government to a focus upon the practice of governance' (Scanlon, 2001, p.483). This, however, as the prior discussion of regional resilience governance has highlighted, inevitably creates problems and tensions within a multi-level governance framework as there is a requirement to both centralize decision-making to get strategic focus and meet performance targets (and some might argue in a Focuadian sense to retain control), as well as for devolution and decentralization to gain stakeholder inclusivity and co-operation.

In relation to the development of a regionally specific resilience tier, the prescriptive model of conformance developed in the CCA and associated with the 'London model' was deemed inappropriate in the peripheral regions, despite pressures to operationalize speedy reform. What we wish to argue here is that in the English regions a pragmatic 'policy imprint' (Shields, 2004) has developed where civil servants have taken mandates, directives or guidance and translated them into workable policy on the ground, not just 'what works, but what works here'. The requirement for regional civil contingency processes that *did not* follow the 'one size fits all' regional model was summed up in draft civil contingencies legalization in 2003:

> The envisaged regional tier will not in all circumstances suit the demands of a particular emergency, or even the contingency planning to cope with it ... [and] needs to recognise that a 'one size fits all' approach is undesirable and provide for greater flexibility in response arrangements for regional (proclaimed) emergencies.[13]

The London model

In the United Kingdom, since the 1970s, London has understandably remained the focus of attention for terrorists, and this did not change after September 11. As a result, in 2002 and pre-dating the CCA, a specialist emergency planning partnership, the London Resilience Forum, was established to address the strategic emergency planning needs of London (the London Resilience Team was established 2001), which were seen as 'well-developed' for dealing with conventional emergencies but required re-evaluating in the light of September 11 attacks:

> 11 September 2001 brought sharply into focus the need for London to be able to respond quickly and effectively if a similar incident occurred in the capital. A coalition of key agencies – known as the London Resilience Partnership – joined forces in May 2002 to plan and prepare for potential emergencies. This was the first time a strategic, pan-London regime was established that could co-ordinate planning across London. (London Prepared, 2003)

Given London's size and profile as a core global city, its arrangements have been developed so that in an event of an emergency there is no effective difference between a local and regional response. As UK Resilience Guidance (2005) notes:

> London's position as the capital and as a city which is a region in its own right, combined with its political and economic significance, and the regional nature of the emergency services, make it more likely that the response to an emergency will be regional. In the context of London's arrangements, no distinction is made in handling an emergency between the regional and local tiers.

The main London response post September 11 was based on restricting the opportunities for terrorists to strike and in preparing the capital for the inevitable attack (which came in July 2005). In broad terms the role of the London Resilience Forum in countering the threat and impact of terrorist attack (and by implication other emergencies) is fourfold and based predominantly on attempts to retain a competitive business edge for London.

First, disseminating information to Londoners and local governments (and tourists) so that they might be better prepared to protect themselves and improve the development of 'community resilience'. Second, to encourage Business Continuity Planning which involves liaison with individual business and business associations to promote contingency and security plans to be updated and regularly tested so as to facilitate a return to 'business as usual' as soon as possible after an incident. Third, the development of a series of strategic emergency plans, for example for mass fatality planning, the setting up of Humanitarian Assistance centres, or the development of evacuation plans for London (*Operation Sassoon*). Fourth, London Resilience Forum is involved in the emerging security agenda surrounding the 2012 Summer Olympic Games (London Prepared, 2007).

The peripheral model

Initially the London experience formed a 'blueprint' for regional resilience governance nationwide. This might not have been a formal responsibility but was certainly the initial 'impression' local responders had. However, provincial regions had different resilience planning priorities focused not predominantly on terrorism, but upon localized threats from non-terrorist sources. As we highlighted in Chapter 7, there was a feeling amongst many emergency planners and disaster management experts that the rhetoric and expenditure on resiliency issues is disproportionately placed upon terrorism. As such we can observe a core-periphery model of resilience governance that has emerged in the United Kingdom, based upon different regionally specific institutional fixes, risk profiles and funding streams, as opposed to developing the standard export of a centralized 'blueprint'. This was for a number of reasons. First, there were massive disparities in funding and staffing. Whereas the London model had significant funds which allowed it to engage in very detailed strategic work and exercising, the other regional teams had far fewer staff (3–5 as opposed to around 40 in London) and resources. Second, as previously mentioned, the risk profiling in the regions was distinctly different, requiring a different type of response. Whereas London focus was on a large-scale terror attack, the peripheral regions were more concerned about gearing up for weather abnormalities or a flu pandemic. Thirdly, in terms of organizational geographies, there were also some very practical reasons why regions were developing differential resilience response plans linked to the co-terminosity of resilience tiers and responder areas. As previously noted, the RRT in London, unlike other regions in England, operates the local level functions as well as the regional tier, with London effectively acting as a 'city-region' in its own right. This is made easier by the fact that many local responder agencies have boundaries that align with those of the resilience regional boundaries. This means that there are no local issues to concern the strategic governance, and few problems liaising with emergency services. In the peripheral regions, despite attempts to regionalize the 'blue light' services a much more complicated spatial geography presented itself.

Summary

This chapter has explored the establishment of a regional tier of resilience and highlighted some of the tensions in the development of this level of resilient governance, part of a broader 'governing at a distance' approach to UK Resilience. The relationships between agencies at this tier have been both obfuscated and clarified during the establishment of the RRFs and RCCs, and through the development of risk profiling and the creation and testing of response plans. The most significant impact of this restructuring is in the *modus operandi* of regional governance, and the influence of the regional tier as a communicative pathway between central and regional government, linking to local practitioners and harnessing the expertise for the co-ordination of best practice within resilient planning. The process has not, however, been without its tensions and has necessitated a pragmatic approach be adopted on behalf of primary operatives and responders. These are tensions that will be unpacked further in the next chapter that focuses on the relationship between the local tier and the regional tier and the impact of the national agenda on local practices within core urban areas.

10
Local Resilience Planning

The history of local emergency planning is in many ways a combination of social, political and cultural inertia tied to a series of questions raised by particular geo-political circumstances, and grounded in both historical context and the requirements of civil defence and protection at different points in time. In Chapter 4 we highlighted that the local government tier has for many decades been given overall responsibility for managing emergencies. The CCA (2004) reinforced the key role of the local area as the key building block of resilience planning and emergency preparedness which aims to bring together a diverse range of national policy goals, legislative reforms and regional managers with local practitioners, in forms of governance partnership that have been largely successful. However, the variation in the adoption of the local resilience agenda, along with the range and speed with which 'a state of readiness' has been developed, is highly contingent itself on the relationships, previous experience and embedded practices – or lack thereof – in given localities.

In the last chapter we highlighted how the regional resilience tier has evolved and how it sought to connect to the local or sub-regional tier. In this chapter we seek to unpack the role and influence of the sub-regional (or city-regional), and city, response to both the introduction of civil contingency reform and the ability to respond to the increased threat from terrorism. The latter of these features was a significant driver of change at the national planning and strategic level, whilst at the local level the impact was more nuanced with a great concern expressed regarding the likely occurrence of natural disasters and health pandemics.

Broader governance priorities of Central Government have helped shape the introduction of resilience through ideas based on principles of subsidiarity, embodying a neoliberal form of governmentality, where efficient government is sought through decentralizing responsibility whilst retaining control through requirements of assessment and the issuing of guidance. In Chapter 9 we unpacked this through ideas of new regionalism. At the local level similar reform has been forthcoming, rooted in the concepts of 'third way' politics (Giddens, 1998) and 'new localism' (Corry and Stoker, 2002) which has attempted to morph existing local operations into a system of greater decentralized decision-making, collaboration between service sectors and wider participatory structures involving the private sector and local communities. This provides a wider policy framework for the introduction of the local resilience agenda.

In further broadening out the impact of restructuring from a national and regional scale, and addressing the local impact of shifting patterns and processes of governance, this chapter is divided into four parts. The first part will explore the role of sub-regional partnerships – Local Resilience Forums – that have been established to co-ordinate the emergency response between different local authorities, service providers and the emergency services. The second part will highlight the practical experiences of emergency planners working under the LRF system, as well as noting the emerging linkages (and tensions of practice) between the LRF and the regional equivalent: the RRF. The third part of the chapter will focus specifically on how the UK peripheral 'Core Cities' have addressed the challenge of becoming more 'resilient'. The fourth and final part of the chapter illuminates a very practical application of emerging local resilience policy, through the management of high-profile events, often deemed a significant terrorist risk or at the very least an event which might lead to significant civil disorder.

Local resilience forum structures and workstream priorities

The principle mechanism to ensure multi-agency co-operation at the sub-regional or city-regional level is the Local Resilience Forum (LRF). As LRFs have developed they have often been based on pre-existing collaborative working relationships between several Local Authority areas, each with their own Emergency Planning Unit or EPU.[1]

LRFs are intended to map onto the geographical boundaries of local policing areas – though this is not always possible – and are usually chaired by the Local Chief Constable. Summing up the role and remit of LRF, the Government (HM Government Preparing for Emergencies, 2007) notes that the aim of LRFs is to:

... bring together all the organizations that have a duty to co-operate under the Civil Contingencies Act, along with others who would be involved in the response to an emergency. Local Resilience Forums ... need to be developed in a multi-agency environment. In other words they ensure that preparing for emergencies is done in a co-ordinated, effective way by all local responders working together.

The LRF is not a statutory body and it is not in a legal position to be able to direct its members, but it does perform a statutory process and aims towards the development of a multi-agency environment for building resilience, which should deliver a number of goals (see Box 10.1):

Box 10.1 The deliverable goals for a LRF (Northumbria Local Resilience Forum, 2005)

---

a) The compilation of agreed risk profiles from an area, through a Community Risk Register.
b) A systematic, planned and co-ordinated approach to encourage Category 1 responders, according to their functions, to address all aspects of policy in relation to:

- risk;

- planning for emergencies;

- planning for business continuity management;

- publishing information about risk assessment and plans;

- arrangements to warn and inform the public;

- other aspects of the civil protection duty.

c) Support the preparation, by all or some of its members, of multi-agency plans and other documents, including protocols and agreements and the co-ordination of multi-agency exercises and other training events.

The operation of LRFs is structurally comparable to the operation of the regional tier, but also allows for local derivations to address need as required. The LRF operates as a two-way funnel into the RRF, where at regional level senior managers often report back to the RRF on organizational progress at the LRF level. These are more often middle-tier operatives and practitioners working under senior officials, and interpreting the roll-out of operational requirements within the broader policy themes and workstreams identified at RRT. This is shown in Figure 10.1 which highlights the LRF structure in Greater Manchester. More can be said on the tensions of developing these structures in different locations. Each city and city-region has specific concerns; there are competitive economic concerns between cities, and different locally specific governance arrangements that have to be incorporated into the working of the LRF and RRF structures across the same breadth of agencies. However, at local level the idiosyncrasies of government and 'blue light' service delivery is far more distinct.

Most emergency planning restructuring and the existing conditions of preparedness were historically established through previous exposure to events.[2] As such, emergency planning has been very much a local experience embedded in key practitioners who had personal practice of managing these disruptive incidents. New conformance to the CCA required widespread capability to become an everyday practice across both civil and emergency services, and develop 'partnership teams' from stakeholders who that had often previously operated in relative institutional isolation. Often this has not meant a wholesale change in the operation of local emergency planning networks, but a formalization and expansion upon pre-existing arrangements.

The resilience governance system broadened the scope and the resources within the new structure. It allowed LRFs – with in many cases a sub-group to the LRF (often called a Resilience Development Group) – to evolve and act as a co-ordination buffer between the LRF and the local working groups below it. The LRF could then plan pre-emptively according to the CCA criteria or priorities that emerge from risk assessments. Since 2005 such judgements have been informed by Community Risk Registers (CRRs) compiled by LRFs every five years in order to assist in identifying gaps in organizational ability, and inform the planning process regarding the scale of response required. The CRR provides an agreed position on the risks that affect a local area and gives a set of priorities on planning and resourcing. CRR from sub-regional LRFs are also fed into the Regional Risk Register (Chapter 9).

The compilation and public dissemination of the CCR – excluding security risks – is often undertaken by co-operation between the Local Authority EPUs in the LRF. A key reason for compiling and making public the CRR was to reassure the public that adequate risk management was being carried out, the result of which they could access as part of a

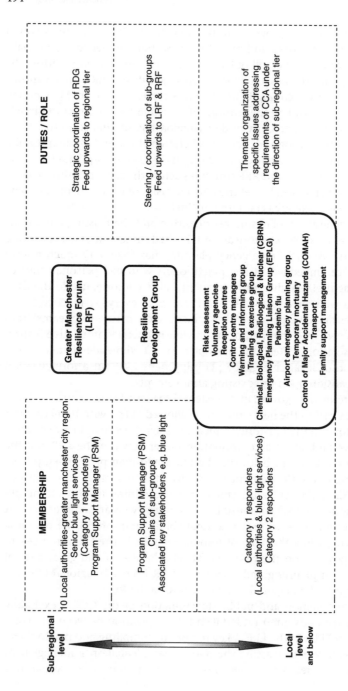

Figure 10.1 The sub-regional Greater Manchester Local Resilience Forum (in 2006)

fledging 'warning and informing' theme of LRF work. As Northumbria Police (North East England) noted upon the dissemination of their CRR in 2005:

> The most important issue for the public is that they can have confidence that we [the LRF] have assessed the potential hazards in our area, and have arrangements in place to respond effectively should an incident occur.

Practical local emergency planning

The LRF acting as communicative structures and conduits for flows of information, along with a massive increase in Government investment in civil contingencies at the local level, required local authorities to restructure their emergency planning divisions. This was a statutory requirement of the CCA and importance was placed upon them becoming 'fit for purpose' as soon as possible. There are a number of diverse issues here for different agencies. In particular, there were concerns about the sphere of influence and experience in emergency management that was often very different between local authorities and 'blue light' agencies. In particular, there were concerns that the local resiliency agenda would get swept up within the traditional police 'service culture' given the LRF boundaries being directed by Police force territories (see Walker and Broderick, 2006).

Previous arrangements under legislation for emergency management required only a lip-service presence to be active within Local Authorities as the majority of civil risks were dealt with by the Police and Fire service. As a result many local authority EPUs lacked critical mass and experience.

With the introduction of the CCA a massive expansion in the Local Authority funding for emergency management[3] propelled emergency planning into the core activities of local government. Emergency Planning teams were established or reformed in all local authorities around the country with the aim of pulling together the personnel with prior experience of disaster management and response in the local civil sector, in order to co-ordinate and collaborate meaningfully with the relevant partner agencies and formalize the diverse local preparedness arrangements, as well as developing an internal programme of corporate resilience. For example, emergency response in the city of Newcastle upon Tyne in North East England underwent a significant scaling-up in terms of personnel and funding. The existing emergency planning

Box 10.2   Local Authority statutory duties (Newcastle)

- To assess the risks of an emergency occurring
- To plan so that if an emergency occurs, the Council can continue to perform its functions
- To plan to prevent or mitigate the effects of an emergency
- To provide warning and informing to the public
- To provide business continuity advice and information to commercial bodies
- To provide internal business and service continuity planning

section was renamed the 'Resilience Planning Team', and tasked with two key aims: first, the maintenance of normal services during times of disruption including major incidents (service continuity), and second, delivering services to support communities directly affected by major incidents and the mechanisms by which such services are delivered (emergency planning) (Newcastle City Council, 2004). They also had a set of statutory duties placed on them by the CCA (2004) as a Category 1 responder (see Box 10.2)

It is also at the Local Authority level that the statutory requirement to deliver a consistent degree of resilience is formally assessed. At the local level, risk management evaluation is being pushed to the forefront of the government modernization agenda. From 2005 it has been embedded within every Local Authority Comprehensive Performance Assessment (CPA) as part of a 'Safer and Stronger Communities priorities' block (Coaffee and Murakami Wood, 2006).[4] In specific relation to the CCA, local authorities' duty to deal with major disruptive challenges were the focus of this assessment; in particular, to continue to deliver critical local services; improve 'partner processes'; and provide advice to businesses about continuity in an event of an emergency incident.

Tensions in practical operation of local resilience

A key concern for many of these emerging and restructured EPUs at a Local Authority level was funding to develop IEM and enhance levels of resilience against a range of 'disruptive challenges', which was not, and to date in many local areas is still not, protected. This lack of 'ring fencing' raised concerns amongst practitioners that the inflated bubble of resilience funding may dissipate, even as the workstreams and areas of governance function into which emergency planning reaches are expanding; or that other areas of local government would 'dip into the pot' to fund other areas of work considered more important at the local level. Though this was a worry, it is not an urgent concern as there is no solid evidence of this occurring, particularly given the high profile of emergency planning at the current time and the high workload associated with statutory conformance requirements. However, the sustainability of resilience planning at local level remains a long-term concern.

This is particularly the case when it comes to preparatory work for the impact of a terrorist attack where many local authorities that may feel their area is not 'at risk' could potentially be caught under-prepared. There is an ongoing Government concern that many provincial cities appeared not to be 'gearing up' for the threat of terrorism despite constant advice and guidance and participation in live exercises for terrorist-response. However, spending much time and effort on terrorism was for some deemed disproportionate especially given the challenges of much more important workstreams that are presenting themselves, most notably pandemic flu planning. There was also a concern that London-based terrorism-response procedures were seen by central Government as appropriate for the regional cities despite obvious differences in capacity to respond and risk profile. This mirrors previous work in the domestic management of terrorist attacks where it was argued that:

> The capital was not the only place targeted by the IRA and there have been numerous concerns outside of London since 9/11. This critique acted as a barrier to sharing information and good practice, with central government being perceived as unwilling to listen to 'lessons from the provinces'.
>
> (Pratchett and Dale, 2004, p. 14)

Another challenge at the local level was getting the right balance between Local Authority expansion of emergency planning and collaboration with the established experience of 'blue light' agencies, many of whom saw the regional tier in particular as added bureaucracy, and had concerns over the expertise of and remit that practicing civil servants were being given at the local level (see Chapter 9).

This was counter-balanced with the role of Local Authority as a communication node in response. Here, whilst the 'blue light' experts deal with the 'hard' response (disaster management on the ground) and the transition of authority to the Local Authority, whose primary responsibility in the management of events was focussed on the 'soft' recovery element of the disaster cycle (taking care of the affected citizens). 'Blue light' agencies are the front line of response and act on the ground at 'Gold' and 'Silver' level response commands,[5] but beyond these requirements the management of recovery falls squarely under the remit of Local Authorities. This was highlighted most prominently in the results of testing for CBRN responses across different regions (see Chapter 9), where the police managed the street event, the fire service co-ordinated and managed the decontamination equipment and post-decontamination, whilst many Local Authorities were unprepared for the housing and management of affected citizens. The reports emerging from the London experience of bombings in 2005 also heightened the priority of establishing swift and effective procedures for dealing with the aftermath of an attack, not just in infrastructure protection but in dealing with the fallout for citizens. As a result, emergency centres in situ, the planning for temporary humanitarian assistance centres and mass fatalities planning were pushed to the fore in the LRF's workstreams as a key responsibility of localities.

Tensions of co-operation between the local practice and regional strategic tiers

At the local level there have been a series of tensions in the evolution and development of the broader agenda of resilience governance restructuring. Linking to the discussion of regionally driven restructuring (Chapter 9), it was evident that initially there was a level of mistrust of the bureaucracy embedded in regional government amongst the civil service at local level, and concern that the civil servants at regional level would be acting in a directive capacity during response to events – a role for which they had neither training nor experience. A general lack of clarity on the remit of this new regional tier added to this mistrust that the central government agenda would lead to regional resilience operatives acting as a roadblock, not a conduit, between central government and 'Gold' and 'Silver' and commands on the ground at the site of emergency response. This was exacerbated by the proposed regionalization 'blue light' agencies (Chapter 9).[6]

This initial uncertainty, often expressed as a lack of trust, slowly changed as the RRF and LRF structures became more embedded into the practice of multi-level resilient governance, and the workstreams became more focussed after the initial melee of conformance to statutory obligations and of practice through 'testing' for emergencies. Over time, the familiarity of key staff with the interoperability of different local agencies has bred more confidence in the process and for the role of the regional tier as a co-ordinator of strategy, and not a director of policy and response.

Negotiations between local and regional agendas for the structure, sustainability and service delivery of resilience across the disaster cycle will only be resolved over time. As the new civil contingencies structure becomes more embedded in everyday government practice then the structural reformations will settle as the workstreams coalesce into more grounded issues. It is also worth noting that in the rush to conform to the statutory obligations of preparedness and response, certain elements of the Capabilities Programme (Chapter 8) were put on the 'back-burner' during the rush to be ready for Local Authority CPA. Amongst the issues that were de-prioritized were the 'warning and informing' stream. There were also new high-priority workstreams that was beginning to come under the remit, at least in part, of the LRF and constituent EPU – most notably, issues linked to anti-radicalization (Prevent) strategies and the need to plan for different faith groups and requirements of improving community cohesion. We shall return to these emerging concerns in Chapter 11.

The focus of different Core-City responses

The UK Core Cities group – comprising the cities of Birmingham, Bristol, Leeds, Liverpool, Manchester, Newcastle, Nottingham and Sheffield – was set up in 1995 as a collective counter-balance to the power of London in economic policy making. In 2002 the Chief emergency planning officer in each of the Core Cities established a Core Cities Emergency Planning Group. The rationale for this mutual working was that many emergency planning-related issues and challenges were similar across all Core Cities. This group, as it has developed, has been successful in sharing good practice in resiliency issues and have developed a strong support network. In addition, the group also uses each other's experiences as a 'benchmarking' exercise to inform their individual practice. Since 2004, annual study meetings have been held, where emergency planners and a host of Category 1 and 2 responders from the Core Cities share experiences and undertake collective training.

Despite the obvious similarities between civil contingency challenges faced, the Core Cities have developed their strategies in different ways.[7] Below is a summary of such activities which occurred in each Core City, followed by a discussion of the similarities and differences in approach.

Birmingham

In 2005 Birmingham was hit by a number of 'disaster events' which tested the teams' ability to respond, including the evacuation of a large portion of the city centre, as well as an unseasonal tornado which caused largely superficial damage but required activation of emergency response mechanisms across the city. A focus on structural reformation in 2005/2006 saw the establishment and expansion of the Emergency Planning Unit (EPU) and Business Continuity Teams (BCT) and the development of a resilience hub for developing expertise and training strategies and administrating the emerging structure and development of social resilience as a key element of practice. Although social resilience was a key priority, it was focussed on easier to reach elements of the voluntary sector and business community rather than developing plans for embedding resilience in local communities. In support of this work, more recently Birmingham City Council has produced a tailored guide for 'Preparing for Emergencies in Birmingham' and an 'In Case of Emergency' wallet which provides advice to the public about storing vital telephone numbers and other information for use in an emergency.[8]

Bristol

The focus of Bristol's resiliency effort was initially on the development of a Bristol Prepared corporate brand for the Civil Contingencies Unit, similar to the corporate strategy of London. Bristol also appointed local 'Contingency Champions' within their structure and set about consultation on the requirements for embedding telecommunications systems that would facilitate response to emergencies. The 'Bristol Prepared' brand was developed through public events with key stakeholders and responders. This also saw the team roll-out consultations on business continuity practices in the city centre and the beginning of co-ordination with crime prevention strategies in the local community. In 2006/2007 more grounded response protocols were established, such as rota's for co-ordination, training with specialist organizations and the beginning of tests on CBRN issues, the establishment of a core emergencies plan as well as specific plans for City Centre Evacuation, a City Flood Response and a Control of Major Accident Hazards (COMAH) plan. The Civil Contingencies Unit (CCU) has also been active in developing multi-agency and sub-regional plans including the Avon Area Joint Media Response Plan, and a CBRN Plan. The CCU is also increasingly developing its programme of exercises in mainly non-terrorist areas.[9]

Leeds

In 2004/2005 Leeds was active in focussing on the statutory conformance and rigorous testing of existing and new emergency plans by the Peace and Emergency Plans Unit and partners. The city has also established an emergency control centre in the city centre, significantly improving the co-ordination capabilities of the previous Cold War apparatus and technology, including computerized Incident Management Systems. There was also a focus on embedding business continuity practices within partner agencies and key responders, as well as highlighting risk assessment, service continuity planning and warning and informing the public as areas in need of further development. In 2006/2007 this was followed up with extensive progress on the established fronts of partnership working, strategic plan development, flood response planning, business continuity planning and response to the emerging threat of pandemic influenza.[10]

Liverpool

In Liverpool during 2004/2005 there was an extensive reorientation and restructuring required in order to make local emergency service systems compatible with the new recommendations and guidelines. The establishment of a full-time Emergency Planning Unit was well connected with Merseyside Local Authorities Contingency Planning Group (MLACPG). In this locale the focus was on the development of the CRR, the establishment of key thematic work groups for risk assessment, and sharing information for raising awareness amongst Category 1 and Category 2 responders. This also included establishing 'service level agreements' between local authorities, fire and defence services and a focus on bringing technology for emergency response up-to-date. Involvement in the *Stratos* local exercises saw the testing of this and other new equipment and protocols in line with CBRN as well as the re-issue of an updated City Centre Evacuation Plan and the rolling-out of a Priority Alert Scheme. In 2006/2007 the focus also shifted towards developing business continuity management (BCM) practice which involved distribution of booklet information to local businesses to develop the awareness of the involvement of city businesses in local resilience.[11]

Manchester

Manchester was another city, like Liverpool, that had a comparatively well-established network of practitioners for civil defence and emergency response activities due to prior experience of disaster events (such as the IRA bombs in the 1990s). This made liaison between the Local Authorities in Greater Manchester relatively unproblematic with regard to collaboration on the collection of the information required for the CRR. Likewise, Manchester has played a leading role on the LRF Mass Planning Steering Group, for co-ordinating strategic policy for response to large-scale events and terrorist attack. This saw regular feedback and collaboration between LRF and RRF level agents and the development of a Local Authority Mass Planning Project in collaboration with the Association of Greater Manchester Authorities (AGMA).

Within Manchester specifically, the EPU has established of a Business Continuity Management programme and the rolling-out of a programme of testing and practice events. This also saw the development of contracts and memoranda of understanding with a number of Category 1 and 2 responders for the supply of key services in the event of a major incident. Equally there has been the development of a comprehensive city centre evacuation plan and the development of a locally specific Preparing for Emergency pack developed for the local population.[12]

Newcastle upon Tyne

Newcastle's Resilience Planning Team collaborates with the county-based EPU, but have focused development work at the Local Authority level. The main focus of this group was to ensure that the city was in line with statutory conformance for the Comprehensive Performance Assessment on local emergency planning arrangements. This included the development of a city-specific branded strategic plan under the banner of 'Resilient Newcastle' which was subsequently used to raise public awareness and form and umbrella over related local emergency planning, business continuity, and exercise and testing practices in the city. Also noted as high priorities were developing a strategic risk register, a policy focus on influenza, a testing agenda for widespread public CBRN exposure, and the importance of maintaining security as a high strategic priority in ensuring the growing reputation of the city as a vibrant regional capital for the attraction of inward investment and 'high-profile events'.

The strategic risk management strategy placed a further emphasis on service continuity planning at a range of levels and the aim of incorporating resilience planning team practice into the mainstream of service planning. The latest priorities include the need to further develop community resilience. Most recently 'Resilient Newcastle' have developed a comprehensive Pandemic Influenza Response Plan, which was validated by an exercise during October 2006, and updated their Notifiable Animal Disease Outbreak Plan to deal with suspected or confirmed cases of avian influenza within Newcastle. There is also a rising concern about flash flooding given recent localized incidents in the summer of 2005. This had not previously been considered a risk, and work is now being undertaken to improve response to such 'unexpected' incidents.[13]

Nottingham

The growth of funding following the CCA in 2004 gave a welcome boost to Nottingham's arrangements for emergency planning and saw, along with many of the other Core Cities, the expansion of their team to a small number of dedicated full-time staff. The launch of a four-year plan for the improvement and restructuring of the emergency planning practice across the Local Authority structure saw the development of an Emergency Accommodation plan, which focussed the step-change towards compliance with CCA regulations. This was rolled out alongside a Nottingham City Centre Emergency Plan, although the partnership agencies noted the vital need to involve the local community in the process. As a result, the distribution of information regarding the plans, advice on response practice, safeguarding people and property before, during and after an incident are increasingly shared across the local community, and supported by visible exercising of strategic plans for response to events.

In the light of the 2005 London bombings, in 2006 this emphasis shifted towards Humanitarian Assistance Centres and the strategic development of an Emergency Accommodation Plan. In particular, the rolling-out of further training events and sharing of best practice amongst the local agencies were developed further and broader advice on business continuity was pushed from the consultation phase to the development and distribution of promotional and advice materials. This included plans for public events the following year – including the distribution of school education packs and radio exposure. The establishment of an Emergency Control Centre in the immediate region also gave a hard site for the co-ordination of civil contingencies-related events and incidents. The Emergency Planning team has also initiated a series of 'exercises' to train City Council staff to respond to an emergency, and to test plans both internally and in conjunction with other agencies.[14]

Sheffield

In 2004/2005 the focus on Sheffield was on a balance between conformance and promotion of the city; linking the internal restructuring of the council to the regeneration of the city as a whole. Tied to the broader multi-agency planning approach, the Local Authority focussed on developing strong links between the local Police and emergency services and the city council, and the rolling-out of technological developments such as the SMS message public subscription-based system – for information provisionally about traffic management, but also emergencies. There was also a strong focus on co-ordination of response practice which saw participation in a number of multi-agency exercises for CBRN, communications and table-top exercises for events management risks, as well as business continuity events with a number of South Yorkshire organizations. The emphasis here was twofold, one part on the civil contingencies framework and the other on economic concerns for the broader city. Most recently focus has been placed upon flood prevention and preparing for unexpected scenarios given events in June 2007 when Sheffield experienced its worst flooding for over 140 years, the response to which, at the time of writing, is still ongoing.[15]

Different challenges, different threats

The different local Core City teams have rolled out their response in different ways using variable levels of funding and most importantly different strategic emphases, based on civic requirements and upon the varying levels of expertise embedded in previous experience of disaster events or incidents. For example, in Newcastle, before the requirements of the CCA, there was a fragmented emergency planning operation which was only exposed during a simulated counter-terrorist exercise – *Operation Magpie* – which took place in the city in 2004 to test response to a CBRN attack. This was the first such simulated counter-terrorist exercise carried out in the United Kingdom outside of London and involved a variety of local and regional responders, including the Emergency planners at Newcastle City Council. From this test it was clear that the multi-agency response and individual responder capability, including that of the City Council could, and should, be drastically improved.

There are widespread variations in the speed, format and prioritization of capabilities across the Core Cities, idiosyncratic to the particular institutional contexts One issue that has been perpetually raised is a concern that emergency planning, despite being encouraged to develop collaborative relationships with other responders and agencies, and with the private sector and general public, are being driven back into silo thinking by pressures to conform to the CAA and associated performance assessment. That said, over time it is clear that good practice in emergency preparedness is being mainstreamed throughout local authorities as a whole, boosted by the increased profile and staffing of emergency planning. Here institutional cultural change is occurring slowing, but surely, and resilience is becoming embedded with the corporate 'way of working'. In many ways we might characterize how emergency planning is being developed as a cross-cutting corporate priority, which is formally assessed and which his making strategic linkages to an array of external stakeholders (responders) as emblematic of broader shifts in local government modernization.

Common to all of the Core Cities areas in 2004 and 2005 was an awareness of CBRN testing as a key area of conformance. Following the July 7 bombings there also saw a two-tiered refocusing of workstreams ex post facto. This entailed, in practical response and recovery on the ground, an increase in the emphasis on communications between agencies – compatibility of radio's, synchronized command and control structures and so on. However, there was an awareness amongst practitioners that developing 'warning and informing' strategies was a more complex issue than simply hypodermically injecting the public with knowledge on risks, hazards and threats, such as stockpiling bottled water, blankets and preserved food (as seen with the Home Offices Preparing for Emergencies publication in 2004). Local warning and informing, it was commonly argued, could also be expanded to include community resilience strategies that move beyond the communication of risk to interventions in radicalization and social cohesion issues, also part of the Government's Counter-terrorism strategy (Chapter 10).

As indicated by the Core City snapshots, different practical approaches to certain elements were adopted in some cities, such as the public information and media events in Nottingham, whereas other cities focussed on prevention and response, such as the Mancunian comprehensive testing arrangements, strategic documentation development and ensuring collaborative arrangements between key stakeholders were in place. In contrast, others limited their activities to the bare minimum of conformance to the CCA and CPA, or forged objective links between wider regeneration and marketing initiative in the embedding of resilience in governance, for example Newcastle and Bristol's branded approaches to resilience policy and Sheffield's thematic links to regeneration and urban renewal agendas. There were also some cities where there was an additional focus upon city-regional work, such as in Manchester and Liverpool, where pre-existing groupings were used to develop strategic response scenarios at larger geographical scales.

There are also topical drivers to the focus of policy as well that bring national pressures to the workstreams of the Core Cities. The rise, worldwide, of concern associated with the potential viral pandemics (stimulated first by SARS, then avian flu) saw a host of national, regional and local plans hastily developed, creating tensions in the communication between tiers and the responsibility of tasking diverse agencies with a range of locally specific modes of practice; for example, would the Police protect the vaccines, would the NHS staff or fire and civil service be tasked with organizing control centres and so on. More generally the nature and scale of planning for pandemics have to be treated very differently from natural disaster events.

In large part, security against counter-terrorism is not normally a prioritized issue in the Core Cities. That said, where security in particular remains a central focus of the everyday operation of local authorities in concert with emergency services is in the management of high-profile sporting, cultural and political events in order to ensure preparedness for any emergencies that might occur. It is to this notion of resiliency and event planning that we now turn.

Securing the resilient event

The impact of resilience planning is often subtle and goes unnoticed by many as so much of the local endeavour is grounded in process management and plan preparation. However, resilience planning becomes very visible when high-profile events are hosted, requiring intense security operations (Coaffee and Murakami Wood, 2006). This is also where the merging of civil contingencies and counter-terrorist policy also becomes noticeable, and an integration of fortification, surveillance and emergency management techniques is highly advanced.

In this sense, the development of a 'resilient city' often has a temporal dimension – the construction of short-term 'resilient sites' for the hosting of events – which seek to pump-prime the local economy and stimulate further inward investment. Importantly the temporary retrofitting of such security 'stage sets' provides a resolute test of the emerging resilience governance infrastructure, especially joined-up government and cross-agency working.

In the United Kingdom in recent years the ruling Labour Party's annual political conferences have become large-scale security events, which require careful resilience management. The conference location has been highly changeable as a variety of cities have actively competed to host the event, seeing it as a perfect opportunity to boost their local economy and raise their national, or global, profile for 'meetings tourism'. Inevitably, such events have high security risks. In the following section, we explore the linkages between such events and resiliency issues through case studies in both Newcastle/Gateshead (2005) and Manchester (2006) which demonstrated in practice the operation of resilience governance arrangements, but also the broader implications of resilience policy for the general public.

The Gateshead 'lockdown'

In February 2005 the Labour Party's annual spring conference took place at venues on the Gateshead riverside (North East England) overlooking Newcastle quayside. The conference was located in the new Sage Music Centre, built with £70m of Arts Council Lottery money. Many of the delegates at the conference were located in the nearby Hilton Hotel, another of the regeneration initiatives occurring along the Gateshead side of the River Tyne. Along with the Baltic Arts 'Factory' and the award-winning Gateshead Millennium pedestrian bridge these buildings form integral pieces of a wider regeneration master plan.

The event itself required a security 'lockdown' of most of this public regeneration zone for the protection of the delegates (a large number of whom were members of the incumbent Government) against the risk of terrorism, as well as shielding them from the high numbers of anti-war (and other) protesters who were expected to descend upon the city.

As such a comprehensive security strategy for the event was pre-planned from six months in advance and led by a special team from the local Police who took primary authority for the design of security strategy, despite having little in-house experience of managing this type of event. This also involved liaison with local and regional resilience teams and the security services. Initial preparations were focussed on detailed data-gathering and surveillance operations that saw the vetting of those employed by local businesses (and their vehicles), establishing a strategy for 'securing' the perimeter of the area to be used by delegates, and plans for the diversion and control of traffic from the area for the duration of the event. The conference venue itself was closed to the public one week in advance of the conference to allow thorough internal and external searches of the site and surrounds by the Police and national security agencies.

In the days immediately before the event random armed police roadchecks were also carried out on major roads around the conference site, and in the areas close to the proposed police cordon, using powers from

Section 44 of the 2000 Terrorism Act. A public information campaign rolled out in local media also requested that the general vigilance from the wider public, and recommended the reporting of any suspicious people or vehicles. The stated aim of the police was to balance the aims of security with the needs of local businesses and residents.

As the conference drew near, a 'ring of steel' security cordon was thrown around the conference venues, being put in place only the day before the arrival of the delegates to minimize disruption to the local community – particularly as the Hilton Hotel and Sage Music Centre (as the main conference venue) sat either side of one of the major transit arteries into the city centre. The roads surrounding the site were closed or had restricted access arrangements and a flight exclusion zone was put in place over the immediate area. This geographical extent of the 'locking down' of this large public funded regeneration area is shown in Plate 10.1.

During the conference itself, security became even more overt, with snipers on higher buildings, Police on jet skis on the River Tyne, and mobile CCTV units and Police vehicles lining the length of the road around the conference venue (Plate 10.2). River searches and boat patrols also regularly took place.

During the conference, a large visible police presence was felt throughout the city with up to 1000 officers on duty at any one time, including specialized personnel. Many of the expected protests took place; however, these were largely contained by both legal and territorial measures on a small stretch of the Newcastle Quayside on the northern bank of the Tyne.[16]

The high levels of 'lockdown' security were seen as an essential part of the resiliency operation, and were put in place to ensure no major breaches of security occurred and that delegates and conference organizers felt safe (and would recommend the return of the conference at a future date).

The impacts of the conference in economic terms are hard to quantify with any accuracy. Security costs for the event were estimated to be around £3m, but conveniently the expected 'economic boom' as a result was also estimated to be the same amount. From questioning traders in the immediate vicinity of the conference, it became apparent that the benefits were far from evenly spread, with claimed loss of trade for some local businesses, but with hotels in particular benefiting from advance bookings. The costs of the inconvenience and temporary loss of civil liberties and freedom of movement are also hard to factor in, but for some businesses it was clear that

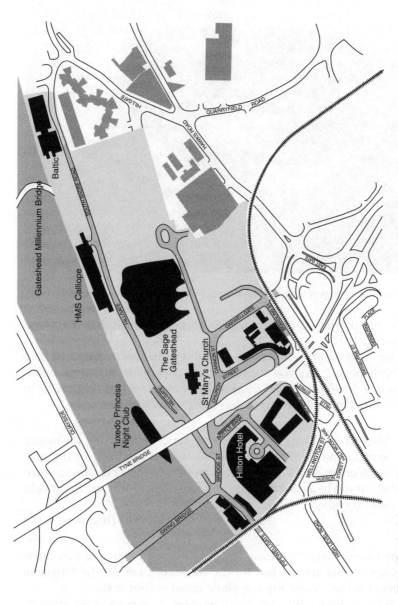

Plate 10.1 The 'lockdown' Zone

Plate 10.2   A highly visible police presence alongside conference venue

the inconvenience outweighed any benefits (Murakami Wood and Coaffee, 2007).

For Gateshead, one benefit touted by the Local Authority and Northumbria Police was the retrofitting of permanent security infrastructure (especially CCTV) linked to crime reduction and safety in Gateshead in the longer term. According to the Police:

> Many of the things seen over the weekend are not where the money went in the security operation. Around £1.5 million of the total was spent on CCTV, radio communications and technical equipment which will be available for use in future major events and in the fight against crime.
>
> (cited in Thompson, 2005)

The Labour Party Chairman, Ian McCartney, also stressed that 'these improvements are not just for the conference but for the long-term benefit of the community as a whole' (cited in Ford, 2005).

We can also see this conference in the wider picture of the attempts by the city and its immediate region to attract further conferences. Such trade was estimated to be worth £72m per annum to the regional economy. Despite the projected economic benefits, we have to question the links between the rolling-out of anti-terror polices like stop and search, automated surveillance, the use of anti-terrorism 'stage-set' security measures in these provincial and largely unthreatened cities, especially when such measures impact so intensely on the ability of ordinary people to use the spaces paid for from the public purse, and which are overtly part of economic development and urban renaissance initiatives aimed at improving their lives (Murakami Wood and Coaffee, 2007).

The Mancunian security island

In Manchester the resiliency issues related to hosting such events are very similar to the Gateshead example, though the location of the event was significantly different. The context of preparations also differed, particularly in terms of experience, as Manchester had previously hosted major party political events, as well as the Commonwealth Games in 2002. As such, the resilience operation was 'tried and tested'. For example, for these previous events significant pre-preparation work was conducted including an extensive search of the city where 'every inch of the city, from its sewers to its waterways, streets, alleys and public buildings, [was] scoured for any sign of weapons, explosives or any other potential threat' (BBC News, 2002). These events had also helped with developing as high degree of embedded co-operation amongst those charged with ensuring resiliency.

The Labour Party Autumn conference in 2006 in Manchester was on a much larger scale than the spring affair in Gateshead, and was based at the publically regenerated G-MEX centre in the heart of the city. The event was significantly of a higher profile than at Gateshead, given not only tensions over a range of proposed national security powers linked to extended detentions for suspected terrorists, but also because it was occurring in the aftermath of the July 2005 bombings in London. The threat level in both the public eye and from the perspective of the security forces had increased.

The G-MEX as a location was, in principle, a more complicated security operation than in Gateshead. First the site was surrounded by alleyways and connections into a shopping complex and leisure facilities and integrated into the heart of Manchester city centre. Equally, the London bombings had highlighted the difficulties of securing public transport networks and the G-MEX both sat next to a series of transport interchanges and is bisected by a light-rail system. It was also decided to secure both the conference venue itself and the hotels (and surrounding streets) in which delegates would be staying through a series of no-go police controlled areas creating a series of 'sterile' or 'dead' spaces in the heart of the city for the duration of the conference (Plates 10.3 and 10.4)

As well as constructing what police referred to as 'island security' around the conference site, procedures to deal with evacuation, contamination and decontamination sites and major incident access were considered and role-played on table-top exercise by resiliency responders so that decision-making could be analysed and any weakness and vulnerabilities could be planned-out in advance. Technical information was also scrutinized for all buildings, regarding, for example, structure and supply points for utility provision, fire exits and air conditioning systems. This utilized state-of-the-art 3D graphics packages.

Manchester's previous experiences of securing the city and its response to the IRA bombs in Manchester (most notably in 1996) led to a relatively smooth development of the resilience and counter-terror planning process and at the local level for this event. The security operation (code-named Operation Protector) was led by Greater Manchester Police in tandem with national security services with the assistance of local and regional resilience responders.[17]

Plate 10.3   No-go areas around the conference venues

Plate 10.4 No-go areas around the conference venues

Given the ease of access to the area and the high likelihood of political demonstrations, a co-ordinated policing strategy was developed. Twenty-four hour helicopter surveillance was supported by armed police units on rooftops and street level during the conference itself. A similar level of preparation went into the conference management with co-ordination between the local police and military organizations, and the provision made for 'airport-style' scanning of all delegates, as well as vehicles, general produce and post heading into the secured event area.

As in Gateshead a large number of protesters were found throughout the city centre on the days of the conference, though in this case the police took a much more interventionist approach setting specific march routes and controlling the flow of protesters around the secured cordon, policing the protest using similar tactics to larger police actions during the Iraq anti-war protests in London in 2003.

Again the economic impact of hosting the conference for the city is difficult to quantify in real terms. Whilst the Labour Party Spring conference held in Manchester in 2004 entailed security costs of around £1m, the larger autumn conference cost over £4m for security alone. As with in the case in Gateshead a number of the technological aspects (such as

CCTV) were incorporated in to the wider city security infrastructure ex post facto.

Overall, despite significant restrictions on public movement and the lockdown of many public spaces, the event was seen in marketing terms as 'another great opportunity to raise the profile of the area, while at the same time stimulating growth in the local economy' (MEN, 2006c). Post-conference it was estimated that the conference brought an extra 17,000 visitors to the city and has boosted the local economy by an initial £15m with the potential of a regional gain of £100m per year. This represented a 30% increase in business tourism if high-profile conferencing becomes a regular part of the urban scene (MEN, 2006d). In December 2006 it was announced that the Labour party will return to Manchester in 2008 and 2010, as a result of the high quality facilities in the conference quarter and perhaps most importantly, the sophisticated security operation that provided an unprecedented feeling of safety for delegates and which is now an almost compulsory element of such event planning (Coaffee and Rogers, 2008).

The combination of these elements of place-marketing, security and resilience in this context come together to form a strategy of regenerative resilience alongside the civil contingencies framework for preparation, prevention, response and recovery that uses 'secure' event management as a launch-pad for economic place-marketing. The aim is as such reputational enhancement through implicit concept management – not explicitly mentioning risk – which fosters an awareness of resilience and competence underpinning the national, or global, profile for investment and 'meetings tourism'.

Although the preceding examples have focused upon the rolling-out of temporary security and resilience for high-profile conferences, we wish to argue here that both the security design and management techniques used, and the intended and unintended impacts, are applicable to the majority of major events. These key elements of 'resilience' planning for events are sixfold:

1. *Intense pre-planning.* Such operations were many months in the planning, involving the development of control zones around the site, procedures to deal with evacuation, contamination and decontamination, major incident access, which were considered and role-played on table-top exercise. Technical information was also scrutinized for all spaces and structures regarding supply points for utility provision, fire exits, air conditioning systems and so on, so that any weakness and vulnerabilities could be planned-out in advance.

2. *The development of 'island security'.* This involved the 'locking down' of strategic areas of cities often with large expanses of steel fencing and concrete blocks surrounding the conference venue. This combined with a high visibility police presence, backed up by private security, the security services and a vast array of permanent and temporary CCTV cameras and airport-style checkpoints to screen delegates. Often such events are also used for trialling 'new' technologies (see Chapter 11).

3. *The setting up of peripheral buffer zones.* Several days before the conferences began the police set up 'buffer zones' in the areas immediately outside the 'island sites' containing a significant visible police presence including police helicopters and fleets of mobile CCTV vans with automatic number plate recording capabilities. Random Police road-checks and stop and search procedures were also widespread both before and during the security operation.

4. *Rebordering the public city.* The Police's stated aim is always to keep disruption to the general population to a minimum whilst ensuring security is robust and visible although in such instances 'rings of security' become 'rings of exclusion' for the general public, often using anti-terror legal measures and often in areas that have undergone publically funded renewal. Restrictions involve not only the immediate conference site but also limitations on road access, the use of public footpaths and vehicle parking. Equally much of the information regarding the security operation is not made publicly available until immediately before the event because of 'security concerns'.

5. *Resilience as a future selling point.* High-profile events bring many thousands of extra visitors to the host city and provide a massive boost to local and regional economies. Sophisticated security operations that provide an unprecedented feeling of safety for spectators or delegates is now an almost compulsory element of such event planning, and as such, the ability to host such a conference in a safe and secure fashion is of significant importance in attracting future conferences and in branding a city as a major events venue. There is now a clear and emerging link between city growth strategies and security planning, with security often seen as a vital selling point for urban competitiveness.

6. *Retrofitting of permanent infrastructure.* One lasting benefit of such events includes the retrofitting of permanent security infrastructure linked to a longer-term crime reduction strategy (see Chapter 11).

Towards local resilience

In this chapter we have focused upon the operation of the local tier of resilience, and unpacked how it operates and how, in particular situations, the vast amount of civil contingencies work that has been undertaken in the localities and sub-regions is 'exercised' through emergency testing and during high-profile events. We have also argued that, just as with the regional tier, there is no 'one size fits all model' of local working, and locally contingent and pragmatic approaches have been adopted, to take account of differences in risk prioritization, staffing, funding, experience and expertise, as well as the institutional context of local agencies and the relationships they have with each other. Here it has often been left up to local EPUs to interpret CCA guidance and then develop, and test, their own emergency procedures in order to demonstrate conformance. As such, the development of resilience has been an ongoing negotiation between those involved in managing risks for the best way of ensuring the process as well as resources, infrastructure and citizenry are as resilient as possible.

It would be fair to say, especially with regard to the Core Cities, that there has been a broad strategy employed during the first years of the implementation and conformance to statutory obligations embedded in the CCA, that has drawn much from the regional and national guidance. Here the focus of work, given the pressures of performance assessment, was upon getting the structures in place and developing a set of generic emergency plans for city-centre evacuation, mass fatalities, emergency and humanitarian assistance centres and so on. Inevitably, this has meant that certain obligations have taken a back seat, particularly those associated with participation of the public in community resilience, public information dissemination and the potential for public resilience training sessions in schools and communities.

The story so far in Chapters 6 and 7 has focussed on the concept and strategic development of an agenda for resilience. Chapters 8, 9 and 10 have then grounded this into the practical structures of governance and key actions in particular urban areas to show that there has been widespread change in the management of risks, hazards and threats as a result. The discussion has foregrounded the nature and extent of the roll-out of resilience policy – from national to regional to local levels – and it is clear that the changes to the focus, practice and structure of governance brought in by resilience are wide ranging, and as such will have wide-ranging implication for urban populations. In the next chapter we synthesize this information in a discussion of the 'everyday' resilience of the city as responsibility for the implementation and practice of resilience been increasingly diffused amongst different stakeholders and agencies highlighting different strategies of governmentality.

11
Urban Resilience and Everyday Life

In the last chapter we highlighted the array of reform activities occurring in the provincial Core Cities to modernize resilience governance, encompassing different expertise and harnessing a range of approaches to contingency, threat, hazard and risk by multiple agencies and stakeholders. Much of this discussion has focused on multi-tier governance and multi-partnership working, illustrating the institutional perceptions of such methods as pre-requisites for developing practicable resilience.

In this chapter we wish to focus upon the impact and implications of resilience in situ, unpacking further the impact of the 'security' emphasis underpinning policy rhetoric on the everyday city. We use the term 'everyday' rather in the way that Alan Hunt (2003) does, in order to avoid any unnecessary distinctions between macro- and micro-levels in considering urban risks and urban life, and how these everyday risks impact upon individual and collective decision-making. As we noted in the first chapter, we draw in particular on the theory of governmentality in which government is considered as 'the conduct of conduct' (Foucault, 1991).

This chapter therefore has two main parts. The first part will focus on the city scale and unpack the spatial practices of urban resilience from the formal governance end of the spectrum. Here we will argue that what is occurring is an interlinked combination of militarization, modernization (or industrialization) and managerialization. Military understandings of space through fortification and division are combined with modern industrial techniques of surveillance and neoliberal private managerial forms of government. This shift in emphasis allows us to understand the process of embedding best practice in resilient governance alongside the spatial impact of change on the fabric of the city itself, with implications for the way in which the citizenry are able to enter, pass through, leave and 'use' the city as a series of alternately interconnected, fractured and blurred public and private spaces (see Graham and Marvin, 2001). However, we emphasize too the often temporally specific nature of these trajectories through the way they are often centred around 'island security' and staged events that we discussed in Chapter 10. Here we tie this into the wider impact of security on the city before and after the event, and the redefinitions of urban spaces through expert security rhetoric and practice.

The shift in emphasis also alludes to the broader implications for the participation and responsibility of the citizen as an actor in embedding resilience into everyday life. The second part of the chapter will draw further on a different aspect of the way Foucauldian governmentality theory has been developed, particularly through the work of Rose (2000) and Hunt (2003) to concentrate on the twin notions of 'responsibilization' and 'deresponsibilization'. We will demonstrate the ways *everyone* is now intended to be involved in either the performance of resilience as an agent of surveillance or counter-terrorism or alternatively in the performance of vulnerability, as a victim of actions from the most horrific (for example, terrorism) to the most mundane or simply irritating (for example, anti-social behaviour). In this section, we will highlight the ways in which the rhetoric of counter-terrorism has been put into practice at the local, community and individual levels.

These trajectories clearly have broader implications for democratic governance of urban spaces and society in relation to other public uses of the city, such as political protest, as well as the governance of security and hazards in future. We shall return to these implications in Chapter 12.

Militarism, modernism, managerialism

Resilience and militarization

Since the events on September 11, and indeed before this event (Coaffee, 2000; Pawley, 1998), many commentators have argued that the way in which authorities responded to the current 'war on terrorism' would have serious consequences for urban living (Coaffee, 2003; Swanstrom, 2002). In the last 20 years, a vast literature has developed around the concept of 'militarizing' or 'securitizing' cities and in particular the policy responses to the occurrence of crime, fear of crime (see, for example, Crawford, 2002; Nunn, 2001; Williams and Johnstone, 2000) and the evaluation of cities as strategic sites for a spectrum of large-scale increasingly destructive interventions from protest and riot to terrorism and war (see, for example, Ashworth, 1991; Cutter *et al.*, 2003; Schneider and Susser, 2003).

The work of the RAND Corporation in the United States has also been crucial in setting the terms of military strategic thinking in this area as part of the so-called Revolution in Military Affairs (RMA), a vast literature in itself (Glenn, 1996), but which has facilitated the merging of military and civilian security agendas. As Bishop and Phillips (2002, p. 94) have argued:

> The military use has merged fully and completely with civil defence, protecting the populace from disasters... Emergency – being on alert, preparedness – has been our steady state for some half a century now; only now, we have more of it and the stakes get even higher.

These bodies of literature have developed alongside an ever-expanding interest in the vulnerability and resilience of cities against natural disasters (which is generally held to include human-induced risk from such events) (Kreimer and Arnold, 2003; Mitchell, 1999; Pelling, 2003).

Lately the three streams of discourse have begun to hybridize through consideration of the ability of cities to continue to thrive against an ever-present threat of terrorism and disorder by building in resilient features to policy processes and practice (Coaffee, 2004; Harrigan and Martin, 2002). Resilience in this sense has physical, economic and social foci – for example, through the development of 'landscapes of defence' (Gold and Revill, 2000), the provision of adequate insurance facilities (Mills, 2002), the development of civic and institutional frameworks to deal with risk management (Beck, 2002) and even individualized responses (Safir and Whitman, 2003).

Resilience is not a new type of policy response but rather, it has been argued, events such as September 11 and the attacks in London, Madrid and elsewhere, allow a surge in the introduction of control technologies, when they are easier to adopt (politically) in the civic realm and particularly at an *urban* level. This is particularly important given the relationships between cities, wars and violent acts of terrorism. Graham (2004, p. 6) for example suggests that 'the world's geo-political struggles increasingly articulate around violent conflicts over very local, urban, strategic sites'. In such a context, the ability of policy-makers to analyse the city through a 'military gaze' has given new insights to the risks cities face from new security challenges, and in particular, how they can protect the networks and information systems of critical urban infrastructures, long seen as vulnerable.

The military gaze, or what we saw Mumford calling the pathology of the city in Chapter 2, can be seen through the return of physical and symbolic forms of boundary and territorial closure, in the superficial image-saturated world of late capitalism. These include defended civic buildings, residential gated communities and major financial districts into which access is conditioned or restricted, as well much larger lines of fortification like those along the US–Mexico border or the Israel–Palestine 'security fence' (Chapter 6).

Resilience and (reflexive) modernity

So what did change? September 11 highlighted the growing awareness that established traditional approaches to disaster management, and in particular security, were inadequate for the contemporary state of risks. In the global risk society (Beck, 1992; 2002), modernity has become increasingly *anticipatory*. Security policy began to shift to proactive and pre-emptive (resilience) solutions at a number of sub-national spatial scales.

In practice, this has forced a rethinking of traditional emergency planning and counter-terrorist agendas, given the increased magnitude of the threats faced, especially those from CBRN sources. In response, new counter-measures have been required, focusing on worst-case scenarios – the *inevitable* attack – representing a shift in emphasis from previous emergency planning and security philosophies which emphasized stopping the threat at source.

That having been said, the resultant policy responses have often amounted to little more than extrapolations of ongoing trends for countering the occurrence events and perception of risk associated with crime and terrorism. The stimulus of September 11 did not necessarily serve to create new urban responses but to reinforce pre-existing trends in and across the field of relevant actors who were, and are, tasked with reacting to new forms of terrorist risk (Chernick, 2005). A renewed focus on fortification has been one of these responses from the military perspective, but in the particular context of the form of modernity and modernization of the city, one can see intensified surveillance as the predominant trajectory, and in particular the movement to increasingly automated software-driven systems (Graham and Wood, 2003; Graham, 2005; Lyon, 2003a). September 11 has undoubtedly proved a catalytic event for the mass introduction of hi-tech surveillance systems – a 'surveillance surge' with the intensification and expansion of existing systems and the adoption of ever more refined technologies initially developed for military purposes (Wood *et al.*, 2003).

This latest wave of technology for crime reduction and anti-terrorism highlights the interconnections of the military and modernity that continue to be as pervasive as when Eisenhower referred to the military-industrial complex in 1961 and, as we saw in Chapter 4, already for a long time before this. The rolling-out of surveillance cameras developed with Automatic Number Plate Recognition (ANPR) technology for use in counter-terrorism are now commonly seen deployed for motorway traffic control and increasingly in civic CCTV systems, and now even supermarket car parks and petrol stations (see Plate 11.1). Such systems are increasingly biometrically embedded despite the technological limitations of biometric recognition (Introna and Wood, 2004), extending so far as proposals by the New York Police Department to blanket Manhattan with cameras that will automatically swivel at the sound of a gunshot. Such 'blue-light' cameras have also been deployed in several notorious housing estates in major US cities such as Cabrini-Green in north Chicago. Likewise, at the time of writing, the suggestion that terahertz wave (T-wave) imaging techniques, a form of 'virtual strip search', could also be employed in conjunction with CCTV (Leake, 2008; Leppard, 2006) and fMRI ('brain scanning').

The introduction of such technologies is testimony to the way in which surveillance is increasingly bound up with the notion of ensuring everyday urban resilience (Coaffee and Murakami Wood, 2006). However, it is also evidence of the continuing industrialization of the social, a cycle of observation, categorization and enforcement that has always been one of the pillars of modernity (Giddens, 1985), but now without the moral project of the enlightenment (Deleuze, 1992), where the social itself is stripped out of the business of government (Rose, 1996), which tends merely towards an institutional concern with orderly flows of goods and information (Lianos, 2001).

Resilience and neoliberal managerialism

This concern with orderly flows, combined of course with the traditional 'culture of secrecy' in Britain (Ponting, 1990), means that there appears to be an acceptance that ordinary citizens should be entirely excluded from the decision-making processes regarding this new securitization of the city. The construction of a resilient urban environment, and the reduction of risk from a wide and unpredictable variety of threats, is seen

Plate 11.1 ANPR cameras at the entrance to a supermarket car park in Salford, Greater Manchester, installed in early 2008

to require an adaptable and holistic security effort that encompasses both fortification and surveillance solutions, as well as reformed governance and management arrangements. This, as Wood *et al.* (2003, p. 144) note, is part of the ever-growing 'cross-fertilization' between the military and the managerial in the governance of urban areas.

These introverted forms of government have succeeded in assisting the 'rebordering' of the city in response to safety and security concerns and predominantly in line with the preferences of city managers and security agencies (Coaffee and Rogers, 2008). In this respect, 'the public' are chiefly deresponsibilized passive recipients within an increasingly controlled and regulated urban society where the knowledge of professionals and experts appears to be overly privileged (Rose, 1993, 2000). This approach is exemplified by Little (2004, p. 57), who notes in relation to the terrorist threat that:

> Threats are unpredictable and the full range of threats probably unknowable... Security in this situation needs to be flexible and agile and capable of addressing new threats as they emerge. Protective technologies have a key role to play in making our cities safer *but only* if supported by organizations and people who can develop pre-attack security strategies, manage the response to an attack, and hasten recovery from it.

Importance here is placed here on a networked managerial form of government based on a business model, and using the language of commercial organizations. The network should be extended therefore not to the demos, but to selected 'stakeholders':

> Developing a successful strategy for urban security requires that these interactions be understood and enabled *by all involved stakeholders*. Security will be neither holistic nor effective if it is restricted to narrow professional or disciplinary stovepipes or if interactions among government officials, security professionals, program and financial staff, and emergency responders occurs only on a product-by-product basis. (ibid., emphasis added)

The impact of this economically focused neoliberal solution to the problems of Government can be seen at many scales. In particular we see the increasing sophistication and cost of security and contingency planning undertaken by organizations and different levels of government, intended to decrease their vulnerability to attack and increase preparedness and 'bouncebackability' in the event of attack. Most institutions are reviewing and re-evaluating individual risk assessments in order to become more resilient and create more effective emergency planning, including locally and regionally focused strategic resilience partnerships, and the adoption of military threat-response tactics and technologies. Full-scale testing and post-evaluation of disaster plans are also now increasingly common. Here importance is placed upon risk assessment through 'horizon scanning' and the detection and response to emergent threats and disaster events, in a way that assures stakeholders or investors that all is 'under control' and that the company has the ability to recover from such disruptions.

This links the achievement of resilience and new security strategies to competition for footloose global capital. Many cities are now overtly linking security to sustainable development or urban regeneration, in terms of both the micro-management of new 'cultural quarters' and gentrification. This is also part of a wider trend towards the privatization of public spaces and the retreat of the state from government in favour of more economically oriented public–private governance arrangements, which include Town Centre Management (TCM), Business Improvements Districts (BIDs) (Rogers and Coaffee, 2005) and the creation of themed urban quarters (Sorkin, 1992; Zukin, 1995) and nostalgic 'retroscapes' (Brown and Sherry, 2005).

Increasingly, such homogenized micro-managed cities are also macro-managed by urban image-making linked to 'city marketing' initiatives, which increasingly play on the importance of the 'safety' of cities as places of business, utilizing security as a vital selling point in their global city 'offer'. The broader place-marketing and place-branding literature is also beginning to focus upon how strategies might be developed to counter unfavourable images associated with such crisis events and to market places perceived to be in crisis (Avraham, 2004; Avraham and Ketter, 2008; Glaesser, 2006).

Strongly embedded resilience will therefore increase the positive reputation of the locale whilst an external perception of an inability to respond (as so aptly demonstrated by the slow reaction to Hurricane Katrina in New Orleans) can significantly damage a city's reputation. Resilience, safety and security and the development of enhanced 'reputational risk' (Coaffee and Rogers, 2008) have thus become an increasingly important tool in the armoury of reputation managers and place promoters as security, economic development and regeneration, marketing and sustainability have become intertwined.

Stage-set security and the event

The previous section has looked at the spatial dimensions of urban planning and resilience management as they have evolved in recent years. We have also made an argument in Chapter 10 that such resilience has a significant *temporal* dimension related to the hosting of high-profile events and developed a series of characteristics of such event planning specifically in relation to UK experiences. We now wish to return to this discussion through a discussion of what we term *stage-set security*

(Murakami Wood and Coaffee, 2006) and to draw out the wider lessons for cities.

The hosting of high-profile events is once again connected to the neoliberal governmental agenda. It is a direct response to the pressure for cities to be competitive in a globalizing world economy. Because of the importance of such events and the intense levels of media coverage, there is a significant perceived threat to them and they have thus become increasingly influential in urban security policy and resilience. The reputationally driven neoliberal urban redevelopment agenda relies heavily on attracting such 'meetings tourism' as both evidence and product of regional, national or global urban economic status. The hybridizing of those trajectories heralds an era of a renewed pragmatic and open control of the city by an emerging 'transnational ruling class' (van der Pijl, 1998) or 'kinetic elites' (Sloterdijk, quoted in Koolhaas and Whiting, 1999), who whilst participating little in the slow, difficult and more dangerous lives of ordinary people are able to move rapidly between and through urban spaces with little risk to themselves (Murakami Wood and Graham, 2006). However, such controls, like the regeneration strategies they seek to protect, are in many ways superficial and image-centred, or what Williams (2004, p. 229) calls, the city 'not so much materialized, as staged', undermining many of the claims to resilience.

One of the issues is that, like the 'travelling circuses' they seek to protect, spatio-temporarily limited security operations – referred to as 'island sites' in the police lexicon – have become a standardized procedure where the security infrastructure is merely assembled at a given location, and then dismantled, moved on and reassembled at the next chosen site. The temporary retrofitting of such security 'stage sets' frequently provides a resolute test of the emerging resilience governance infrastructure, and in particular the extent of joined-up government and cross-agency working (Chapter 10).

However, there is a second issue; increasingly the event often leaves a permanent legacy of fixed security infrastructure or at the very least rhetoric around extension of the existing infrastructure that was supposedly shown up as inadequate by the travelling security show. Many examples of the extension of supposedly temporary resilience operations can be documented. The Olympic Games, a top-level marker of global city status, are perhaps the pre-eminent example. Before and during the staging of the 2004 Summer Olympic Games, and in the midst of the 'war on terror', Athens deployed over 70,000 specially trained police and soldiers as well as another 35,000 military personnel to patrol the streets. Military hardware utilized included a network of 13,000 surveillance cameras, mobile surveillance vans, chemical detectors, a number of Patriot anti-aircraft missile sites, NATO troops specializing in weapons of mass destruction, AWAC early warning surveillance planes, police helicopters, fighter jets, minesweepers and monitoring airships (Coaffee and Murakami Wood, 2006; Samatas, 2004).

The Olympics forced the Greek authorities to speed up the modernization of its state security system, with Athens for the duration of the games becoming a 'panoptic fortress' to give assurances to the rest of the world that the city was safe and secure to host the world's greatest sporting spectacle (Samatas, 2004, p. 115). However, the retrofitting of such security systems was envisioned as a long-term project which was to be maintained *after* the Olympics and which critics have argued will become a menace to privacy and civil liberties:

> With the pretext of security for the Olympics, since July 1 2004 more than 1500 CCTV cameras have been in operation across the country. The permit that was at first issued for their operation by the Data Protection Authority expired on the 4th of October of 2004. However after they were outrageously renamed 'traffic control cameras', their permit was extended until the 24th of May, 2005. The evident contravention of their use on an every-day level, social control, repressive attacks aiming to the criminalization of social resistance now comprise elements integrated into everyday life. The cameras moved out of the Olympic venues and into the streets – and they're watching us....
>
> (Athens Indymedia, 2005)

Kiyoshi Abe (2004) has also uncovered a similar link between securitization and the football World Cup in Japan and South Korea in 2002[1] and Klauser (2007) has also noted such developments with regard to the football World Cup in Germany in 2006.

It is not just CCTV that ends up becoming permanent fixtures in the city after temporary events that require high levels of temporary security. In Sydney, Australia, the hosting of the Asia Pacific Economic Co-operation (APEC) summit led to large-scale concrete and steel fences being built across the city centre of with over 5000 security personnel deployed to keep protesters out (BBC News, 2007a). The permanent legacy of the summit are 49 loudspeakers and sirens – a permanent public address network – which were installed in central Sydney and which have 'remained' in the light of the ongoing terrorist threat

Plate 11.2   The public alert system in central Sydney in 2007

to alert people to any major security incidents and direct people to evacuation points (Plate 11.2).

Officially this is part of a planned security upgrade as part of a roll-out of the Government's counter-terrorism initiatives announced in 2005, although the timing of their embedding within central Sydney, just before the APEC summit, make many believe their real purpose was linked directly to this event.

Finally, we should also note the opportunity high-profile events present for two different aspects of social control. The first is the pre-event 'crackdown' on unwanted 'others' in the city and nation concerned. For example, as we finished this book, the Chinese government were talking of the threat of Tibetan and Uighur 'splittists' to the 2008 Olympic Games as a reason for heightened security and repressive action prior to and during the event. The second is the field-testing of new surveillance technologies. Stanley and Steinhardt (2002), for example, highlighted that facial recognition software had been used in surveillance systems at a number of major airports in the United States as well as at prominent sporting fixtures, most notably the Super Bowl. For example, the 2006 Super Bowl in Detroit provides perhaps the starkest example with what was referred to as 'supersize security' involving one of the largest security operations in US history. Inside the event security cordon, fans were screened by metal and radiation detectors; special security forces and bomb disposal teams were on standby; computer-linked high-resolution CCTV was utilized along with real-time satellite imagery to allow instant response; and the area was guarded by 10,000 police and private security guards (Coaffee and Murakami Wood, 2006).

This event also allowed the Michigan National Guard troops to test new equipment such as 'sensor fusion' that combined readings from portable and fixed devices that can potentially detect terrorist threats in real time and upload them to a central, secure Web server, where security staff anywhere can monitor conditions at the event, forming what might be termed militarily adapted 'virtualized battle spaces' and 'network-centric-warfare' systems. While sensors capable of detecting chemical, biological or radiological threats have been used at previous Super Bowls, the readings had to be communicated by radio between different security personnel. This event for some resembled military or fortress urbanism at its nadir:

> Detroit, overnight becomes an instant battle city seen by everyone. A nomadic capital for an exercise in U.S. deployed fortress urbanism; a Rumsfeldian monument to the commercialization of the spectacle of war. Fort Field, in a matter of hours, turns into a spontaneous and controlled past-time riot town, a fortified urban temple designed for such abuse. Of course, it's also the ultimate training center for the Department of Homeland Security; the football stadium as the ideal city waiting to be attacked. (Subtopia website, 2006)

Likewise at the football World Cup in 2006, new independently mobile robotic bomb-detection devices were tested around football stadia in Germany (Klauser, 2007). However, the surveillance surge can even occur as part of the competition for such temporary events. The city of Tokyo has already announced that it will deploy advanced three-dimensional facial recognition technology to supplement the networks of cameras put in place for the 2002 World Cup, as part of its candidacy for the Olympics in 2016.

We are all spies now

We have seen how an intertwined combination of militarism, modernism and management has affected the spatial control of the city. We now move to the level of the community and the individual. Government rhetoric is increasingly explicit in linking security into everyday life, presenting different scales from international defence against global threats through 'homeland security' right down to personal safety as one continuous spectrum of security. In particular, a broad trajectory of responsibilization (Rose, 2000) is increasingly underpinning both the governance of security and urban resilience, and particularly the interactions between citizen and state. We will argue in the remainder of this chapter that the way in which resilience policy has been rolled out in recent years is increasingly putting the onus of preventing and preparing for emergencies onto institutions, professions, communities and individuals. We argue that we are all expected to be counter-terrorists, agents of surveillance or spies now; everybody has a moral responsibility, whether vague or defined, in the everyday urban response to the 'war on terror'.

However, as we have seen, in parallel with this agenda of responsibilization is a process of deresponsibilization (Hunt, 2003) that can be deployed both by individuals and organizations to themselves or to others, in order to emphasize their status either as victims or as the passive recipients of expert judgement. These processes do not necessarily work in complementary ways and the roles of responsible moral subject and innocent victim can often be performed by the same individual or group at different times, or even at the same time from different perspectives.

Developing responsibilization for resilience

Discourses regarding security and resilience are still largely closed, privileging specialist and corporate interest and not citizen concerns. In practice, the policies to tackle the ongoing terrorist threat and develop everyday resilience should be a hybrid of effective emergency management and situational measures to design-out or restrict the opportunity for terrorism to occur. More recently Government rhetoric appears to be shifting towards engaging citizens, local communities, institutions and employers in developing strategies for community and economic resilience as well as personal risk management.

This is in many ways an entirely expected consequence of the risk society where formal government and reliance on the state is increasingly supplemented or replaced entirely with 'active' citizenship involving the self-regulation of conduct within communities (Rose, 2000). It is considered essential for 'individuals and communities to take more responsibility for their own security, whether this be through schemes of "target hardening" or by setting up neighbourhood watch' (ibid., p. 322). Government functions traditionally exercised by the state have been diffused throughout a host of other 'authorities' and 'institutions' and 'communities' who are in many cases guided merely by vague instructions from above. The justification is that

national governments should no longer aspire to be the guarantor and ultimate provider of security: instead the state should be a partner, animator and facilitator for a variety of independent agents and powers, and should exercise only limited powers of its own, steering and regulating rather than rowing and providing.

(ibid., pp. 323–4)

In this sense Rose further argues that individuals, families, firms, organizations, communities are urged to take upon themselves the responsibility for the security of their property and their persons, and for their own families (ibid., p. 327).

Thus it can be seen that security policy increasingly encourages the development of community or institutional resilience, and the development of the 'responsible citizen', where the state passes responsibility to others as a supplement to more detailed institutional strategies.

Institutional responsibility

We have shown in previous chapters how resilience has been governed through the decentralization of responsibility, but with ultimate control retained at the national state level through policy guidance, strategy-making, the addition of a regional tier of resilience governance and enhanced performance management requirements for local partnerships. We also highlighted how multi-stakeholder partnership working at local and regional levels between Category 1 and Category 2 responders were seen as a prerequisite of successful resilience strategies.

Most recently this idea of institutional responsibilization has been especially stark in the field of education, particularly in the context of the war on terrorism. In his 'Statement on Security' in July 2007, the British Prime Minister, Gordon Brown, emphasized the risk of the transformation of young people into terrorists since the attacks on the London transport network in July 2005, a process referred to as 'radicalization', and argued that a range of institutions, particularly those linked to education, should have roles in combating it, and that:

> ...this requires not just the security measures...but that we work with all communities and all countries through debate, discussion, dialogue and education as we tackle at root the evils that risk driving people, particularly vulnerable young people, into the hands of violent extremists.

In his speech, Brown continued that 'schools, colleges, universities, civil society, faith groups...*indeed every institution in our country*, have a part to play' (ibid., emphasis added; see also Brown, 2006).

This has led to attempts to enforce this responsibility. For example, in early 2008, the Department for Innovation, Universities and Skills issued consultation guidance to colleges and universities regarding their role in tackling violent extremism in a document entitled *Promoting Freedom of Speech to Achieve Shared Values and Prevent Violent Extremism on Campus* (DIUS, 2008).

The discourse of radicalization is a curious one in that it simultaneously deresponsibilizes the individuals and groups involved in specific terrorist acts, portraying them as victims of radicalization and, further, moves the responsibility for addressing this to institutions. We suggest it is as much as a means of disciplining those institutions, and instilling habits of mutual surveillance on the supposedly overly liberal and radical individuals and ideas within them, as it is about dealing realistically with those who are genuinely involved or likely to be involved in terrorist acts.

Personal responsibilization

A key, but as yet underdeveloped, strand of resiliency work in the United Kingdom has been dialogue with the general public about threat and emergency – the so-called 'warning and informing' strand. We have argued in Chapter 8 that initial attempts to undertake this in 2004 through the publication of the *Preparing for Emergencies* leaflet were less than successful. This aspect of resilience policy is currently being given a higher priority. Many local governments are beginning to develop increasingly nuanced ways of risk communication with the public and to develop a dialogue with individuals and community groups. This emerging 'warning and informing' stream, unlike other elements of resilient planning work which have been characterized by a professional and exclusive remit, aims to focus upon consulting the public about a variety of themes, for example: what new measures might the public like to see in place; what are the problems local communities have faced in previous emergency (not necessarily terrorist related) incidents; and how citizens would like to be kept informed about threats and emergency incidents.

More positively a range of resilience planning activities focussing on an active model of engagement with citizens, as opposed to hypodermic models of information distribution are now emerging at the local level. For example, this is framed in Greater Manchester by a '10 step' programme which is currently being rolled through the local resilience forum (see Figure 11.1)[2].

Communicating with the public by resilience planners is increasingly seen by local-level practitioners as a two-way process, although much of the work at local levels still follows a more 'passive' model of the citizen as a 'subject' to be informed of appropriate actions rather than a stakeholder, with the same status as the partner agencies engaged in decision-making and response.

From a grass-roots community perspective, of perhaps more concern have been announcements by the security services and police that the public are now to be enrolled in the fight against terrorism – a message reinforced by a series of recent high-profile advertisements in the

---

1. Set up a Public Warning Task Group
2. Use the Community Risk Register as your starting point to determine priority risks
3. Identify and agree lead responders for all major risks
4. Audit current systems of communication in place
5. Determine target audience (including vulnerable groups)
6. Consult the public in your area
7. Decide what is sufficient in terms of communicating with and/or involving the public
8. Implement a comprehensive training and exercising regime to test warning and informing arrangements
9. Ensure all stakeholder communities and communities are kept informed through the design and implementation of a regularly updated educational awareness-raising campaign
10. Measure the effectiveness of your warning and informing system and adjust as appropriate.

Figure 11.1 The 10-step cycle for communicating with the public

media. For example, in a press release in February 2008 – *Police launch new counter-terrorism campaign* (Security Service, 2008) it was argued that 'terrorists will not succeed if suspicious activity is reported to the police':

> We want people to look out for the unusual – some activity or behaviour which shrikes them as not quite right and out of place in their normal day-to-day lives. Terrorists live within our communities, making their plans whilst doing everything they can to blend in, and trying not to raise suspicions about their activities. (ibid.)

Such suspicion, it was noted, should, as with previous campaigns, be reported to an anti-terrorism hotline.[3]

One of the initial poster used in this campaign focused upon what the security services term 'hostile reconnaissance' – the actions that a terrorist would take to reconnoitre target areas in advance of an attack. Against a background of digital cameras, this poster asks 'Thousands of people take photos every day. What if one of them seems odd?' It continues:

> Terrorists use surveillance to help plan attacks, taking photos and making notes about security measures like the location of CCTV cameras. If you see someone doing that, we need to know. Let experienced officers decide what action to take.[4]

A week after this poster first appeared a new advertisement was launched which focused upon the potential of terrorists living within communities. This time against the backdrop of an everyday front door, the new poster asked 'You see hundreds of houses every day. What if one has unusual activity and seems suspicious?' It continued:

> Terrorists live within our communities, planning attacks and storing chemicals, if you're suspicious of a property where there's unusual activity that doesn't fit normal day-to-day life, we need to know...

The campaign clearly aims at turning citizens into spies (see, for example, Kackman, 2005). As we saw in Chapter 3, informers and spies have a long history as an apparatus for urban social control; however, in most cases, such spies were either full-time employees of the police or military state or were organized and regularly paid informers. This campaign is different and, as in the case of the radicalization agenda, is aimed at *everyone* as part of their supposed moral duty as a responsible citizen.

However, the responsibilization is only taken so far. There is at the same time a deliberate curtailing of the role of the citizen-spy to the duty of reporting suspicious activity without further judgement. The significance of what has been reported is to be reserved to the expert in terrorist risk; at the moment of judgement there is a deresponsibilization. As the poster campaign produces only very limited understanding in the citizen-spy, it must also have broader intentions, that is first, to encourage a general climate of categorical suspicion (Norris, 2003) and second, to generate a further responsibilizing movement in inculcating the habit of self-surveillance (Foucault, 1977).

The governmental aim is a generalized form of discipline. However, this is not entirely the panoptic discipline that Foucault identified as being symptomatic of the enlightenment project. Nor in fact is it entirely the impersonal control of flows identified by Deleuze (1992). It has elements of both, but as it involves the many watching the particular, it is in fact strongly *synoptic* (Mathiesen, 1997); however, it is also *mutual* and *moral*. It is more like the moral suasion we saw in Chapter 3 as characteristic of modern Japanese state control (Garon, 1997), or the efforts to regulate behaviour in modern Europe (Hunt, 1999). Mark Andrejevic (2005, 2007), for example, has argued that in the complex web of surveillance relationships between state and citizen in a neoliberal economy, responsibilization creates a new kind of productive capacity, a kind of moral economy of surveillance in which the labour is undertaken as much by the watched as the watcher. Here we can see this contemporary form of the regulation of morals in action.

Private sector responsibilization

In Chapter 5 we highlighted how during the IRA bombing campaign against the financial zones of London, the private sector worked in partnership with the public sector and the police to reduce the threat of attack or minimize disruption if one were to occur.

This private sector role is embedded within civil contingencies legislation wherein service providers in areas such as mobile telecommunications, water and sewerage and transport and logistics have an obligation to share information with Category 1 responders. More broadly a range of industrial or commercial organizations may also play a direct role in the preparation for emergencies through liaison with local resilience forums about evaluation planned or in response to emergencies, if their company is affected. Local authorities also have a duty to develop business contingency plans in conjunction with the private sector, especially if such organizations are the cause of an emergency (for example, industrial accident at their premises); is affected by an emergency (for example, staff need to be evacuated); or can provide resources required to mitigate the effects of an emergency (for example, food retailers and caterers). In the recovery phase, the private sector will play a significant part, given the size of the resources, specialist expertise and capabilities (for example, site clearance, decontamination and engineering) at its disposal. The insurance industry is a key player in both the assessment of risk and the financing of rebuilding.

With particular regard to countering the terrorist threat the private sector has both self-interest and social responsibility. Many businesses especially in vulnerable parts of major cities are themselves potential targets of attack and have a duty of care to their employees to protect them from undue risk through the development of adequate contingency and security planning. According to Briggs (2002, p. 7), businesses are an 'unlikely' but nonetheless important counter-terrorist actor, but that this must be done in partnership and with the backing of Government:

> Public-private partnership should not be regarded as being one directional – the government depends on business in a number of ways. The business community is responsible for developing the software and technology that can help tackle cyber and other forms of terrorism; many of the country's critical infrastructures are now privately-owned; the long-term stability of the UK following an attack depends on the business community getting back on its feet as quickly as possible; and there are now infinite dependencies between systems. Public-private partnership in tackling terrorism must be based on genuine principles of partnership. Businessmen may be unlikely counter-terrorists, but a national policy without them will make the UK a softer target for attack.

In this sprit of multi-sector partnership working, there are increasingly efforts made to train and skill the private sector for coping with terrorist threat. Since 2001, counter-terrorist initiatives to assist business to deal with both traditional and new forms of terrorist attack have emerged out of London's experience of dealing with terrorism, which have been rolled out across the United Kingdom in order to heighten the speed of response as well as aid business continuity. Such initiatives include *Project Griffin* and *Project Argus* which seek to train private security staff and security managers so that they are better equipped to: be of assistance to the police in the event of a major incident; deal with their organization's security challenges on a day-to-day basis and in the event of a major incident; disrupt hostile reconnaissance; and to reflect upon their existing security and contingency plans, in order to build capacity to react in the event of an attack and to help safeguard staff, customers and company assets.

Local responder responsibilization

Local responders have been at the forefront of resilience work over recent years in improving preparedness for emergencies. As we have shown in previous chapters, at the local level resiliency is managed largely by a combination of local authority run emergency planning units in conjunction with the Police. These Category 1 responders have already had to bear a burden of responsibility in terms of resilience governance, but their role is dynamic and ever-changing and is likely to be increased in the future. We noted in Chapter 9 how UK local government is assessed in terms of the effectiveness of its emergency planning function under Comprehensive Performance Assessment. In November 2007 the Department of Communities and Local Government launched a consultation into a new performance management framework for local government which contained 198 key indicators of performance – three of which (35–37), under the theme of policing and community safety, were directly linked to resilience (DCLG, 2007b).

National Indicator (NI) 35 related to the Prevent strand of CONTEST and specifically to building resilience to violent extremism. Here it was argued that 'a security based response is not enough – we must stop people being drawn to violent extremism in the first instance' (ibid., p. 58). This indicator will therefore measure the standard of local areas' arrangements to engage with Muslim communities.

Connected to this stream of work, in February 2008, the Association of Chief Police Officers announced that they had drawn up plans for so-called 'neighbourhood profiling', described by one commentator as 'a radical strategy to stop British Muslims turning to violence which will see every neighbourhood in the country mapped for its potential to produce extremists and supporters of Al-Qaida' (Dodd, 2008). This overtly racially and religiously focused form of geo-demographic profiling has the potential to create a new form of 'post-code discrimination' where having the 'wrong' name, or even just living in the 'wrong' place could see whole groups of entirely innocent people being regarded as categorically suspect and subjected to further more targeted forms of investigation. It could also lead to them suffering from other adverse economic and social effects such as the decline in the value of their homes or the inability to get jobs, once knowledge, accurate or inaccurate, about the targeted neighbourhoods becomes common.

National Indicator 36, on the other hand, focuses on so-called 'soft' targets – unprotected areas where large numbers of people congregate – deemed to be at risk from terrorist attack, and for which local government would now appear to be partially responsible. NI 36 focused on the Protect strand of CONTEST and particularly protecting against terrorist attack where 'local authorities are increasingly seen as key to delivery of the overarching aim . . . by the inclusion/development of counter terrorism protective security' (DCLG, 2007b, p. 60).

National Indicator 37 by contrast focuses specifically upon the 'Prepare' strand of CONTEST as well as more broadly on the requirements under the Civil Contingencies Act 2004. Specifically it relates to 'awareness of civil protection arrangements in the local area' (ibid., p. 61). This will involve responsibility for developing responders' capability to deal with emergencies. This NI also links to our previous discussions on individual responsibility, with the local state being judged on its ability to ensure its citizens are prepared:

> . . . so that they can sustain their own safety and that of their families; and citizens being prepared to help neighbours and communities. An essential pre-condition to that will be citizens being made aware of risks in their areas (e.g. of flooding), and of relevant emergency plans (e.g. those of their local agencies). An informed public are better prepared to deal with the consequences of an emergency. The indicator is designed to measure the impact of local agencies arrangements for communicating/educating citizens regarding civil protection matters, by measuring how informed they feel, by organizations in their local area, about what they should do in the event of a large scale emergency. (ibid.)

The responsible urban planner

David Godschalk (2003) argued that when designing resilient cities a collaborative partnership is required between state actors and a variety of built environment professions. He notes that:

> If we are to take the achievement of urban resilience seriously, we need to build the goal of the resilient city into the everyday practice of city planners, engineers, architects, emergency managers,

developers and other urban professionals. This will require a long-term collaborative effort to increase knowledge and awareness about resilient city planning and design. (p. 42)

As we have emphasized in previous chapters, the role of the planner and other built environment professionals in protective counter-terrorist security has been limited: usually this is a task led by the police and military. However, as we have seen, enhancing community safety in crowded places – the 'soft targets' – has been a key current concern of Government and has been backed up by large and ongoing streams of work being conducted by the National Counter Terrorism Security Office (NaCTSO) on disseminating protective security advice to places deemed vulnerable to targeting such as shopping centres, bars pubs and clubs and sports stadia. This concern for protecting crowded places was further reinforced in the Home Office review (West Review) in November 2007, following the London/Glasgow terror attacks, which called for counter-terrorism measures to be embedded within the design, planning and construction of public places (Home Office, 2007c; Thompson, 2007). The West Review emphasized the importance of counter-terror measures being incorporated into the pre-planning and design stages of new developments as well as security, being made as unobtrusive as possible so to avoid a fortress mentality (West, 2008).

Although there is to be no primary legalization as yet to 'force' planners and the architects, developers or designers they work with to adopt counter-terrorism measures there are concerns that the planning profession is having responsibility passed to it to protect areas of the city. Concern has been expressed that National Indicator 36 mentioned above and additional fears that corporate manslaughter legislation (to be enforced from April 2008) could potentially leave planners or architects liable to legal redress if an attack occurs against a structure of space deemed a target, but which has been inadequately protected. This is not a new concern. After September 11 there were concerns that planners and architects could be legally responsible for deaths, injury and damage caused by a terrorist strike (Hyam, 2002).

We have seen how governmental strategies have affected the spatio-temporal form of the city, and are envisaged to impact on the everyday activities of citizens. However, it is worth noting that much of our analysis would be regarded as overly critical by many conservative commentators. For example, Savitch (2008) has recently criticized many academic discussions of urban resilience to terrorism as unrealistically dystopian. Instead he focuses on the experience of the citizen and discovers positive commonalities across people in targeted cities from New York to Jerusalem. However, the move is at least partly political: Savitch chooses to focus on the role of victimhood in the cities of allies in the war on terror, at the expense of victims of those allies, and at the expense of the political and military responsibility of national authorities.[5]

The impression one gets from his book then is that it is almost a celebration of the New Yorker, the Londoner or the Jerusalemite because of 'the strength of their social fabric, the dynamism of their economies, and the optimism of their citizenry' (Savitch, 2008 p. 159). This analysis ignores differences in class, race, gender and social position that we have shown are all implicated within discussion of what is to be secured and what is to be made resilient. It also ignores the fact that the happy citizens of these happy cities are also resilient because they are thoroughly enmeshed in global networks of capitalism, modernity and privilege. This leads to curious ambiguities, where after a discussion of the post-September 11 surveillance surge, it is argued that on the one hand things have changed in hardly any noticeable way in response to terrorism, yet on the other hand 'Tom Wolfe's maxim that "you can't ever go home again" rings ever so true' (p. 160). It is to this latter question, that of home, and the directions in which the relationship between citizen and state may go, that we turn in the final chapter.

12
Security is Coming Home

In this book we have examined the relationship between the vulnerability and resilience of the city, focusing on the UK national, regional and sub-regional governance architectures for civil contingencies and security that are developing in the Twenty-First Century. These were primarily developed in order to build up a consistent degree of resilience across the country in order to prepare for, and respond to, a variety of threats faced. Although this has been driven since the 1980s by a concern for Integrated Emergency Management (IEM), and despite the concerns of provincial cities over flooding and the threat of animal disease pandemics to rural areas, it is clear that the threat of terrorism has become the predominant driver at state level. This has enabled emergency planning to enjoy unprecedented funding and profile at all scales. In the last chapter, we explored what this might mean for the everyday life of the city from spatial governance to institutional and personal responsibilization.

In this chapter we reflect on these current trajectories. The chapter is divided into three parts. The first part deals with the *future of resilience policy*, focusing on the United Kingdom's first national security strategy published in March 2008, a strategy which for the first time attempted to draw together responsibility and organization for threat from terrorism and natural disasters in a co-ordinated and coherent manner.

The second part of the chapter examines the *impact of resilience politics*, and the relationship between technological, political and social change in the resilient city. In particular, we question the common notion that there is a 'balance' or a trade-off between security and accountability, democracy, liberty and privacy. This means returning to the question Lewis Mumford raised in his discussion of the origins of war and the city as to whether there is an inherent pathology within 'dreams' of security which leads inevitably to violence. In this we ask what are the implications of a permanent state of emergency or exception, contrasting the bleak assessment of Giorgio Agamben (2005) to the pragmatic acceptance of the necessity of surveillance measures of more conservative commentators.

Finally, the third part will examine the *future of resilience* itself, and ask whether in becoming subordinate to anxious globalization, 'resilience' might, like 'competitive' or 'sustainable', become just another empty metaphor to add to urban policy statements. However, we also ask whether resilience might become a term around which genuinely new and beneficial policy agendas may emerge linking social and economic concerns and facilitating and enhancement of multi-tier and multi-agency partnership working and strengthening civil society: a type of 'third way security' solution? (Coaffee and O'Hare, 2008)

The future of resilience policy

The path to a new national security strategy

The dynamic nature of threats has meant that initial attempts to rescale the security state and generate resilience to emergencies or disaster events has laid bare the need for a comprehensive reform of emergency planning. As detailed in Chapter 8, even as the new structures of resilience were being established, there were critical voices arguing that issues of cross-governmental working, multi-tier devolution and a general sense that too much was being asked of local responders too quickly and was limiting the effectiveness of the reforms. The need to pause and introduce a greater element of critical reflection was recognized at the top levels of government and was alluded to by Gordon Brown in 2006 when he was still the Chancellor of the Exchequer,[1] who noted a need:

> ... to stand back and reflect and ... make the long-term cool-headed assessment we need to have about the likely repetition of such events and to decide what, for the long term, need to be done to strengthen our security.
>
> (Brown, 2006, cited in DEMOS, 2007, p. 21)

Such reflection subsequently did begin. In July 2007, in the wake of terrorist attacks in London and Glasgow, Gordon Brown, as Prime Minister, announced in *The Governance of Britain* (HM Government, 2007a) that the executive would be made more accountable through a reformed intelligence and security infrastructure and that a national security strategy would be forthcoming in 2008 'and provide the basis for deciding on changes in priorities to reflect changed circumstances' (ibid., p. 33).

There was clearly a strong element of influence of the American model of national security governance. This is not simply further evidence of the subservient 'special relationship' that Britain has had for some time with US strategic priorities. New Labour and Gordon Brown in particular have a distinct personal Americanophilia (Ramsay, 1998). Thus, the planned strategy was also to include a committee whose name mirrors the US National Security Council, adjusted by the Britishness of being a 'committee':

> In order to ensure that the delivery of such polices on the ground is more 'joined-up', a new National Security Committee was to be created 'to ensure that its policies and their delivery are coordinated and appropriate to the changing nature of the risks and challenges facing us in the 21st century'.[2] (ibid.)

In a further 'Statement on Security', Brown (2007) reinforced the need for a new National Security Strategy and Committee and noted that for the first time there will now be a single security budget.[3] This acknowledgment of a need for a more co-ordinated security strategy followed the restructuring of the 'not fit for purpose' Home Office (Travis, 2007) into two new units: the Office for Security and Counter-Terrorism to work 'in partnership with other departments and agencies to ensure a more effective and co-coordinated response to the threats to our security' (Home Office, 2007b); and a cross-government Research, Information and Communication Unit to tackle the spread of radical Islam. This has reinforced the Home Office's 'Lead Department' role for counter-terrorism and therefore left the Civil Contingencies Secretariat to focus on its overarching role on generic resiliency issues.

In addition, from April 2007 four regional Counter-Terrorism Units (CTUs) were established in Greater Manchester, West Yorkshire, the West Midlands and London to work in partnership with the security services, with a focus on intelligence gathering and on tackling 'violent extremism'. The development of this CTU structure coincided with the publication of a new Government strategy action plan *Preventing Violent Extremism, Winning Hearts and Minds* (DCLG, 2007a) in which the Government pledged to step-up work with Muslim communities to isolate, prevent and defeat violent extremism, much of which as we saw in the previous chapter, relies on the responsibilization of citizens and their transformation into citizen-spies.

The National Security Strategy 2008

On 19 March 2008, the British Prime Minister launched the long-awaited National Security Strategy (NSS): *The National Security Strategy of the United Kingdom: Security in an Interdependent World* (Cabinet Office, 2008). The 'single overarching national security objective' was articulated in this report as:

> ...protecting the United Kingdom and its interests, enabling its people to go about their daily lives freely and with confidence, in a more secure, stable, just and prosperous world. (p. 6)

The NSS set out the rationale and logic underpinning this plan which was seen as 'the next building blocks' (ibid., p. 5) to add to recently enacted reform of civil contingences and counter-terrorism, and was required to deal with an increasingly complex 'security landscape' – linking national authorities with those at a local level, as well as assessing Britain's place in an ever-more interdependent global world. The NSS argued that increased funding and staffing of the security services would also be required.[4] In this section we focus primarily on threats to the United Kingdom whilst acknowledging the key strand of this strategy that focuses on the United Kingdom's approach to international security.

In the Prime Minister's statement to the House of Commons (BBC News, 2008) it was noted that the NSS was a response to the requirement of new risk management in a changing world and argued that the threat, particularly from international terrorism, was real and ever-changing and that it could not be ignored in an increasingly interdependent global society that has moved from the paranoid Cold War rhetoric of civil defence (Chapter 5) and IRA terrorism (Chapter 6):

> As the strategy makes clear, new threats demand new approaches. A radically updated and much more coordinated response is now required. For most of the last half century the main threat was unmistakable: a Cold War adversary. Today, the potential threats we face come from far less predictable sources: both state and non-state. 20 years ago the terrorist threat to Britain was principally that from the IRA. Now it comes from loosely affiliated global networks that threaten us and other nations across continents. Once, when there was instability in faraway regions or countries, we had a choice – to become involved or not.
>
> (BBC News, 2008)

The NSS, noted Brown, was far more than just a counter-terrorism plan but a broader strategy to tackle a complex array of risk capable of causing insecurity that might result from 'climate change, poverty, mass population movements and even organized crime [which] reverberate quickly round the globe' (BBC News, 2008). Here the NSS makes it clear that the 'view of international security has broadened' and that 'this strategy deals with trans-national crime, pandemics and flooding, not part of the traditional idea of national security' (Cabinet Office 2008, p. 3). In particular, ideas of resilience are prominent:

> Our new approach to security also means improved local resilience against emergencies, building and strengthening local capacity to respond effectively in a range of circumstances from floods to possible terrorism incidents... not the old cold war idea of civil defence but a new form of civil protection that combines expert preparedness for potential emergencies with greater local engagement of individuals and families themselves.
>
> (BBC News, 2008)

Leaving aside aspects of the NSS relating to international relations,[5] at the UK level it was argued that new innovative governance configurations are the solution to insecurity:

> At home, we will favour a partnership approach... we will build on the coalition of public, private and third sectors already involved in counter-terrorism. We will work with owners or operators to protect critical sites and essential services; with business to improve resilience; with local authorities and communities to plan for emergencies and to counter violent extremism; and with individuals, where changing people's behaviour is the best way to mitigate risk.
>
> (Cabinet Office, 2008, p. 8)

The NSS also had a forward planning focus and argued that the Joint Terrorism Analysis Centre (JTAC) – which co-ordinates the work of all Government departments including the police and intelligence agencies – will be given a 'new focus on the longer-term challenge of investigating the path to violent extremism' (BBC News, 2008). As the NSS reinforces 'the most effective way to tackle all the major security challenges involves early engagement. The most effective way to reduce the long-term threat from terrorism is to tackle the causes of violent extremism, both at home and overseas' (Cabinet Office, 2008, p. 7).

The strategy placed added emphasis upon developing new approaches to 'warn and inform' the public which, as noted in previous chapters, has been an often-neglected, or even ridiculed, aspect of resiliency. The Prime Minister noted:

> We will openly publish for the first time a national register of risks – information that was previously held confidentially within Government – so the British public can see at first hand the challenges we face and the levels of threat we have assessed.
>
> (BBC News, 2008)

The contribution of individual citizens and local communities to the national security effort, it was argued, would be bolstered by this received risk assessment information:

> Individuals have an essential role to play in national security. We can all contribute, for example by being vigilant against terrorism, and by planning for, and taking a more active role in responding to, civil emergencies, on the basis of new and improved information on the risks we face.
>
> (Cabinet Office, 2008, p. 59)[6]

Plans were also announced in the NSS to set up an unpaid 'Civil Protection Network' where members of the public will be trained to respond to emergencies. This appears to be a variation on the World War Two Air Raid Precaution (ARP) wardens or the Cold War Civil Defence Volunteers (see Chapter 4), and has also been likened to a strengthened Neighbourhood Watch scheme. This network it is contended will build on civil emergency plans developed by council-controlled local resilience forums (see Hope, 2008).

Despite the strategy paying lip-service to both terrorist and non-terrorist arrangements that 'will retain, strong, balanced and flexible capabilities' (Cabinet Office, 2008, p. 9), the Prime Minister's statement to the House made it clear that terrorism was still the main driver of security/resilience. In this regard, the statement to the House was also used to signpost recent and emergent policy that has evolved in the light of 'security threats' including compulsory ID cards for foreign nationals and the contentious issues within the Counter-Terrorism bill that in special circumstances periods of extending detention (at the time of writing, proposed to be 42 days) can be allowed for 'terror' suspects to be held without charge.

Compared to terrorism, the notion of civil emergencies is only given a fleeting mention in the text of the NSS with emphasis given to infectious diseases (especially influenza-type pandemics), extreme weather and coastal and inland flooding. Dealing with such risks is, however, framed through the discourse of terrorist threat:

> Because of the scale and speed of the risk they pose, those phenomena [civil emergencies] have similar potential to other security challenges to threaten our normal way of life across significant areas of the country...is similar to our approach to other national security challenges, including terrorism.
>
> (Cabinet Office, 2008, p. 15)

In large part the NSS seems to offer little new in terms of Government action. That said it does reiterate the commitment for CONTEST, the national counter-terrorism strategy, and planning for civil emergencies in terms of building the resilience to respond. Of particular use in this regard was the mapping of key future priorities in both these streams of resiliency work.

In terms of CONTEST the NSS argued that Government 'will continue to learn, adapt, and invest' (Cabinet Office, 2008, p. 27) in counter-terrorism but that this must be done with civil and democratic values in mind and that 'we need to respond robustly, bringing those involved to justice while defending our shared values, and resisting the provocation to over-react' (ibid., p. 28).

As such, the Government argued that their response should be proportionate:

> The threat from terrorism is real...But we must also keep it firmly in perspective...we are also determined to maintain the balance of security and liberty, and above all to maintain normal life, whether at airports, on the train or underground networks, or in our communities. (ibid.)

A sixfold list of future priorities for countering terrorism was also given (see Box 12.1).

Box 12.1 The counter-terrorism priorities contained in the National Security Strategy (2008, p. 28)

- Delivering the Government's Public Service Agreement – to 'reduce the risk to the United Kingdom and its interests overseas from international terrorism';
- Continuing to build our capability to detect and disrupt terrorists, in the United Kingdom and overseas, through investment in the police and the security and intelligence agencies;
- Enhancing the protection against terrorism provided by new border technology and the new UK Border Agency;
- Increasing our capacity to deal with the consequences of a terrorist attack;
- Delivering the improved range of projects and programmes to tackle violent extremism, including working with partners overseas; and
- Addressing grievances and challenging the violent extremism narrative, for example highlighting our active support for the Middle East Peace Process.

In terms of civil contingencies the NSS reinforces the need to retain and enhance capability to respond through additional funding and training. There are also particular links to prioritize flood management and pandemic planning to ensure effective mechanisms are in place at local and regional levels to deal these 'high probability' risks. The key feature of this approach appears to be the increased need to develop social and community resilience:

> Human and social resilience, often at the community level, will continue to be crucial...The British people have repeatedly shown their resilience in the face of severe disruptions whether from war, terrorism, or natural disasters. Communities and individuals harness local resources and expertise to help themselves, in a way that complements the response of the emergency services. That kind of community resilience is already well organized in some parts of the United Kingdom, and we will consider what contribution we can make to support and extend it, building on the foundations of the

Civil Contingencies Act and on the lessons of emergencies over the past few years.

(Cabinet Office, 2008, pp. 42–3)

This focus upon community involvement/responsibility was seen by one commentator as trying 'to incorporate the growing role of volunteerism and non-governmental organizations' (*The Times*, 2008, p. 20) and to which the rhetoric of resilience in Britain still frequently returns.

As with counter-terrorism, future priorities for this stream of resilience work are given (Box 12.2).

However, if the announcement of the NSS was intended to represent a defining statement on the issue, there was little positive news for the Prime Minister upon its release. Opposition media highlighted the fact that although heavily focused on terrorism and international issues and that the NSS does highlight the link between counter-terrorism and civil contingences, it 'largely amounted to a review of what is happening and what is expected in terms of threat assessment – the new strategy is a damp squib. Short on vision, managerial, rather than thought provoking, it simply pulls together many existing policy strands' (*Daily Telegraph*, 2008, p. 25). The establishment 'newspaper

---

Box 12.2 Planning for civil emergencies and building resilience priorities contained in the National Security Strategy (p. 43)

- Continuing to increase expenditure on flood management in England, from £600 million in 2007/08 to £800 million in 2010/11;

- Continuing to build domestic capacity to respond to an influenza pandemic;

- Continuing to build the extensive network of organizations engaged in preparing for and responding to domestic emergencies;

- Publishing a national-level risk register covering the full range of risks; and

- Reviewing the Civil Contingencies Act to ensure an effective legislative and regulatory framework.

of record', *The Times*, saw the NSS as 'a security blanket' and 'more of a framework to cope with uncertainty than a strategy' (*The Times*, 2008, p. 20). Here it was argued that some sensible elements were incorporated including keeping the public informed about threats faced and attempting to identify immediate and long-term threats though risk assessment and horizon scanning (ibid.). More critically, the leader of the Conservative Party, David Cameron, noted that it 'sounded more like a list than a strategy' whilst Nick Clegg, the leader of the UK third political party, the Liberal Democrats, noted that 'the plans were more as assessment of the threats to Britain rather than a strategy for tackling them' (cited in Morris, 2008, p. 6).

However, it was not warmly received even by those on the other end of the (increasingly narrow) mainstream political spectrum in the United Kingdom. A spokesperson from the Institute of Public Policy Research (IPPR), one of the key think tanks behind the New Labour project, noted that the NSS was 'weaker on policy substance and weaker still on necessary policy changes to the machinery of government' (cited in Norton-Taylor, 2008). Worse, the editorial in left-leaning *Independent* newspaper noted that the NSS 'was an old fashioned mishmash of an agenda, thrown down in a rather take-it-or-leave-it fashion, in the apparent hope that MPs would appreciate its nutritional value' (*The Independent*, 2008, p. 44). It continued by arguing that the strategy itself was full of scare tactics and emotive language that contributed to a sense of fear, especially from terrorism, 'with so many thousand individuals being watched, so many plots detected, so many mortal dangers out there' (ibid.). In this sense it was argued that 'the whole construct is revealed for what it is: nothing more than a political game' (*The Independent*, 2008, p. 44) where crisis is constantly evoked, where legal measures to increase the detention period of terrorist suspects are legitimized and which might lead to a further expansion of the surveillance state; for example unlimited security service access to CCTV cameras across the country (for example, Hope, 2008).

In summary, the NSS did try and pull together the vast amount number of existing workstreams from across Government in this area of policy and this may make for more co-ordinated policy in the future. However, it failed to deliver much that was new in terms of the resilience agenda, and further was accused of contributing to a fear-mongering agenda and the onward march of the 'surveillance society'. It is to this and the questions of the broader political debates from which resilience is drawn that we now turn.

The impact of resilience politics

Since the birth of the nation state, the study of security, across many disciplines, has been conceived of on a national, trans-regional or global scale and largely in terms of broad governance coalitions or macroeconomic institutions or 'interests' (Booth, 2004). In this book we have demonstrated the movement of the historically contingent and temporally variably nature of this conception of security, and have detailed how it is currently being re-evaluated and rescaled. Partly this challenge comes from the emerging ideas of 'human security', which from the 1990s have tried to wrench security away from its institutional bias, to focus it on the needs of people and populations (Paris, 2001) or from the recognition of the shared threat of climate change, and partly from the particular threat of contemporary Jihadist terrorism. However, as we have seen, these challenges exist during a time of intense problematization of the notion of 'Government' at nation-state level, and thus facing new security challenges of terrorism has meant an emphasis on responsibilization, which requires analysis through different frames of reference from the 'realist security studies orthodoxy' (Coaffee and Murakami Wood, 2006, p. 504). For academics, we would suggest, these frames of reference are increasingly based in the trans-disciplinary field of 'Surveillance Studies' (Lyon, 2007), which draws on a combination of anthropology, sociology, political science, criminology, geography and new media and communication studies.

Many countries are now adopting increasingly introspective approaches to their own security and are rethinking traditional polices which seem outdated in the contemporary world. In the United Kingdom, as we have shown in preceding chapters, a new protective and regulatory state has emerged and is articulated through the rhetoric of resilience, replacing Cold War era conceptions of emergency planning and civic protection and leading to the dispersion of security responsibilities through all levels of government and beyond. This 'reterritorialization' of security can be seen as part of a process of social fragmentation or splintering that has been occurring since the late 1960s and early 1970s, and which has accelerated since the end of the Cold War. Neoliberalism has also helped spread regimes of privatization and has increasingly transformed security into a commodity which is the responsibility of all levels of global society, rather than coterminous with national borders or existing in the context of a consensual international order (Coaffee and Murakami Wood, 2006, p. 514).

In preceding chapters we have sought to demonstrate that the concept of security is now being rescaled and is increasingly ubiquitous, through the particular example of the way in which major global cities, and increasingly provincial cities, are dealing with terrorist threats to both core business and financial and state functions, and also to temporary high-profile events. Security as a concept is 'coming home': in other words, the discourses, procedures and often materials of national and international security are influencing, or are directly employed at, smaller scales from the urban to the community, domestic and personal. However, at the same time, the threats are positioned as global, and 'terrorism' – or now more commonly simply 'terror' – rather like the market or democracy with which it is juxtaposed, is both everywhere and nowhere (ibid., p. 504).

In this sense we must be prepared for life in a constant state of emergency (Wood *et al.*, 2003), or what Giorgio Agamben (2005) calls a 'state of exception'. In this regard the UK Government, like others, is constantly accused on peddling a 'politics of fear' (Furedi, 2005, p. 125, see also Bauman, 2006). The British state is of course not solely responsible for the existence of this fear, but draws on it as a resource, and by doing so feeds back into the what the Dutch architect, Lieven De Cauter (2004), calls a 'hallucinatory world' (p. 118). He breaks this fear down into six current types: first, *demographic fear*, the fear of the human species out of control of its own numbers and its environmental effect on the world; second, *dromophobia*, the fear of the pace of change, or more accurately the fear of being left behind 'left in the wake of acceleration' (p. 119) of the information society; third, *economic fear*, the fear of losing out in the competitive neoliberal economy; fourth, *xenophobia*, the fear of outsiders, foreigners and 'others'; fifth, *agoraphobia*, the fear of the disintegration of the space of politics at every level from economic globalization to the incivility of public spaces; and finally, the *fear of terrorism*.

What is interesting is the rhetorical and policy movement that constantly occurs between these types. Emotive and militarized rhetoric which talks of not only the war on terror but a war on drugs, crime, binge-drinking, anti-social behaviour and so on, as well as constant reminders of Government 'threat and risk assessments' through the media and even email distribution lists reinforce the culture of fear.

The state and surveillance

The ubiquity of 'fear' within Government rhetoric was witnessed in the Queen's Speech at the State Opening of Parliament in 2004.[7] The narrative of forthcoming policy in this speech implicitly linked terrorism to a whole raft of other proposed legislation including that on the National Identity Register and ID cards, serious crime, drug and alcohol abuse and hence to public order and anti-social behaviour (BBC News, 2004). Through the exploitation of fear, security is thus becoming part of every policy domain.

A normalized notion of security and resilience has begun to pervade everyday life posing critical questions regarding the relationship between broader resilience policy for dealing with new security challenges and other emergent social polices directed at the civic realm (Coaffee and Wood, 2006). In the United Kingdom, the Government and interest groups are playing on the whole range of types of fear to justify technologically driven control strategies to counter anti-social behaviour, democratic protest, to exclude the dangerous 'other' from public space and to introduce Identity Cards which link citizens to state-held databases.

The apparatus of counter-terrorism, security and resilience – from video surveillance, through barriers against suicide car bombs, to body screening systems at transport hubs – is increasingly integrated into the urban fabric of major cities. Although it is often justified as protecting the critical infrastructure of the city, the security apparatus itself is now seen by policy-makers as critical infrastructure (Graham, 1999). The continued technological innovation, spawned by the constant iteration between military, civil and academic research and development now means that more sophisticated and increasingly intrusive surveillance technologies continue to be developed and marketed to media-savvy politicians and bureaucrats always looking for that simple 'silver bullet' (Marx, 1995) to solve complex problems. As the authors of the *Report on the Surveillance Society* argued in 2006, this can also lead to a closed and technologically dependent policy world:

> the more that states, organizations, communities and people become dependent on surveillance technologies, the more there is an apparent 'lock-in' which prevents other options from being considered, and a comprehension gap which increases a dependence on expertise outside the democratic system. (Murakami Wood *et al.*, 2006, p. 29)

The adoption and diffusion of such technologies and associated practices have increasingly been seen as technical or managerial not political issues. Until recently, they had rarely been scrutinized in public discourse. However, in the United Kingdom, the Office of the Information

Commissioner (ICO), the watchdog for Data Protection and Freedom of Information, has, however, changed this by going beyond the technical limits of its remit as a regulatory agency. There have been many reports from pressure groups, such as Liberty (the British equivalent of ACLU in the United States), Privacy International and the No2ID campaign; however, it was the intervention of the Information Commissioner, Richard Thomas, in a speech in 2004 in which he argued that we were 'sleepwalking into a surveillance society' and the subsequent commissioning of a report from the Surveillance Studies Network to detail the nature of that surveillance society (Murakami Wood *et al.*, 2006) that has finally brought more attention to the politics of surveillance in the United Kingdom. This has been followed by other reports, increased media coverage of surveillance and two separate parliamentary inquiries by the House of Commons Home Affairs Committee and the House of Lords Constitution Committee, both of which were still ongoing at the time of writing. Whether their reports or the belated media interest in these issues makes any long-term difference remains to be seen.

Resilience and civil liberties

The merging of crime prevention, anti-social behaviour measures and security within an array of policy agendas, underpinned by the rhetoric that we are living in a changing, uncertain and dangerous world, is leading to serious questions regarding civil liberties and the extent to which Western democracies are moving towards security states and surveillance societies. The rhetorical links between the narratives of social order, quality of life, fear of crime and threat of terrorism increasingly appear to implicitly underpin the wider legislative agenda of reform in the United Kingdom. Similar trends have also been documented elsewhere. Wekerle and Jackson (2004) have argued with regard to North American cities that numerous policies have 'hitchhiked' on the anti-terrorism agenda and been implicitly and explicitly embedded within numerous social and planning policy discourses and that 'anti-terrorism is such a hegemonic project that it insinuates itself into the interstices of everyday life, reframing policies relating to urban form, transportation and public space' (p. 36).

Commenting upon not dissimilar Australian experiences of the 'war on terror', McDonald (2005) has also discussed how the public discourse surround counter-terrorism is carefully constructed or 'spun' to resonate with concerns of domestic population and to justify an ever-advancing security state. Here 'political responses that potentially undermine individual security' and which are only 'marginally related' to the war on terror have been evoked as the government has sought to develop a broad discourse of the need for 'militarized vigilance in protecting Australia's security in an insecure world' (ibid., p. 298). Significantly, links can be made between the shifts in the emphasis and focus of the state-driven rhetoric through which the tightening of state interventions is legitimated and the socio-spatial retrofitting of temporary security into permanent security infrastructure. Resilience as a policy metaphor and governance structure seems to be a more nuanced approach to embedding security than the 'hard spaces' and 'zero-tolerance' approaches seen in broad policy shift towards crime reduction in New York, following the Giuliani era, or in the mass policing of high-profile events.

The resilience agenda assumes a softer and more subtle approach to embedding security into the broader experience of governance, through stakeholder partnerships and responsibilization of stakeholders and citizens alike for ensuring resilience. Yet there remains an undercurrent of paranoia and suspicion unsuited to idealized liberal democracies. For example, central Government appeared to encourage the use of anti-terror laws and detention protocols in the policing of recent climate change protests at Heathrow airport to ensure a 'robust' police response (Vidal and Pidd, 2007), highlighting the broader implications of how such powers can be used, or abused, and ongoing tensions which are likely to be a central issue in making sure resilience does not isolate the state from the citizens it seeks to protect. The co-ordinated policing of civil disturbance as a form of implicit terrorist activity have been increasingly legitimized in state discourse by the 'home-grown' origins of the terrorists responsible for the 2005 London bombings, and, more broadly, embedding an institutionalized mistrust of the citizen in state policies.

Security thus ties into crime and social order policies blurring the boundaries and legal distinctions between terrorism, crime and anti-social behaviour. Likewise, resilience planning now has broad applications extending vastly beyond a reworked framework of emergency planning and counter-terrorism strategy, with resilience often being brought into focus under the guise of improving security, safety and quality of life in the community (Coaffee and Rogers, 2008). Mike Raco (2003, 2007) has shown how security has gradually infiltrated the UK Government's policies for sustainable communities and security has consequently become a major pillar of urban sustainability in official discourse. For example, the so-called 'Respect' agenda is leading to the micro-management of anti-social behaviour in public spaces, for instance 'Respect Zones' in which even the CCTV cameras are linked to public address systems used to publically shame 'flawed consumers' (Bauman, 2006) for their misdemeanours, or the use of ultrasonic nonlethal weapons such as the 'Mosquito' for displacing youths from 'hanging around' outside shops.

Ironically, both the use of anti-terrorist legislation against protestors and the militarization of anti-social behaviour management demonstrate not 'respect' in any meaningful sense of the word, but the state's own *agoraphobia* (De Cauter, 2004), its fear of the citizen. This is the paradox that has existed since the creation of the first city walls, which both protected the liberty of the citizen and acted as a means of control. Here the state is both acknowledging that it cannot trust the citizen, whilst at the same time wanting to make the citizen responsible for self-policing. In one sense the problem remains the same as in the Nineteenth Century moral panic over urban disorder: how can one know the good citizen from the bad?

The advancing 'security for all, by all' rhetoric is having significant impacts upon a range of civil liberties and citizenship and is being utilized to justify an ever-advancing security state. Such measures therefore often provoke considerable criticism within political institutions and in wider civil society not least with regard to issues of freedom of movement, the pervasive monitoring of activities and the impact on community cohesion and multiculturalism (see, for example, Murakami Wood *et al.*, 2006). This is creating a situation which some are terming 'creeping authoritarianism' (Jenkins, 2006). Although the use of a sense of impending risk and danger to enact new civic policy is of course not a new political strategy, the potential impact, broadening scale and unquantifiable nature of impending 'new' global risks (most notably, but not exclusively, terrorism), combined with political leaders' claims of 'unique' and 'classified' knowledge of potential threats, is increasingly justifying the implementation of a raft of resilience policies, without critical civic consultation (ibid.).

Of particular concern are the ways that the security, counter-terrorism and resilience agendas may sacrifice what is supposedly to be safeguarded by those polices – that is the values and freedoms of liberal democracy. The danger comes from the assumption that some civil rights and liberties impede an effective counter-terrorist strategy, and that the solution is to find an appropriate 'balance' of the two that is inevitably weighted more towards security than liberty. We would argue, as did Lustgarten and Leigh in 1994, in *In from the Cold*, that this comes from a misconception of security. Weighing fundamental human rights in a balance against national security (or indeed simply civil order) is to miss the point that the legitimacy of the nation state or the civil order depends on the guaranteeing of those rights and freedoms. Without them, the state ceases to have a purpose beyond its self-perpetuation: it becomes, like Mumford's early defended city (see Chapter 2), pathological.

The justification for such a move has traditionally been one of a 'state of exception', that is the abnormal circumstances of war or national emergency. Giorgio Agamben has provided a comprehensive analysis of this concept, arguing that it has now become 'the dominant paradigm of government in contemporary politics' (2005, p. 2) and the displacement of the law by authority. It is through the consideration of states of exception that we can understand the return to the wall and fortification; for Agamben, the quintessential apparatus is not the Panopticon but the concentration camp. One can therefore see the state of exception as a shift back to the predominant use of sovereign power in Foucault's triad of governmentality.

In contrast, recent work by more conservative commentators entirely disagrees with this analysis or at least with the implications that Agamben draws. For example, Savitch (2008) argues that even though 'barriers have been known to block off civic space [and] intensive surveillance coupled with forbidden space can deaden city life [...] for all its drawbacks, surveillance has become necessary. In fact, urban populations have demanded protection' (2008, p. 147). His conclusion is that 'local resilience is a long-term and inherent condition of cities. It is nonetheless helped along and sustained by the political order' (ibid., p. 174).

The truth is between the two. In many ways the reliance of the state on the discourse of responsibilization shows up the weakness of the contemporary nation state in neoliberal capitalism. It might well be able to declare a state of exception, but it cannot sustain its enforcement in the way that a mediaeval city state could. In addition, liberal Western states are certainly more responsive to the needs of citizens than Agamben's pessimistic view. This is not to say that we should not be concerned. As the *Report on the Surveillance Society* argued:

> ... getting surveillance into proper perspective as the outcome of bureaucracy and the desire for efficiency, speed, control and coordination does not mean that all is well. All it means is that we have to be careful identifying the key issues and vigilant in calling attention to them.
>
> (Murakami Wood *et al.*, 2006, p. 2)

The future of resilience

Towards 'third way' security

We have argued that resilience is a multi-faceted term that has been applied in many different ways in policy and politics. Indeed as Vale and Campenella (2005, p. 339) say, historically 'resilience is primarily a rhetorical device intended to enhance or restore the legitimacy of whatever government was in power at the time the disaster occurred'. Moreover, 'urban resilience is an interpretive framework proposed by local and national leaders and shaped and accepted by citizens in the wake of disaster' (ibid., p. 353).

In the United Kingdom since 1997 the dominant political framework through which the resilience debate has evolved has been that of 'third way' politics, the underpinning elements of which are important in understanding how resilience policy has developed and been transmuted into what may be described as 'third way security' (Coaffee and O'Hare, 2008).

'Third way' politics – a normative agenda for centre-left politics throughout the Western world (Giddens, 1998; Scanlon, 2001) – emerged alongside the perceived need to reform public administration and public services in response to the ongoing restructuring of the global economy, and was most notably adopted by the Clinton administration in the United States and the Blair Government in the United Kingdom. There are a number of features of this approach to politics that are of direct relevance here to our discussion on the future of resilience.

First, the 'third way' is a broad concept that developed in order to rearticulate the need to manage the complexities of the increasingly globalized world. We saw this quite clearly in the prior discussion of the new National Security Strategy where the concerns regarding security, and the need for added resilience, were highlighted in terms of an array of interconnected local and global issues. Whereas, in the past, security was seen as broadly related to international relationships, today we can argue that increasingly security has 'come home' to focus not only upon traditional as well as new international security threats from a wide range of sources, not just terrorism, but also increasingly upon the civil, urbane and domestic notions, embodying ideas of human security.

Second, under 'third way' ideas, the need for effective government has led to the vertical decentralization of power and responsibility – subsidiarity – to different tiers of government premised upon the twin concerns of unleashing enterprise and market forces, whilst at the same time ensuring the provision of key social support services. In this regard, the resilience agenda has been significant, especially against the backdrop of a highly centralized state. As a result of the need to improve UK resilience, power and responsibility has, in very real ways, been devolved to localities (Chapter 10) and facilitated by the addition of a regional resilience tier (Chapter 9). The aim of such multi-level working has also been to provide civic frameworks where citizens receive a certain level of protection, whilst commercial enterprises are made more resistant to events which might stop the orderly flow of commerce.

Third, the 'third way' is also connected to ideas of efficiency with an emphasis upon accountability, evidence and performance management. We have seen, particularly in Chapters 10 and 11, how the evaluation of resilience as a key priority at local government level has been paralleled by the development of assessment frameworks and the creation of indicators, not only for effective emergency planning, but also for tackling violent extremism and protecting crowded public places from terrorism. The aim here has been for national government to 'steer' local government into particular workstreams that will ultimately, in their view, lead to a guaranteed minimum level of resilience across the United Kingdom.

Fourth, the 'third way' theory of change is also characterized by a belief in the value of community and the promotion of active citizenship, based on ideas of social capital and communitarianism (Etzioni, 1998; Putnam, 2000). In short, this has aspired to strengthen 'bottom-up' approaches and increase local responsibility. In our previous discussions we have clearly seen how one of the key elements of UK resilience is an appreciation of community and social resilience, and an acknowledgement that local citizens have a key role to play in building resilience as individuals and as part of communities to supplement more strategic guidance from the local and national state. The Government has facilitated this through streams of work called 'warning and informing', although we might argue that from a Foucauldian governmental perspective this appears to be an agenda of civil responsibilization, and the passing on of the risk management baton from state to citizen.

Fifth, the promotion of a 'stakeholder society' emphasizing a broader shift in decentralized decision-making, conceptualized as a transformation from 'providing' to 'enabling' state and from 'government' to 'governance', is also a key idea of the 'third way'. Once again the resiliency agenda provides a tangible example of where multi-stakeholder partnerships between public and private sectors, and at all tiers of Government, have been developed between statutory and non-statutory 'responders' in order to prepare for emergencies and mitigate threat. We have also seen how the ideas of partnership working have most recently been centrally reinforced within the 2008 NSS.

Security governance without government

Critiques of the 'third way' are also illuminating in terms of our discussion of resilience. The 'third way' as a political concept can also be seen as an articulation of a new mode of governance and governmentality. Viewing the 'third way' as a new method of governing illuminates the rescaling of the state, ideas of subsidiarity and locally pragmatic working, an increased emphasis on partnership working and a greater role and reasonability being afforded to civil society for the management and control of their everyday life. Here the state's role is seen as a facilitator rather than a manager, keen to regulate direct 'hands-on' responsibility (see Furedi, 2005). We must, however, counter-pose this idealistic idea with ideas of responsibilization (Chapter 11) where it is argued that governments and institutions having lost their ability to manage contemporary risk, diffuse their responsibility to a plethora of 'authorities' and 'institutions' and 'communities' who are subtly steered by the hand of supposedly apolitical 'experts'. This for many is seen as an expression of 'neoliberal governmentality' and represents 'not the end but a transformation of politics that restructures the power relations in society... between statehood and a new relation between state and civil society actors' (Lemke, 2002, p. 58).

What is clear is that in the United Kingdom, a new protective and regulatory state has emerged, which is commonly articulated through the rhetoric of resilience and has led to the dispersion of security responsibilities through all levels of Government and beyond. This balancing of the responsibility of the state and the individual is at the heart of the resilience agenda and is becoming far more evident as indicated by agendas for 'warning and informing the public' about security risks faced, providing public assessments of threats faced, encouraging individuals to phone anti-terror hotlines if they see suspicious activity and the development of voluntaristic civil protection networks.

Another conception of the 'third way' is as an act of political marketing, in other words as a brand (Arvidsson, 2006). The many facets of the 'third way' have meant that its actual meaning has proved difficult to pin down leading to much confusion, especially over terminology. As Arnoldi (2007, p. 67) has articulated the third way 'becomes a brand, a "free-floating signifier", detached from a fixed referent, and thus capable of attaching itself to any flow of desire'. This ambiguity as has been argued can in fact be a positive element that allows the agenda to become colonized by other, not necessarily related, agendas that 'allows unlimited ideological flexibility (and) the right to change policies as a matter of principle' (Temple, 2000, p. 310).

Here the political argument for using such 'empty phraseology', which lacks any meaningful substance, is entirely logical. As Furedi (2005, p. 7) notes, 'take some of the Hurrah words that trip off the tongue of public figures. Everybody is for diversity, transparency social cohesion, inclusion, best practice, added value, stakeholding and sustainability . . . it is evident that its purpose is to signal approval. Sustainability is good because unsustainability is bad'. Likewise we could easily make a similar case for terms like security, preparedness and resilience. With regard to resilience we have identified how resilience is now used as a label, and a framework, for a host of polices broadly connected to security, and particularly to the 'war on terror'. The way in which the concept and practice of resilience has recently become embedded within public policy, particularly in the United Kingdom, is the result of both historical precedent and the extrapolation of pre-existing trends, as well as more contemporary concerns embedded within a complex mixture of social concerns, economic considerations and political rhetoric.

Another key example of this trend was the publication, in August 2008, of the UK's first National Risk Register (NRR) which pulled together the evidence from the national Capabilities Programme and from community (local) and regional risk registers (Cabinet Office, 2008). This publically available document, promised as part of the earlier National Security Strategy, sets out the range of risks seen as either natural events, major accidents (collectively know as hazards) or malicious attacks (collectively known as threats). This document, although highlighting the greater likelihood of terrorist attacks against transport networks and crowded public places, acknowledges that the greatest risk currently facing the UK comes from an influenza pandemic. The NRR was predominantly aimed at increasing the awareness amongst individuals, and the public and private sectors, of the multitude of risks the UK faces, and encouraging proactive preparedness planning to be initiated and constantly updated.

In our discussion, the key argument is that resilience has become a 'catch-all' phrase for expressing responses to threat of many kinds (although usually terrorism) and leading to the increasing ubiquity of security and surveillance in urban areas. As we have argued in this, and the preceding chapter, there is a normalized notion of resilience that pervades everyday life, posing critical questions regarding the relationship between broader resilience policy for dealing with new security challenges and other emergent social policies directed at the civic realm. Most noticeably the opportunities offered by the terrorist threat for Governments to adopt social control technologies in the 'national interest' and for 'homeland security', amidst the ongoing climate of fear, are almost unprecedented. As Graham notes, 'in the wake of 9/11 and other catastrophic terrorist acts of the last few years, the design of buildings, the management of traffic, the physical planning of cities and neighbourhoods, are being brought under the widening umbrellas of "national security" ' (Graham, 2004, p. 11).

Conclusion: blending resilience with sustainable urbanism

As we have noted, urban policy in the United Kingdom is now adopting a discourse of 'sustainable communities' that seems to be locating 'security' as a key component, or even foundational principle of sustainability (Atkinson and Helms, 2007; Raco, 2007). And if the exact term 'resilience' is not used here, we would argue that resilience fundamentally *is* the union of sustainability and security, with the former redefined by the latter. Rather than security by design, we have security by sustainable development or community development. Many commentators have argued that how authorities respond to the current 'war on terrorism' will have serious consequences for urbanity. For example, as Swanstrom (2002) noted 'the main threat to cities comes not from terrorism but from the policy responses to terrorism that could undermine the freedom of thought and movement that are the lifeblood of cities...' This must be real 'human security' not the superficial, macho, image-centred security show of the stage-set city (Murakami Wood and Coaffee, 2007). A permanent theme-park security is not helpful although it might be a considered a temporary necessity to cope with high-profile events or other 'states of exception'. Vulnerability and resilience are not just properties of the form and inhuman components of cities, but also of personal psychology and identity – how they feel and perform in space – and this is nowhere better shown than in relation to the supposedly safe, or resilient, city.

We are not arguing for no security or the de-prioritization of building resilience: we agree with Campbell (1984) when he suggests that a policy which hints at the absence of civil defence suggests to the citizen that there is no protection. However, the discursive and material shifts and the underlying 'fears' and 'threats' must be the subject of our research and analysis in this area, to enable the variety of potential outcomes from the totalitarian to the liberatory that can result, to be understood and to make the case for following hope, not fear (Murakami Wood and Coaffee, 2007).

The development of everyday resilience in, and for the city, is as old as urbanism itself although it has been articulated in different ways and has surged and retreated in response to events. All managers of urban areas consider how they might plan and prepare for a host of threats that present themselves, be they natural disaster or human-induced risks. Seldom are such plans utilized, but this does not mean they should not be made or practiced. As Vale and Campenella (2005, p. 352) note, 'inevitably such plans prove to be of limited value and have often been held up to ridicule. Basement bomb shelters lined with cans of Campbell's soup, or the infamous "duck and cover" films of the Cold War era are still routinely parodied'. Likewise the UK Government's announcement in the NSS that they are to set up a civil protection force was roundly greeted in the press with humour, and caricatured as a 'Dads Army', in reference to the accident-prone Home Guard unit of the popular 1970s television programme.

Importantly, what the development of urban resilience and its accompanying plans and strategies tells us about Government priorities and governmentality is illuminating. For example, in the United Kingdom we have seen the threat of terrorism take centre stage in discussion regarding security, civil contingencies and resilience, despite other threats from flooding, climate change and especially pandemic, which provide much greater logical risk in terms of impact, damage, disruption and death toll. Likewise the rhetoric of partnership and decentred responsibility give the impression that we are all being subsumed into the resilience agenda, whether we like it or not.

Our suggestion would be for resilience to be acknowledged as the sustenance of a living, civil society. The rhetoric of fear and suspicion and the increasing use made of fortification and technologies of surveillance further drain the already declining reservoir of mutual public trust, even if people's belief in them have become convinced that they need them. Instead the focus should be on rebuilding democracy and accountability and making them resilient. Cities in which citizens are engaged and feel part of are places that will indeed be able to celebrate their resilience and survival without the need for the imposition of a more permanent state of exception.

Notes

Chapter 2

1. De Boer and Sanders unfortunately confuse the moral admonitions of Nichiren with the actual, far more gradual and politically centred decline of the regime: socio-political histories of the period give the role of natural disaster little credit in this regard (see, for example, Souyri, 2002 [1998]).
2. Ironically, the city had been almost as devastated by its sacking by Crusader forces supposedly on the same side, during the Fourth Crusade of 1204 (see Harris, 2004), whose armies were equally destructive of the Islamic cities they captured in the Levant during the *al-furub al-salibiyyah* (crusader wars) (see Hillenbrand, 1999).
3. There were at least three attempts to wall the 'north-west frontier': the last being the best known by the Emperor Hadrian (Johnson, 2004); but there were also the Antonine Wall (Hanson and Maxwell, 1983) and the earlier wall along the Gask Ridge, still being investigated (Wooliscroft, 2002).
4. See John Pike's GlobalSecurity website 'US-Mexico Border Fence/ Great Wall of Mexico Secure Fence' http://www.globalsecurity.org/security/systems/mexico-wall.htm (accessed 20/12/2007).

Chapter 3

1. It was not just humans that were regulated. See Blancou (2001) on the history of control of animals and diseases.
2. However, Higonnet (2002) has disputed at least any primarily repressive military motivation for the rebuilding.

Chapter 4

1. The amateur historian, Matthew White (2005), uses the term 'hemoclysm' (lit. blood-letting) to refer to the massive and unprecedented series of linked wars, massacres and exterminations which characterized the Twentieth Century. As a *longue durée* analysis, this echoes Zygmunt Bauman's view that the Twentieth Century was characterized by 'fast and efficient killing, scientifically designed and administered genocide' (1995, p. 193).
2. Other significant advocates were Basil Liddell-Hart in the United Kingdom, and in Italy, Giulio Douhet.
3. For the official rationale, see Stimson (1947); for a consideration of the different views on this, see Sherwin (1995).
4. These agreements, including the Geneva and Hague Conventions and the multiple agreements and treaties on nuclear weapons, are outside the scope of this book.

Chapter 5

1. This idea saw mixed land-use in the city as contributing to greater safety as this would increase the times of day the streets were frequented.
2. Not only did SBD prove successful in reducing criminality but were also often able to elicit a significant discount on household insurance (Conzens *et al.*, 1999).
3. During the first years of the 'Troubles' (1968–1970) the commercial core of the city was seen as a relatively neutral space within the segregated sectarian landscape and was relatively unaffected by terrorism. All this changed in July 1970 when a large bomb was detonated in the area without warning.
4. This initially led to fears that these measures would destroy the city centre in a way the Provisional IRA never could, by keeping the customers out (see Brown, 1985; Boal, 1995).
5. It is believed that the term 'ring of steel' was first used in 1976 to refer to the amalgamation of the four individual security zones around Belfast City Centre into one large security sector ringed by seventeen 10–12 foot high, steel gates (Coaffee, 2003).
6. Place promotion campaigns were also been used to re-image the stigmatized Central Belfast area in an attempt to shake of its image of terrorist violence (see Gold, 1994; Neil, 1995).
7. Soffer and Minghi highlight that the security landscape evolved over the course of the Twentieth Century but intensified after 1948 with the establishment of the state and again in the late 1960 and early 1970 linked to a series of Middle Eastern regional conflicts.
8. For a detailed account, see Segal and Weizman (eds.) (2003).
9. For a detailed account of the history of CCTV in Britain, see Norris and Armstrong, 1999.
10. Furedi (2006), utilizing the work of criminologist David Garland (2001), referred to the lack of statistics relationship between crime figures and fear of crime as part of a 'crime complex' that 'encompasses a cluster of attitudes that are shaped by the belief that high crime rates are a normal part of life' and that 'these attitudes are expressed through a consciousness of crime that is moulded by popular culture and institutionalized in the organization of everyday life' (p. 3).

Chapter 6

1. Jones and Newman also illuminated how there existed a 'benign co-existence' (p. 181) between the local police force and the private security agencies who tended to operate in different geographical spaces – the police in the public realm and the private security professionals in the spaces of commerce.
2. The City at this time employed around 130,000–140,000 people and generated an estimated output of £10–15 billion a year for the UK economy (Corporation of London, 1995).
3. Locally the ring of steel was often called 'the ring of plastic' as initially access restrictions were based on funnelling traffic through strategically placed rows of traffic cones (Coaffee, 2004).
4. This cordon was again expanded in August 2005.

5. Here preparation involved assessing the likelihood of terrorist attack on your organization; preparing your staff for the possibility of telephoned bomb threats; choosing the mix of protective measures that best suits your premises and that will deter or detect the terrorist; encouraging your staff to remain vigilant; and testing security plans regularly.

Chapter 7

1. See also Harvey and Delfabbro (2004) for an overview.
2. The rhetoric of resilience in the media is also often emotive in this way, building on the positive psychological sense of strength gained from exposure, thus underpinning much of the 'spin' of resilience as a metaphor which can be deployed strategically in a broader framework of policies.
3. Institutional resilience to change in the context of cross-national collaboration and convergence is another approach to resilience not discussed here in depth; for an example of this see Jordan (2003).
4. Whilst economic resilience is useful in itself, its conceptual orientation often excludes socio-cultural and spatial factors (underpinning the reason for adopting a resiliency approach) at the cost of over-privileging the orderly flow of capital.
5. It has also been noted that the risk and frequency of disease outbreaks is increasing, affecting every corner of the globe (see, for example, Hayman, 2004).

Chapter 8

1. This demonstrates the global scale of natural hazards planning alongside the global terror threat, but also the need to operate proactively across several scales efficiently (international, national, regional, local).
2. Cited in Walker and Broderick (2006, p. 24).
3. There was also another booklet called *Emergency Response and Recovery* which dealt with further aspects of IEM published at the same time.
4. A discussion of the detail of the CCA legislation lies beyond the scope of this chapter (for a detailed expose and commentary on the Act, see Walker and Broderick, 2006).
5. A discussion the resiliency arrangements lie beyond the scope of our discussion here. For further information see http://www.scotland.gov.uk/ Topics/Justice/emergencies; http://www.walesresilience.org/; http://cepu. nics.gov.uk/.
6. National Government's further commitment to this fledgling 'warning and informing' strategy was to formalize, from 2003, a National Media Emergency Forum (subsequent regional and local variations have since emerged). This was initially a voluntary body set up in 1996.
7. For example, the urban riots in a number of northern English towns during the summer of 2001, some of the worst in 20 years, were sparked in part by accusations of racial segregation. This increased concerns regarding existing approaches to area-based regeneration and the need to prioritize measures that would improve the integration of different ethnic groupings.

8. To date this aspect of countering radicalization has involved numerous meetings and discussions between Government misters and senior members of UK Muslim communities, detailed work undertaken by the Foreign and Commonwealth Office in local communities, and the development of grass-roots projects to engage with Muslim youth.

9. The 'MI' in MI5 and MI6 stands for 'Military Intelligence' and is a hangover from a much older system of classification of the British intelligence community.

10. This Act uses a clause in the European Convention on Human Rights (ECHR, Article 5) which allows the Secretary of State to apply to the courts for 'derogating' order. The 2005 Act has in recent years been challenged in the UK courts, where under Article 6 of the ECHR (right to a fair hearing) it was successfully argued that this, in certain circumstances, amount to a 'deprivation of liberty' (HM Government, 2006, p. 20).

11. Notably this included the creation of a new European Union Counter-Terrorism Strategy in 2005; achieved whilst the United Kingdom held the rotating EU presidency.

12. At present, *Project Semaphore* – a pilot system – is assessing how this might best be done, and this will be superseded after 2008 with a roll-out of a full e-borders system.

13. CPNI was formed in early 2007 from the merger of the National Infrastructure Security Coordination Centre (NISCC) and a part of MI5 (the Security Service) – the National Security Advice Centre (NSAC).

14. Depending on the nature of the event, different representatives will attend the meeting and advise on contingency arrangements.

15. Under such powers, Parliament could, in theory, be suspended and a bank holiday declared to shut down businesses. Property could be destroyed or requisitioned, mass assemblies banned and freedom of movement limited. In extreme cases, the armed forces can be mobilized and special courts set up to deal with suspects if it was felt another atrocity was planned (*The Independent*, 2007).

16. In the United Kingdom a combination of JTAC and the Security Service (MI5) are responsible for setting international and domestic terrorism threat levels, respectively.

17. http://www.preparingforemergencies.gov.uk/ (accessed 1 March 2008).

18. http://www.preparingforemergencies.co.uk/ (accessed 1 March 2008).

Chapter 9

1. In the United Kingdom in the last decade such constitutional modernization has been widespread and has led to a devolution and decentralization drive which has resulted in the formation of a Parliament for Scotland, a National Assembly for Wales, an Assembly for Northern Ireland and an Elected Major for London.

2. This was within a broader structural context of 43 police services of drastically differing sizes operating through England, Northern Ireland and Wales. The eventual proposals suggested 24 forces should be created.

3. Other key areas include major crime (murder), serious and organized crime, public order and strategic roads policing.

4. Formerly the Office of the Deputy Prime Minister (ODPM).
5. In England there are nine regions – North East, North West, Yorkshire and Humber, West Midlands, East Midlands, South East, South West, East of England and London.
6. Historically, some EPU emerged at the county level.
7. Based on reflections from a series of interviews conducted with local emergency planners during 2005–2006.
8. Control of major accident hazards (COMAH).
9. There is a tendency, given the amount of testing that now occurs to assume this is a reaction to the events of September 11. It is important to note, however, that in London tests have been an ongoing part of emergency planning for many years and tests on the underground network have been a regular occurrence since the mid-1990s, stimulated by the Tokyo subway attack.
10. *Exercise Atlantic Blue* was conducted in April 2005 involving the United Kingdom, the United States and Canada (known as TopOff 3 in the United States and Triple Play in Canada). This was a major counter-terrorism exercise that simulated internationally linked terrorist incidents.
11. The findings of the Government enquiry into the response on July 7 stimulated another round of investment and refined certain areas of the capability targets for future development; in particular, a focus upon immediate 'first hour' of the response for rescue and treatment of the injured and walking wounded (London Assembly, 2006).
12. In the light of national disaster RCCCs will co-ordinate with COBR(A), which may still convene in relation to smaller scale disaster events and liaise with local command and control, but the RCCC should only come into force if the scale of event affects more than one region.
13. Joint Committee on Draft Civil Contingencies Bill First Report (2003) at http://www.publications.parliament.uk/pa/jt200203/jtselect/jtdcc/184/18 410.htm.

Chapter 10

1. For example, the Greater Manchester LRF in North West England – *GM Resilience* – covers a conurbation of approximately 500 square miles with a population of over 2.5 million. Geographically, the area encompasses ten Local Authority areas: Bolton, Bury, Manchester, Oldham, Rochdale, Salford, Stockport, Tameside, Trafford, and Wigan.
2. For example, stimulated by such high-profile events as the Hillsborough disaster (1989), experience of rioting in ethnically diverse Core Cities (1981, 1992, 2001), public protest such as the miners strikes and police confrontations in the 1980's or widespread flooding (2001, 2007).
3. As a result of the introduction of the statutory requirements under the CCA, Central Government increased funding for emergency planning by 113%, although this extra resource might not be applied across local authorities equitably (Newcastle City Council, 2004).
4. Operating since 2002, CPA is the mechanism by which a Local Authority's service delivery is 'judged' by the Audit Commission and then supported to deliver service improvement. From 2009 a new mechanism – the Comprehensive Area Assessment with replace the CPA (see also Chapter 11)

5. In the response to an emergency event there are several tiers of response set up as a part of the emergency services procedures. Gold command operates strategic co-ordination, silver command (often on site or close by) logistics and tactics and bronze command on-site operations. There are often several silver and bronze commands operating in a multi-scalar or multiple site event; Gold command will be the focus for feedback into an RCCC, should one be convened.

6. This was a particular concern with relation to the Police, whose current operational boundaries had formed the spatial territory covered by the LRF. The boundaries of police and LRF responsibility were more or less coterminous in different sub-regions. In Greater Manchester, for example, this was not a problem as all the sub-regional LRF areas corresponded to the police operational area. However, in the North East, for example, the regionalization of the police force would have had significant implications for the role and function of the three existing LRF structures and slowing down the larger process of conformance to broader regulations such as the CCA.

7. This can be seen in the annual conference reports (see Core Cites, 2005, 2006), whereby the group met to update each other formally and feed back on best practice, challenges and accomplishments over the previous period.

8. For more information visit – http://www.birmingham.gov.uk/Generate Content?CONTENT_ITEM_ID=79595&CONTENT_ITEM_TYPE=0&MENU_ID =14305.

9. See for further information: http://www.bristol.gov.uk/ccm/content/Advice-Benefits/Emergencies/civil-contingencies-unit.en.

10. See for further information: http://www.leeds.gov.uk/page.aspx? pageidentifier=9EBBB45B4ED319AD80256E1500545065.

11. For further information see http://www.liverpool.gov.uk/Policing_ and_public_safety/Accidents_emergencies_and_safety/emergency_planning/ Partnerships/index.asp.

12. For further information see http://www.manchester.gov.uk/site/ scripts/documents_info.php?categoryID=200039&documentID=2610&page Number=3.

13. For further information see http://www.newcastle.gov.uk/core.nsf/a/ emergencyservice.

14. For further information see http://www.nottinghamcity.gov.uk/ emergency_planning.

15. For further information see http://www.sheffield.gov.uk/your-city-council/ emergency-planning.

16. Protest occurred from groups including Fathers 4 Justice (F4J), the Countryside Alliance, Stop the War Coalition and the Association of University Teachers. One F4J protestor, dressed as Spiderman, did manage to get past the supposedly tight security and climbed high onto a high-level bridge overlooking the conference site, presenting a possible security risk, where he remained for several hours, before voluntarily descending.

17. Despite the high levels of security, the local news reported a number of potential threats and risks after an army vehicle for transporting mortars was stolen from a base in Stockport only days before the conference began (MEN, 2006a) and a laptop containing the security details for the conference was stolen from an army officials' car (MEN, 2006b).

Chapter 11

1. For more details, see Murakami Wood *et al.* (2007).
2. This cycle has been adopted by Greater Manchester Local Resilience forum in 2007. It is based upon a model developed by the National Steering Committee on Warning and Informing the Public (NSCWIP).
3. From March 2008 advertising campaigns went into operation in London, Greater Manchester, West Yorkshire and the West Midlands and focusing upon specific aspects of the terrorist threat.
4. This advert appeared in the *Manchester Evening News*, March 6, p. 19.
5. He makes several attacks on scholars who have criticized both the military 'urbicide' of Israeli armed forces in the occupied Palestinian territories and US domestic responses to the attacks on the World Trade Center and the Pentagon.

Chapter 12

1. The Chancellor of the Exchequer is the UK equivalent of the Minister for Finance.
2. The Committee will meet regularly, and will be chaired by the Prime Minister. It replaces the existing Ministerial Committees on Defence and Overseas Policy, Security and Terrorism, and Europe.
3. This statement set in motion a review of the Government counter-terrorism effort placing significant emphasis upon: the protection and resilience of critical national infrastructure and crowded public places; a new proposed Counter Terrorism Bill; and priority given under the existing e-border programme.
4. In terms of resources, it was announced that in order to meet the impending threats facing the United Kingdom, the number of personnel in the security services will be enhanced and funding increased. The growth of funding for counter-terrorism and intelligence will rise from £1 billion in 2001 to £2.5 in 2007/2008 which will increase to £3.5 billion by 2010/2011 (Cabinet Office, 2008, p. 5).
5. International security concerns, energy security and armed forces retention and deployment formed a key segment of the NSS. This included the creation of a 1000-strong UK civilian standby capacity including police, emergency service professionals for overseas reconstruction work. This, however, lies outside of our discussion here.
6. As well as a greater commitment to informing the public about threat, it was also announced that knowledge and skills held outside Government would be leveraged through the creation of a National Security Forum that will advise the recently constituted National Security Committee and 'harness a much wider range of expertise and experience from outside government' (BBC News, 2008).
7. The monarch reads a prepared speech to a complete session of both Houses of Parliament, outlining the government's agenda for the coming year.

Bibliography

Abdallatif, T.F., Mousa, S.E. and Elbassiony, A. (2003) 'Geophysical investigation for mapping the archaeological features at Qantir, Sharqyia, Egypt', *Archaeological Prospection*, 10, 1, 27–42.

Abe, K. (2004) 'Everyday policing in Japan: surveillance, media, government and public opinion', *International Sociology*, 19, 2, 215–31.

Abu-Lughod, J.L. (1989) *Before European Hegemony: The World System AD 1250–1350* (Oxford: Oxford University Press).

Addison, P. and Jones, H. (eds.) (2005) *A Companion to Contemporary Britain, 1939–2000* (Oxford: Blackwell).

Adger, W.N. (2000) 'Social and ecological resilience: are they related?', *Progress in Human Geography*, 24, 3, 347–64.

Africa, T.W. (1971) 'Urban violence in imperial Rome', *Journal of Interdisciplinary History*, 2, 1, 3–21.

Agamben, G. (2005) *State of Exception* (trans. K. Attell) (Chicago: University of Chicago Press).

Al Tamimi, A. (2003) 'The Wall's path is based on ultimate control over Palestinian water', in Palestinian Environmental NGO Network (PENGON) *Stop the Wall in Palestine*, pp. 138–40 see: http://stopthewall.org/downloads/pdf/book/guestarticles.pdf (accessed 12 December 2007), 61–74.

Alberti, L.B. (1991 [1485]) *On the Art of Building [De Re Aedificatoria]* (Cambridge MA: MIT Press).

Alexander, D. (2002) 'From civil defence to civil protection and back again', *Disaster Prevention and Management*, 1, 3, 209–13.

Ambraseys, N.N. (2004) 'The 12th Century seismic paroxysm in the Middle East: a historical perspective', *Annals of Geophysics*, 47, 2/3, 733–58.

Amin, A. (1999) 'An institutionalist perspective on regional economic development', *International Journal of Urban and Regional Research*, 23, 2, 365–78.

Anderson, D. and Killingray, D. (ed.) (1991) *Policing the Empire: Government, Authority and Control, 1830–1940* (Manchester: Manchester University Press).

Anderson, D. and Rathbone, R. (eds.) (2000) *Africa's Urban Past* (Oxford: James Currey).

Anderson, P. (1996 [1974]) *Passages from Antiquity to Feudalism* (London: Verso [London: New Left Books]).

Anderton, C. (1990) 'The inherent propensity toward peace or war embodied in weaponry', *Defence and Peace Economics*, 1, 197–219.

Andrejevic, M. (2005) 'The work of watching one another: lateral surveillance, risk, and governance', *Surveillance and Society*, 2, 4, 479–97.

Andrejevic, M. (2007) *iSpy: Surveillance and Power in the Interactive Era* (University of Kansas Press).

Antonopoulos, J. (1992) 'The great Minoan eruption of the Thera volcano and the ensuing tsunami in the Greek Archipelago', *Journal of Natural Hazards*, 5, 2, 153–68.

Applebaum, A. (2003) *Gulag: A History* (New York: Doubleday).

Applebaum, A. (2006) *Gulag: A History of the Soviet Camps* (London: Allen Lane).

Arnold, T.F. (1995) 'Fortifications and the Military Revolution: the Gonzaga experience, 1530–1630', in C.J. Rogers (ed.) *The Military Revolution Debate: Readings on the Military Transformation of Early Modern Europe* (Boulder CO: Westview Press), pp. 201–26.

Arnoldi, J. (2007) 'Informational ideas', *Thesis Eleven*, 89, 58.

Arvidsson, A. (2006) *Brands: Meaning and Value in Media Culture* (London: Routledge).

Asher, C. (2000) 'Delhi walled: changing boundaries', in J.D. Tracy (ed.) *City Walls: The Urban Enceinte in Comparative Perspective* (Cambridge: Cambridge University Press), pp. 247–81.

Ashworth, G.J. (1991) *War and the City* (London: Routledge).

Athens Indymedia (2005) 'CCTV cameras all around us (but some destroyed)', see: http://athens.indymedia.org/features.php3?id=394 (accessed 1 April 2008).

Atkins, P.J. (1993) 'How the West End was won: the struggle to remove street barriers in Victorian London', *Journal of Historical Geography*, 19, 3, 265–77.

Atkinson, R. (2003) 'Domestication by cappuccino or a revenge on urban space? Control and empowerment in the management of public space', *Urban Studies*, 40, 9, 1829–43.

Atkinson, R. and Helms, G. (eds.) (2007) *Securing and Urban Renaissance: Crime, Community and British Urban Policy* (Bristol: The Policy Press).

Augustine of Hippo (2003 [413–426]) *City of God [De Civitate Dei]* (Harmondsworth: Penguin).

Avraham, E. (2004) 'Media strategies for improving an unfavourable city image', *Cities*, 21, 6, 471–9.

Avraham, E. and Ketter, E. (2008) *Media strategies for Marketing Places in Crisis* (Oxford: Butterworth-Heinemann).

Azaryahu, M. (2000) 'Israeli securityscapes', in J.R. Gold and G. Revill (eds.) *Landscapes of Defence* (Harlow: Prentice Hall), pp. 102–13.

Azzaro, R., Barbano, M.S., Moroni., A., Mucciarelli, M. and Stucchi, M. (1999) 'The seismic history of Catania', *Journal of Seismology*, 3, 3, 235–52.

Bache, I. and Jones, R. (2000) 'Has EU regional policy empowered the regions? A study of Spain and the United Kingdom', *Regional and Federal Studies*, 10, 3, 1–20.

Bachrach, B.S. (2000) 'Imperial walled cities in the West: an examination of the earlier mediaeval *Nachleben*', in J.D. Tracy (ed.) (2000) *City Walls: The Urban Enceinte in Comparative Perspective* (Cambridge: Cambridge University Press), pp. 192–218.

Baer, M., Heron, K., Morton, O., and Ratliff, E. (eds.) (2005) *Safe: The Race to Protect Ourselves in a Newly Dangerous World* (New York: Harper Collins).

Ball, K. and Webster, F. (eds.) (2003) *The Intensification of Surveillance: Crime, Terrorism and Warfare in the Information Age* (London: Pluto Press).

Balmer, B. (2002) 'Biological warfare: the threat in historical perspective', *Medicine, Conflict, and Survival*, 18, April/June, 120–37.

Bamford, J. (1983) *The Puzzle Palace* (Harmondsworth: Penguin).

Bankoff, G., Frerks, G. and Hilhorst, D. (eds.) (2004) *Mapping Vulnerability: Disasters, Development and People* (London: Earthscan).

Barker, G. (2002) 'A tale of two deserts: contrasting desertification histories on Rome's desert frontiers', *World Archaeology*, 33, 3, 488–507.

Bauman, Z. (1995) *Life in Fragments: Essays in Postmodern Modernity* (Oxford: Blackwell).

Bauman, Z. (2006) *Liquid Fear* (Cambridge UK: Polity Press).

BBC (2007) 'Regional anti-terror unit formed', 2 April, see: http://news.bbc.co.uk/1/hi/england/6516829.stm (accessed 2 February 2008).

BBC News (2002) 'Security tight for Games', 23 July, see: http://news.bbc.co.uk/sport3/commonwealthgames2002/hi/front_page/newsid_2146000/2146550.stm (accessed 23 November 2007).

BBC News (2004) Security takes election stage, see: http://news.bbc.co.uk/1/hi/uk_politics/4034903.stm (accessed 23 November 2007).

BBC News (2007a) 'Sydney fenced in for Apec summit', 1 September, see: http://news.bbc.co.uk/1/hi/world/asia-pacific/6973631.stm (accessed 23 November 2007).

BBC News (2007b) 'UK security policy out of date', 10 December, see: http://news.bbc.co.uk/1/hi/uk/7133508.stm (accessed 10 December 2007).

BBC News (2008) 'In full: Brown security statement' (19 March), see: http://news.bbc.co.uk/1/hi/uk_politics/7304999.stm (accessed 19 March 2008).

Beck, U. (1992) *Risk Society: Towards a New Modernity* (London: Sage).

Beck, U. (2002) 'The terrorist threat: world risk society revisited', *Theory, Culture and Society*, 19, 4, 39–55.

Beck, U. (2003) 'The silence of words: on terror and war', *Security Dialogue*, 34, 3, 255–67.

Beito, D.T. and Smith, B. (1990) 'The formation of urban infrastructure through nongovernmental planning: the private places of St. Louis, 1869–1920', *Journal of Urban History*, 16, 3, 263–303.

Belinda, B. and Helms, G. (2003) 'Zero tolerance for the industrial past and other threats: policing and urban entrepreneurialism in Britain and Germany', *Urban Studies*, 40, 9, 1845–67.

Benjamin, W. (1999) *The Arcades Project* (Cambridge MA: Belknap Press).

Berger, S. (ed.) (2006) *A Companion to Nineteenth-Century Europe, 1789–1914* (Oxford: Blackwell).

Berque, A. (1993) *Du Geste à la Cité: Formes Urbaines et Lien Social au Japon* (Paris: Gallimard).

Bishop, R. and Phillips, J. (2002) 'Manufacturing emergencies', *Theory, Culture and Society*, 19, 4, 91–102.

Bissell, W.C. (2000) 'Conservation and the colonial past: urban planning, space and power in Zanzibar', in D. Anderson and R. Rathbone (eds.) *Africa's Urban Past* (Oxford: James Currey), pp. 246–61.

Black, E. (2002) *IBM and the Holocaust: The Strategic Alliance Between Nazi Germany and America's Most Powerful Corporation* (New York: Crown).

Black, J. (1998) *War and the World: Military Power and the Fate of Continents, 1450–200* (New Haven CT: Yale University Press).

Black, J. (2003) *World War Two: A Military History* (London: Routledge).

Blair, T. (2003) Speech to US Congress, Thursday, 17 July, see: http://www.cnn.com/2003/US/07/17/blair.transcript/ (accessed 20 July 2003).

Blakely, E.J. and Snyder, M.G. (1995) Fortress America: Gated and Walled Communities in the US (*Lincoln institute of Land Policy, Working papers*).

Blancou, J. (2001) 'History of the traceability of animals and animal products', *Revue Scientifique et Technique Office International de Epizooites*, 20, 2, 420–5.

Boal, F.W. (1969) 'Territoriality on the Shankhill-Falls Divide, Belfast', *Irish Geography*, 6, 30–50.

Boal, F.W. (1971) 'Territoriality and class: a study of two residential areas in Belfast', *Irish Geography*, 6, 229–48.

Boal, F.W. (1975) 'Belfast 1980: A segregated city?', *Graticule*, Department of Geography, Queens University of Belfast.

Bollens, S. (1999) *Urban Peace Building in Divided Societies: Belfast and Johannesburg* (Colorado: Westview Press).

Bonanno, G.A. (2004) 'Loss, trauma, and human resilience: have we underestimated the human capacity to thrive after extremely aversive events?', *American Psychologist*, 59, 1, 20–8.

Bonanno, G.A., Galea, S., Bucciarelli, A. and Vlahov, D. (2006) 'Psychological resilience after disaster: New York City in the aftermath of the September 11th terrorist attack', *Psychological Science*, 17, 3, 181–6.

Bonner, D. (1985) *Emergency Powers in Peacetime* (London: Sweet & Maxwell).

Booth, K. (2004) 'Realities of security', *International Relations*, 18, 1, 5–8.

Bosovic, M. (ed.) (1995) *The Panopticon Writings: Introduction* (London: Verso).

Botsman, D.V. (2005) *Punishment and Power in the Making of Modern Japan* (Princeton NJ: Princeton University Press).

Bowker, G.C. and Star, S.L. (1999) *Sorting Things Out: Classification and its Consequences* (Cambridge MA: MIT Press).

Boyer, P. (1978) *Urban Masses and Moral Order in America: 1820–1920* (Cambridge MA: Harvard University Press).

Braudel, F. (1986 [1979]) *The Perspective of the World (Civilisation and Capitalism 15th –18th Century: Volume 3)* (New York: Harper and Row).

Bray, W. (1972) 'The city state in Central Mexico at the time of the Spanish conquest', *Journal of Latin American Studies*, 4, 2, 161–85.

Briggs, R. (ed.) (2002) *The Unlikely Counter Terrorist* (London: Foreign Policy Centre).

Briguglio, L. (2004) 'Economic vulnerability and resilience: concepts and measurements', in L. Briguglio and E.J. Kisanga (eds.) *Economic Vulnerability and Resilience of Small States* (Malta: Islands and Small States Institute and Commonwealth Secretariat) 43–53.

Brigulio, L., Cordina, G., Bugeja, S. and Farrugia, N. (2005) *Conceptualising and Measuring Economic Resilience* (Malta: Island and Small States Institute).

Brogden, M. (1987) 'The emergence of the police: the colonial dimension', *British Journal of Criminology*, 27, 1, 4–14.

Brower, D.R. (1986) 'Urban revolution in the late Russian empire', in M.F. Hamm (ed.) *The City in Late Imperial Russia* (Bloomington IL: Indiana University Press), 319–50.

Brown, G. (2006) Speech at Royal United Services Institute, London, 13 February.

Brown, G. (2007) 'Statement on Security', 25 July, see: http://www.number10.gov.uk/output/Page12675.asp (accessed 26 July 2007).

Brown, P.L. (1995) Designs in a Land of Bombs and Guns, *New York Times*, 28 May.

Brown, S. (1985a) 'City centre commercial revitalisation: the Belfast experience', *The Planner*, 9–12 June.

Brown, S. (1985b) 'Central Belfast's security segment: an urban phenomenon', *Area*, 17, 1, 1–8.

Brown, S. (1987) 'Shopping centre development in Belfast', *Land Development Studies*, 4, 193–207.

Brown, S. and Sherry, J.F. (eds.) (2005) *Time, Space, and the Market: Retroscapes Rising* (New York: M.E. Sharpe).

Bryan, D. (2003) Belfast: Urban space, 'policing' and sectarian polarization, in J. Schneider and I. Susser (eds.), *Wounded Cities: Destruction and Reconstruction in a Globalized World* (Oxford: Berg), pp. 251–70.

Buckle, P., Mars, G. and Smale, S. (2000) 'New approaches to assessing vulnerability and resilience', *Australian Journal of Emergency Management*, 15, 2, 8–14.

Buckley, J. (1999) *Air Power in the Age of Total War* (Bloomington IL: Indiana University Press).

Bugliarelio, G. (2003) 'Urban security in perspective', *Technology in Society*, 25, 4, 499–507.

Bull-Kamanga, L., Diagne, K., Lavell, A., Leon, E., Lerise, F. and MacGregor, H. (2003) 'From everyday hazards to disasters: the accumulation of risk in urban areas', *Environment and Urbanisation*, 15, 1, 193–203.

Bunyan, T. (1977) *The History and Practice of the Political Police in Britain* (London: Quartet Books).

Burns, J. (1993) 'IRA Exploited Reduction in Spot Security Checks', *Financial Times*, 26 April, 7.

Burrows, W. (1987) *Deep Black: Space Espionage and National Security* (New York: Random House).

Cabinet Office (2003) *Dealing with Disaster (Revised Third Edition)* (London: Cabinet Office).

Cabinet Office (2005) *Emergency Preparedness* (London: Cabinet Office).

Cabinet Office (2006) *Civil Contingencies Act 2004: A Short Guide (revised)* (London: Cabinet Office).

Cabinet Office (2007) *Civil Contingences*, see: http://www.cabinetoffice.gov.uk/secretariats/civil_contingencies.aspx (accessed 1 February 2007).

Cabinet Office (2008) *The National Security Strategy of the United Kingdom: Security in an Interdependent World* (London: The Stationary Office).

Cabinet Office (2008) *National Risk Register* (London: Cabinet Office).

Caldwell, D.R., Ehlen, J. and Harmon, R.S. (eds.) (2005) *Studies in Military Geography And Geology* (Netherlands: Springer).

Campbell, B. (2002) *War and Society in Imperial Rome, 31 BC–AD 284* (London: Routledge).

Campbell, D. (1982) *War Plan UK: The Truth About Civil Defence in Britain* (London: Burnett Books).

Campbell, D. (1984) *The Unsinkable Aircraft Carrier: American Military Power in Britain* (London: Michael Joseph).

Campbell, D.B. (2006) *Besieged: Siege Warfare in the Ancient World* (Oxford: Osprey Publishing).

Camporesi, P. (1988) *The Incorruptible Flesh: Bodily Mutation and Mortification in Religion and Folklore* (trans. T. Croft-Murray) (Cambridge: Cambridge University Press).

Carpenter, S., Walker, B., Anderies, J.M. and Abel, N. (2001) 'From metaphor to measurement: resilience of what to what?' *Ecosystems*, 4, 765–81.

Carter, A., Deutch, J. and Zelikow, P. (1998) 'Catastrophic terrorism: tackling the new danger', *Foreign Affairs*, November/December, 80–94.

Castells, M. (1996) *The Information Age: Economy, Society and Culture Vol. 1: The Rise of the Network Society* (Oxford: Blackwell).

Central Office of Information (COI) (1980 [1976]) *Protect and Survive* (London: HMSO).

Chang, K., Filer, L. and Ying, Y. (2002) 'A structural decomposition of business cycles in Taiwan', *China Economic Review*, 13, 53–64.

Chang, N. (2002) *The Silencing of Political Dissent: How the USA Patriot Act Undermines the Constitution* (New York: Seven Stories press).

Chang, S. (1970) 'Some observations on the morphology of Chinese walled cities', *Annals of the Association of American Geographers*, 60, 1, 63–91.

Chen, A.H. and Siems, T.F. (2004) 'The effects of terrorism on global capital markets', *European Journal of Political Economy*, 20, 349–66.

Chernick, H. (ed.) (2005) *Resilient City: The Economic impact of 9/11* (New York: Russell Sage Foundation).

Chester, D.K. (2001) 'The 1755 Lisbon earthquake', *Progress in Physical Geography*, 25, 3, 363–83.

Chester, D.K., Degg, M., Duncan, A.M. and Guest, J.E. (2000) 'The increasing exposure of cities to the effects of volcanic eruptions: a global survey', *Global Environmental Change Part B: Environmental Hazards*, 2, 3, 89–103.

Christiensen, P. (1993) *The Decline of Iranshahr: Irrigation and Environments in the History of the Middle East 500 BC–AD 1500* (Copenhagen: Museum Tusculanum Press).

Christopherson, S. (1994) 'The fortress city: privatized spaces, consumer citizenship', in A. Amin (ed.) *Post-Fordism – a reader* (Oxford: Blackwell), pp. 409–27.

Clarke, D. (2004) *Technology and Terrorism* (London: Transaction).

Clarke, I.F. (1966) *Voices Prophesying War, 1763–1984* (Oxford: Oxford University Press).

Clay, G. (1973) *Close-up: How to Read the American City* (London: Pall Mall).

Coaffee, J. (1996) 'Beating the bombers – Landscapes of Defence in London and Belfast', 28th *International Geographical Congress*, The Hague, Netherlands, 4–10 August 1996.

Coaffee, J. (2000) 'Fortification, fragmentation and the threat of terrorism in the city of London', in J.R Gold and G.E. Revill (eds.) *Landscapes of Defence* (London: Addison Wesley Longman), pp. 114–29.

Coaffee, J. (2003) *Terrorism, Risk and the City: The Making of a Contemporary Urban Landscape* (Aldershot: Ashgate).

Coaffee, J. (2004) 'Rings of steel, rings of concrete and rings of confidence: designing out terrorism in central London pre and post 9/11', *International Journal of Urban and Regional Research*, 28, 1, 201–11.

Coaffee, J. (2005) 'Urban renaissance in the age of terrorism:revanchism, social control or the end of reflection?', *International Journal of Urban and Regional Research*, 29, 2, 447–54.

Coaffee, J. (2006) 'From counter-terrorism to resilience – new security challenges and the multidisciplinary counter-challenge in the 'age of terror', *European Legacy – Journal of the International Society for the Study of European Ideas*, 11, 4, 389–403.

Coaffee, J. (2008) 'Redesigning counter-terrorism for soft targets', *RUSI Monitor*, March, 16–17.

Coaffee, J. and Headlam, N. (2008) 'Pragmatic localism uncovered: The search for locally contingent solutions to national reform agendas', *Geoforum*, 39, 4, 1585–99.

Coaffee, J. and Murakami Wood, D. (2006) 'Security is coming home: rethinking scale and constructing resilience in the global urban response to terrorist risk', *International Relations*, 20, 4, 503–17.

Coaffee, J. and O'Hare, P. (2008) 'The ethical challenges of dealing with counter-terrorism strategy in the planning classroom', paper presented at The UK-Ireland Planning Research Conference 2008, Queen's University, Belfast, 18–20 March.

Coaffee, J. and Rogers, P. (2008) 'Rebordering the city for new security challenges', *Space and Polity*, 12, 1, 101–118

Coaffee, J., Moore, C., Fletcher, D. and Bosher, L. (2008) 'Resilient design for community safety and terror-resistant cities', *Proceedings of the Institute of Civil Engineers: Municipal Engineer* (in press).

Coates-Stephens, R. (1998) 'The walls and aqueducts of Rome in the early middle ages, A.D. 500–1000', *The Journal of Roman Studies*, 88, 166–78.

Cohn, N. (2001) *Cosmos, Chaos and the World to Come: The Ancient Roots of Apocalyptic Faith* (London: Yale University Press).

Coleman, A. (1984) 'Trouble in Utopia: I. Design influences in blocks of flats', *Geographical Journal*, 150, 351–62.

Coleman, A. (1985) *Utopia on Trial: Vision and Reality in Planned Housing* (London: Hilary Shipman).

Coleman, R. (2004) Watching the degenerate: street camera surveillance and urban regeneration, *Local Economy*, 19, 3, 199–211.

Coles, E. (1998) 'What price emergency planning? Local authority civil protection in the UK', *Public Money and Management*, 18, 4, 27–32.

Collinson, P. (1963) *The Cutteslowe Walls* (London: Faber and Faber).

Committee on Homeland Security and Governmental Affairs (CHSGA) (2006) *Hurricane Katrina: A Nation Still Unprepared, Special Report of the Committee Homeland Security and Governmental Affairs* (Washington: U.S. Government Printing Office).

Communities and Local Government Committee (2006) *Fire and Rescue Service: Fourth Report of Session 2005–06* (London: House of Commons/TSO).

Connah, G. (2000a) 'African city walls: a neglected source?', in D. Anderson and R. Rathbone (eds.) *Africa's Urban Past*. (Oxford: James Currey), pp. 36–51.

Connah, G. (2000b) 'Contained communities in tropical Africa', in J.D. Tracy (ed.) (2000) *City Walls: The Urban Enceinte in Comparative Perspective* (Cambridge: Cambridge University Press), pp. 19–45.

Cooper, D. (1998) 'Regard between strangers: diversity, equality and the reconstruction of public space', *Critical Social Policy*, 18, 4, 465–92.

Cooper, F.A. (2000) 'The fortifications of Epaminondas and the rise of the monumental Greek city', in J.D. Tracy (ed.) (2000) *City Walls: The Urban Enceinte in Comparative Perspective* (Cambridge: Cambridge University Press), pp. 155–91.

Core Cities (2005) *Are We Meeting the Challenge? 2nd Core Cities Study* (Easingwold: Emergency Planning College).

Core Cities (2006) *CBRN Capabilities: Core Cities Study 2006* (Easingwold: Emergency Planning College).

Cornell, T.J. (2000) 'The city-states in Latium', in M.H. Hansen (ed.) *A Comparative Study of Thirty City-State Cultures* (Copenhagen: Kgl. Danske Videnskabernes Selskab), pp. 209–28.

Corporation of London (1993a) *The Way Ahead – Traffic and the Environment, Draft Consultation Paper* (London: Corporation of London).

Corporation of London (1993b) *Security Initiatives, Draft Consultation Paper* (London: Corporation of London).

Corporation of London (1995) *City Research Project: Final Report* – The Competitive Position of London's Financial Services (London: Corporation of London).

Correia, F., Santos, M. and Rodrigues, R. (1987) 'Engineering risk in regional drought studies', in L. Dickstein and E. Plate (eds.) *Engineering Reliability and Risk in Water Resources* (Dordrecht: Martinus Nijhoff), pp. 61–86.

Corry, D. and Stoker, G. (2002) *New Localism Refashioning the Centre-Local Relationship* (London: NLGN).

Cozens, P. (2002) 'Sustainable urban development and crime prevention through environmental design for the British city. Towards and effective Environmentalism for the 21st century', *Cities*, 19, 2, 129–37.

Cozens, P. Hillier, D. and Prescott, G. (1999) 'Crime and design of new build housing', *Town and Country Planning*, 68, 7 July, 231–3.

Cozens, P., Saville, G. and Hillier, D. (2005) 'Crime Prevention through Environmental Design (CPTED): a review and modern bibliography', *Property Management*, 23, 5, 328–56.

Crawford, A. (2002) *Crime and Insecurity: The Governance of Safety in Europe* (Devon: Willan).

Crawford, C. (1995) 'Protecting building from explosions', *City Security*, 8, 16–18.

Creamer, M. (1994) 'Community recovery from trauma', in R. Watts and D.J. De la Horne (eds.) *Coping with Trauma: The Victim and the Helper* (Brisbane: Australian Academic Press), pp. 37–52.

Crowe, T. (2000) *Crime Prevention Through Environmental Design: Applications for Architectural Design and Space Management* (Oxford: Butterworth-Heinemann).

Cutter, S.L., Richardson, D. and Wilbanks, T.J. (2003) *The Geographical Dimensions of Terrorism* (New York: Routledge).

Daily Telegraph (2008) 'Seeking security in a dangerous world', Comment, 20 March, p. 25.

Davic, R.D. and Welsh Jr. H.H. (2004) 'On the ecological roles of salamanders', *Annual Review of Ecology, Evolution, and Systematics*, 35, 405–34.

Davies, S. (1996a) *Big Brother – Britain's Web of Surveillance and the New Technological Order* (London: Pan Books).

Davies, S. (1996b) 'The case against: CCTV should not be introduced', *International Journal of Risk, Security and Crime Prevention*, 1, 4, 327–31.

Davis, J.K. (1992) *Spying on America: The FBI's Domestic Counterintelligence Program* (Westport CT: Praeger).

Davis, M. (1990) *City of Quartz: Excavating the Future in Los Angeles* (London: Verso).

Davis, M. (1992) *Beyond Blade Runner: Urban Control – The Ecology of Fear* (Westfield, New Jersey: Open Magazine Pamphlet series).

Davis, M. (1998) *Ecology of Fear: Los Angeles and the Imagination of Disaster* (New York: Metropolitan Books).

Davis, R.C. and Ravid, B.C.I. (eds.) (2001) *The Jews of Early Modern Venice* (Baltimore: JHU Press).

Davison, C. (1925) 'The Japanese earthquake of 1 September 1923', *The Geographical Journal*, 65, 1, 41–61.

Daws, I. (2005) 'Critical condition', *Fire Prevention and Fire Engineers Journals*, 65, 259, 50–1.

Dawson, G.M. (1984) 'Defensive planning in Belfast', *Irish Geography*, 17, 27–41.

De Boer, J.Z. and Sanders, D.T. (2002) *Volcanoes in Human History: The Far-Reaching Effects of Major Eruptions* (Princeton NJ: Princeton University Press).

De Boer, J.Z. and Sanders, D.T. (2005) *Earthquakes in Human History: The Far-Reaching Effects of Seismic Disruption* (Princeton NJ: Princeton University Press).

De Cauter, L. (2004) *The Capsular Civilization. On the City in the Age of Fear* (Rotterdam: NAi Publishers).

De la Croix, H. (1963) 'The literature on fortification in Renaissance Italy', *Technology and Culture*, 4, 1, 30–50.

De la Croix, H. (1972) '*Military Considerations in City Planning* (New York: Braziller).

De Medeiros, C.A. (2003) 'The post-war American technological development as a military enterprise', *Contributions to Political Economy*, 22, 1, 41–62.

De Vries, J. (1974) *The Dutch Rural Economy in the Golden Age, 1500–1700* (New Haven, CN: Yale University Press).

Dean, M. (1999) *Governmentality: Power and Rule in Modern Society* (Thousand Oaks CA: Sage).

Dear, M. and Flusty, S. (1998) 'Postmodern urbanism', *Annals of the Association of American Geographers*, 88, 1, 50–72.

Dear, M.J. (1999) *The Postmodern Urban Condition* (Oxford: Blackwell).

Deas, I and Ward, K. (2000) 'From the 'new localism' to the 'new regionalism'? The implications of regional development agencies for city–regional relations', *Political Geography'*, 19, 3, 273–92.

Del Monte-Luna, P., Brook, B.W., Zetina-Rejón, M.J. and Cruz-Escalona, V.H. (2004) 'The carrying capacity of ecosystems', *Global Ecology and Biogeography*, 13, 6, 485–95.

Deleuze, G. (1992) 'Postscript on the societies of control' (trans. M. Joughin) *October* 59 (Cambridge: MIT press), 3–7.

DEMOS (2007) *National Security for the Twenty-First Century* (London: DEMOS).

Department for Communities and Local Government (DCLG) (2006) *Fire and Resilience*, see: http://www.communities.gov.uk/fire/resilienceresponse/regionalresilience/ (accessed 10 December 2006).

Department for Communities and Local Government (DCLG) (2007a) *Preventing Violent Extremism, Winning Hearts and Minds* (London: HMSO).

Department of Communities and Local government (DCLG) (2007b) *National Indicators for Local Authorities and Local Authority Partnerships: Handbook of Definitions – Draft for Consultation* (London: HM Government).

Department for Innovation Universities and Skills (DIUS) (2008) 'Promoting freedom of speech to achieve shared values and prevent violent extremism on campus', Press Release, 22 January, see: http://www.dius.gov.uk/press/22-01-08.html (accessed 22 January 2008).

Derbes, V.J. (1966) 'De Mussis and the great plague of 1348. A forgotten episode of bacteriological warfare', *Journal of the American Medical Association*, 196, 1, 59–62.

Desmarais, R.H. (1971) 'The British Government's strikebreaking organization and Black Friday', *Journal of Contemporary History*, 6, 2, 112–27.

Dillon, D. (1994) 'Fortress America', *Planning*, 60, 8–12.

Dobson, R.B. (1983) *The Peasants' Revolt* (2nd Edition) (Basingstoke: Macmillan).

Dodd, V. (2008) 'New strategy to stem the flow of terror recruits', *The Guardian*, 28 February, p. 1.

Doeksen, H. (1997) 'Reducing crime and the fear of crime by reclaiming New Zealand's suburban street', *Landscape and Urban Planning*, 39, 243–52.

Doherty, F., Hurwitz, K., Massimino, E., McClintock, M., Purohit, R., Smith, C. and Thornton, R. (2005) *Imbalance of Powers: How changes to U.S. Law and Policy since 9–11 Erode Human Rights and Civil Liberties* (Washington: New York: Lawyers Committee for Human Rights).

Donegan, L. (1993) 'City Traffic Ban to Help Fight Bombers', *The Guardian*, 22 May, 9.

Donson, F., Chesters, G., Welsh, I. and Tickle, A. (2004) 'Rebels with a cause, folk devils without a panic: Press jingoism, policing tactics and anti-capitalist protest in London and Prague'. *Internet Journal of Criminology*, see: http://www.internetjournalofcriminology.com/ijcarticles.html (accessed 30 November 2006).

Dower, J.W. (2000) *Embracing Defeat: Japan in the Wake of World War II* (New York: Norton).

Downey, G. (1955) 'Earthquakes at Constantinople and vicinity, A.D. 342–1454', *Speculum*, 30, 4, 596–600.

Downey, G. (1958) 'The size of the population of Antioch', *Transactions and Proceedings of the American Philological Association*, 89, 84–91.

Dray-Novey, A. (1993) 'Spatial order and police in imperial Beijing', *Journal of Asian Studies*, 52, 4, 885–922.

Dunbabin, J. (2002) *Captivity and Imprisonment in Medieval Europe, 1000–1300* (Basingstoke: Palgrave MacMillan).

Durham, P. (1995) 'Villains in the frame', *Police Review*, 20 January, 20–21.

Durodie, B. (2005) 'Terrorism and community resilience: A UK perspective', *Chatham House – ISP/NSC Briefing Paper* 05/01, 4–5.

Durodie, B. and Wessely, S. (2002) 'Resilience or panic: the public and terrorism attack', *The Lancet*, 130, 1901–2.

Durodie, W. (2006) 'What can the science and technology community contribute?', in A.D. James (ed.) *Science and Technology Policies for the Counter Terrorism Era* (Amsterdam: IOL Press).

Dynes, R.R. (1997) *The Lisbon Earthquake In 1755: Contested Meanings In The First Modern Disaster*, Disaster Research Center Preliminary Papers 255, University of Delaware.

Dynes, R.R. (1999) *The Dialogue Between Voltaire And Rousseau On The Lisbon Earthquake: The Emergence Of A Social Science View*, Disaster Research Center Preliminary Papers 293, University of Delaware.

Eastler, T.E. (2005) 'Military use of underground terrain: a brief historical perspective', in D.R. Caldwell, J. Ehlen and R.S. Harmon (eds.) (2005) *Studies In Military Geography and Geology* (Netherlands: Springer), pp. 21–38.

Edgerton, D. (1991) *England and the Aeroplane: An Essay on a Militant and Technological Nation* (Basingstoke: Macmillan).

Edgerton, D. (2006) *Warfare State: Britain, 1920–1970* (Cambridge: Cambridge University Press).

Edwards, P.M. (1996) *The Closed World: Computers and the Politics of Discourse in Cold War America* (Cambridge MA: MIT Press).

Ellin, N. (1996) *Postmodern Urbanism* (Oxford: Blackwell)

Ellin, N. (ed.) (1997) *Architecture of Fear* (New York: Princeton Architectural Press).

Elvin, M. (1998) 'The environmental legacy of imperial China', *The China Quarterly*, 156, 733–56.

Ericson, R.V. and Doyle, A. (eds.) (2003) *Risk and Morality* (Toronto: University of Toronto Press).

Ericson, R.V. and Haggerty, K.D. (1997) *Policing the Risk Society* (Toronto: University of Toronto Press).

Etzioni, A. (ed.) (1998) *The Essential Communitarian Reader* (Lanham, MD: Rowman & Littlefield Publishers).

Fairweather, L. (1975) 'The evolution of the prison', in S. Lenci, L. Fairweather, E. Vetere, B. Cacciapuoti, T. Eriksson and U. Leone (eds.) (1975) *Prison Architecture: An International Survey of Representative Closed Institutions and Analysis of Current Trends in Prison Design* (London: Architectural Press).

Farish, M. (2003) 'Disaster and decentralization: American cities and the Cold War', *Cultural Geographies*, 10, 2, 125–48.

Farmer, E.L. (2000) 'The hierarchy of Ming city walls', in J. Tracy (ed.) *City Walls: The Urban Enceinte in Comparative Perspective* (Cambridge: Cambridge University Press), pp. 461–87.

Finch, P. (1996) 'The fortress city is not an option', *The Architects' Journal*, February 15, 25.

Finn, J. (2005) 'Photographing fingerprints: data collection and state surveillance', *Surveillance & Society*, 3, 1, 21–44.

Flusty, S. (1994) *Building Paranoia: The Proliferation of Interdictory Space and the Erosion of Spatial Justice* (Los Angeles Forum for Architecture and Urban Design, 11).

Flynn, S. (2007) *The Edge of Disaster: Rebuilding a Resilient Nation* (New York: Random House).

Ford, C. (2005) Conference good for North says Labour, *Sunday Sun*, February 6, p. 2.

Ford, L.R. (1993) 'A model of Indonesian city structure', *The Geographical Review*, 83, 374–96.

Foucault, M. (1977) *Discipline and Punish: The Birth of the Prison* (Harmondsworth: Penguin).

Foucault, M. (with G. Burchell and C. Gordon) (1991) *The Foucault Effect: Studies in Governmentality* (Chicago: University of Chicago Press).

Fraser, M.W., Richman, J.M. and Galinsky, M.J. (1999) 'Risk, protection, and resilience: toward a conceptual framework for social work practice', *Social Work Research*, 23, 3, 131–43.

Freedman, L. (1989 [1981]) *The Evolution of Nuclear Strategy (2nd Edition)* (Basingstoke: Macmillan)

Frost, C. (1994) 'Effective responses for proactive enterprises: Business continuity planning, *Disaster Prevention and Management*, 3, 1, 7–15.

Frykenberg, R.E. (ed.) (1986) *Delhi Through the Ages: Essays in Urban History, Culture, and Society* (Delhi: Oxford University Press).

Fulbrook, M. (1995) *Anatomy of a Dictatorship: Inside the GDR, 1949–1989* (Oxford: Oxford University Press).

Fuller, J.F. (1992 [1961]) *The Conduct of War, 1789–1961: A Study of the Impact of the French, Industrial, and Russian Revolutions on War and Its Conduct* (New Brunswick NJ: Da Capo Press).

Furedi, F. (2005) *The Politics of Fear; Beyond Left and Right* (London: Continuum).

Furedi, F. (2006) *Culture of Fear Revisited* (Fourth Edition) (Trowbridge: Continuum).

Fyfe, N.R. (ed.) (1998) *Images of the Street: Planning, Identity and Control in Public Space* (London: Routledge).

Gabba, E. (1994) *Italia Romana* (Como: New Press).

Ganse, R.A. and Nelson, J.B. (1982) 'Catalogue of significant earthquakes 2000 B.C. to 1979, including quantitative casualties and damage', *Bulletin of the Seismological Society of America*, 72, 3, 873–7.

Garber, M. and Walkowitz, R. (ed.) (1995) *Secret Agents: The Rosenberg Case, McCarthyism and Fifties America* (New York: Routledge).

Garland, D. (2001) *The Culture of Control: Crime and Social Order in Contemporary Society* (Oxford: Oxford University Press).

Garon, S. (1997) *Molding Japanese Minds: The State in Everyday Life* (New York: Princeton University Press).

Gat, A. (1998) *Fascist and Liberal Visions of War: Fuller, Liddell Hart, Douhet, and Other Modernists* (Oxford: Oxford University Press).

Gat, A. (2002) 'Why city-states existed: riddles and clues of urbanisation and fortifications', in M.H. Hansen (ed.) (2002) *A Comparative Study of Six City-State Cultures.* (Copenhagen: Kgl. Danske Videnskabernes Selskab), pp. 125–39.

Genosko, G. and Thompson, S. (2005) 'Administrative surveillance of alcohol consumption in Ontario, Canada: pre-electronic technologies of control', *Surveillance & Society*, 4, 1/2, 1–28.

Gernet, J. (1985 [1972]) *A History of Chinese Civilization* (Cambridge: Cambridge University Press).

Giddens, A. (1998) *The Third Way: The Renewal of Social Democracy* (Cambridge: Polity Press).

Glaesar, E. and Shapiro, J. (2001) *Cities and Warfare: The Impact of Terrorism on Urban Form* (Cambridge: Harvard Institute of Academic Research).

Glaesser, D. (2006) 'Crisis management in the tourism industry', in Y. Mansfield and A. Pizam (eds.) *Tourism, Security and Safety; From Theory to Practice* (Burlington MA: Butterworth Heinemann).

Glassner, B. (1999) *The Culture of Fear* (New York: Basic Books).

Glenn, R.W. (1996) *Combat in Hell: A Consideration of Constrained Urban Warfare* (Santa Monica: RAND).

Gloyn, W.J. (1993) *Insurance Against Terrorism* (London: Witherby).

Goble, A. (1995) 'Social change, knowledge, and history: Hanazono's admonitions to the crown prince', *Harvard Journal of Asiatic Studies*, 55, 1, 61–128.

Godschalk, D.R. (2003) 'Urban hazard mitigation: creating resilient cities', *Natural Hazards Review*, 4, 3, 136–43.

Gold, J.R. (1982) 'Territoriality and human spatial behaviour', *Progress in Human Geography*, 6, 44–67.

Gold, J.R. (1994) 'Locating the message: place promotional image communication', in J.R. Gold and S.V. Ward (eds.) *Place Promotion* (Chichester: Wiley), pp. 19–37.

Gold, J.R. (2007) *The Practice of Modernism: Modern Architects and the Urban Transformation, 1954–1972* (London: Routledge).

Gold, J.R. and Revill, G. (1999) 'Landscapes of defence', *Landscape Research*, 24, 3, 229–39.

Gold, J.R. and Revill, G. (eds.) *(2000) Landscapes of Defence* (London: Prentice Hall).

Gold, R. (1970) 'Urban violence and contemporary defensive cities', *Journal of the American Institute of Planning*, 36, 146–59.

Goldsmith, M. (2002) 'Central control over local government – a western European comparison', *Local Government Studies*, 28,3, 91–112.

Gollin, A.M. (1981) 'England is no longer an island: the phantom airship scare of 1909', *Albion: A Quarterly Journal Concerned with British Studies*, 13, 1, 43–57.

Gollin, A.M. (1989) *The Impact of Airpower on the British People and Their Government, 1909–1914* (Basingstoke: Macmillan).

Goodchild, R.G. (1952) 'The decline of Libyan agriculture', *The Geographical Magazine*, 25, 147–56.

Goodey, B. and Gold, J.R. (1987) 'Environmental perception: the relationship with urban design', *Progress in Human Geography*, 11, 126–32.

Gotham, K.F. (2007) '(Re)Branding the Big Easy: tourism rebuilding in post-Katrina New Orleans', *Urban Affairs Review*, 42, 6, 823–50.

Government Office Network (2007) *Partnering with Whitehall*, see: http://www.gose.gov.uk/common/docs/239393/partnering_with_whitehall.pdf (accessed 10 October 2007).

Graham, S and Marvin, S. (2001) *Splintering Urbanism: Networked Infrastructures, Technological Mobility and the Urban Condition* (London: Routledge).

Graham, S. (1999), 'The eyes have it: CCTV as the fifth utility', *Town and Country Planning*, 68, 10, 312–5.

Graham, S. (2002) 'Special collection: Reflections on Cities. September 11th and the "war on terrorism." One year on', *International Journal of Urban and Regional Research*, 26, 3, 589–90.

Graham, S. (2003) 'Lessons in Urbicide', *New Left Review*, 19, 63–77.

Graham, S. (2004) 'Postmortem city: towards an urban geo-politics', *City*, 8, 2, 165–96.

Graham, S. (2005) 'Software-sorted geographies', *Progress in Human Geography*, 29, 5, 562–80.

Graham, S. (ed.) (2004) *Cities, War and Terrorism* (Oxford: Blackwell).

Graham, S. and Wood, D. (2003) 'Digitizing surveillance: categorization, space, inequality', *Critical Social Policy*, 23, 2, 227–48.

Graham, S., Brooks, J. and Heery, D. (1996) 'Towns on the television: closed circuit TV systems in British towns and cities', *Local Government Studies*, 22, 3, 3–27.

Grant, J. (2001) 'The dark side of the grid: power and urban design', *Planning Perspectives*, 16, 3, 219–41.

Gras, M.L. (2004) 'The legal regulation of CTV in Europe', *Surveillance & Society*, 2, 2/3, 216–29.

Grattan, J. (2006) 'Aspects of Armageddon: An exploration of the role of volcanic eruptions in human history and civilization', *Quaternary International*, 151, 1, 10–18.

Green, D. (1984) 'Veins of resemblance: photography and eugenics', *Oxford Art Journal*, 7, 2, 3–16.

Greenberg. M.R, Lahr, M. and Mantell, N. (2007) 'Understanding the economic costs and benefits of catastrophes and their aftermath: a review and suggestions for the U.S. Federal Government', *Risk Analysis*, 27, 1, 83–96.

Gregory, F. (2007) 'UK Draft Civil Contingencies Bill 2003 and the subsequent Act: building block for homeland security?' in P. Wilkinson (ed.) *Homeland Security: Future Preparations for Terrorist Attack Since 9/11* (London: Routledge), pp. 333–42.

Gregory, F. and Wilkinson, P. (2005) 'Riding pillion for tackling terrorism is a high risk policy', *Chatham House, ISP/NSC Briefing Paper*, 2–3 July.

Griffith, R. (2000) 'The Hausa City-States from 1450–1804', in M.H. Hansen (ed.) *A Comparative Study of Thirty City-State Cultures* (Copenhagen: Kgl. Danske Videnskabernes Selskab), pp. 483–506.

Groebner, V. (2007) *Who Are You? Identification, Deception and Surveillance in Early Modern Europe* (New York: Zone).

Grogger, J. and Weatherford, M.S. (1995) 'Crime, policing and the perception of neighbourhood safety', *Political Geography*, 14, 6–7, 521–41.

Guillemin, J. (2005) *Biological Weapons: From the Invention of State-sponsored Programs to Contemporary Bioterrorism* (Irvington NY: Columbia University Press).

Gunderson, L.H. (2000) 'Ecological resilience: in theory and application', *Annual Review of Ecology and Systematics*, 31, 425–39.

Gunderson, L.H., Holling, C.S., Pritchard, L. and Peterson, G.D. (2002) 'Resilience', in H.A. Mooney and J.G. Canadell (eds.) *Encyclopedia of Global Environmental Change* (London: John Wiley), pp. 530–1.

Haas, J., Creamer, W. and Ruiz, A. (2004) 'Power and the emergence of complex polities in the Peruvian preceramic', *Archaeological Papers of the American Anthropological Association*, 14, 1, 37–52.

Haldon, J. (1999) *Warfare, State and Society in the Byzantine World, 565–1204* (London: Routledge).

Hall, P. (1998) *Cities in Civilization: Culture, Innovation, and Urban Order* (London: Weidenfeld & Nicolson).

Hamilton, D. and Joaquin, A. (2000) 'Urban planning for flood, hazards, risk and vulnerability', in E.E. Wohl (ed.) *Inland Flood Hazards: Human, Riparian, and Aquatic* (Cambridge: Cambridge University Press), pp. 469–90.

Hamilton, R.F. and Herwig, H.H. (2003) *The Origins of World War I* (Cambridge: Cambridge University Press).

Hamm, M.F. (ed.) (1986) *The City in Late Imperial Russia* (Bloomington IL: Indiana University Press).

Hanes, J.E. (2000) 'Urban planning as an urban problem: the reconstruction of Tokyo after the Great Kanto Earthquake', *Policy Science*, 7, 3, 123–37.

Hansen, M.H. (2000a) 'The concepts of city-state and city-state culture', in M.H. Hansen (ed.) *A Comparative Study of Thirty City-State Cultures* (Copenhagen: Kgl. Danske Videnskabernes Selskab), pp. 11–34.

Hansen, M.H. (2000b) 'The Hellenic polis', in M.H. Hansen (ed.) *A Comparative Study of Thirty City-State Cultures* (Copenhagen: Kgl. Danske Videnskabernes Selskab), pp. 141–88.

Hansen, M.H. (ed.) (2002) *A Comparative Study of Six City-State Cultures* (Copenhagen: Kgl. Danske Videnskabernes Selskab).

Hanson, W.S. and Maxwell, G.S. (1983) *Rome's North West Frontier: The Antonine Wall* (Edinburgh: Edinburgh University Press).

Harrigan, J. and Martin, P. (2002) 'Terrorism and the resilience of cities', *FRBNY Economic Policy Review*, November, 97–116.

Harring, S.L. (1983) *Policing a Class Society: The Experience of American Cities, 1865–1915* (New Brunswick, N.J.: Rutgers University Press).

Harrisson, T. (1976) *Living Through the Blitz* (London: William Collins/Mass Observation).

Harvey, J. and Delfabbro, P.H. (2004) 'Psychological resilience in disadvantaged youth: a critical overview', *Australian Psychologist*, 39, 1, 3–13.

Hashimoto, N. (2000) 'Public organizations in an emergency: the 1995 Hanshin-Awaji earthquake and municipal government', *Journal of Contingencies and Crisis Management*, 8, 1, 15–22.

Haubrich, D. (2006) 'Anti-terrorism Laws and slippery slopes: reply to Waddington', *Policing and Society: An International Journal of Research and Policy*, 16, 4, 405–14.

Haussig, R. (1992) *War and Society in Ancient Mesoamerica* (Berkeley: University of California Press).

Hayman, D. (2004) 'The international response to the outbreak of SARS in 2003', *Philosophical Transactions of the Royal Society*, 359, 1447, 1127–9.

Haywood, K.J. (2004) *City Limits: Crime, Consumer Culture and the Urban Experience* (London: Glasshouse).

Heater, D.B. (2004) *A History of Education for Citizenship* (London: Routledge-Farmer).

Heberer, T. and Jakobi, S. (2000) 'Henan – the model: from hegemonism to fragmentism. portrait of the political culture of China's most populated province' (Duisburg Working Papers on East Asian Studies, No. 32) (Duisburg: Gerhard-Mercator-Universität).

Heiman, T. (2002) 'Parents of children with disabilities: resilience, coping, and future expectations', *Journal of Developmental and Physical Disabilities*, 14, 2, 159–71.

Hempel, L. (2006) 'In the eye of the beholder? Representations of video surveillance in German public television', *Surveillance & Society*, 4, 1/2, 85–100.

Henig, R. (2001) *The Origins of the First World War* (London: Routledge).

Henstra, D. Kovacs, P., McBean, G. and Sweeting, R. (2004) *Disaster resilient cities* (Background paper) (Canada: Institute for Catastrophic Loss Reduction, Infrastructure).

Herbert, S. (1997a) *Policing Space: Territoriality and the Los Angeles Police Department* (Minneapolis: University of Minnesota Press).

Herbert, S. (1997b) 'On prolonging the conversation: some correctives and continuities', *Urban Geography*, 18, 5, 398–402.

Hess, G. (2005) 'Rethinking energy policy: hurricane damage has Congress considering legislation to open more gas and oil resources', *Chemical and Engineering News*, 83, 40, 31–4.

Heyman D.L. and Rodier G. Global surveillance, national surveillance, and SARS. Emerging Infectious Diseases [serial online] 2003 Feb [*date cited*]. Available from: URL: http://www.cdc.gov/ncidod/EID/vol10no2/03-1038.htm.

Higgs, E. (2004) *The Information State in England: The Central Collection of on Citizens since 1500* (Basingstoke: Palgrave Macmillan).

Higonnet, P. (2002) *Paris: Capital of the World* (trans. Goldhammer, A.) (Cambridge MA: Harvard University Press).

Hill, C.N. (2001) *A Vertical Empire: The History of the UK Rocket and Space Programme, 1950–1971* (London: Imperial College Press).

Hillenbrand, C. (1999) *The Crusades: Islamic Perspectives* (London: Routledge).

Hilliard, L. (1986) 'Local government, civil defence and emergency planning: heading for disaster?', *The Modern Law Review*, 49, 4, 476–88.

Hinman, E.E. and Hammond, D.J. (1997) *Lessons From the Oklahoma City Bombing: Defensive Design Techniques*. (Reston, VA: American Society of Civil Engineers).

Hirst, J. (1995) 'The Australian experience: the convict colony', in N. Morris and D.J. Rotham (eds.) *Oxford History of the Prison* (New York: Oxford University Press), pp. 263–96.

Hirst, P.Q. and Thompson, G. (1999) *Globalization in Question: The International Economy and the Possibilities of Governance* (Cambridge: Polity Press).

HM Fire Services Inspectorate (FSI) (2003) *Regional Control: National Resilience* (London: Her Majesties Fire Service Inspectorate).

HM Government (2004) *Civil Contingencies Act* (London: HMSO).

HM Government (2006) *Countering International Terrorism: The United Kingdom's Strategy*, CM 688 (London: HM Government).

HM Government (2006a) *Countering International Terrorism: The United Kingdom's Strategy*, CM 688 (London: HMSO).

HM Government (2006b) *Threat Levels: The System to Assess the Threat from International Terrorism*, July 2006 (London: TSO).

HM Government (2007a) *The Governance of Britain* (London: HMSO).

HM Government (2007b) *The United Kingdom Security and Counter-Terrorism Science and Innovation Strategy* (London: HMSO).

HM Government (2008) *Preventing Violent Extremism: A Strategy for Delivery* (London: HM Government).

HM Government Preparing for Emergencies (2007) 'Local Resilience', see: http://www.preparingforemergencies.gov.uk/government/local.shtm (accessed 30 March 2007).

HM Treasury and Office of the Deputy Prime Minister (2006) *Review of Government Offices* (London: HM Treasury).

Hobbes, T. (2006 [1651]) *Leviathan* (eds. G. Alan, J. Rogers and K. Schuhmann) (New York: Continuum).

Hobsbaum, E. (1994) *Age of Extremes: The Short Twentieth Century* (London: Abacus).

Hogan, J. (2003) 'Smart software linked to CCTV can spot dubious behaviour', *New Scientist*, 11 July, see: http://www.newscientist.com/article/dn3918-smart-software-linked-to-cctv-can-spot-dubious-behaviour.html (accessed 10 December 2006).

Holden, A. and Iveson, K. (2003) 'Designs on the urban: new labour's urban renaissance and the spaces of citizenship', *City*, 7, 1, 57–72.

Hollander, J.B. and Whitfield, C. (2005) 'The appearance of security zones in US cities after 9/11', *Property Management*, 23, 4, 244–56.

Holling, C.S. (1973) 'Resilience and stability of ecological systems', *Annual Review of Ecology and Systematics*, 4, 1–23.

Holling, C.S. (1994) 'Simplifying the complex: the paradigms of ecological function and structure', *Futures*, 26, 6, 598–609.

Home Office (1982) *Domestic Nuclear Shelters: Technical Guidance* (A Home Office Guide. London: HMSO).

Home Office (2001) *Building Cohesive Communities: A Report of the Ministerial Group on Public Order and Community Cohesion* (London: HMSO).

Home Office (2004) *Preparing for Emergencies: What you Need to Know* (London: HMSO).

Home Office (2007a) *Counter Terrorism Strategy*, see: http://security.homeoffice. gov.uk/counter-terrorism-strategy/about-the-strategy/ (accessed 21 July 2007).

Home Office (2007b) 'Home Office Structure', see: http://www.homeoffice.gov. uk/about-us/organisation/home-office-structure/ (accessed 10 August 2007).

Home Office (2007c) 'Lord West Reviews on Protective Security' (Press Release) (London: Home Office).

Hope, C. (2008) 'Dads Army volunteers will tackle threats to UK security', *The Daily Telegraph*, 20 March, 10.

Horne, C.J. (1996) 'The case for: should CCTV be introduced', *International Journal of Risk, Security and Crime Prevention*, 1, 4, 317–26.

Hounshell, D.A. (1984) *From the American System to Mass Production, 1800–1932: The Development of Manufacturing Technology in the United States* (Baltimore: JHU Press).

House of Commons Communities and Local Government Committee (2006) *Fire and Rescue Service: Fourth Report of Session 2005–2006* (London: TSO).

Howell, D.L. (2005) *Geographies of Identity in Nineteenth Century Japan* (Berkeley: University of California Press).

Hoyt, L. (2005) Do business improvement district organizations make a difference? Crime in and around commercial areas in Philadelphia, *Journal of Planning Education and Research*, 25, 2, 185–99.

Hughes, J. (2003) 'The Strath Report: Britain confronts the H-bomb, 1954–1955', *History and Technology*, 19, 3, 257–75.

Hughes, S.C. (1994) *Crime, Disorder and the Risorgiemento: The Politics of Policing in Bologna* (Cambridge: Cambridge University Press).

Hunt, A. (1996) *Governance of the Consuming Passions: A History of Sumptuary Law* (Basingstoke: Palgrave Macmillan).

Hunt, A. (1999) *Governing Morals: A Social History of Moral Regulation* (Cambridge: Cambridge University Press).

Hunt, A. (2003) 'Risk and morality in everyday life', in R.V. Ericson and A. Doyle (eds.) (2003) *Risk and Morality* (Toronto: University of Toronto Press), pp. 165–92.

Hunt, A. (2004) 'Getting Marx and Foucault into bed together!', *Journal of Law and Society*, 31, 4, 592–609.

Hyam, T. (2007) 'Architects' may be liable for terrorism', *Building Design*, September 13, 1.

Hyde, M. (1976) *British Air Policy Between the Wars: 1918–1939* (London: Heinemann).

Hyett, P. (1996) 'Damage limitation in the age of terrorism', *The Architects Journal*, February 15, 29.

Ignatieff, M. (1978) *A Just Measure of Pain: The Penitentiary in the Industrial Revolution, 1750–185* (New York: Pantheon).

Introna, L. and Wood, D. (2004) 'Picturing Algorithmic Surveillance: The Politics of Facial Recognition Systems', *Surveillance and Society*, 2, 2/3, 177–98.

Israel, J.I. (1995) *The Dutch Republic: Its Rise, Greatness, and Fall, 1407–1806* (Oxford: Oxford University Press).

Jacobs, J. (1961) *The Death and Life of Great American Cities* (London: Peregrine).

Jarman, N. (1993) 'Intersecting Belfast', in B. Bender (ed.) *Landscape – Politics and Perspectives* (Oxford: Berg), pp. 107–38.

Jeffery, C.R. (1971) *Crime Prevention Through Environmental Design* (Beverly Hills: Sage).

Jenkins, S. (2006) 'Not totalitarianism – but guilty of creeping authoritarianism', *The Guardian*, 26 April, 19.

Jinnai, H. (1995[1985]) *Tokyo: A Spatial Anthropology* (Berkeley: University of California Press).

Johnson, L.C. (1995) 'China's Pompeii: Twelfth-Century Dongjing', *The Historian*, 58, 1, 49–68.

Johnson, N. and Mueller, J. (2002) 'Global mortality of the 1918–1920 "Spanish" influenza pandemic', *Bulletin of the History of Medicine*, 76, 1, 105–15.

Johnson, S. (1973) 'A group of late Roman city walls in Gallia Belgica', *Britannia*, 4, 210–23.

Johnson, S. (2004) *Hadrian's Wall* (Batsford: Sterling Publishing).

Joint Committee on Draft Civil Contingencies Bill (2003) *First Report*, see: http://www.publications.parliament.uk/pa/jt200203/jtselect/jtdcc/184/18410. htm (accessed 20 February 2005).

Jones, G.S. (1971) *Outcast London: A Study in the Relationship Between Classes in Victorian Society* (Oxford: Oxford University Press).

Jones, H. (2005) 'The impact of the Cold War', in P. Addison and H. Jones (eds.) *A Companion to Contemporary Britain, 1939–2000* (Oxford: Blackwell), pp. 22–41.

Jones, M. and MacLeod, G. (2004) 'Regional spaces, spaces of regionalism: territory, insurgent politics and the English question', *Transactions of the Institute of British Geographers*, 29, 4, 433–52.

Jones, N. (1987) *The Beginning of Strategic Air Power: A History of the British Bomber Force, 1922–1939* (London: Frank Cass).

Jones, T. (1993) 'Company Chiefs Want Steel Gates Over roads', *The Times*, 27 April, 3.

Jones, T. and Newburn, T. (1998) *Private Security and Public Policing* (Oxford: Clarendon Press).

Juergensmeyer, M. (1997) 'Terror mandated by God', *Terrorism and Political Violence*, 9, 2, 16–23.

Juma, J. (2003) 'How does a 21st Century version of apartheid look like? Palestine knows', in Palestinian Environmental NGO Network (PENGON) *Stop the Wall in Palestine*, see: http://stopthewall.org/downloads/pdf/book/guestarticles.pdf (accessed 12 December 2007), pp. 138–40.

Jungk, R. (1958) *Brighter Than a Thousand Suns: A Personal History of the Atomic Scientists* (trans. J. Cleugh) (Harmondsworth: Penguin).

Jürgens, U. Gnad, M. (2002a) "Gated communities in South Africa-experiences from Johannesburg", *Environment and Planning B: Planning and Design*, 29, 337–53.

Kackman, M. (2005) *Citizen Spy: Television, Espionage, and Cold War Culture* (Minneapolis: University of Minnesota Press).

Kahn, H. (1984) *Thinking About the Unthinkable in the 1980s* (New York: Simon and Schuster).

Kaijser, A. (2002) 'System building from below institutional change in Dutch water control systems', *Technology and Culture*, 43, 3, 521–48.

Kaku, M. and Axelrod, D. (1987) *To Win a Nuclear War: The Pentagon's Secret Plans* (London: Zed Books).

Kaplan, J. (2006) 'Islamaphobia in America?: September 11 and islamophobic hate crime', *Terrorism and Political Violence*, 18, 1, 1–33.

Karan, P.P. (1997) 'The city in Japan', in P.P. Karan and K. Stapleton (eds.) (1997) *The Japanese City* (Lexington: University of Kentucky Press), pp. 12–39.

Karan, P.P. and Stapleton, K. (eds.) (1997) *The Japanese City* (Lexington: University of Kentucky Press).

Kearon, T., Mythen, G. and Walklate, S. (2007) 'Making sense of emergency advice; public perceptions of terrorist risk', *Security Journal*, 20, 77–95.

Keeley, L.H. (1996) *War Before Civilisation* (Oxford: Oxford University Press).

Kendal, B. (2003) 'An overview of the development and introduction of ground radar to 1945', *Journal of Navigation*, 56, 343–52.

Kern, P.B. (1999) *Ancient Siege Warfare* (Bloomington: Indiana University Press).

Kettering, S. (1994) 'State control and municipal authority in France', in J.L. McClain, J.M. Merriman and K. Ugawa (eds.) (1994) *Edo and Paris: Urban Life and the State in the Early Modern Era* (New York: Cornell University Press), pp. 86–103.

Keys, D. (2000) *Catastrophe: An Investigation into the Origins of the Modern World* (London: Arrow).

Kincade, W.H. (1978) 'Repeating history: the civil defense debate renewed', *International Security*, 2, 3, 99–120.

King, B. and Kutta, T.J. (2003) *Impact: The History of Germany's V-Weapons in World War II* (New Brunswick NJ: Da Capo Press).

Klauser, F. (2007) 'Surveillance and urban space FIFAland 2006TM: security and surveillance strategies during the football World Cup 2006 in Germany', paper presented at *Technologies of (In)security*, University of Oslo, 19–20 April.

Klein, R.J.T., Nicholls, R.J. and Thomalla, F. (2003) 'Resilience to natural hazards: how useful is this concept?', *Environmental Hazards*, 5, 34–5.

Koch, H.W. (1988) 'Operation Barbarossa: the current state of the debate', *The Historical Journal*, 31, 2, 377–90.

Kohl, P.L. (1985) 'Recent research in Central Asia', *American Antiquity*, 50, 4, 789–95.

Kohl, P.L. and Fawcett, C.P. (eds.) (1995) *Nationalism, Politics, and the Practice of Archaeology* (Cambridge: Cambridge University Press).

Koolhaas, R. and Whiting, S. (1999) 'Spot check: a conversation between Rem Koolhaas and Sarah Whiting', *Assemblage*, 40, 36–55.

Kreimer, A. and Arnold, M. (2003) *Building Safer Cities: the Future of Disaster Risk* (Washington DC: World Bank).

Kunstler, J. and Salingaros, N.A. (2001) 'The End of Tall Buildings', published electronically by PLANetizen [online], 17 September, see: http://www.planetizen.com/ (accessed 30 December 2001).

Ladd, B. (1997) The Ghosts of Berlin: Confronting German History in the Urban Landscape (Chicago: University of Chicago Press).

Ladd, B. (2005) 'Double restoration: rebuilding Berlin after 1945', in L. Vale and T. Campenella (eds.) The Resilient City: How Modern Cites Recover from Disaster (Oxford: Oxford University Press), 117–34.

Lao Tzu (1963) Tao Te Ching (Harmondsworth: Penguin).

Laqueur, W. (1996) 'Post-modern terrorism', Foreign Affairs, 75, 5, 24–36.

Larsen, M.T. (2000) 'The old Assyrian city-state', in M.H. Hansen (ed.) (2000) A Comparative Study of Thirty City-State Cultures 9 (Copenhagen: Kgl. Danske Videnskabernes Selskab), pp. 77–87.

Lawford, J. and Eiser, C. (2001) 'Exploring links between the concepts of quality of life and resilience', Paediatric Rehabilitation, 4, 4, 209–16.

Lawson, A.C. (1969 [1908]) The California Earthquake of April 18, 1906. Report of the State Earthquake Investigation Commission, Pub. no. 87 (2 Volumes) (Washington DC: Carnegie Institution of Washington).

Leake, J. (2008) 'Strip search: camera that sees through clothes from 80ft away', The Times, 9 March, see: http://www.timesonline.co.uk/tol/news/uk/science/article3512019.ece (accessed 10 March 2008).

Lees. L. (1998) 'Urban resistance and the street: Spaces of control and contestation', in N. R. Fyfe (ed.) Images on the Street (London: Routledge).

Lemke, T. (2002) 'Foucault, governmentality, and critique', Rethinking Marxism, 14, 3, 49–64.

Leppard, D. (2006) ' "Superman" scanner to spot bombers', The Sunday Times, 5 November, see: http://www.timesonline.co.uk/tol/news/uk/article625572.ece (accessed 10 March 2008).

Ley, D. (1974) The Black Inner City as Frontier Outpost: Images and Behaviour of a Philadelphia Neighbourhood (Washington D.C: Monograph No. 7, Association of American Geographers).

Lianos, M. (2001) Le Nouveau Contrôle Social: toile institutionnelle, normativité et lien social (Paris : L'Harmattan-Logiques Sociales).

Liberty (2006) Terrorism Act 2006, see: http://www.liberty-human-rights.org.uk/issues/6-free-speech/terrorism-act-2006/index.shtml (accessed 29 December 2006).

Lieberman, R. (1991) 'Real architecture, imaginary history: the Arsenale gate as Venetian mythology', Journal of the Warburg and Courtauld Institutes, 54, 117–26.

Ling, R. (1990) 'A stranger in town: finding the way in an ancient city', Greece & Rome (2nd Series), 37, 2, 204–14.

Little, R. (2004) 'Holistic strategy for urban security', Journal of Infrastructure Systems, 10, 2, 52–9.

Loader, I. (1997) 'Thinking normatively about private security', Journal of Law and Society, 34, 3, 377–94.

London Assembly (2006) Report of the 7 July Review Committee (London: Greater London Authority).

London Prepared (2003) 'Emergency advice for London', see: http://www.londonprepared.gov.uk/ (accessed 20 December 2003).

London Prepared (2006) 'London exercises', see: http://www.londonprepared.gov.
uk/londonsplans/londonexercises/ (accessed 2 December 2006).

London Prepared (2007) 'Emergency plans: Olympics', see: http://www.london
prepared.gov.uk/londonsplans/index.jsp (accessed 6 February 2008).

London Resilience (2006) 'Looking back moving forward: the multi agency
debrief', see: http://www.londonprepared.gov.uk/downloads/lookingback
movingforward.pdf (accessed 13 December 2006).

Lowndes, V. and Skelcher, C. (1998) 'The dynamics of multi-organisational partnerships: an analysis of changing modes of governance', *Public Administration*,
76, 2, 313–33.

Lustgarten, L. and Leigh, I. (1994) *In From the Cold: National Security and
Parliamentary Democracy* (Oxford: Clarendon Press).

Lyon, D. (1994) *The Electronic Eye: The Rise of Surveillance Society* (Cambridge:
Polity Press).

Lyon, D. (2003a) *Surveillance After September 11* (Cambridge: Polity).

Lyon, D. (2003b) 'Technology vs "terrorism": circuits of city surveillance since
September 11th', *International Journal of Urban and Regional Research*, 27, 3,
666–78.

Lyon, D. (2007) 'Sociological perspectives and Surveillance Studies: "slow jour-
nalism" and the critique of social sorting', *Contemporary Sociology: A Journal of
Reviews*, 36, 2, 107–11.

MacLeod, G. (2002) 'From urban entrepreneurialism to a "Revanchist City"?
On the spatial injustices of Glasgow's renaissance', *Antipode*, 34, 3,
602–24.

MacKenzie, D. and Spinardi, G. (1995) 'Tacit knowledge, weapons design, and
the uninvention of nuclear weapons', *The American Journal of Sociology*, 101, 1,
44–99.

Maeda, A. (2004 [1981]) 'Utopia of the prisonhouse: a reading of *In Darkest Tokyo*',
in J.A. Fuji (ed.) *Text and the City: Essays on Japanese Modernity* (Durham NC:
Duke University Press).

Maier, C.C. (2005) 'Targeting the city: debates and silences about the aerial
bombing of World War II', *International Review of the Red Cross*, 87, 859,
429–44.

Major, A.J. (1999) 'State and criminal tribes in colonial Punjab: surveillance,
control and reclamation of the "dangerous classes",' *Modern Asian Studies*, 33,
657–88.

Mallory, K. and Ottar, A. (1973) *Architecture of Aggression: A History of Military
Architecture in North West Europe 1900–1945* (London: Architectural Press).

Manchester Evening News (MEN) (2006a) 'Security alert at TA centre' 27 September,
see: http://www.manchestereveningnews.co.uk/ (accessed 14 January 2007).

Manchester Evening News (MEN) (2006b) 'Labour security secrets stolen',
20 September, see: http://www.manchestereveningnews.co.uk/ (accessed 14
January 2007).

Manchester Evening News (MEN) (2006c) '£4.2m bill to shield Labour MPs',
Manchester Evening News, 28 February, 3.

Manchester Evening News (MEN) (2006d) '£100M: Manchester to cash in on
windfall following success of Labour Party Conference', 29 September, 1.

Mansfield, Y. and Pizam, A. (eds.) (2006) *Tourism, Security and Safety; From Theory
to Practice* (Burlington MA: Butterworth Heinemann).

Marcuse, P. (1993) 'What's so new about divided cities?', *International Journal of Urban and Regional Research*, 17, 353–65.

Marcuse, P. (2002) 'Afterword', in P. Marcuse and R. van Kempen (eds.) *Of States and Cities: The Partitioning of Urban Space* (Oxford: Oxford University Press).

Marcuse, P. (2002) 'Urban form and globalization after September 11th: the view from New York', *International Journal of Urban and Regional Research*, 26, 3, 596–606.

Marcuse, P. and van Kempton, R. (2002) *Of States and Cities: The Partitioning of Urban Space* (Oxford: Oxford University Press).

Marx, G.T. (1985) 'The surveillance society: the threat of 1984-style techniques', *The Futurist*, June, 21–6.

Marx, G. (1988) *Undercover* (Berkeley: University of California Press).

Marx, G. (1995) 'The engineering of social control: the search for silver bullets', in J. Hagan and R. Peterson (eds.) *Crime and Inequality* (Stanford: Stanford University Press), pp. 225–46.

Mathiesen, T. (1997) 'The viewer society: Michel Foucault's "Panopticon" revisited", *Theoretical Criminology*, 1, 2, 215–34.

Mawson, J. and Spencer, K. (1997) 'The Government Offices for the English regions: towards regional governance?', *Policy and Politics*, 25, 1, 71–84.

Mazower, M. (1998) *Dark Continent: Europe's Twentieth Century* (London: Allen Lane).

Mazower, M. (2002) 'Review essay: violence and the state in the Twentieth Century.' *The American Historical Review*, 107, 4, no page numbers, see: http://historycooperative.press.uiuc.edu/journals/ahr/107.4/ah0402001158. html (accessed 20 March 2008).

Mazower, M. (ed.) (1997) *The Policing of Politics in the Twentieth Century* (Providence RI: Berghahn Books).

McCahill, M. and Norris, C. (2002) *CCTV in Britain*, Working Paper 3, Centre for Criminology and Criminal Justice, University of Hull.

McCamley, N.J. (1988) *Secret Underground Cities: An Account of Some of Britain's Subterranean Defence, Factory and Storage Sites in the Second World War* (Barnsley: Pen and Sword Books).

McCauley, M. (2003) *The Origins of the Cold War, 1941–1949 (3rd Edition)* (Edinburgh: Pearson Educational).

McClain, J.L., Merriman, J.M. and Ugawa, K. (eds.) (1994) *Edo and Paris: Urban Life and the State in the Early Modern Era* (New York: Cornell University Press).

McDonald, M. (2005) 'Constructing insecurity: Australian security discourse and policy post-2001', *International Relations*, 19, 3, 297–320.

McEntire, D. and Myers, A. (2004) 'Preparing communities for disaster: issues and processes for local government', *Disaster prevention and management*, 13, 4, 140–52.

McGuire, W.J., Griffiths, D.R., Hancock, P.L. and Stewart, I.S. (2000) *The Archaeology of Geological Catastrophes* (Special Publication 171) (London: The Geological Society).

McNeil, W.H. (1982) *The Pursuit of Power: Technology, Armed Force and Society Since A.D.1000* (Chicago: University of Chicago Press).

McNeil, W.H. (1994 [1976]) *Plagues and Peoples* (Harmondsworth: Penguin).

Meisel, J.S. (1994) 'Air raid shelter policy and its critics in Britain before the Second World War', *Twentieth Century British History*, 5, 3, 300–19.

Melossi, D. and Pavarini, M. (1981 [1977]) *The Prison and the Factory: Origins of the Penitentiary System* (Basingstoke: Macmillan).

Merrifield, A. and Swyngedouw, E. (eds.) (1997) *The Urbanization of Injustice* (London: Lawrence and Wishart).

Milgram, S. (1970) 'The experience of living in cities', *Science*, 167, 1461–8.

Milliken, J. (1999) 'The study of discourse in International Relations: a critique of research and methods', *European Journal of International Relations*, 5, 2, 236.

Mills, E.S. (2002) 'Terrorism and U.S. real estate', *Journal of Urban Economics*, 51, 2, 198–204.

Millward, D. (1996) 'TV cameras have limited effect on town centre crime', *Electronic Telegraph*, 2 January.

Milner, G.R. (2000) 'Pallisaded settlements in prehistoric eastern North America', in J.D. Tracy (ed.) *City Walls: The Urban Enceinte in Comparative Perspective* (Cambridge: Cambridge University Press), pp. 46–70.

Ministry of Information (MI) (1941) *The Battle of Britain: An Air ministry Account of the Great Days from 8th August–31st October 1940* (London: HMSO).

Mitchell, J.K. (1999) *Crucibles of Hazard: Mega-cities and Disasters in Transition* (New York: United Nations University Press).

Moffat, R. (1983) 'Crime Prevention Through Environmental Design: a management perspective', *Canadian Journal of Criminology*, 25, 4, 19–31.

Molotch, H. and McClain, N. (2003) 'Dealing with urban terror: heritages of control, varieties of intervention, strategies of research', *International Journal of Urban and Regional Research*, 27, 3, 679–98.

Morris, N. (2008) 'Brown publishes first national security strategy', *The Independent*, 20 March, 6.

Morris, N. and Rothman, D.J. (1995) *The Oxford History of the Prison: The Practice of Punishment in Western Society* (Oxford: Oxford University Press).

Moss, T. (2004) 'Geopolitical upheaval and embedded infrastructures: securing energy and water services in a divided Berlin', IRS Working Paper (Erkner, Germany: Liebnitz Institute for Regional Development and Structural Planning) see: http://www.irs-net.de/download/Infrastructures.pdf (accessed 20 March 2008).

Mumford, L. (1961) *The City in History: Its Origins, Its Transformations, and Its Prospects* (Harmondsworth: Penguin).

Mundill, R.R. (2002) *England's Jewish Solution: Experiment and Expulsion, 1262–1290* (Cambridge: Cambridge University Press).

Murakami Wood, D. (ed.), Ball, K., Lyon, D., Norris, C. and Raab, C. (2006) *A Report on the Surveillance Society*. Wilmslow, UK: Office of the Information Commissioner (ICO).

Murakami Wood, D. and Coaffee, J. (2007) 'Lockdown! Resilience, resurgence and the stage-set city', in R. Atkinson and G. Helms (eds.) *Securing the Urban Renaissance* (Bristol: Policy Press), pp. 91–106.

Murakami Wood, D., Lyon, D. and Abe, K. (2007) 'Surveillance in Urban Japan: A Critical Introduction', *Urban Studies*, 44, 3, 551–68.

Mythen, G. and Walklate, S. (2006), 'Communicating the terrorist risk: Harnessing a culture of fear', *Crime, Media and Culture*, 2, 2, 123–44.

Naimark, N.M. (2007) 'War and Genocide on the Eastern Front, 1941–1945', *Contemporary European History*, 16, 259–74.

National Capital Planning Commission (2001) *Designing for Security in the Nation's Capital* (Washington: NCPC).

Neill, W. (1992) 'Re-imaging Belfast', *The Planner*, 2 October, 8–10.

Neill, W.J.V., Fitzsimons, D.S. and Murtagh, B. (1995) *Reimaging the Pariah City – Urban Development in Belfast and Detroit* (Aldershot: Avebury).

Neufeld, M.J. (1995) *The Rocket and the Reich: Peenemünde and the Coming of the Ballistic Missile Era* (New York: Free Press).

Neufeld, M.J. (2007) 'Wernher von Braun's ultimate weapon', *Bulletin of the Atomic Scientists*, 63, 4, 50–78.

Neufeld, M.J. and Berenbaum, M. (2000) *The Bombing of Auschwitz: Should the Allies Have Attempted It?* (New York: St Martin's Press).

New Left Review (ed.) (1982) *Exterminism and Cold War* (London: New Left Review).

Newcastle City Council (2004) 'Resilience planning/Civil Contingencies Act', *Minutes of the Executive*, 15 December.

Newman, O. (1972) *Defensible Space: Crime Prevention Through Urban Design* (New York: Macmillan).

Newman, O. (1973) *Defensible Space: People and Design in the Violent City* (London: Architectural Press).

Newman, O. (1995) 'Defensible space – a new physical planning tool for urban revitalisation', *Journal of the American Planning Association*, 61, 2, Spring, 149–55.

Nijenhuis, W. (1991) 'City frontiers and their disappearance', *Assemblage*, 16, 42–53.

Norfolk, S. (1994) 'Houston streets: A world apart', *The Independent*, 9 November, p. 26.

Norris, C. (2003) 'From personal to digital: CCTV, the panopticon and the technological mediation of suspicion and social control', in D. Lyon (ed.) *Surveillance as Social Sorting: Privacy, Risk and Digital Discimination* (London: Routledge), pp. 249–81.

Norris, C. and Armstrong, G. (1999) *The Maximum Surveillance Society: The Rise of CCTV* (Oxford: Berg).

Norris, C., McCahill, M. and Wood, D. (2004) 'Editorial. The growth of CCTV: a global perspective on the international diffusion of video surveillance in publicly accessible space', *Surveillance and Society*, 2, 2/3, 110–35.

Northumbria Local Resilience Forum (2005) *Handbook* (Newcastle: NLRF).

Northumbria Police (2005) 'Northumbria Local Resilience Forum – publication of Community Risk Register', *News Statement*, 15 November.

Norton-Taylor, R. (2008) 'Brown plans to send British civilian force to conflict zones', *The Guardian*, 20 March, 15.

Nunn, S. (2001) 'Cities, space, and the new world of urban law enforcement technologies', *Journal of Urban Affairs*, 23, 3–4, 259–78.

O'Shea, S. (2006) *Sea of Faith* (London: Pergamon Press).

O'Brien, T. (1955) *Civil Defence* (London: HMSO).

O'Connor, D. (2005) *Closing the Gap: A review of the 'fitness for purpose' of the current policing structure in England and Wales* (London: Her Majesty's Inspectorate of the Constabulary).

O'Brien, G. and Reid, P. (2005) 'The future of UK emergency management: new wine, old skin?', *Disaster Prevention and Management*, 14, 3, 353–61.

Obura, D.O. (2004) 'Resilience and climate change: lessons from coral reefs and bleaching in the Western Indian Ocean', *Estuarine, Coastal and Shelf Science*, 63, 3, 353–72.

Oc, T. and Tiesdell, S. (2000) 'Urban design approaches to safer city centres: the fortress, the panoptic, the regulatory and the animated', in J.R. Gold and G. Revill (eds.) *Landscapes of Defence* (London: Prentice Hall) 188–208.

Oc, T. and Tiesdell, S. (1997) *Safer City Centres – Reviving the Public Realm* (London: Paul Chapman).

Odell, K.A. and Weidenmier, M.D. (2004) 'Real shock, monetary aftershock: the 1906 San Francisco earthquake and the panic of 1907', *The Journal of Economic History*, 64, 1002–27.

Office of the Deputy Prime Minister (ODPM) (2003) *Our Fire and Rescue Service* (London: ODPM/HMSO).

Office of the Deputy Prime Minister (ODPM) (2003) *Sustainable Communities: Building for the Future* (London: ODPM).

Office of the Deputy Prime Minister (ODPM) (2004) *Civil Resilience* see: www.odpm.gov.uk/stellent/groups/odpm_civilres/documents/sectionhome page/odpm_civilres_page.hcsp (accessed 4 December 2004).

Ogawa, T., Hashimoto, K. and Sunohara, H. (2007) 'The Aneha scandal and amendment of Japan's Building Standard Law' *Building Safety Journal*, December, 54–5.

Oliver-Smith, A. (2004) 'Theorizing vulnerability in a globalized world: A political ecological perspective', in G. Bankoff, G. Frerks and D. Hilhorst (2004) *Mapping Vulnerability: Disasters, Development and People* (London: Earthscan), pp. 10–24.

Owens, E.J. (1999) *The City in the Greek and Roman World* (London: Routledge).

Palmer, S.H. (1988) *Police and Protest in England and Ireland, 1780–1850* (Cambridge: Cambridge University Press).

Paris, R. (2001) 'Human security: paradigm shift or hot air?', *International Security*, 26, 2, 88–103.

Parker, G. (1996) *The Military Revolution: Military Innovation and the Rise of the West, 1500–1800* (Cambridge: Cambridge University Press).

Parssinen, T.M. (1974) 'Popular science and society: the phrenology movement in early Victorian Britain', *Journal of Social History*, 8, 1, 1–20.

Paton, D., Millar, M. and Johnston, D. (2001) 'Community resilience to volcanic hazard consequences', *Natural Hazards*, 24, 157–69.

Pawley, M. (1998) *Terminal Architecture* (London: Reaktion).

Peck, L. (2004) 'How I strolled into the heart of the Games', *The Times*, 14 May, 4.

Pelling, M. (2003). *The Vulnerability of Cities: Natural Disasters and Social Resilience*. (London: Earthscan).

Pelling, M. and High, C. (2005) 'Understanding adaption: what can social capital offer assessments of adaptive capacity?', *Global Environmental Change*, 15, 308–19.

Peters, E.M. (1995) 'Prison before prison: the ancient and mediaeval worlds', in N. Morris and D.J. Rothman (eds.) *The Oxford History of the Prison: The Practice of Punishment in Western Society* (Oxford: Oxford University Press), 3–43.

Pickett, S.T.A., Cadenasso, M.L. and Grove, J.M. (2004) 'Resilient cities: meaning, model, and metaphor for integrating the ecological, socio-economic, and planning realms', *Landscape and Urban Planning*, 69, 369–84.

Plunket, P. and Uruñuela, G. (2006) 'Social and cultural consequences of a late Holocene eruption of Popocatépetl in central Mexico', *Quaternary International*, 151, 1, 19–28.

Ponting, C. (1990) *Secrecy in Britain* (Oxford: Basil Blackwell).

Poole, S. (2006) 'War of the words', *The Guardian*, 18 February, see: http://www.guardian.co.uk/comment/story/0,1712407,1712400.html (accessed 19 February 2006).

Porter, B. (1987) *The Origins of the Vigilant State: The London Metropolitan Police Before the First World War* (London: Weidenfeld & Nicholson).

Porter, D. (1999) *Health, Civilization and the State: A History of Public Health from Ancient to Modern Times* (London: Routledge).

Powell, M. (2000) 'New Labour and the third way in the British welfare state: a new and distinctive approach?', *Critical Social Policy*, 20, 1, 39–60.

Powers, T. (2000) *Heisenberg's War: The Secret History of the German Bomb* (New Brunswick NJ: Da Capo).

Poyner, B. (1983) *Design Against Crime: Beyond Defensible Space* (London: Butterworth).

Poynting, S. and Mason, V. (2007) 'The resistible rise of islamophobia: anti-Muslim racism in the UK and Australia before 11 September 2001', *Journal of Sociology*, 43, 1, 61–86.

Pratchett, L. and Dale, A. (2004) 'The domestic management of terrorist attack: the local dimension' (Leicester: Local government Research Unit, De Montfort University).

Putnam R.D. (2000) *Bowling Alone: The Collapse and Revival of American Community* (New York: Simon & Schuster).

Raco, M. (2003) 'Remaking place and securitising space: urban regeneration and the strategies, tactics and practices of policing in the UK', *Urban Studies*, 40, 9, 1869–87.

Raco, M. (2007) 'The planning, design and governance of sustainable communities in the UK', in R. Atkinson and G. Helms (eds.) *Securing and Urban Renaissance: Crime, Community and British Urban Policy* (Bristol: The Policy Press), pp. 39–56.

Raeff, M. (1975) 'The well-ordered police state and the development of modernity in Seventeenth and Eighteenth-Century Europe: an attempt at a comparative approach', *The American Historical Review*, 80, 5, 1221–43.

Ramsay, R. (1998) 'Uncle Sam's New Labour', *Variant* 6, see: http://www.variant.org.uk (accessed 1 March 2008).

Raven, S. (1993) *Rome in Africa* (3rd Edition) (London: Routledge).

Ravid, B.C.I. (1976) 'The first charter of the Jewish merchants of Venice', *AJS Review*, 1, 187–222.

Raymond, A. (1991) 'Soldiers in trade: the case of Ottoman Cairo', *British Journal of Middle Eastern Studies*, 18, 1, 16–37.

Reader, J. (2004) *Cities* (London: Heineman).

Reale, O. and Dirmeyer, P. (2000) 'Modeling the effects of vegetation on Mediterranean climate during the Roman classical period Part I: climate history and model sensitivity', *Global and Planetary Change*, 25, 3/4, 163–84.

Reeve, A. (1996) 'The private realm of the managed town centre', *Urban Design International*, 1,1, 61–80.

Rhodes, R. (1986) *The Making of the Atomic Bomb* (New York: Simon & Schuster).

Richards, A. (2007) 'Terrorism and public information', in P. Wilkinson (ed.) *Homeland Security: Future Preparations for Terrorist Attack Since 9/11*, 288–95.

Richelson, J. (1999) *America's Space Sentinels: DSP Satellites and National Security* (Kansas: University Press of Kansas).

Richmond, J. (1930) *The City Wall of Imperial Rome* (Oxford: Clarendon Press).

Ridley, R.T. (1986) 'To be taken with a pinch of salt: the destruction of Carthage', *Classical Philology*, 81, 2, 140–6.

Roberts, M.J.D. (2004) *Making English Morals: Voluntary Association and Moral Reform in England* (Cambridge: Cambridge University Press).

Robinson, G.W.S. (1953) 'West Berlin: the geography of an enclave', *Geographical Review*, 43, 4, 540–57.

Rockett, J.P. (1994) 'Constructive critique of United Kingdom emergency planning', *United Kingdom Emergency Planning*, 3, 1, 47–60.

Rogers, C.J. (ed.) (1995) *The Military Revolution Debate: Readings on the Military Transformation of Early Modern Europe* (Boulder CO: Westview Press).

Rogers, P. (1996) *Economic Targeting and Provisional IRA Strategy*, University of Bradford, Department of Peace Studies, Paper 96.1.

Rogers, P. (2006) Are you normal? Young people's participation in the renaissance of public space – a case study of Newcastle upon Tyne; UK, child, youth & the Environment International Perspectives on child & youth Participation', 16, 2, 102–16.

Rogers, P. and Coaffee, J. (2005) 'Moral panics and urban renaissance: policy, tactics and lived experiences in public space', *City*, 9, 3, 321–40.

Rose, A. (2003) 'Defining and measuring economic resilience to disasters', *Disaster Prevention and Management*, 13, 4, 307–14.

Rose, A. (2004) 'Defining and measuring economic resilience to earthquakes', *MCEER Research Progress and Accomplishments: 2003–2004*, 4, 1, 41–54.

Rose, A. (2007) Economic resilience to natural and man-made disasters: multi-disciplinary origins and contextual dimensions, *Environmental Hazards*, 7, 383–98.

Rose, N. (1993) 'Government, authority and expertise in advanced liberalism', *Economy and Society*, 22, 3, 283–99.

Rose, N. (1996) 'The death of the social? Re-figuring the territory of government', *Economy and Society*, 25, 3, 327–56.

Rose, N. (2000) 'Government and control', *British Journal of Criminology*, 40, 2, 321–39.

Rose, N. and Miller, P. (1992) 'Political power beyond the state: problematics of government', *The British Journal of Sociology*, 43, 2, 173–205.

Rousseau, J. (1999 [1755]) *Discourse on the Origin of Inequality* (Oxford: Oxford University Press).

Rubenstein, J. (1973) *City Police* (New York: Ballentine).

Rubey, W. (1969) 'Introduction', in A.C. Lawson (1969 [1908]) *The California Earthquake of April 18, 1906. Report of the State Earthquake Investigation Commission*, Pub. No. 87 (2 Volumes) (Washington DC: Carnegie Institution of Washington).

Runciman, P. (1990 [1965]) *The Fall of Constantinople 1453* (Cambridge: Cambridge University Press).

Ruttan, V.W. (2006) *Is War Necessary for Economic Growth? Military Procurement and Technology* (New York: Oxford University Press).

Sack, R.P. (1986) *Human Territoriality: Its Theory and History* (Cambridge: Cambridge University Press).

Safir, H. and Whitman, E. (2003) *Security: Policing Your Homeland, Your City, Yourself* (New York: Thomas Dunne Books).

Samatas, M. (2004) *Surveillance in Greece: From Anticommunist to Consumer Surveillance* (New York: Pella Publishing).

Savage, C.C. (1987) *Architecture of the Private Streets of St. Louis: The Architects and the Houses They Designed* (Columbia: University of Missouri Press).

Savitch, H.V. (2008) *Cities in a Time of Terror: Space, Territory and Local Resilience* (New York: M.E. Sharpe).

Sawyer, R.D. (2004) *Fire and Water: The Art of Incendiary and Aquatic Warfare* (Boulder CO: Westview Press).

Scanlon, C. (2001) 'A step to the left or just a jump to the right? Making sense of the third way on government and governance', *Australian Journal of Political Science*, 36, 3, 481–98.

Schencking, J.C. (2006) 'Catastrophe, opportunism, contestation: the fractured politics of reconstructing Tokyo following the Great Kanto Earthquake of 1923', *Modern Asian Studies*, 40, 833–73.

Scheppele, K.L. (2006) 'North American emergencies: the use of emergency powers in Canada and the United States', *International Journal of Constitutional Law*, 4, 213–43.

Schneider, J. and Susser, I. (2003) *Wounded Cities: Destruction and Reconstruction in a Globalized World* (Oxford: Berg).

Security Service (MI5) (2006) *Protecting Against Terrorism* (London: TSO).

Security Service (Mi5) (2008) 'Police launch new counter-terrorism campaign' *Mi5 News Update*, 25 February (message from the Security Service/Mi5 mailing list).

Segal, R. and Weizman, E. (eds.) (2003) *A Civilian Occupation: The Politics of Israeli Architecture* (London: Verso).

Sekula, A. (1986) 'The body and the archive', *October*, 39, 3–64.

Shaw, R. and Goda, K. (2004) 'From disaster to sustainable civil society: the Kobe experience', *Disasters*, 28, 1, 16–40.

Shearing, C.D. and Stenning, P. (1985) 'From the Panopticon to Disneyworld: the development of discipline', in A.N. Doob and E.L. Greenspan (eds.) *Perspectives in Criminal Law* (Aurora: Canada Law Books), pp. 335–49.

Sheffi, Y. (2005) *The Resilient Enterprise: Overcoming Vulnerability for Competitive Advantage* (Cambridge: MIT Press).

Sheldon, R.M. (2005) *Intelligence Activities in Ancient Rome: Trust in the Gods, but Verify* (London: Routledge).

Shelley. L.I. (1996) *Policing Soviet Society: The Evolution of State Control* (London: Routledge).

Shelton, B. (1999) *Learning from the Japanese City: East Meets West in Urban Design.* (London: Spon).

Shepard, W.S. (2002) 'The ETA: Spain fights Europe's last active terrorist group', *Mediterranean Quarterly,* 13, 1, 54–68.

Sherry, M.S. (1987) *The Rise of American Air Power: The Creation of Armageddon* (New Haven CY: Yale University Press).

Sherwin, M.J. (1995) 'Hiroshima as politics and history', *The Journal of American History*, 82, 3, 1085–93.

Shields, P.M. (2004) 'Classical pragmatism: engaging practitioner experience', *Administration and Society*, 36, 3, 351–61.

Shimada, I., Schaff, C.B., Thompson, L.G. and Mosley-Thompson, E. (1991) 'Cultural impacts of severe droughts in the prehistoric Andes: application of a 1500-year ice core precipitation record', *World Archaeology*, 22, 3, 247–70.

Shirlow, P. and Murtagh, B. (2006) *Belfast: Segregation, Violence and the City* (London: Pluto press).

Shriver, T.E. and Kennedy, D.K. (2005) 'Contested environmental hazards and community conflict over relocation', *Rural Sociology*, 70, 4, 491–513.

Sibley, D. (1995) *Geographies of Exclusion: Society and Difference in the West* (London: Routledge).

Sinnigen, W.G. (1961) 'The Roman secret service', *The Classical Journal*, 57, 2, 65–72.

Smith, H. (1993) 'Checkpoints mark fortress London', *Evening Standard*, 7 June, 6.

Smith, C. (1995) *Urban Disorder and the Shape of Belief: The Great Chicago Fire, the Haymarket Bomb, and the Model Town of Pullman* (Chicago: University of Chicago Press).

Smith, J. (2003) 'Civil contingencies planning in government', *Parliamentary Affairs*, 56, 410–22.

Smith, N. (1996) *The New Urban Frontier: Gentrification and the Revanchist City* (London: Routledge).

Smith, P.T. (1985) *Policing Victorian London: Political Policing, Public Order and the London Metropolitan Police* (Westport CN: Greenwood).

Snider, K.F. (2000) 'Expertise of experimenting? Pragmatism and American public administration: 1920–1950', *Administration and Society*, 32, 4, 329–54.

Soffer, A. and Minghi, J.V. (1986) 'Israel's security landscapes: the impact of military considerations on land-use', *Political Geographer*, 38, 28–41.

Sofsky, W. (1997) *The Order of Terror: The Concentration Camp* (trans. W. Templer) (Princeton: Princeton University Press).

Soja, E. (1995) 'Postmodern urbanization: the six restructurings of Los Angeles', in S. Watson and K. Gibson (eds.) *Postmodern Cities and Spaces* (Oxford: Blackwell).

Solis, R.S., Haas, J. and Creamer, W. (2001) 'Dating Caral, a preceramic site in the Supe valley on the central coast of Peru', *Science*, 292, 5517, 723–6.

Sorensen, A. (2002) *The Making of Urban Japan: Cities and Planning from Edo to the Twenty-First Century* (London: Routledge).

Sorkin, M. (1992) *Variations on a Theme Park: The New American City and the End of Public Space* (New York: Hill and Wang).

Sorkin, M. (ed.) (1995) *Variations on a Theme Park – The New American City and the End of Public Space* (New York: Hill and Wang).

Sorren, D. (1985) 'An earthquake on Cyprus: new discoveries from Kourion', *Archaeology*, 38, 52–9.

Southall, A. (1998) *The City in Time and Space* (Cambridge: Cambridge University Press).

Southern, A. (2001) 'What matters is what works? The management of regeneration', *Local Economy*, 16, 4, 264–71.

Souyri, P.F. (2002 [1998]) The *World Turned Upside Down: Medieval Japanese Society* (trans. K. Rothe) (London: Pimlico).

Spaatz, C. (1947) 'Evolution of air power: our urgent need for an air force second to none', *Military Affairs*, 1, 11, 2–16.

Spierenberg, P. (1995) 'The body and the state: early modern Europe', in N. Morris and D.J. Rothman (1995) *The Oxford History of the Prison: The Practice of Punishment in Western Society* (Oxford: Oxford University Press), pp. 44–70.

Squires, J.D. (1937) 'Aeronautics in the Civil War', *The American Historical Review*, 42, 4, 652–69.

Stanish, C. (2001) ' The origin of state societies in South America', *Annual Review of Anthropology*, 30, 41–64.

Stanley, J. and Steihardt, B. (2002) *Drawing a Black: The Failure of Facial Recognition in Tampa, Florida* (Washington DC: ACLU).

Stasiulis, D. and Ross, D. (2006) 'Security, flexible sovereignty, and the perils of multiple citizenship', *Citizenship Studies*, 10, 3, 329–48.

Steinberg, D.J. (ed.) (1987) *In Search of Southeast Asia: A Modern History* (Revised Edition) (Sydney: Allen & Unwin).

Steinhardt, N.S. (1999) *Chinese Imperial City Planning* (Honolulu: University of Hawaii Press).

Stimson, H. (1947) 'The decision the use the nuclear bomb', *Harpers*. Reprinted online by the Association for Asian Studies, see: http://www.aasianst. org/EAA/StimsonHarpers.pdf (no page numbers) (accessed 1 March 2008).

Stiros, S.C. (2001) 'The AD 365 Crete earthquake and possible seismic clustering during the Fourth to Sixth Centuries AD in the Eastern Mediterranean: a review of historical and archaeological data', *Journal of Structural Geology*, 23, 2–3, 545–62.

Stocker, J. (2004) *Britain and Ballistic Missile Defence, 1942–2002* (London: Frank Cass).

Strachan, H. (2000) 'Review article: the First World War', *The Historical Journal*, 43, 889–903.

Sturgis, J.L. (1991) 'Whisky detectives' in town: the enforcement of the liquor laws in Hamilton, Ontario, c.1870–1900', in D. Anderson and D. Killingray (eds.) (1991) *Policing the Empire: Government, Authority and Control, 1830–1940* (Manchester: Manchester University of Press), pp. 202–18.

Subtopia (2006) 'Fortress urbanism', see: http://subtopia.blogspot.com/2006/02/fortress-urbanism-super-bowl-city.html (accessed 12 February 2007).

Swanson, G.W. (1972) 'The Ottoman police', *Journal of Contemporary History*, 7, 1/2, 243–60.

Swanstrom, T. (2002) 'Are fear and urbanism at war?', *Urban Affairs Review*, 38, 1, 135–40.

Szinicz, L. (2005) 'History of chemical and biological warfare agents', *Toxicology*, 214, 3, 167–81.

Takamura, Y. and Tone, K. (2003) 'A comparative site evaluation study for relocating Japanese government agencies out of Tokyo', *Socio-Economic Planning Sciences*, 37, 2, 85–102.

Takashi, K. (1994) 'Governing Edo', in J.L., McClain, J.M. Merriman and K. Ugawa (eds.) (1994) *Edo and Paris: Urban Life and the State in the Early Modern Era* (New York: Cornell University Press), pp. 41–67.

Tanaka, S. and Murakami, K. (2006) 'The city of trees': the role of a grand concept for Sendai spatial planning, *Planning Theory and Practice*, 7, 4, 449–60.

Taylor, D. (1997) *The New Police: Crime, Conflict and Control in Nineteenth-Century England* (Manchester: Manchester University Press).

Temple, M. (2000) 'New Labour's third way: pragmatism and governance', *British Journal of Politics and International Relations*, 2, 3, 302–25.

The Independent (2008) 'Generals still fighting the battles of the past', Editorial and Opinion, 20 March, 44.

The Times (2008) 'Security blanket: more of a framework to cope with uncertainly than a strategy', Comment, 20 March, 20.

Thompson, D. (2005) 'Cost to taxpayer of Labour part security: 2.8M', *Newcastle Journal*, 29 January, 1.

Thompson, M. (2007) 'PM calls on architects to design out terror', *Architects Journal*, 14 November, see: http://www.architectsjournal.co.uk/news/dailynews/pm_calls_on_architects_to_design_out_terror.html (accessed 15 November 2007).

Thorpe, K. (2001) 'The "juggernaut method": the 1966 state of emergency and the Wilson government's response to the seamen's strike', *Twentieth Century British History*, 12, 4, 461–85.

Tilly, C. (1992) *Coercion, Capital, and European States, AD 990–1992* (Oxford: Blackwell).

Tilly, C. and Blockmans, W.P. (1994) *Cities and the Rise of States in Europe, A.D. 1000 to 1800* (Boulder CO: Westview Press).

Timmerman, P. (1981) *Vulnerability, Resilience and the Collapse of Society: A Review of Models and Possible Climatic Applications* (Toronto: Institute for Environmental Studies, University of Toronto).

Tobin, G.A. (1999) 'Sustainability and community resilience: the holy grail of hazards planning?', *Environmental Hazards*, 1, 1, 13–25.

Torrence, R. and Grattan, J.P. (2002) *Natural Disasters and Cultural Change* (London: Routledge).

Tracy, J.D. (ed.) (2000) *City Walls: The Urban Enceinte in Comparative Perspective* (Cambridge: Cambridge University Press).

Travis, A. (2007) 'Struggling Home Office split up to combat terrorism', *The Guardian*, 30 March, see: http://www.guardian.co.uk/politics/2007/mar/30/ukcrime.immigrationpolicy (accessed 1 March 2007).

Trench, R. and Hillman, E. (1984) *London Under London: A Subterranean Guide* (London: John Murray).

Trevisanato, S.I. (2007) 'The "Hittite plague", an epidemic of tularaemia and the first record of biological warfare', *Medical Hypotheses*, 69, 6, 1371–4.

Trim, R. (2005) 'An integrative approach to disaster management and planning', *Disaster Prevention and Management*, 13, 3, 218–25.

UK Resilience (2003) 'Communicating Risk', see: http://www.ukresilience.info/upload/assets/www.ukresilience.info/communicatingrisk.pdf (accessed 23 August 2006).

UK Resilience (2005a) 'English Regions', see: http://www.ukresilience.info/response/englishregions.aspx (accessed 12 October 2005).

UK Resilience (2005b) *Exercises*, see: http://www.ukresilience.info/preparedness/exercises.aspx (accessed 12 October 2005).

UK Resilience (2006a) *Communicating Risk Guidance* (London: UK Resilience/HMSO).

UK Resilience (2006b) *National Capabilities Survey*, 2006, see http://www.ukresilience.info/preparedness/ukgovernment/survey.aspx (accessed 30 November 2006).

UK Resilience (2007) *Capabilities Programme*, see http://www.ukresilience.info/preparedness/ukgovernment/capabilities.aspx (accessed 2 August 2007).

UK Resilience Guidance (2005) 'Central government arrangements for responding to an emergency', March (London: UK Resilience).

Um, N. (2003) 'Spatial negotiations in a commercial city: the Red Sea port of Mocha, Yemen, during the first half of the Eighteenth Century', *The Journal of the Society of Architectural Historians*, 62, 2, 178–93.

United Nations (2004) *Reducing Disaster Risk: A Challenge for Development – A Global Report* (New York: UN Publications).

United States Geological Survey (USGS) (nd.) Earthquake Hazards Program 'The Great 1906 San Francisco Earthquake', see: http://earthquake.usgs.gov/regional/nca/1906/18april/index.php (accessed 20 February 2008).

US House of Representatives (2006) *A Failure of Initiative: Final Report of the Select Bipartisan Committee to Investigate the Preparation for and Response to Hurricane Katrina* (Washington: Government Printing Office).

Vale, L.J. (1987) *The Limits of Civil Defence in the USA, Switzerland, Britain and the Soviet Union* (Basingstoke: MacMillan).

Vale, L.J. and Campanella, T.J. (eds.) (2005) *The Resilient City: How Modern Cities Recover From Disaster* (Oxford: Oxford University Press).

Valler, D., Phelps, N. and Wood, A. (2002) 'Devolution, regionalism and local economic development', *Local Economy*, 17, 3, 186–90.

Van Creveld, M. (1991) *Technology and War: From 2000 B.C. to the Present* (New York: Free Press).

Van den Eyde, J. and Veno, A. (1999) 'Coping with disastrous events: an empowerment model of community healing', in R. Gist and B. Lubin (eds.) *Response to Disaster* (Philadelphia: Taylor and Francis), pp. 167–92.

Van der Pijl, K. (1998) *Transnational Classes and International Relations* (London: Routledge).

Van Wyhe, J. (2004) *Phrenology and the Origins of Victorian Scientific Naturalism* (Aldershot: Ashgate).

Vanderbilt, T. (2002) *Survival City: Adventures Among the Ruins of Atomic America* (New York: Princeton Architectural Press).

Varley, P. (1967) *The Onin War* (New York: Columbia University Press).

Vidal, J. and and Pidd H. (2007) 'Police to use terror laws on Heathrow climate protesters: government has encouraged use of stop and search and detention without charge', 11 August, see http://www.guardian.co.uk/uk/2007/aug/11/ukcrime.greenpolitics (accessed 11 August 2007).

Vidler, A. (2001) 'The city transformed: designing defensible space'. *New York Times (online)*, 23 September, see: http://query.nytimes.com/gst/fullpage.html?res=9502E4DB163AF930A1575AC0A9679C8B63 (accessed 24 September 2001).

Virilio, P. (2002) *Desert Screen: War at the Speed of Light* (London: Continuum).

Waldron, A. (1990) *The Great Wall of China* (Cambridge: Cambridge University Press).

Walker, C. (2007) 'The treatment of foreign terror suspects', *Modern Law Review*, 70, 3, 427–57.

Walker, C. and Broderick, J. (2006) *The Civil Contingencies Act 2004: Risk Resilience, and the Law in the United Kingdom* (Oxford: Oxford University Press).

Wallerstein, E. (1989) *The Modern World-System, Vol. III: The Second Great Expansion of the Capitalist World-Economy, 1730–1840* (San Diego: Academic Press).

Warren, R. (2002) 'Situating the city and September 11th: military urban doctrine, "pop-up" armies and spatial chess', *International Journal of Urban and Regional Research*, 26, 3, 614–19.

Weber, M. (1996 [1921]) *The City* (New York: Free Press).

Weinberg, G.L. (1994) *A World at Arms: A Global History of World War II* (Cambridge: Cambridge University Press).

Weiss, H. and Bradley, R.S. (2001) 'What drives societal collapse?', *Science*, 291, 5504, 609–10.

Weizman, E. (2007) *Hollow Land: Israel's Architecture of Occupation* (London: Verso).

Wekerle, G.R.. and Jackson, P.S.B. (2005) Urbanising the security agenda: anti-terrorism, urban sprawl and social movements, City, 9, 33–49.

Wessely, S. (2005) 'The bombs made enough victims – let's not make more', *Spiked Online*, see: http://www.spiked-online.com/Articles/0000000CAC61.htm (accessed 17 June 2006).

West, L. (2008) 'Training to tackle terror', *Planning*, 7 March, 10.

Wetzell, R.F. (2000) *Inventing the Criminal: A History of German Criminology, 1880–1945* (Chapel Hill: UNC Press).

Whaller, M.A. (2001) 'Resilience in an ecosytemic context: evolution of a concept', *American Journal of Orthopsychiatry*, 71, 3, 290–7.

Wheelis M. (2002) 'Biological warfare at the 1346 siege of Caffa', *Emerging Infectious Diseases*, 8 (no page numbers).

Whelan, C.J. (1979) 'Military intervention in industrial disputes', *Industrial Law Journal*, 8, 1, 222–34.

White House (2003) *National Strategy for the Physical Protection of Critical Infrastructures and Key Assets* (Washington DC).

White, G.F., Kates, R.W. and Burton, I. (2001) 'Knowing Better and losing even more: the use of knowledge in hazards management', *Environmental Hazards*, 3, 81–92.

White, M. (2005a) 'Source list and detailed death tolls for the Twentieth Century hemoclysm', see: http://users.erols.com/mwhite28/warstat1.htm (accessed 1 March 2008).

White, M. (2005b) 'Death tolls for the man-made megadeaths of the 20th Century', see: http://users.erols.com/mwhite28/battles.htm (accessed 1 March 2008).

Whitehead, M. (2003) 'In the shadow of hierarchy: metagovernance, policy reform and urban regeneration in the West Midlands', *Area*, 35, 6–14.

Williams, A. (1979) *The Police of Paris, 1718–1789* (Baton Rouge: Louisiana State University Press).

Williams, C. A. (2003) 'Police surveillance and the Emergence of CCTV in the 1960s', in M. Gill (ed.) *CCTV* (Leicester: Perpetuity Press), pp. 9–22.

Williams, C.A. (2006) 'Police and the law', in S. Berger (ed.) (2006) *A Companion to Nineteenth-Century Europe, 1789–1914* (Oxford: Blackwell), pp. 345–454.

Williams, K.S. and Johnston, C. (2000) 'The politics of the selective gaze: closed circuit television and the policing of public space', *Crime Law and Social Change*, 34, 2, 183–210.

Williams, R.J. (2004) *The Anxious City: English Urbanism in the Late Twentieth Century* (London: Routledge).

Wilson, D. (2003) 'Unravelling control freakery: redefining central-local government relations', *British Journal of Politics and International Relations* 5, 3, 317–46.

Wintour, P. (2005) 'Counter-terrorism strategy comes under fire', *The Guardian*, 24 October, 20.

Wirth, L. (1998 [1928]) *The Ghetto* (Chicago: Transaction).

Wohl, E.E. (ed.) (2000) *Inland Flood Hazards: Human, Riparian, and Aquatic* (Cambridge: Cambridge University Press).

Wolfendale, J. (2007) Terrorism, security and the threat of counterterrorism, *Studies in Conflict and Terrorism*, 29, 753–70.

Wood, D. (2001) 'The hidden geography of transnational surveillance'. Unpublished PhD Thesis: Newcastle University, UK.

Wood, D., Konvitz, E. and Ball, K. (2003) 'The constant state of emergency? Surveillance after 9/11', in K. Ball and F. Webster (eds.) *The Intensification of Surveillance – Crime, Terrorism and Warfare in the Information Age* (London: Pluto Press), pp. 137–50.

Wooliscroft, T.D.J. (2002) *The Roman Frontier on the Gask Ridge: Perth and Kinross - An Interim Report on the Roman Gask Project, 1995–2000* (Oxford: Archaeopress).

Wright, R. (1992) *Stolen Continents: The Americas Through Indian Eyes Since 1492* (New York: Houghton Mifflin).

Yiftachel, O. (2006) *Ethnocracy: Land and Identity Politics in Israel/Palestine* (Philadephia: University of Pennsylvania Press).

Ziegler, C.A. (1994) 'Weapons development in context: the case of the World War I balloon bomber', *Technology and Culture*, 35, 4, 750–67.

Zukin, S. (1995) *The Cultures of Cities* (Oxford: Blackwell).

Index

3m

FLORIDA COMMUNITY COLLEGE AT JACKSONVILLE LIBRARY

3 3801 01233264 1